Administrator's Pocket Consultant

Microsoft®
EXCHANGE SERVER 2003

William R. Stanek

PUBLISHED BY
Microsoft Press
A Division of Microsoft Corporation
One Microsoft Way
Redmond, Washington 98052-6399

Library of Congress Cataloging-in-Publication Data
Stanek, William R.
    Microsoft Exchange Server 2003: Administrator's Pocket Consultant / William R. Stanek.
      p. cm.
    Includes index.
    ISBN 0-7356-1978-6
    1. Microsoft Exchange server.   2. Client/server computing.   I. Title.

    QA76.9.C55S785   2003
    005.7'13769--dc21   2003053966

Printed and bound in the United States of America.

5 6 7 8 9   QWE   8 7 6 5 4

Distributed in Canada by H.B. Fenn and Company Ltd.

A CIP catalogue record for this book is available from the British Library.

Microsoft Press books are available through booksellers and distributors worldwide. For further information about international editions, contact your local Microsoft Corporation office or contact Microsoft Press International directly at fax (425) 936-7329. Visit our Web site at www.microsoft.com/mspress. Send comments to *mspinput@microsoft.com*.

For Microsoft:
Acquisitions Editor: Jeff Koch
Project Editor: Valerie Woolley

For nSight Publishing Services (www.nsightworks.com
Project Manager: Carmen Corral-Reid
Technical Editor: Chris Russo
Copyeditor: Teresa Horton
Proofreaders: Kerin Foley, Katie O'Connell
Desktop Publishing Specialist: Patty Fagan
Indexer: Jack Lewis

Body Part No. X09-99961

Contents at a Glance

Part IV

Microsoft Exchange Server 2003 and Group Administration

Table of Contents

Part III
Microsoft Exchange Server 2003 Data Store Administration

Tables

Acknowledgments

Writing *Microsoft Exchange Server 2003 Administrator's Pocket Consultant* was a lot of fun—and a lot of work. As you'll see, Exchange Server 2003 has many enhancements over its predecessors and that meant a lot of research to ensure the book was as accurate as it could be. It is gratifying to see techniques I've used time and again to solve problems put into a printed book so that others may benefit from them. But no man is an island and this book couldn't have been written without the help of some very special people.

As I've stated in *Microsoft IIS 6.0 Administrator's Pocket Consultant* and in *Microsoft Windows Server 2003 Administrator's Pocket Consultant*, the team at Microsoft Press is top-notch. Valerie Woolley was instrumental throughout the writing process. The Microsoft team helped me stay on track and get the tools I needed to write this book. Completing and publishing the book wouldn't have been possible without their help! Carmen Maria Corral-Reid headed up the editorial process for nSight, Inc. As the project manager, she wore many hats and helped out in many ways. Thank you!

Unfortunately for the writer (but fortunately for readers), writing is only one part of the publishing process. Next came editing and author review. I must say, Microsoft Press has the most thorough editorial and technical review process I've seen anywhere—and I've written a lot of books for many different publishers. Chris Russo was the technical editor for the book. I'd also like to thank Teresa Horton for her careful copyediting of this book.

I would also like to thank Al Valvano, Jeff Koch, and Juliana Aldous Atkinson. Thank you for your help throughout my many projects. Thank you also for shepherding this project through the publishing process!

Hopefully I haven't forgotten anyone, but if I have, it was an oversight. *Honest.;-)*

Introduction

Microsoft® Exchange Server 2003 Administrator's Pocket Consultant is designed to be a concise and compulsively usable resource for Microsoft Exchange Server 2003 administrators. This is the readable resource guide that you'll want on your desk at all times. The book covers everything you need to perform the core administrative tasks for Exchange Server 2003. Because the focus is on giving you maximum value in a pocket-sized guide, you don't have to wade through hundreds of pages of extraneous information to find what you're looking for. Instead, you'll find exactly what you need to get the job done.

In short, the book is designed to be the one resource you turn to whenever you have questions regarding Exchange Server 2003 administration. To this end, the book zeroes in on daily administration procedures, frequently used tasks, documented examples, and options that are representative although not necessarily inclusive. One of the goals is to keep the content so concise that the book remains compact and easy to navigate, while ensuring that the book is packed with as much information as possible—making it a valuable resource. Thus, instead of a hefty 1000-page tome or a lightweight 100-page quick reference, you get a valuable resource guide that can help you quickly and easily perform common tasks, solve problems, and implement advanced Exchange Server 2003 technologies like virtual servers, X.400 message stacks, and routing group connectors.

Who Is This Book For?

Microsoft® Exchange Server 2003 Administrator's Pocket Consultant covers the standard, enterprise, and conference versions of Exchange Server 2003. The book is designed for

- Current Exchange Server 2003 administrators
- Current Windows administrators who want to learn Exchange Server 2003
- Administrators upgrading to Exchange Server 2003 from Microsoft Exchange 5.5
- Administrators upgrading to Exchange Server 2003 from Microsoft Exchange 2000
- Administrators transferring from other messaging servers
- Managers and supervisors who have been delegated authority to manage mailboxes or other aspects of Exchange Server 2003

To pack in as much information as possible, I had to assume that you have basic networking skills and a basic understanding of e-mail and messaging servers. With this in mind, I don't devote entire chapters to understanding why e-mail systems are needed or how e-mail systems work. I don't devote entire chapters to installing Exchange Server 2003 either. I do, however, provide complete details on the components of Exchange organizations and how you can use these components to build a fully redundant and highly available messaging environment. You will also find complete details on all the essential Exchange administration tasks.

I also assume that you are fairly familiar with Windows Server 2003. If you need help learning Windows Server 2003, I highly recommend *Microsoft Windows Server 2003 Administrator's Pocket Consultant*.

How Is This Book Organized?

Microsoft® Exchange Server 2003 Administrator's Pocket Consultant is designed to be used in the daily administration of Exchange Server 2003, and as such, the book is organized by job-related tasks rather than by Exchange Server 2003 features. If you are reading this book, you should be aware of the relationship between Pocket Consultants and Administrator's Companions. Both types of books are designed to be a part of an administrator's library. Whereas Pocket Consultants are the down-and-dirty, in-the-trenches books, Administrator's Companions are the comprehensive tutorials and references that cover every aspect of deploying a product or technology in the enterprise.

Speed and ease of reference is an essential part of this hands-on guide. The book has an expanded table of contents and an extensive index for finding answers to problems quickly. Many other quick reference features have been added as well. These features include quick step-by-step instructions, lists, tables with fast facts, and extensive cross-references. The book is broken down into both parts and chapters. Each part contains an opening paragraph or two about the chapters contained in that part.

Part I, "Microsoft Exchange Server 2003 Administration Fundamentals," covers the fundamental tasks you need for Exchange Server 2003 administration. Chapter 1 provides an overview of Exchange Server 2003 administration concepts, tools, and techniques. Chapter 2 covers Exchange client setup and management. Chapter 3 extends the Exchange client discussion and looks at mobile Microsoft Office Outlook users as well as Microsoft Outlook Web Access. With more and more users working on the road or from home, this chapter helps ensure that you can give these mobile users the best support possible.

In Part II, "Active Directory Services and Microsoft Exchange Server 2003," I show you how to manage resources that are stored in the Active Directory database. You'll also learn about the Exchange Server 2003 features that are integrated with Active Directory services. Chapter 4 examines essential concepts and tasks that you need to know to work with Exchange Server 2003. Chapter 5 takes a look at creating and managing users and contacts. You'll learn all about Exchange aliases, enabling and disabling exchange mail for individual users, forwarding mail off-site, and more. Chapter 6 discusses mailbox administration, including techniques for configuring, moving, and recovering mailboxes. In

Chapter 7, you'll find a detailed discussion of how to use address lists, distribution groups, and templates. You'll also learn how to manage these resources. The final chapter in this part covers directory security and Exchange policies.

Part III, "Microsoft Exchange Server 2003 Data Store Administration," covers Exchange Server 2003 data store administration. In Chapter 9, you learn how to manage Exchange data and storage groups. Chapter 10 examines administration of mailbox and public folder stores. Chapter 11 looks at how you can use public folders in the enterprise. Finally, Chapter 12 details how to back up and restore Exchange Server. You'll learn key techniques that can help you reliably back up and more importantly, recover Exchange Server in case of failure.

In Part IV, "Microsoft Exchange Server 2003 and Group Administration," I discuss advanced tasks for managing and maintaining Exchange organizations. Chapter 13 provides the essentials for managing servers, administrative groups, and routing groups. You'll also learn how to configure global settings for the organization. Chapter 14 explores message routing within the organization. The discussion starts with a look at the X.400 Message Transfer Agent and X.400 stacks, then goes on to detail how to install and use connectors for routing groups, SMTP, and X.400. Chapter 15 explores tasks for configuring SMTP, IMAP4, and POP3 virtual servers. Chapter 16 covers HTTP virtual servers and also discusses how they are used with Outlook Web Access and Outlook Mobile Access. Finally, Chapter 17 discusses Exchange maintenance, monitoring, and queuing.

Conventions Used in This Book

I've used a variety of elements to help keep the text clear and easy to follow. You'll find code terms and listings in monospace type, except when I tell you to actually type a command. In that case, the command appears in **bold** type. When I introduce and define a new term, I put it in *italics*.

Other conventions include the following:

Note To provide details on a point that needs emphasis

Best Practices To examine the best technique to use when working with advanced configuration and administration concepts

Caution To warn you when there are potential problems you should look out for

More Info To provide more information on the subject

Real World To provide real-world advice when discussing advanced topics

Security Alert To point out important security issues.

 Tip To offer helpful hints or additional information.

I truly hope you find that *Microsoft Exchange Server 2003 Administrator's Pocket Consultant* provides everything you need to perform essential administrative tasks as quickly and efficiently as possible. You're welcome to send your thoughts to me at williamstanek@aol.com. Thank you.

Support

Every effort has been made to ensure the accuracy of this book. Microsoft Press provides corrections for books through the World Wide Web at the following address:

http://www.microsoft.com/mspress/Support/default.asp

If you have comments, questions, or ideas about this book or the companion disc, please send them to Microsoft Press using either of the following methods:

Postal Mail:

Microsoft Press
Attn: Editor, *Microsoft Exchange Server 2003 Administrator's Pocket Consultant*
One Microsoft Way
Redmond, WA 98052-6399

E-mail:

mspinput@microsoft.com

Please note that product support isn't offered through the mail addresses. For support information about Exchange Server 2003, you can call Exchange Server 2003 Standard Support at (800) 936-4900 weekdays between 6 A.M. and 6 P.M. Pacific time.

Part I

Microsoft Exchange Server 2003 Administration Fundamentals

Part I covers the fundamental tasks you need for Microsoft Exchange Server 2003 administration. Chapter 1 provides an overview of Exchange Server administration concepts, tools, and techniques. Chapter 2 covers Exchange Server client setup and management. Chapter 3 extends the Exchange client discussion and looks at mobile Microsoft Office Outlook 2003 users as well as Microsoft Outlook Web Access. With more and more users working on the road or from home, this chapter helps ensure that you can give these mobile users the best support possible.

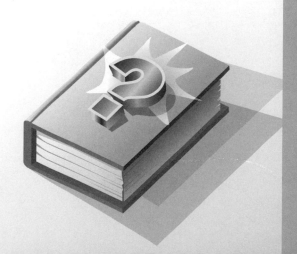

Chapter 1
Overview of Microsoft Exchange Server 2003 Administration

Exchange Server 2003 is designed to meet all the messaging and collaboration needs of any organization, no matter how large or small. Exchange Server has many features and offers wide support for industry-standard mail protocols.

The key features you should focus on initially are those involving scalability, reliability, and availability, including the following:

- **Enhanced wireless and mobile user support**   Exchange Server features built-in support for wireless services and adds remote procedure call (RPC) over Hypertext Transfer Protocol (HTTP) as an option for mobile users. With RPC over HTTP, Outlook 2003 and other RPC clients can use a standard Internet connection to securely access Exchange Server over the Internet. This means mobile users no longer have to rely on a virtual private network (VPN) connection to access Exchange Server as if they were on the corporate network.

Note   RPC over HTTP is made possible through Internet Information Services 6, which is only available when running Exchange Server 2003 on Microsoft Windows Server 2003.

- **Fault-tolerant SMTP support**   Simple Mail Transfer Protocol (SMTP) is the Internet standard for transferring and delivering e-mail. Exchange Server uses SMTP as the default transport protocol for routing messages. SMTP provides major performance and reliability improvements over RPCs, which previous versions of Exchange Server used for message routing. Also, the SMTP implementation for Exchange Server has been enhanced considerably to ensure that the message delivery system is fault tolerant. You'll find more information on fault tolerance in later chapters.

- **Mailbox recovery support** Mailboxes can become disconnected if their associated user account in Active Directory is deleted. With previous editions of Exchange Server, you could only recover these mailboxes one at a time. The new Mailbox Recovery Center allows you to perform recovery or export operations on multiple disconnected mailboxes simultaneously. You can export mailbox information, reassociate user accounts with the mailboxes, and reconnect the mailboxes all from the Mailbox Recovery Center.

- **Multiple message database support** Exchange Server allows you to divide the message store into multiple databases that you can manage either individually or in logical groupings called *storage groups*. You can then store these message databases on one or more Exchange servers. Because you can manage transaction logging and recovery for each of these databases separately, the repair or recovery of one database doesn't affect other databases in the Exchange installation.

- **Multiple protocol and virtual server support** Exchange Server supports many industry-standard messaging protocols, and each of these protocols can be installed on one or more virtual servers. A virtual server is a server process that has its own configuration information, which includes Internet Protocol (IP) addresses, port numbers, and authentication settings. Each messaging protocol configured for use on Exchange Server has its own virtual server. You can create additional virtual servers as well. You can use virtual servers to handle messaging needs for a single domain or for multiple domains. For large installations, you can install virtual servers on separate systems, dividing the workload on a per-protocol basis.

- **Advanced clustering support** Exchange Server Enterprise Edition supports two-node active/active clustering and eight-node active/passive clustering. If a disk drive or server fails on one server, you can distribute the workload to the remaining servers and begin recovery on the failed server. This means that the failure of a single server doesn't halt message processing, and you don't need to have a dedicated failover server.

Exchange Server is tightly integrated with Windows Server 2003, and many of the core features are fully integrated. As you get started with Exchange Server, the operating system integration is a key area that you should focus on. Other areas you should focus on include hardware and component requirements, as well as the availability of administration tools.

Microsoft Exchange Server 2003

Several editions of Exchange Server 2003 are available, including Exchange Server 2003 Standard Edition and Exchange Server 2003 Enterprise Edition. The various server editions support the same core features and administration tools, which means you can use the techniques discussed throughout this book regardless of which Exchange Server 2003 edition you are using. For reference, the specific feature differences between Standard Edition and Enterprise Edition are as follows:

- **Exchange Server 2003 Standard Edition** Designed to provide essential messaging services for small to medium-sized organizations and branch office locations. This server edition supports up to 2 storage groups (with one of the storage groups, called the recovery storage group, being reserved for database recovery operations) and a maximum of 2 databases per storage group. Each database is limited to a maximum size of 16 gigabytes. Additionally, Windows clustering is not supported and the X.400 connector is not included.

- **Exchange Server 2003 Enterprise Edition** Designed to provide essential messaging services for organizations with increased availability, reliability and manageability needs. This server edition supports up to 5 storage groups (with one of the storage groups, called the recovery storage group, being reserved for database recovery operations) and a maximum of 5 databases per storage group. Each database is limited to a maximum size of 16 terabytes (limited only by hardware). Windows clustering is fully supported, and the X.400 connector is included.

Note Throughout this book, I refer to Exchange Server in different ways, and each has a different meaning. Typically, I refer to the software product as Exchange Server. If you see this term, you can take it to mean Microsoft Exchange Server 2003. When necessary, I use Exchange Server 2003 to draw attention to the fact that I am discussing a feature that's new or has changed in the most recent version of the product. Each of these terms means essentially the same thing. If I refer to a previous version of Exchange Server, I always do so specifically, such as Exchange 2000 Server. Finally, I often use the term Exchange server (note the lowercase s in server) to refer to an actual server computer, as in "There are eight Exchange servers in this routing group."

Exchange Server and Windows Integration

Exchange Server 2003 is optimized to run on Windows Server 2003 and can be installed with the following operating systems:

- **Windows Server 2003 Standard Edition** Designed to provide services and resources to other systems on a network. It's a direct replacement for Microsoft Windows NT 4.0 Server and Microsoft Windows 2000 Server. The operating system has a rich set of features and configuration options. Windows Server 2003 Standard Edition supports up to 4 gigabytes (GB) of RAM and two CPUs.

- **Windows Server 2003 Enterprise Edition** Extends the features provided in Windows Server 2003 to include support for Cluster Service, metadirectory services, and Services for Macintosh. It also supports 64-bit Intel Itanium-based computers, hot swappable RAM, and nonuniform memory access (NUMA). Enterprise servers can have up to 32 GB of RAM on x86, 64 GB of RAM on Itanium, and eight CPUs.

- **Windows Server 2003 Datacenter Edition** The most robust Windows server. It has enhanced clustering features and supports very large memory configurations with up to 64 GB of RAM on x86 and 128 GB of RAM on Itanium. It has a minimum CPU requirement of 8 and can support up 32 CPUs in all.

- **Windows Server 2003 Web Edition** Designed to provide Web services for deploying Web sites and Web-based applications. As such, this server edition includes the Microsoft .NET Framework, Microsoft Internet Information Services (IIS), ASP.NET, and network load-balancing features but lacks many other features, including Active Directory. In fact, the only other key Windows features in this edition are the distributed file system (DFS), Encrypting File System (EFS), and Remote Desktop for administration. Windows Server 2003 Web Edition supports up to 2 GB of RAM and two CPUs.

Although Exchange Server 2003 can also be installed on Windows 2000 Server editions with Service Pack 3 or later, running Exchange Server 2003 on Windows Server 2003 has many benefits. It ensures all the latest Exchange features and enhancements are available, including the following:

- **Improved memory allocation** Exchange Server can more efficiently reuse blocks of virtual memory to reduce fragmentation and improve performance. Additionally, using the USERVA switch in the Boot.ini file, administrators can optimize user and kernel mode memory allocations on a per-megabyte basis.

- **Volume Shadow Copy support** Shadow copy backup is a feature of Windows Server 2003 that allows the operating system to create point-in-time snapshots of data. Volume Shadow Copy provides additional options for backup and recovery of Exchange Server.

- **Cross-forest Kerberos authentication support** When using Exchange Server and Outlook 2003, Exchange can use Kerberos to authenticate users, and when transitive trusts are in place, the authentication can take place across forest boundaries, allowing Exchange Servers and user accounts to be in different forests.

- **Improved Active Directory architecture** When using Exchange Server on Windows Server 2003, all Windows Server 2003 Active Directory enhancements are available to improve performance and allow for better integration of the operating system and Exchange server. These improvements improve performance, reduce replication traffic, allow for rollback of Active Directory changes, and provide additional configuration and administration options.

Security Alert It is important to note that on a new Exchange Server 2003 installation, some features are disabled for security reasons. Specifically, you'll find that the Microsoft Exchange POP3, Microsoft Exchange IMAP4 and Microsoft Exchange Site Replication services are disabled. If you use these services with Exchange, you'll need to enable them for automatic startup and then start them using the techniques discussed in the section of Chapter 4 entitled, "Using and Managing Exchange Server Services." You may also find that wireless browsing for Outlook Mobile Access (OMA) is not enabled. To enable wireless browsing, see the section of Chapter 3 entitled, "Managing Wireless Browsing."

In Exchange Server 2003, e-mail addresses, distribution groups, and other directory resources are stored in the directory database provided by Active Directory. Active Directory is a directory service running on Windows domain controllers. When there are multiple domain controllers, the controllers automatically replicate directory data with each other using a multimaster replication model. This model allows any domain controller to process directory changes and then replicate those changes to other domain controllers.

The first time you install Exchange Server 2003 in a Windows domain, the installation process updates and extends Active Directory. The changes made to Active Directory allow you to centrally manage many Exchange functions, including user administration and security. Not only does centralized management reduce the administration workload, it also reduces complexity, making it easier for administrators to manage large Exchange installations.

The Exchange installation process also updates the Active Directory Users And Computers Snap-In for Microsoft Management Console (MMC). These updates are what make Active Directory Users And Computers the tool of choice for performing most Exchange administration tasks. You can use Active Directory Users And Computers to do the following:

- Manage mailboxes and distribution groups.
- Enable and disable messaging features such as instant messaging and voice messaging.

- Set delivery restrictions, delivery options, and storage limits on individual accounts.
- Manage e-mail addresses associated with user accounts.

The main window for Active Directory Users And Computers is shown in Figure 1-1. If you're familiar with Windows Server administration, you'll note that the main window has been updated for Exchange Server. By selecting View, Add/Remove Columns, you can add four new columns as well:

- **E-Mail Address** Shows the e-mail address of the user or group, such as williams@technology.domain.com.
- **Exchange Alias** Shows the e-mail alias for the user or group within Exchange, such as williams. For users, this is also the name of the Exchange mailbox.
- **Exchange Mailbox Store** Shows the identifier for the mailbox store in which the mailbox is stored. (Only users can have mailboxes, so this entry doesn't apply to groups.)
- **X.400 E-mail Address** Shows the e-mail address that is used with the X.400 connector.

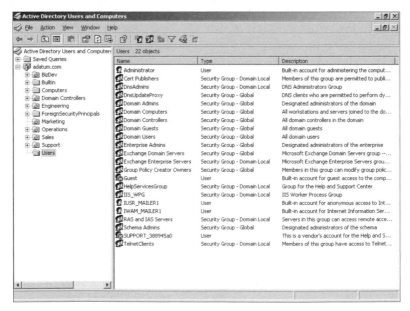

Figure 1-1. *Use Active Directory Users And Computers to manage tasks for mailboxes and distribution groups.*

Although these changes to Windows Server are relatively minor, other changes to Windows Server have far-reaching effects. Security is a prime example.

Exchange Server 2003 fully supports the Windows Server security model and relies on this security mechanism to control access to directory resources. This means you can control access to mailboxes and membership in distribution groups and you can perform other Exchange security administration tasks through the standard Windows Server permission set. For example, to add a user to a distribution group, you simply make the user a member of the distribution group in Active Directory Users And Computers.

Because Exchange Server uses Windows Server security, you can't create a mailbox without first creating a user account that will use the mailbox. Every Exchange mailbox must be associated with a domain account—even those used by Exchange for general messaging tasks. For example, the SMTP and System Attendant mailboxes that Exchange Server uses are associated by default with the built-in System user.

Use of Windows Server security also means that access to Exchange Server is controlled through standard Windows Server groups. The key groups are as follows:

- **Domain Admins** Members of Domain Admins can manage user accounts and related account permissions. They can create mailboxes, modify distribution groups, and perform other Exchange administration functions. They can also manage the configuration of Exchange Server.

- **Enterprise Admins** Members of Enterprise Admins have full access to Exchange Server. They can create mailboxes, modify distribution groups, and perform other Exchange administration functions. They can also delete trees and subelements, tasks that cannot be performed by Domain Admins.

- **Exchange Domain Servers** Computers that are members of this group can manage mail interchange and queues. All Exchange servers should be members of this group. This global group is in turn a member of the domain local group Exchange Enterprise Servers.

Like Windows Server, Exchange Server also supports policy-based administration. You can think of policies as sets of rules that help you effectively manage Exchange Server. You can create two general types of policies:

- **System policies** You use system policies to manage Exchange servers, public data stores, and mailbox data stores.

- **Recipient policies** You use recipient policies to manage e-mail addresses for users.

You can use system and recipient policies to automate many administration tasks. For example, you can create a system policy to automate replication and maintenance of data stores. You could then apply this policy to multiple Exchange servers. This is discussed in more detail in Chapter 8, "Implementing Directory Security and Microsoft Exchange Server 2003 Policies."

Hardware and Component Requirements for Exchange Server

Before you install Exchange Server 2003 you should carefully plan the messaging architecture. Key guidelines for choosing hardware for Exchange Server are as follows:

- **Memory** Minimum of 256 MB of RAM. This is twice the minimum memory suggested by Microsoft. The primary reason for this additional memory is to enhance performance. That said, most of the Exchange installations I run use 512 MB of RAM as a starting point, even in small installations (and especially if you plan to run all Exchange services from a single server).

- **CPU** Exchange Server is designed for Intel x86 and Itanium CPUs. Exchange Server 2003 achieves benchmark performance with Intel Pentium 4 3.06 GHz, Intel Xeon 3.06 GHz and Intel Itanium 2 1.0 GHz. These CPUs provide good starting points for the average Exchange Server 2003 installation.

- **Symmetric multiprocessing** Exchange Server supports symmetric multiprocessors, and you'll see significant performance improvements if you use multiple CPUs. Still, if Exchange Server is supporting a small organization with a single domain, one CPU should be enough. If the server supports a medium or large organization or handles mail for multiple domains, you might want to consider adding processors. An alternative would be to distribute the workload to virtual servers on different systems.

- **Disk drives** The data storage capacity you need depends entirely on the number and the size of the databases that will be on the server. You need enough disk space to store all your data, plus workspace, system files, and virtual memory. Input/output (I/O) throughput is just as important as drive capacity. In most cases, Small Computer System Interface (SCSI) drives are faster than Integrated Device Electronics/Enhanced Integrated Drive Electronics (IDE/EIDE) and are therefore recommended. Rather than use one large drive, you should use several smaller drives, which allows you to configure fault tolerance with redundant array of independent disks (RAID).

- **Data protection** Add protection against unexpected drive failures by using RAID. RAID 0, RAID 1, and RAID 5 are supported by Windows Server. Other RAID levels can be implemented using hardware RAID configurations. I recommend using RAID 1 or RAID 5 for drives containing messaging databases. RAID 1 (disk mirroring) creates duplicate copies of data on separate drives, but recovery from drive failure usually interrupts operations while you restore the failed drive from transaction logs or database backups. RAID 5 (disk striping with parity) offers good protection against single drive failure but has poor write performance.

- **Uninterruptible power supply** Exchange Server 2003 is designed to maintain database integrity at all times and can recover information using transaction logs. This doesn't protect the server hardware, however, from sudden power loss or power spikes, both of which can seriously damage hardware. To prevent this, connect your server to an uninterruptible power supply (UPS). A UPS gives you time to shut down the server or servers properly in the event of a power outage. Proper shutdown is especially important on servers using write-back caching controllers. These controllers temporarily store data in cache, and without proper shutdown, this data can be lost before it is written to disk.

Many Exchange Server features require IIS 5.0 or later. Before you install Exchange Server, you should ensure that the target server is configured properly. With Windows 2000 Server using Service Pack 3 or later, any required IIS components are installed automatically prior to installing Exchange Server 2003. However, with Windows Server 2003, the following IIS components must be installed prior to installing Exchange Server 2003 for it to run properly:

- Windows .NET Framework
- ASP.NET
- SMTP Service
- NNTP Service
- World Wide Web Service

On a Windows 2003 Server system, you can determine if these components are installed or add necessary components by completing the following steps:

1. In Control Panel, double-click Add/Remove Programs.
2. Start the Windows Components Wizard by clicking Add/Remove Windows Components. You should now see the Windows Components Wizard page shown in Figure 1-2.

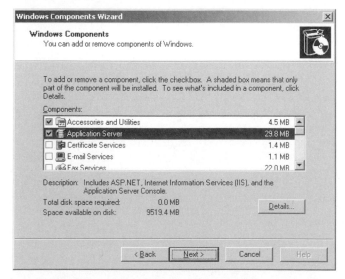

Figure 1-2. *IIS and Exchange Server are tightly integrated. You'll need to install IIS before deploying most messaging and collaboration services.*

3. With Windows Server 2003, IIS is now under Application Server, so the Application Server entry should be selected in the Components list box. If it isn't, select it.

 Note Throughout this book, I refer to double-clicking, which is the most common technique used for accessing folders and running programs. With a double-click, the first click selects the item and the second click opens or runs it, or both. In Windows Server 2003 you can also configure single-click open/run. Here, moving the mouse over the item selects it and a click opens or runs it, or both. You can change the mouse click options with the Folder Options utility in Control Panel. To do this, select the General tab, and then choose Single-Click To Open Item or Double-Click To Open Item as appropriate.

4. Click Details, then select .NET Framework, ASP.NET, and Internet Information Services (IIS).

5. Select (but do not clear) Internet Information Services (IIS) and then click Details. Select these subcomponents of IIS:
   - Common Files
   - Internet Information Services Manager
   - SMTP Service
   - NNTP Service
   - World Wide Web Service

6. Click OK twice.

7. Complete the installation process by clicking Next and then clicking Finish.

If you follow these hardware and component guidelines, you'll be well on your way to success with Exchange Server 2003.

Exchange Server Administration Tools

Several types of tools are available for Exchange administration. The ones you'll use the most for managing local and remote servers are the graphical administration tools. With proper configuration, these tools let you centrally manage Exchange servers regardless of where they're located.

One of the key tools for Exchange administration is Active Directory Users And Computers, which was discussed previously in this chapter. Another key tool is System Manager. System Manager provides an integrated toolbox for managing Exchange installations, and it's the equivalent of the Exchange Administrator in previous versions of Exchange Server. As Figure 1-3 shows, you can use System Manager to manage the following:

- Global settings for all Exchange servers in the organization
- Policies, address lists, and address templates for recipients

- Server protocols and information stores
- System policies for servers, mailbox stores, and public folder stores
- Connectors—including connectors for Lotus Notes and Novell GroupWise
- Site replication, message tracking, and monitors
- Public folders

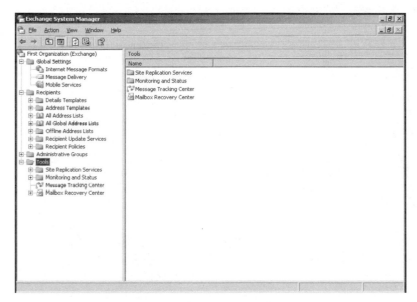

Figure 1-3. *Use System Manager to manage Exchange sites, servers, and settings.*

If you selected the Exchange System Management Tools component when you installed Exchange Server, you'll find that Active Directory Users And Computers and System Manager are already installed on your server. In this case, you can find these tools by clicking Start, choosing Programs or All Programs, and then choosing Microsoft Exchange.

You don't have to run Active Directory Users And Computers or System Manager from the Exchange server. You can install these tools on any Microsoft Windows XP Professional, Windows 2000 Server, or Windows Server 2003 system by completing the following steps:

1. Log on to the system using an account with full Exchange administrator privileges. Insert the Exchange Server 2003 CD-ROM into the CD-ROM drive.

2. If Autorun is enabled, an introductory dialog box should be displayed automatically. Select Exchange Server Setup to start the Microsoft Exchange Server Installation Wizard. Otherwise, you'll need to start the Setup program on the CD-ROM.

3. If you are prompted to provide administrator credentials prior to installation, select Run The Program As The Following User, and then provide the user name and password of a domain administrator account.

4. On the Microsoft Exchange Server Installation Wizard page, click Next to continue. Accept the end user license agreement by selecting I Agree and then click Next.

5. As Figure 1-4 shows, you should now see the Component Selection Wizard page. You need to install the Microsoft Exchange Server component and the Microsoft Exchange System Management Tools. Once you've selected these options for installation, click Next, and then complete the installation process.

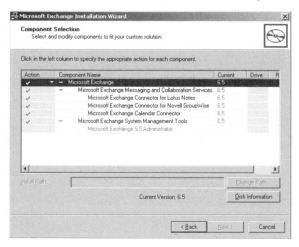

Figure 1-4. *Use the Microsoft Exchange Server Installation Wizard to install the components labeled Microsoft Exchange Server and Microsoft Exchange System Management Tools.*

Other administration tools that you might want to use with Exchange Server are summarized in Table 1-1.

Table 1-1. Quick Reference Administration Tools to Use with Exchange Server 2003

Administrative Tool	Purpose
Active Directory Cleanup Wizard	Identify and merge multiple accounts that refer to the same person.
Computer Management	Start and stop services, manage disks, and access other system management tools.
Configure Your Server	Add, remove, and configure Windows services for the network.
DNS	Manage the Domain Name System (DNS) service.

Table 1-1. Quick Reference Administration Tools to Use with Exchange Server 2003

Administrative Tool	Purpose
Event Viewer	Manage events and logs.
Exchange Server Migration Wizard	Migrate user accounts from other e-mail servers to Exchange Server.
Internet Information Services (IIS) Manager	Manage Web, File Transfer Protocol (FTP) and SMTP servers.
Microsoft Network Monitor	Monitor network traffic and troubleshoot networking problems.
Performance	Display graphs of system performance and configure data logs and alerts.

Most of the tools listed in Table 1-1 are accessible from the Administrative Tools program group. Click Start, point to Programs or All Programs, and then point to Administrative Tools.

Chapter 2

Managing Microsoft Exchange Server 2003 Clients

As a Microsoft Exchange administrator, you need to know how to configure and maintain Exchange clients. With Microsoft Exchange Server 2003 you can use any mail client that supports standard mail protocols. Some of the clients you can use include the following:

- Microsoft Office Outlook 2003
- Microsoft Outlook Express
- Microsoft Outlook for the Mac
- Microsoft Outlook Web Access

For ease of administration you'll want to choose a specific client for on-site users as a standard and supplement it with a specific client for off-site or mobile users. The on-site and off-site clients can be the same. I recommend focusing on Outlook Express, Outlook 2003, and Outlook Web Access. Each client supports a slightly different set of features and messaging protocols, and each client has its advantages and disadvantages, including the following:

- With Outlook 2003, you get a full-featured client that on-site, off-site, and mobile users can use. Outlook 2003 is part of the Microsoft Office system of applications and is the only mail client spotlighted here that features full support for the latest messaging features in Exchange Server. Outlook 2003 is more difficult to configure than Outlook Express, but corporate and workgroup users often need its rich support for calendars, scheduling, and e-mail management.

- With Outlook Express, you get a lightweight client that's best suited for off-site or mobile users. Outlook Express is freeware that is available with Microsoft Internet Explorer. Although Outlook Express supports standard messaging protocols, the client doesn't support calendars, scheduling, voice mail, or key messaging features of Exchange Server. It is, however, fairly easy to configure.

- With Outlook Web Access, you get a mail client that you can access securely through a standard Web browser. With Internet Explorer 5.0 or later, Outlook Web Access supports most of the features found in Outlook 2003, including calendars, scheduling, and voice mail. With other browsers the client functionality remains the same, but some features, such as voice mail, might not be supported. You don't need to configure Outlook Web Access on the client, and it's ideal for users who want to access e-mail while away from the office.

Outlook 2003 is the most common Exchange client for corporate and workgroup environments. With the introduction of remote procedure call (RPC) over Hypertext Transfer Protocol (HTTP), which eliminates the need for a virtual private network (VPN) to access Exchange Server over the Internet, Outlook 2003 might also be your client of choice for off-site and mobile users. The catch with RPC over HTTP is that the technology requires a complicated back-end configuration and is only supported when Exchange Server 2003 is running on Microsoft Windows Server 2003.

Outlook Express and Outlook Web Access, on the other hand, aren't designed for corporate users and are really meant for off-site or mobile users. Both clients are easy to configure and require relatively little back-end configuration. In fact, Exchange Server can be configured quickly and easily to work with these clients.

This chapter shows you how to manage Outlook 2003 and Outlook Express. Chapter 3, "Managing Mobile Outlook Users for Wireless, Web and Dial-Up Access," looks at using Outlook 2003 with RPC over HTTP and Outlook Web Access.

Configuring Mail Support for Outlook 2003 and Outlook Express

You can install both Outlook 2003 and Outlook Express as clients on a user's computer. The following sections look at these topics:

- Configuring Outlook 2003 and Outlook Express mail support for the first time
- Configuring Outlook 2003 for Exchange Server
- Adding Internet mail accounts to Outlook 2003 and Outlook Express
- Reconfiguring Outlook 2003 mail support
- Setting advanced mail options

Configuring Outlook 2003 for the First Time

You can install Outlook 2003 as a stand-alone product or as part of Office 2003. If another e-mail application is already installed on the computer, you'll have the opportunity:

- **Upgrade**   Select Upgrade From, choose the e-mail program to upgrade from, such as Outlook Express, and then click Next to start the Internet Connection Wizard. Afterward proceed through the steps as discussed in the section of this chapter entitled, "Configuring Outlook Express for the First Time." When you finish, you'll be able to import existing e-mail, contacts and other information into Outlook by clicking Yes when prompted. Keep in mind you are configuring a POP3, IMAP4 or HTTP server configuration rather than a direct connection to Exchange Server and you will probably need to reconfigure the mail account to connect directly to Exchange Server after you complete the upgrade and import process.

- **Not Upgrade**   Select Do Not Upgrade and then click Next to go right to the Yes/No prompt discussed below. You can then configure the user to connect directly to Exchange, POP3, IMAP4, HTTP or other server types. You will not, however, have the opportunity to import existing e-mail, contacts or data. This data will be available only in the previously configured e-mail program.

If no other e-mail application is installed on the computer, you won't get the import option. Instead, during installation of the stand-alone product—or the first time you run Outlook that was installed with Office 2003—you'll be prompted to configure Outlook to connect to a Microsoft Exchange Server, Internet e-mail, or other e-mail server. If you click Yes, you'll have the following options:

- **Microsoft Exchange Server**   Connect directly to Exchange Server; best for users who are connected to the organization's local area network (LAN). Users will have full access to Exchange Server. If users plan to connect to Exchange Server using RPC over HTTP, this is the option to choose as well.

- **POP3**   Connect to Exchange or another Post Office Protocol 3 (POP3) e-mail server through the Internet; best for users who are connecting from a remote location, such as home or a remote office, using dial-up or broadband Internet access. With POP3, users can download e-mail but cannot synchronize mailbox folders.

- **IMAP**   Connect to Exchange or another Internet Message Access Protocol (IMAP) e-mail server through the Internet; best for users who are connecting from a remote location, such as home or a remote office, using dial-up or broadband Internet access. With IMAP, users can download e-mail and also synchronize mailbox folders.

- **HTTP**   Connect to an HTTP e-mail server, such as Hotmail, through the Internet; best as an additional e-mail configuration option. Here, users can have an external e-mail account with a Web-based e-mail service that they want to check in addition to corporate e-mail.

- **Additional Server Types** Connect to a third-party mail server. If your organization has multiple types of mail servers, including Exchange Server, you'll probably want to configure a connection to Exchange Server first and then add additional e-mail account configurations later.

The sections that follow detail how you can configure Outlook 2003 to connect to Exchange, Internet e-mail, and other e-mail servers.

First-Time Configuration: Connecting to Exchange

The steps you follow to configure Outlook 2003 to connect to Exchange Server are as follows:

1. Click Yes when prompted to configure Outlook to connect to a Microsoft Exchange Server, Internet e-mail, or other e-mail server. Then, as shown in Figure 2-1, select Microsoft Exchange Server as the server type to use with Outlook 2003. Click Next.

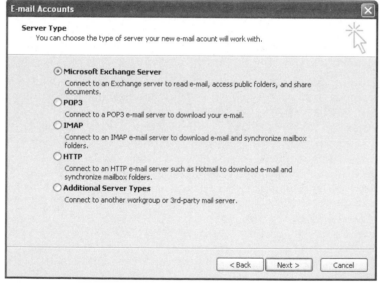

Figure 2-1. *In the Microsoft Outlook Setup Wizard, select the information services to install with Outlook 2003.*

2. In the Microsoft Exchange Server field, type the host name of the mail server, such as **mailer1**. You can also enter the fully qualified domain name of the mail server, such as **mailer1.adatum.com**. Using the full domain name can help ensure a successful connection when the mail server is in a different domain or forest.

3. In the User Name field, enter the user's domain logon name or domain user name, such as **Williams** or **William Stanek**. Click Check Name to confirm that you've entered the correct user name for the mailbox.

4. In most cases, you'll want to store a local copy of the user's e-mail on his or her computer. If this is the case, click Next to continue. If the computer has limited hard drive space, if it is a temporary computer, or if the user has several different computers that he or she uses for e-mail, you might not want to store a local copy of the user's mail on the computer. In this case, clear the Use Local Copy Of Mailbox check box and then click Next.

5. When you click Finish, Outlook configures itself and generates a Welcome message for the user. If the user also wants to connect to POP3, IMAP, or HTTP e-mail servers, follow the steps listed in the section of this chapter entitled "Adding Internet Mail Accounts to Outlook 2003 and Outlook Express."

First-Time Configuration: Connecting to Internet E-Mail or Other E-Mail Servers

The steps for configuring Outlook 2003 to use Internet e-mail or other e-mail servers are as follows:

1. Click Yes when prompted to configure Outlook to connect to a Microsoft Exchange Server, Internet e-mail, or other e-mail server. Before clicking Next, select the e-mail server type:

   - POP3 is used to check mail on an e-mail server and download the mail to the user's inbox. The user can't access private or public folders on the server. By using advanced configuration settings, the user can elect to download the mail and leave it on the server for future use. By leaving the mail on the server, the user can check mail on a home computer and still download it to an office computer later.

   - IMAP is used to check mail on an e-mail server and download message headers. The user can then access each e-mail individually and download it. Unlike POP3, IMAP has no option to leave mail on the server. IMAP also lets users access public and private folders on an Exchange server. It is best suited for users who have a single computer, such as a laptop, that they use to check mail both at the office and away from it.

   - HTTP is used to connect to an HTTP e-mail server, such as Hotmail, through the Internet; best as an additional e-mail configuration option. Here, users might have an external e-mail account with a Web-based e-mail service that they want to check in addition to corporate e-mail.

2. Under User Information, type the name that will appear in the From field of outgoing messages for this user, such as **William Stanek**, and then type the

e-mail address of the user. Be sure to type the e-mail alias as well as the server name, such as **williams@adatum.com**.

3. Under Logon Information, type the user's e-mail logon name and password or have the user type this information. For some mail servers, you might need to enter the name of the domain as well. With POP3 and IMAP, you type this information in the form ***domain\e-mail_alias***, such as **technology\williams**. In some cases, you might need to type this information in the form ***domain/e-mail_alias***, such as **technology/williams**.

4. If you selected POP3 or IMAP, you must enter the fully qualified domain name for the incoming and outgoing mail servers. Although these entries are often the same, some organizations have different incoming and outgoing mail servers. If you are not certain of your fully qualified domain name, contact your network administrator.

 Note If you're connecting to Exchange with POP3 or IMAP, enter the fully qualified domain name for the Exchange server instead of the host name. For example, you would use MailServer.adatum.com instead of MailServer.

5. If you selected HTTP, you can select the HTTP mail service provider as MSN, Hotmail, or Other. With the Other option, you must enter the Uniform Resource Locator (URL) to the main e-mail page of the HTTP service, such as *http://mail.yahoo.com/*.

6. For security, you might want to select Log On Using Secure Password Authentication. This option ensures that passwords aren't passed as clear text over the Internet and that some form of encryption is used.

7. Check the account settings by clicking Test Account Settings. If you've configured e-mail properly, Outlook should be able to successfully send a test message. Be sure that all steps pass. Click Close.

8. Click Next and then click Finish to complete the configuration.

 Tip If you configure Outlook to use an Internet e-mail or other e-mail server and later need to connect directly to Exchange, you'll need to reconfigure mail support. See the section of this chapter entitled "Configuring Outlook 2003 for Exchange."

Configuring Outlook Express for the First Time

When you install Internet Explorer you have the option of installing Outlook Express as well. Outlook Express runs the Internet Connection Wizard the first time the application is started. You configure the user's Internet connection for startup by completing the following steps:

1. In the Display Name field, type the name that will appear in the From field of outgoing messages for this user, such as **William Stanek**. Click Next.

2. Type the e-mail address of the user. Be sure to type the e-mail username as well as the domain name, such as **williams@adatum.com**. Click Next.

3. As shown in Figure 2-2, select the type of protocol to use for the incoming mail server as POP3, IMAP, or HTTP. The advantages and disadvantages of these protocols are as follows:

- POP3 is used to check mail on an e-mail server and download the mail to the user's inbox. The user can't access private or public folders on the server. By using advanced configuration settings, the user can elect to download the mail *and* leave it on the server for future use. By leaving the mail on the server, the user can check mail on a home computer and still download it to an office computer later.

- IMAP is used to check mail on an e-mail server and download message headers. The user can then access each e-mail individually and download it. Unlike POP3, IMAP has no option to leave mail on the server. IMAP also lets users access public and private folders on an Exchange server. It is best suited for users who have a single computer, such as a laptop, that they use to check mail both at the office and away from it.

- HTTP is used to connect to an HTTP e-mail server, such as Hotmail, through the Internet; best as an additional e-mail configuration option. Here, users might have an external e-mail account with a Web-based e-mail service that they want to check in addition to corporate e-mail.

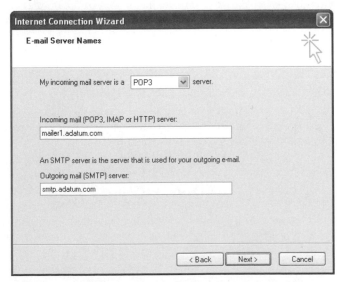

Figure 2-2. *Specify incoming and outgoing mail server options with the Internet Connection Wizard.*

4. If you select POP3 or IMAP, you must enter the fully qualified domain name for the incoming and outgoing mail servers. Although these entries are often the same, some organizations have different incoming and outgoing mail servers. If you are not certain of your fully qualified domain name, contact your network administrator. Click Next.

 Note If you're connecting to Exchange with POP3 or IMAP, enter the fully qualified domain name for the Exchange server instead of the host name. For example, you would use MailServer.adatum.com instead of MailServer.

5. If you select HTTP, you can select the mail service provider as MSN, Hotmail, or Other. With the Other option, you must enter the URL to the main e-mail page of the HTTP service, such as *http://mail.yahoo.com/*. Click Next.

6. Type the account name and password for the user or have the user type this information. The account name is usually the same as the e-mail username. For some mail servers, however, you might need to enter the name of the domain as well. You type this information in the form ***domain\e-mail_alias***, such as **technology\williams**. In some cases, you might need to type this information in the form ***domain\e-mail_alias***, such as **technology/williams**.

7. For security, you might want to select Log On Using Secure Password Authentication. This option ensures that passwords aren't passed as clear text over the Internet and that some form of encryption is used. Click Next.

8. Click Next and then click Finish to complete the configuration. If other e-mail applications are configured on the computer, the Outlook Express Import wizard is started and you have the option of importing the user's messages and address book. Be careful, because the import process deletes the user's mailbox from Outlook 2003.

Configuring Outlook 2003 for Exchange

If you didn't configure Outlook 2003 to use Exchange Server the first time it was started, don't worry: you can change the Outlook configuration to use Exchange. It does take a bit of extra work, however.

To get started, you need to close Outlook if it is started and then run the Mail utility in Control Panel. If Control Panel is in Category View, click Switch To Classic View and then double-click Mail. Otherwise, simply double-click Mail. Then follow these steps to configure Outlook 2003 to use Exchange:

1. In the Mail Setup–Outlook dialog box, click E-mail Accounts. This starts the E-Mail Accounts Wizard.

2. Select Add A New E-Mail Account and then click Next.

3. Select Microsoft Exchange Server and then click Next.

4. In the Microsoft Exchange Server field, type the host name of the mail server, such as **mailer1**. You can also enter the fully qualified domain name

of the mail server, such as **mailer1.adatum.com**. Using the full domain name can help ensure a successful connection when the mail server is in a different domain or forest.

5. In the User Name field, enter the user's domain logon name or domain user name, such as **Williams** or **William Stanek**. Click Check Name to confirm that you've entered the correct user name for the mailbox.

6. In most cases, you'll want to store a local copy of the user's e-mail on his or her computer. If this is the case, click Next to continue. If the computer has limited hard drive space, if it is a temporary computer, or if the user has several different computers that he or she uses for e-mail, you might not want to store a local copy of the user's mail on the computer. In this case, clear the Use Local Copy Of Mailbox check box and then click Next.

7. Click Finish to close the E-Mail Accounts Wizard and then click Close in the Mail Setup–Outlook dialog box.

8. Start Outlook 2003. If you elected to use a local copy of the user's mailbox, Outlook begins creating this local copy. The creation process can take several minutes.

Adding Internet Mail Accounts to Outlook 2003 and Outlook Express

Both Outlook 2003 and Outlook Express allow you to retrieve mail from multiple servers. For example, you could configure Outlook to check mail on the corporate Exchange server, a personal account on Earthlink, and a personal account on Hotmail.

Adding Internet Mail Accounts in Outlook 2003

You add Internet mail accounts to Outlook 2003 by completing the following steps:

1. Display the E-Mail Accounts dialog box by selecting Tools, E-Mail Accounts.

2. Select Add A New E-Mail Account and then click Next.

3. Select the e-mail server type as POP3, IMAP, or HTTP and then click Next.

4. Follow Steps 2 through 8 outlined previously in the section of this chapter entitled, "First-Time Configuration: Connecting to Internet E-Mail or Other E-Mail Servers."

Adding Internet Mail Accounts in Outlook Express

With Outlook Express, you add Internet mail accounts by completing the following steps:

1. Select Accounts from the Tools menu. In the Internet Accounts dialog box, click Add, and then select Mail. This starts the Internet Connection Wizard.

2. Follow the steps outlined previously in the section of this chapter entitled "Configuring Outlook Express for the First Time."

Reconfiguring Outlook 2003 Mail Support

When you first configure Outlook 2003 on a computer, you can configure it to connect to a Microsoft Exchange Server, Internet e-mail, or other e-mail server. You can change this e-mail configuration at any time by completing the following steps:

1. Start Outlook 2003, and then select Tools, E-Mail Accounts.

2. In the E-Mail Accounts dialog box, select View Or Change Existing E-Mail Accounts and then click Next.

3. As Figure 2-3 shows, the currently configured accounts are listed in the order in which e-mail is processed. The e-mail account listed first is the primary or default account for sending e-mail. Further, incoming and outgoing mail for this account is processed before mail for other accounts.

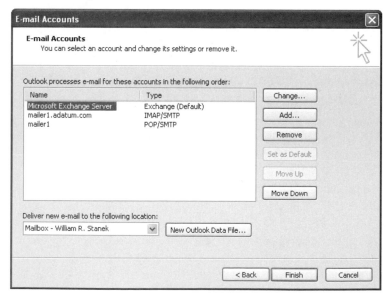

Figure 2-3. *Currently configured accounts are listed in the order in which e-mail is processed.*

4. To change the default account for sending mail, select the account you want to use as the default and then click Set As Default. This effectively reconfigures Outlook 2003 to use the designated e-mail server as its primary e-mail server.

5. To change the settings of an e-mail account, click Change, make any edits necessary, and then click Next.

6. To remove an e-mail account, click Remove and then click Yes when prompted to confirm the action.

7. Click Finish when you are done reconfiguring Outlook mail support.

Leaving Mail on the Server with POP3

If the user connects to an Internet e-mail server, an advantage of POP3 is that it lets the user leave mail on the server. By leaving the mail on the server, the user can check mail on a home computer and still download it to an office computer later.

Leaving Mail on the Server: Outlook 2003

With Outlook 2003, you can configure POP3 accounts to leave mail on the server by completing the following steps:

1. Start Outlook 2003 and then select E-Mail Accounts from the Tools menu.

2. In the E-Mail Accounts dialog box, click Next. After you select the POP3 mail account you want to modify, click Change.

3. Click More Settings to display the Internet E-Mail Settings dialog box.

4. In the Internet E-Mail Settings dialog box, select the Advanced tab, as shown in Figure 2-4.

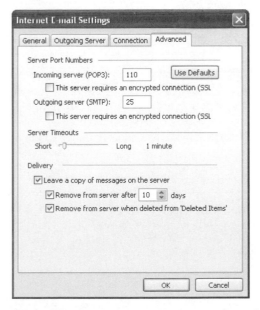

Figure 2-4. *Use the Advanced tab to configure how and when mail should be left on the server.*

5. Use the Delivery options to configure how and when mail should be left on the server. To enable this option, select the Leave A Copy Of Messages On

The Server check box. The additional options depend on the client configuration. Options you might see include the following:

- **Remove From Server After *N* Days**   Select this option if you're connecting to an Internet service provider (ISP) and want to delete messages from the server after a specified number of days. By deleting ISP mail periodically, you ensure that your mailbox size doesn't exceed your limit.

- **Remove From Server When Deleted From "Deleted Items"**
  Select this option to delete messages from the server when you delete them from the Deleted Items folder. You'll see this option with Internet Only Outlook 2003 configurations.

6. Click OK when you've finished changing the account settings.

7. Click Next and then click Finish.

Leaving Mail on the Server: Outlook Express

With Outlook Express 2003, you can configure POP3 accounts to leave mail on the server by completing the following steps:

1. Start Outlook Express, and then select Accounts from the Tools menu.

2. Select the POP3 mail account you want to modify, and then click Properties.

3. In the Properties dialog box, select the Advanced tab.

4. Use the Delivery options to configure how and when mail should be left on the server. To enable this option, select Leave A Copy Of Messages On The Server. The additional options depend on the client configuration. Options you might see include the following:

- **Remove From Server After *N* Days**   Select this option if you're connecting to an Internet service provider (ISP) and want to delete messages from the server after a specified number of days. By deleting ISP mail periodically, you ensure that your mailbox size doesn't exceed your limit.

- **Remove From Server When Deleted From "Deleted Items"**
  Select this option to delete messages from the server when you delete them from the Deleted Items folder. You'll see this option with Internet Only Outlook 2003 configurations.

5. Click OK and then click Close.

Checking Private and Public Folders with IMAP and UNIX Mail Servers

With IMAP you can check public and private folders on a mail server. This option is enabled by default, but the default settings might not work properly with UNIX mail servers.

Checking Folders: Outlook 2003

With Outlook 2003, you can check or change the folder settings used by IMAP by completing the following steps:

1. Start Outlook 2003, and then select E-Mail Accounts from the Tools menu.
2. In the E-Mail Accounts dialog box, click Next. After you select the IMAP mail account you want to modify, click Change.
3. Click More Settings to display the Internet E-Mail Settings dialog box.
4. In the Internet E-Mail Settings dialog box, select the Advanced tab.
5. If the account connects to a UNIX mail server, enter the path to the mailbox folder on the server, such as **~wrstanek/mail**. Don't end the folder path with a forward slash (/). Click OK.
6. Click Next and then click Finish.

Checking Folders: Outlook Express

With Outlook Express, you can check or change the folder settings used by IMAP by completing the following steps:

1. Start Outlook Express, and then select Accounts from the Tools menu.
2. Select the IMAP mail account you want to modify and then click Properties.
3. In the Properties dialog box, select the IMAP tab, as shown in Figure 2-5.

Figure 2-5. *Use the IMAP tab to configure how folders are used with IMAP mail accounts.*

4. If the account connects to a UNIX mail server, enter the path to the mailbox folder on the server, such as **~wrstanek/mail**. Don't end the folder path with a forward slash (/).

5. To automatically check for new messages in all public, private, and hidden folders, make sure the Check For New Messages In All Folders check box is selected.

6. To store sent items and draft messages on the IMAP server, select the Store Special Folders On IMAP Server check box and then type the name for these folders. The default names are Sent Items and Drafts, respectively.

7. Click OK and then click Close.

Managing the Exchange Server Service in Outlook 2003

Whenever you use Outlook 2003 to connect to Exchange Server, you can use the Exchange Server Service to optimize the way mail is handled. This service has many advanced configuration and management options, including those for the following:

- E-mail delivery and processing
- Remote mail
- Scheduled connections
- Multiple mailboxes

Each of these options is examined in the sections that follow.

Managing Delivery and Processing E-Mail Messages

When Outlook 2003 uses Exchange Server, you have strict control over how e-mail is delivered and processed. Exchange mail can be delivered to one of three locations:

- Server mailboxes
- Local copies of server mailboxes
- Personal folders

Exchange mail can be processed by any of the information services configured for use in Outlook 2003. These information services include the following:

- Microsoft Exchange
- Internet E-mail

Let's look at how you use each of these delivery and processing options.

Using Server Mailboxes

Server mailboxes are the default configuration option. With server mailboxes, new e-mail is delivered to a mailbox on the Exchange server and you can only view or receive new mail when you're connected to Exchange. Server mailboxes are best suited for corporate users with dedicated connections and users who can remotely access Exchange through a dial-up connection or through RPC over HTTP.

With server mailboxes, you have the option of storing a local copy of e-mail on the user's computer in addition to the e-mail stored on Exchange Server or storing e-mail only on the Exchange Server. The default configuration is to use a local copy of the user's mailbox. In most cases, this is a good configuration. You might want to change this configuration if the user's computer has limited hard disk space or if the user doesn't have a dedicated computer. Another reason for changing this configuration is if the user makes use of multiple computers for e-mail and you don't want local copies of mail stored on several different computers.

Changing the configuration doesn't necessarily mean storing e-mail only on the server. You can also configure Outlook to download only message headers. In this configuration, the e-mail body is only downloaded from Exchange when the user opens the message.

Tip   You can think of local copies as mirror images of the user's mailbox on Exchange Server. Local copies of Exchange mailboxes are stored in .ost files. With Microsoft Windows XP, the default location of an .ost file is %SystemDrive%\%HomePath%\Local Settings\Application Data\Microsoft\Outlook where %SystemDrive% and %HomePath% are system- and user-specific environment variables.

Local mailbox copies are similar to offline folders used with previous versions of Outlook. However, they are configured automatically (as long as you select Use Local Copy) and are much easier to use and manage.

To configure how server mailboxes and local copies of server mailboxes are used, complete the following steps:

1. Start Outlook 2003, and then select E-Mail Accounts from the Tools menu. This displays the E-Mail Accounts dialog box. Click Next.

2. The Deliver New E-Mail To The Following Location list shows where mail is being delivered. Select the Mailbox-*username* option where *username* is the name of the account you are logged in under to ensure mail is delivered to the Exchange Server mailbox rather than to a personal folder.

3. Select the Exchange mail account you want to modify and then click Change.

4. On the Exchange Server Settings page, click More Settings to display the Microsoft Exchange Server dialog box.

5. Click the Advanced tab, shown in Figure 2-6.

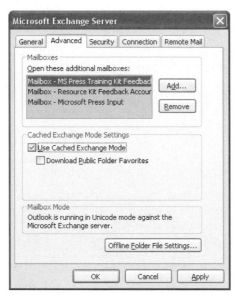

Figure 2-6. *On the Advanced tab, select the mailbox settings that you want to use.*

6. The Use Cached Exchange Mode box should be selected by default. Clear this check box if you want to store e-mail only on the server and then skip to Step 8.

7. Click OK to close the Microsoft Exchange Server dialog box.

8. Click Next and then click Finish.

Using Personal Folders

An alternative to using server mailboxes is to use personal folders. Personal folders are stored in a file on the user's computer. With personal folders, mail delivered to the user's Inbox is no longer stored on the server. Users have personal folders when Outlook 2003 is configured to use Internet e-mail or other e-mail servers. Users might also have personal folders if the auto-archive feature is used to archive messages. Users can also change to personal folders rather than using server-stored e-mail, or server-stored messages with a local copy of their e-mail.

Real World   Personal folders are stored in .pst files. With Windows XP, the default location of a .pst file is %SystemDrive%\%Home-Path%\Local Settings\Application Data\Microsoft\Outlook where %SystemDrive% and %HomePath% are system and user-specific environment variables. Personal folders are best suited for mobile users who check mail through dial-up connections and who might not be able to use a dial-up connection to connect directly to Exchange.

Users with personal folders lose the advantages that server-based folders offer—namely, single-instance storage and the ability to have a single point of recovery in case of failure. In addition, .pst files have many disadvantages. They get corrupted frequently and on these occasions, the Inbox Repair Tool must be used to restore the file. If the hard disk on a user's computer fails, you can only recover the mail if the .pst file has been backed up. Unfortunately, most workstations aren't backed up regularly (if at all) and the onus of backing up the .pst file falls on the user who might or might not understand how to back up the .pst file.

Determining the Presence of Personal Folders   You can determine the presence of personal folders using either of these techniques:

- In the Outlook mail folder list, look for the Personal Folders node and related Deleted Items, Inbox, Outbox, and Sent Items folders.
- Select Accounts from the Tools menu. Click Next in the E-Mail Accounts dialog box and then check the Deliver New E-Mail To The Following Location list to see if Personal Folders is listed as an option.

Creating Personal Folders   If personal folders aren't available and you want to configure them, follow these steps:

1. Select E-Mail Accounts from the Tools menu. Click Next in the E-Mail Accounts dialog box.

2. On the E-Mail Accounts page, click New Outlook Data File.

3. Microsoft Outlook Personal Folders File (.pst) should be selected by default. Click OK.

4. This displays the Create Or Open Outlook Data File dialog box shown in Figure 2-7. Use this dialog box to look for an existing .pst file or to create a new one.

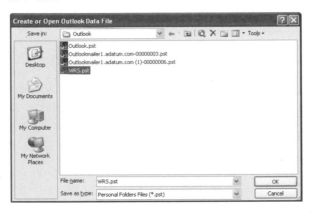

Figure 2-7. *Use the Create Or Open Outlook Data File dialog box to search for an existing .pst file or to create a new one.*

5. If you create a new .pst file, you'll see the Create Microsoft Personal Folders dialog box. In the Name field, enter the name for the personal folders. Then, as necessary, select an encryption option and set a password on the .pst file.

Note   It is important to be aware that Exchange Server does not ship with any password recovery utility for .pst files. If a user sets a password on a .pst file and forgets it, the Exchange administrator has no way to reset it. You might find third-party vendors who make password-cracking or recovery tools, but they are not guaranteed to work and they are not supported by Microsoft.

6. Click OK and then click Finish. The personal folder you've selected or created is displayed in the Outlook folder list. You should see related subfolders as well.

Delivering Mail to Personal Folders   If you want mail to be delivered to a personal folder, complete the following steps:

1. Select E-Mail Accounts from the Tools menu. Click Next in the E-Mail Accounts dialog box.

2. Using the Deliver New E-Mail To The Following Location drop-down list, select the Personal Folders option, as shown in Figure 2-8.

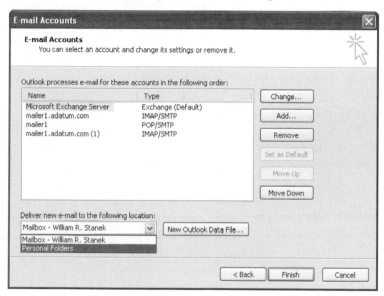

Figure 2-8. *To deliver mail directly to a personal folder and not store mail on the server, select the Personal Folders option from the Deliver New E-Mail To The Following Location drop-down list on the Delivery tab.*

3. Click Finish and confirm the action by clicking OK.

4. Exit and restart Outlook. Outlook will now use personal folders.

Accessing Multiple Exchange Server Mailboxes

Earlier in the chapter, I discussed how users could check multiple Internet mail accounts in Outlook 2003. You might have wondered if users could check multiple Exchange mailboxes as well—and they can. Users often need to access multiple Exchange mailboxes for many reasons:

- Help Desk administrators might need access to the Help Desk mailbox in addition to their own mailboxes.

- Managers might need temporary access to the mailboxes of subordinates who are on vacation.

- Mailboxes might need to be set up for long-term projects, and project members need access to those mailboxes.

- Resource mailboxes might need to be set up for accounts payable, human resources, corporate information, and so on.

Normally, there is a one-to-one relationship between user accounts and Exchange mailboxes. You create a user account and assign a mailbox to the account; only this user can access the mailbox directly through Exchange. To change this behavior, you must do the following:

1. Log on to Exchange as the owner of the mailbox.

2. Delegate access to the mailbox to one or more additional users.

3. Have users with delegated access log on to Exchange and open the mailbox.

The sections that follow examine each of these steps in detail.

Logging On to Exchange as the Mailbox Owner

Logging on to Exchange as the mailbox owner allows you to delegate access to the mailbox. Before you can log on as the mailbox owner, you must complete the following steps:

1. Create a domain user account for the mailbox, if one doesn't already exist.

2. Log on as the user. You'll need to know the account name and password for the domain.

3. Start Outlook 2003. Make sure that mail support is configured to use Exchange Server. If necessary, configure support for Exchange Server, which creates the mail profile for the user.

4. Once you configure Outlook to use Exchange Server, you should be able to log on to Exchange Server as the mailbox owner.

 Tip You should configure the mailbox to deliver mail to the server rather than to a personal folder. In this way, the mail is available to be checked by one or more mailbox users.

Delegating Mailbox Access

Once you've logged on as the mailbox owner, you can delegate access to the mailbox by completing these steps:

1. In Outlook 2003, choose Options from the Tools menu. Select the Delegates tab, and then click Add.

2. The Add Users dialog box is shown in Figure 2-9. To add users, double-click the name of a user who needs access to the mailbox. Repeat this step as necessary for other users. Click OK when you're finished.

Figure 2-9. *Use the Add Users dialog box to delegate access to mailboxes.*

3. In the Delegate Permissions dialog box, assign permissions to the delegates for Calendar, Tasks, Inbox, Contacts, Notes, and Journal items. The available permissions are as follows:

- **None**   No permissions
- **Reviewer**   Grants read permission only
- **Author**   Grants read and create permissions
- **Editor**   Grants read, create, and modify permissions

Note   If the user needs total control over the mailbox, you should grant the user Editor permission for all items.

4. Click OK twice. These changes take place when a user restarts Outlook.
5. Delegated users can access the mailbox and send mail on behalf of the mailbox owner. To change this behavior, set folder permissions as described in the section of this chapter entitled "Granting Permission to Access Folders Without Delegating Access."

Opening Additional Exchange Mailboxes

The final step is to let Exchange Server know about the additional mailboxes the user wants to open. To do this, follow these steps:

1. Have the user who wants access to additional mailboxes log on and start Outlook 2003.

2. In Outlook 2003, select E-Mail Accounts from the Tools menu. Click Next in the E-Mail Accounts dialog box.

3. Select the Microsoft Exchange Server account and then click Change.

4. Click More Settings to display the Microsoft Exchange Server dialog box.

5. Select the Advanced tab and then click Add. Afterward, type the name of a mailbox to open. Generally, this is the same as the mail alias for the user or account associated with the mailbox. Click OK, and then repeat this step to add other mailboxes.

6. Click OK again.

7. Click Next and then click Finish. The additional mailboxes are displayed in the Outlook folder list.

Granting Permission to Access Folders Without Delegating Access

When a mailbox is stored on the server, you can grant access to individual folders in the mailbox. Granting access allows users to add the mailbox to their mail profiles and work with the folder. Users can only perform tasks for which you've granted permission.

To grant access to folders individually, follow these steps:

1. Right-click the folder for which you want to grant access and then select Properties.

2. Select the Permissions tab, as shown in Figure 2-10.

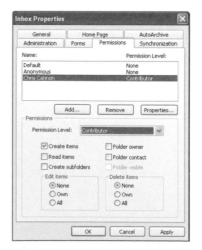

Figure 2-10. *Grant access to a folder through the Permissions tab.*

3. The Name and Permission Level lists display account names and their permissions on the folder. Two special names might be listed:
   - **Default**   Provides default permissions for all users.
   - **Anonymous**   Provides permissions for anonymous users, such as those who anonymously access a published public folder through the Web.

4. If you want to grant users permission that differs from the default permission, click Add.

5. In the Add Users dialog box, double-click the name of a user who needs access to the mailbox. Click Add to put the name in the Add Users list. Repeat this step as necessary for other users. Click OK when you're finished.

6. In the Name and Role lists, select one or more users whose permissions you want to modify. Afterward, use the Roles list to assign permissions or select individual permission items. The roles are defined as follows:
   - **Owner**   Grants all permissions in the folder. Users with this role can create, read, modify, and delete all items in the folder. They can create subfolders and change permissions on folders as well.
   - **Publishing Editor**   Grants permission to create, read, modify, and delete all items in the folder. Users with this role can create subfolders as well.
   - **Editor**   Grants permission to create, read, modify, and delete all items in the folder.
   - **Publishing Author**   Grants permission to create and read items in the folder, to modify and delete items the user created, and to create subfolders.
   - **Author**   Grants permission to create and read items in the folder and to modify and delete items the user created.
   - **Nonediting Author**   Grants permission to create and read items in the folder.
   - **Reviewer**   Grants read-only permission.
   - **Contributor**   Grants permission to create items but not to view the contents of the folder.
   - **None**   Grants no permission in the folder.

7. When you're finished granting permissions, click OK.

Using Mail Profiles to Customize the Mail Environment

The mail profile used with Outlook 2003 determines which information services are available and how they are configured. A default mail profile is created when you install and configure Outlook 2003 for the first time. This mail profile is usually called Outlook.

The active mail profile defines the service setup for the user who is logged on to the computer. You can define additional profiles for the user as well. You can use these additional profiles to customize the user's mail environment for different situations. Here are two scenarios:

- A manager needs to check Technical Support and Customer Support mailboxes only on Mondays when she writes summary reports. On other days the manager doesn't want to see these mailboxes. To solve this problem, you create two mail profiles: Support and Standard. The Support profile displays the manager's mailbox as well as the Technical Support and Customer Support mailboxes. The Standard profile displays only the manager's mailbox. The manager can then switch between these mail profiles as necessary.

- A laptop user wants to check Exchange mail directly while connected to the LAN. When at home, the user wants to use remote mail with scheduled connections. On business trips, the user wants to use Simple Mail Transfer Protocol (SMTP) and POP3. To solve this problem, you create three mail profiles: On-Site, Off-Site, and Home. The On-Site profile uses the Exchange Server service with a standard configuration. The Off-Site profile configures Exchange Server for remote mail and scheduled connections. The Home profile doesn't use the Exchange information service and uses the Internet Mail service instead.

Common tasks you'll use to manage mail profiles are examined in the sections that follow.

Creating, Copying, and Removing Mail Profiles

You manage mail profiles through the Mail utility. To access this utility and manage profiles, follow these steps:

1. In Control Panel, double-click Mail. If you are using Category View for Control Panel, click Switch To Classic View and then double-click Mail.
2. In the Mail Setup – Outlook dialog box, click Show Profiles.
3. As Figure 2-11 shows, you should see a list of mail profiles for the current user. Mail profiles for other users aren't displayed. You can now perform the following actions:
   - Click Add to create a new mail profile using the E-Mail Accounts Wizard.
   - Delete a profile by selecting it and clicking Remove.

- Copy an existing profile by selecting it and clicking Copy.
- View a profile by selecting it and clicking Properties.

Figure 2-11. *To add, remove, or edit mail profiles, click Show Profiles to display this dialog box.*

Selecting a Specific Profile to Use on Startup

You can configure Outlook to use a specific profile on startup or to prompt for a profile to use. To start with a specific profile, follow these steps:

1. In Control Panel, double-click Mail.
2. In the Mail Setup – Outlook dialog box, click Show Profiles.
3. After selecting Always Use This Profile, use the drop-down list to choose the startup profile.
4. Click OK.

To prompt for a profile before starting Outlook, follow these steps:

1. In Control Panel, double-click Mail.
2. In the Mail Setup – Outlook dialog box, click Show Profiles.
3. Select Prompt For A Profile To Be Used.
4. Click OK.

The user will be prompted for a profile the next time Outlook is started.

Chapter 3
Managing Mobile Outlook Users for Wireless, Web and Dial-Up Access

Most users want to be able to access e-mail, calendars, contacts, and scheduled tasks no matter what time it is or where they are, and with Microsoft Exchange Server 2003, you can make anywhere, anytime access to Exchange data a real possibility. How? Start by using Exchange's built-in mobile and Web access features to allow users to connect to Exchange using wireless networks and over the Internet using Web browsers. Afterward, configure your network to allow direct dial-up connections or to use remote procedure calls (RPCs) over Hypertext Transfer Protocol (HTTP), and then create Microsoft Outlook profiles that use these configurations.

Mastering Outlook Web Access Essentials

Microsoft Outlook Web Access is a standard Microsoft Exchange Server 2003 technology that allows users to access their mailboxes and public folder data using a Web browser. The technology works with standard Internet protocols, including Web Distributed Authoring and Versioning (WebDAV).

WebDAV is an extension to HTTP that allows remote clients to create and manage server-based files, folders, and data. When users access mailboxes and public folders over the Web, an HTTP virtual server hosted by Exchange Server 2003 is working behind the scenes to grant access and transfer files to the browser. Because Outlook Web Access doesn't need to be configured on the client, it's ideally suited for users who want to access e-mail while away from the office.

When you install Exchange Server 2003, Outlook Web Access is automatically configured for use. This makes Outlook Web Access fairly easy to manage, but there are some essential concepts that you should know to manage it more effectively. This section explains these concepts.

Using Outlook Web Access

Outlook Web Access and a default HTTP virtual server are installed automatically when you install Exchange Server 2003. In most cases you only need to open the appropriate ports on your organization's firewall, as discussed in Chapter 16, "Managing HTTP Virtual Servers for Web and Mobile Access Users," to allow users to access mailboxes and public folder data over the Web. After that, you simply tell users the Uniform Resource Locator (URL) path that they need to type into their browser's Address field. The users can then access Outlook Web Access when they're off-site.

Outlook Web Access is optimized for screen resolutions of 800 × 600 or higher. Two different versions of Outlook Web Access are available:

- **Basic Experience** Basic Experience is designed to work with standard Web browsers, provided that the browsers support HTML 3.2 and JavaScript [European Computer Manufacturers Association (ECMA)] script. This means users could use Microsoft Internet Explorer, Netscape Navigator, and other browsers to access Outlook Web Access. However, Microsoft recommends that you use Internet Explorer 5.0 or later versions or Netscape Navigator 4.7 or later. Both browsers have been tested for compatibility with Outlook Web Access.

- **Rich Experience** Rich Experience is designed for Internet Explorer 5.0 or later, and it has significant enhancements. Its performance closely approximates Microsoft Office Outlook 2003, including a folder hierarchy that you can expand or collapse, drag-and-drop functionality, and shortcut menus that you can access by right-clicking. In addition, you can also view the Outlook search folders, use Preview pane and Two Line view, mark items as read or unread, resize Hypertext Markup Language (HTML) frames, sort and spell check, and create and manage server-side rules.

 Note The application programming interface (API) for Microsoft Internet Explorer 6.0 has extensions for Outlook Web Access as well. These extensions allow Internet Explorer to compress message data using GZip compression technology, provided that Exchange is running on Microsoft Windows Server 2003. GZip compression gives about a 30 percent performance improvement when transferring data.

Figure 3-1 shows the Rich Experience view of Outlook Web Access. Most users with Internet Explorer 5.0 or later get this view of Outlook Web Access automatically. If their browser doesn't support a necessary technology for the Rich Experience view or this technology has been disabled, they might get the Basic View instead. If they can right-click and see a shortcut menu, they have the Rich Experience view.

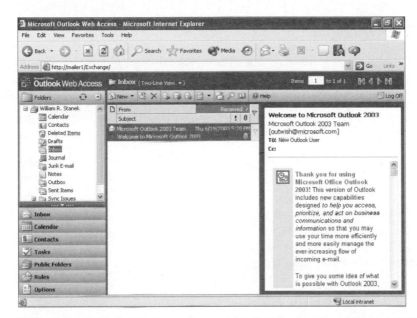

Figure 3-1. *Outlook Web Access has nearly all of the features of Outlook 2003.*

In addition to being able to manage their inbox, calendar, contacts, tasks, public folders, and mailbox rules, users can also set the following Outlook Web Access options by clicking Options in the task pane, making whatever changes are desired, and then clicking Save And Close:

- **Out of Office Assistant**   Allows you to specify whether you are in the office or out of the office. If out of the office, you can enter the text of the AutoReply message to be sent to anyone who sends you e-mail.

- **Messaging Options**   Allows you to set key messaging options. By default, 25 items are displayed per page, but this can be set to from 5 to 100 items per page if desired. You can also edit your signature and specify a preferred font to use for messages. The default font is 10-point Arial.

- **Reading Pane Options**   Allows you to specify whether and how messages are marked as read.

- **Spelling Options**   Allows you to set options for the spell checker, including the dictionary language. The default language is set per the browser's language setting.

- **E-mail Security**   Allows you to download the latest version of the Secure/Multipurpose Internet Mail Extensions (S/MIME) control.

Note When you are using Internet Explorer 6.0 Service Pack 1 or later, and Microsoft Windows 2000 or later, you can sign mail using a secure digital signature. At the time of this writing, only cleartext-signed messages are supported, which means encrypted S/MIME cannot be used.

- **Privacy and Junk E-mail Prevention** Allows you to filter junk e-mail, choose how to respond to requests for read receipts, and block external content in HTML e-mail messages.

 Tip One of the reasons for blocking external content in HTML e-mail messages is that images and other types of external content are used as e-mail beacons by those who send unsolicited (spam) e-mail. If you open a message containing external content, your e-mail address might be validated for the spammer, therefore indicating to the spammer that the e-mail address is valid and encouraging more spam.

- **Appearance** Allows you to select the color scheme used by Outlook Web Access. The default color scheme is blue.

- **Date and Time Formats** Allows you to set the format for dates and times. You can also set the current time zone. Although this changes the time zone used when sending e-mail messages, it doesn't change the time zone on the computer.

- **Calendar Options** Allows you specify when the first day of the week is and when the workday starts and ends for the purposes of calendar scheduling.

- **Reminder Options** Allows you to enable or disable reminders for calendars and tasks.

- **Contact Options** Allows you to specify whether the Global Address Lists or your personal contacts are checked first when resolving e-mail addresses in messages you are composing. By default, the Global Address List is checked first.

- **Recover Deleted Items** Allows you to view and recover items that were recently emptied from the Deleted Items folder. Any items you recover are moved back to the Deleted Items folder.

Enabling and Disabling Web Access for Users

Exchange Server 2003 enables Outlook Web Access for each user by default. If necessary, you can disable Outlook Web Access for specific users. To do this, complete the following steps:

1. Start Active Directory Users And Computers.
2. Select Advanced Features from the View menu. Advanced features should now be enabled for viewing and configuring.
3. Double-click the user's name in Active Directory Users And Computers. This opens the Properties dialog box for the user account.

4. Click the Exchange Features tab. The enabled mobile and Web access features for the user are displayed as shown in Figure 3-2.

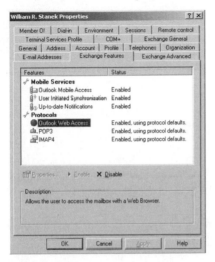

Figure 3-2. *Use the Exchange Features tab to manage a user's mobile and Web access settings.*

- To disable Outlook Web Access for this user, select Outlook Web Access under Protocols and then click Disable.

- To enable Outlook Web Access for this user, select Outlook Web Access under Protocols and then click Enable.

5. Click OK.

Connecting to Mailboxes and Public Folders over the Web

You use WebDAV to access mailboxes and public folders over the Web and the corporate intranet. With WebDAV, clients can do the following:

- **Access mailboxes**   To access a user's mailbox, type the Exchange URL into Internet Explorer's Address field and then enter the user name and password for the mailbox you want to access. For example, to access the mailbox for the Exchange alias williams, type **http://***servername***/Exchange**, where ***servername*** is a placeholder for the HTTP virtual server hosted by Exchange Server 2003. When prompted, type the user name **williams** and the mailbox password.

- **Access default public folders tree**   To access the default public folder, access the user's mailbox and then click the Public Folders tab. Or type the folder's URL into Internet Explorer's Address field. For example, to access the public folder tree in a browser, type **http://***servername***/public/**, where *servername* is a placeholder for the HTTP virtual server hosted by Exchange Server 2003 and *public* is the default name of the Public Folders Web share.

- **Access alternate public folder trees** To access alternate public folder trees, type the folder's URL into Internet Explorer's Address field. For example, to access a public folder called Marketing, type **http://*servername*/ marketing/**, where *servername* is a placeholder for the HTTP virtual server hosted by Exchange Server 2003 and *marketing* is the name of the alternate public folder tree.

 Note To perform any of these actions, users need to authenticate themselves to be granted access. If users are unable to authenticate themselves, they see an error page and are denied access to Exchange data.

Mastering Mobile Device and Wireless Access Essentials

Exchange Server 2003 supports wireless access for users with many types of mobile devices, including pocket PCs, personal digital assistants (PDAs), and smart phones. As an Exchange administrator, there are several things you can do to fine-tune the wireless access configuration for your organization. You'll want to take a look at synchronization and notification settings, enable or disable unsupported devices, and update Exchange for the mobile service carriers in your area. Once you've done that, you can test the services and roll Exchange out for users.

Using Outlook Mobile Access

Outlook Mobile Access is a standard feature of Exchange Server 2003. Using Outlook Mobile Access, users with mobile devices can access their e-mail, calendar, contacts, and scheduled tasks. Mobile access services have two key components:

- **Wireless synchronization access** With wireless synchronization, users can use Pocket PC devices to synchronize Exchange data with the Microsoft Exchange Server ActiveSync application. Synchronizing a device to Exchange allows users to keep their Exchange data current without being constantly connected to a wireless network.

- **Wireless browse access** With wireless browsing, users can use their wireless devices to connect to Exchange and browse their Exchange data. On the wireless device, browsing is enabled using the built-in Web browser. The user connects to the Internet using the services of their mobile device, and then browses Exchange using the Outlook Mobile Access URL, such as *http://exchange.adatum.com/oma*.

Both wireless access components are installed by default on Exchange Server 2003, and no installation is required. You will, however, want to configure mobile services carriers and optimize the mobile access configuration for your organization.

Note   Outlook Mobile Access browsing is possible because of the HTTP virtual server that is installed with Exchange. To learn more about possible server configurations for Outlook Mobile Access browsing, read the section of Chapter 16 entitled "Using Front-End and Back-End Server Configurations for Web and Mobile Access."

Configuring Exchange for Mobile Service Carriers

Throughout the United States and the world, there are hundreds and hundreds of carriers that provide services for mobile devices. The mobile service carriers that are used in your area should be configured to make it as easy as possible for users to take advantage of Exchange's wireless access features. You can configure mobile service carriers through the following:

- **Microsoft Corporate Messaging Services**   Using Microsoft Corporate Messaging Services, you can obtain a list of carriers and their settings. You then import these settings.

- **Exchange System Manager**   Using Exchange System Manager, you can configure individual carriers by name and Simple Mail Transfer Protocol (SMTP) domain.

These techniques are discussed in the sections that follow.

Downloading and Installing the Carriers List

You'll probably want to download and install the carriers list the first time you configure mobile services, and then periodically update the list to keep it current. To download and install the carriers list, follow these steps:

1. Visit Microsoft Corporate Messaging Services at the Microsoft Web site for Exchange Server 2003. At the site, you'll need to register your organization.

2. Once you are registered, you'll be able to download the carrier information list and a utility that helps you import the information into Active Directory. The carrier information is then made available to Exchange through Active Directory.

3. Confirm that information was imported properly using Exchange System Manager. Start Exchange System Manager by clicking Start, choosing Programs or All Programs, Microsoft Exchange, and then System Manager. In System Manager, expand the Global Settings node, and then select Mobile Services. You should see a Carriers entry or a list of available carriers.

Configuring Mobile Services Carriers Individually

To configure individual mobile service carriers, follow these steps:

1. Start Exchange System Manager by clicking Start, choosing Programs or All Programs, Microsoft Exchange, and then System Manager.

2. In System Manager, expand the Global Settings node, and then select Mobile Services as shown in Figure 3-3. You can now:

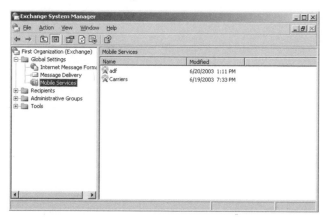

Figure 3-3. *Access the Mobile Services node to view the currently configured carriers.*

- **Add carriers** To add a new carrier, right-click Mobile Services, point to New, and then choose Mobile Carrier. In the Mobile Carrier dialog box, type a name for the carrier and then enter the address of the carrier's SMTP domain, such as @msn.com.

 Note The @ symbol is optional. If you don't enter it, Exchange adds the symbol automatically to the SMTP domain address. This symbol is used to specify any address at the specified domain.

- **View or modify carriers** To view or modify an existing carrier's configuration, right-click the carrier entry in the details pane and then select Properties. You can then change the SMTP domain address for the carrier if desired.

- **Delete carriers** To delete a carrier, right-click the carrier entry in the details pane and then select Delete. When prompted, confirm the action by clicking Yes.

Managing Wireless Synchronization and Exchange Server ActiveSync

Using Exchange Server ActiveSync, users with Pocket PC 2002 devices can initiate synchronization with Exchange to keep their data up to date, and users with Pocket PC 2003 or later devices can receive notices from Exchange that trigger synchronization through the always-up-to-date feature. Always-up-to-date is a key feature that you probably want to know a bit more about. It works like this:

1. The user configures his or her Pocket PC device to synchronize with Exchange, selecting specific Exchange folders that he or she wants to keep up to date.

2. When a new message arrives in a designated sync folder, a control message is sent to the mobile device.

3. The control message initiates a data synchronization session and the device performs background synchronization with Exchange.

Users with third-party synchronization software for their mobile devices can also sync with Exchange, provided the software is compatible with Exchange Server ActiveSync. Once they are synchronized, users can then access their data while they are offline. To view or change wireless synchronization settings, follow these steps:

1. Start Exchange System Manager by clicking Start, choosing Programs or All Programs, Microsoft Exchange, and then System Manager.

2. In System Manager, expand the Global Settings node. Right-click Mobile Services and then choose Properties to display the Mobile Services Properties dialog box shown in Figure 3-4.

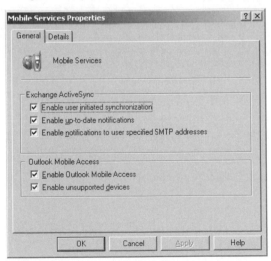

Figure 3-4. *Use the Exchange ActiveSync options to optimize the synchronization settings for your organization.*

3. The synchronization configuration is controlled with the following options in the Exchange ActiveSync panel:

- **Enable User Initiated Synchronization** Allows users to use Pocket PC 2002 or later devices to initiate synchronization with Exchange to keep their data up to date. If you enable this option, users can synchronize manually with Exchange or schedule synchronization at specific times. If you disable this option, no other synchronization options are allowed.

- **Enable Up-To-Date Notifications** Allows users to use Pocket PC 2003 or later devices to receive notices from Exchange that trigger synchronization. If you enable this option, when a new message arrives in a user's mailbox, Exchange sends a notification to the wireless device that allows synchronization to occur automatically.

- **Enable Notifications To User Specified SMTP Addresses** Allows users to use any wireless carrier with the wireless synchronization feature. If you enable this option, users who have mobile devices can receive synchronization notifications regardless of which carrier they are using. Use this option when you do not want to specify the carrier.

4. Click OK to save the configuration changes.

Real World ActiveSync notifications are sent over wireless networks using the Internet. To take advantage of these services, users must subscribe to the Internet services of a wireless carrier. The actual process of receiving synchronization requests and sending synchronization notifications is handled through the HTTP virtual server configured for use with Exchange. Exchange Server ActiveSync is in fact configured as an ASP.NET application on the HTTP virtual server. For Exchange Server ActiveSync to work properly, the HTTP virtual server must be configured properly, as discussed in Chapter 16, "Managing HTTP Virtual Servers for Web and Mobile Access Users." If you want to learn more about Internet Information Services (IIS) and ASP.NET, I recommend IIS 6.0 Administrator's Pocket Consultant (Microsoft Press, 2003).

Managing Wireless Browsing

Wireless browsing allows users to access their Exchange e-mail, calendar, contacts, and scheduled tasks using the built-in Web browser of their mobile devices. To browse Exchange, users must subscribe to the Internet services of a wireless carrier and then access Exchange using the Outlook Mobile Access URL, such as *http://exchange.adatum.com/oma.*

Because of some technology incompatibilities with carrier gateways that alter the markup contained in message data sent between Exchange and wireless devices, wireless browsing is only supported with the following:

- HTML devices, such as Pocket PC 2002 or later and smart phones.
- XHTML devices, such as cell phones, that use Wireless Application Protocol (WAP) 2.0 or later.
- CHTML devices, such as cell phones, that use iMode.

Additionally, the wireless device must be with a wireless carrier whose network uses Global System for Mobile Communications (GSM), General Packet Radio Service (GPRS), or Code Division Multiple Access (CDMA). With these supported devices running on a supported network, you can be sure that a user's wireless browsing experience is consistent from device to device. Any device with a Web browser can use Outlook Mobile Access, but the browsing experience with an unsupported device might not be the same as with supported devices. For example, the formatting of messages might be inconsistent. Regardless, when users access Outlook Mobile Access, they'll have these key options:

- **Inbox** Read, reply to, forward, or flag e-mail messages.
- **Calendar** View calendar and scheduling information, such as meetings and appointments.
- **Contacts** Find important contacts with their address, e-mail, and telephone information or create new contacts.
- **Tasks** Browse current tasks or create new ones.
- **Find Someone** Find information on someone in Exchange's Global Address List.
- **Compose New** Create new e-mail messages
- **Preferences** Configure Outlook Web Access preferences

Note With Exchange, Outlook Mobile Access is configured as an ASP.NET application on an HTTP virtual server being used with Exchange. For Outlook Mobile Access to work properly, the HTTP virtual server must be configured properly as discussed in Chapter 16, "Managing HTTP Virtual Servers for Web and Mobile Access Users."

To view or change the wireless browsing settings, follow these steps:

1. Start Exchange System Manager by clicking Start, choosing Programs or All Programs, Microsoft Exchange, and then System Manager.

2. In System Manager, expand the Global Settings node. Right-click Mobile Services and then choose Properties to display the Mobile Services Properties dialog box shown previously in Figure 3-4.

3. The wireless browsing configuration is controlled with the following options of the Outlook Mobile Access panel:

   - **Enable Outlook Mobile Access**   Allows users to browse Exchange using Outlook Mobile Access. If you enable this option, users can browse Exchange using the Outlook Mobile Access URL. If you disable this option, no wireless browsing is allowed.

   - **Enable Unsupported Devices**   Allows users with unsupported devices to browse Exchange using Outlook Mobile Access. Keep in mind, though, that these users might have inconsistent message formatting or other problems.

4. Click OK to save the configuration changes.

Configuring Devices for Mobile Access and Wireless Browsing

Configuring mobile devices to access Exchange using Outlook Mobile Access is a multipart process. First, users need to subscribe to the Internet service offered by their wireless carrier and configure their mobile devices to use the service. Afterward, they need to start the device's browser, navigate to the Outlook Mobile Access URL, and then, when prompted, log on to Exchange by providing their user name, password, and domain information.

With a Pocket PC, the process works like this:

1. After you configure the mobile device to use the Internet service provided by the user's wireless carrier, on the Today screen, tap Start, and then tap Internet Explorer. This displays the Internet Explorer screen.

2. Tap View and then tap Address Bar to display the address bar in the browser window.

3. Tap anywhere within the address bar and then type the Outlook Mobile Access URL, such as **http://exchange.microsoft.com/oma**. You should automatically connect. If you don't, you might have to connect manually.

4. When prompted, log on to Exchange, provide your user name, password, and domain information.

Enabling and Disabling Mobile Access Features for Individual Users

Exchange Server 2003 enables mobile services for each user by default. If necessary, you can disable mobile services for specific users. To do this, complete the following steps:

1. Start Active Directory Users And Computers.

2. Select Advanced Features from the View menu. Advanced features should now be enabled for viewing and configuring.

3. Double-click the user's name in Active Directory Users And Computers. This opens the Properties dialog box for the user account.

4. Click the Exchange Features tab. You can now do the following:

   - **Enable or disable Outlook Mobile Access** Click Outlook Mobile Access under Mobile Services and then click Enable or Disable as appropriate. If you disable Outlook Mobile Access, the user will not be able to use sync or browse with Exchange.

   - **Enable or disable user-initiated synchronization** Click User Initiated Synchronization under Mobile Services and then click Enable or Disable as appropriate. If you disable synchronization, the user can browse using wireless access but any mobile devices he or she uses cannot send or receive synchronization requests.

   - **Enable or disable up-to-date notifications** Click Up-To-Date Notifications under Mobile Services and then click Enable or Disable as appropriate. If you disable up-to-date notifications, Exchange does not notify the user when new messages are received and because of this background syncs do not occur.

5. Click OK.

Creating Mobile Outlook Profiles for Remote Mail and RPC over HTTP

Remote mail and RPC over HTTP are two of the least understood configuration options for Exchange Server. Using remote mail, you can configure Outlook 2003 to connect to Exchange Server using a dial-up connection to your organization's modem bank. Remote mail is useful in these scenarios:

- Users at a branch office must connect to Exchange Server by means of dial-up connections.

- Laptop users want to connect to Exchange Server through dial-up connections when out of the office. (Here, you might want to configure on-site and off-site mail profiles for the user. See the section of Chapter 2, "Managing Microsoft Exchange Server 2003 Clients," entitled "Using Mail Profiles to Customize the Mail Environment.")

- Users working at home need to connect to Exchange Server by means of dial-up connections.

Using RPC over HTTP, you can configure Outlook 2003 to connect to Exchange Server using RPCs over the Internet. RPC over HTTP is useful in these scenarios:

- Users at a branch office must connect to Exchange Server over a broadband connection, such as Digital Subscriber Line (DSL) or a cable modem, and you don't have a virtual private network (VPN), or you want to simplify the connection process by eliminating the need for a VPN.

- Laptop users want to connect to Exchange Server through broadband or T1 connections when out of the office without having to use VPNs. (Here, you might want to configure on-site and off-site mail profiles for the user. See the section of Chapter 2 entitled "Using Mail Profiles to Customize the Mail Environment.")

- Users working at home need to connect to Exchange Server by means of broadband connections without having to use a VPN.

Both remote mail and RPC over HTTP require fairly complex server implementations on the back end to enable the technology for users, the discussion of which is beyond the scope of this book. The sections that follow discuss how to configure Outlook 2003 clients to use these options.

Creating Outlook Profiles for Dial-Up Connections to Corporate Networks

You configure dial-up connections for Outlook 2003 (also called remote mail) by completing the following steps.

1. Exit Outlook 2003. Then, in Control Panel, double-click Mail. If you aren't using Classic Control Panel View, click Switch To Classic View to display the Mail icon and then double-click it.

2. In the Mail Setup dialog box, click Show Profiles. Then in the Mail windows, click Add.

3. Type the name of the profile, such as Remote Exchange, and then click OK. This starts the E-mail Accounts Wizard.

4. Select Add A New E-mail Account and then click Next.

5. Select Microsoft Exchange Server as the server type and then click Next.

6. In the Microsoft Exchange Server field, type the host name of the mail server, such as **mailer1**. You can also enter the fully qualified domain name (FQDN) of the mail server, such as **mailer1.adatum.com**. Using the full domain name can help ensure a successful connection when the mail server is in a different domain or forest.

7. In the User Name field, enter the user's domain logon name or domain user name, such as **Williams** or **William Stanek**. Click Check Name to confirm that you've entered the correct user name for the mailbox. You'll want to

store a local copy of the user's e-mail on his or her computer, so ensure that the Use Local Copy Of Mailbox check box is selected.

8. Click More Settings. This displays the Microsoft Exchange Server dialog box.

9. With remote mail connections, you'll usually want to work offline and dial up as necessary. Select both Manually Control Connection State and Work Offline And Use Dial-Up Networking, as shown in Figure 3-5.

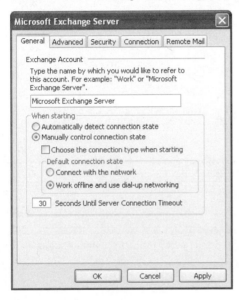

Figure 3-5. *Use manual connection settings for working offline and dial-up networking.*

10. If you want the user to be prompted for connection type, select the Choose The Connection Type When Starting check box.

11. If you want to encrypt message traffic, click the Security tab and under Encryption, select Encrypt Information.

12. On the Connection tab, choose Connect Using My Phone Line and then under Use The Following Dial-Up Networking Connection, choose an existing connection to use for remote mail, as shown in Figure 3-6. If no connection is available, click Add and create a connection.

13. You now need to configure remote mail. Click the Remote Mail tab.

14. If you'd like to remotely send and receive all mail with Exchange, select Process Marked Items and skip Steps 15 and 16.

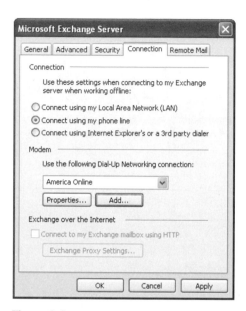

Figure 3-6. *Connect using a phone line and then specify the dial-up networking connection to use.*

15. If you'd like to receive only mail that meets specific criteria, select Retrieve Items That Meet The Following Conditions, and then click Filter. This displays the Filter dialog box shown in Figure 3-7. When using filters, keep in mind that only messages that match all the specified conditions are retrieved.

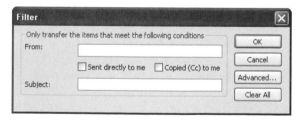

Figure 3-7. *The Filter dialog box lets you filter mail so it meets specified criteria.*

16. Use the following options in the Filter dialog box to configure filters:

- **From** Enter names or e-mail addresses that must appear in the From field of messages. You can use semicolons (;) to separate multiple names or e-mail addresses.

- **Sent Directly To Me** Transfers messages with the user's name in the To field.

Note When Send Directly To Me is selected, messages sent to distri- bution lists of which the user is a member aren't transferred, so be sure this is the behavior you want. If you want to transfer messages sent to distribution lists of which the user is a member, select Copied (Cc) To Me as well.

- **Copied (Cc) To Me** Transfers messages with the user's name in the Cc field or messages sent to distribution lists of which the user is a member.
- **Subject** Transfers messages with a specific subject. Multiple sub- jects can be entered as long as a semicolon separates each one.
- **Advanced** Allows you to specify additional criteria for messages to be transferred, including size, date, and importance.

17. Once you're finished configuring remote mail, click OK. In the E-mail Accounts Wizard, click Next and then click Finish.

18. In the Mail Setup dialog box, click Close and then click OK.

Creating Outlook Profiles for RPC over HTTP

You configure Outlook 2003 to use RPC over HTTP by completing the following steps:

1. In Control Panel, double-click Mail. If you aren't using Classic Control Panel View, click Switch To Classic View to display the Mail icon and then double- click it.

2. In the Mail Setup dialog box, click Show Profiles. Then in the Mail window, click Add.

3. Type the name of the profile, such as **Remote Exchange**, and then click OK. This starts the E-mail Accounts Wizard.

4. Select Add A New E-mail Account and then click Next.

5. Select Microsoft Exchange Server as the server type and then click Next.

6. In the Microsoft Exchange Server field, type the host name of the mail server, such as **mailer1**. You can also enter the FQDN of the mail server, such as **mailer1.adatum.com**. Using the full domain name can help ensure a successful connection when the mail server is in a different domain or forest.

7. In the User Name field, enter the user's domain logon name or domain user name, such as **Williams** or **William Stanek**. Click Check Name to confirm that you've entered the correct user name for the mailbox. You'll want to store a local copy of the user's e-mail on his or her computer, so ensure that the Use Local Copy Of Mailbox check box is selected.

8. Click More Settings. This displays the Microsoft Exchange Server dialog box.

9. With remote mail connections, you'll usually want to work offline and dial up as necessary. Select both Manually Control Connection State and Work Offline And Use Dial-Up Networking, as shown previously in Figure 3-5.

10. If you want the user to be prompted for a connection type, select Choose Connection Type When Starting.

11. If you want to encrypt message traffic, click the Security tab and under Encryption, select Encrypt Information.

12. Click the Connection tab, and then select Connect Using Internet Explorer's Or A Third Party Dialer.

13. Select Connect To My Exchange Mailbox Using HTTP. If this option is unavailable, you might need to apply the most recent service packs for the operating system and Internet Explorer. Then repeat this procedure.

14. Click Exchange Proxy Settings, then configure the proxy settings for the Exchange proxy server. You need to know the URL of the proxy server and the full domain name. Be sure to connect to Exchange using Secure Sockets Layer (SSL) and mutually authenticate the session when connecting with SSL. For proxy authentication, you'll want to use basic authentication in most cases.

15. Once you're finished configuring the mail settings, click OK. In the E-mail Accounts Wizard, click Next and then click Finish.

16. In the Mail Setup dialog box, click Close and then click OK.

Part II

Active Directory Services and Microsoft Exchange Server 2003

Part II of this book shows you how to manage resources that are stored in the Active Directory database. You'll also learn about the Microsoft Exchange Server 2003 features that are integrated with Active Directory services. Chapter 4 examines essential concepts and tasks that you need to know to work with Exchange Server 2003. Chapter 5 takes a look at creating and managing users and contacts. You'll learn all about Exchange aliases, enabling and disabling exchange mail for individual users, forwarding mail offsite, and more. Chapter 6 discusses mailbox administration, including techniques for configuring, moving, and recovering mailboxes. In Chapter 7 you'll find a detailed discussion of how to use address lists, distribution groups, and templates. You'll also learn how to manage these resources. The final chapter in this part covers directory security and Exchange policies.

Chapter 4

Microsoft Exchange Server 2003 Administration Essentials

Whether you're using Microsoft Exchange Server 2003 for the first time or honing your skills, you'll need to master many key concepts to work effectively with Exchange Server. You'll need to know the following:

- How the Exchange environment is organized
- How information is stored in Exchange Server
- Which Microsoft Windows processes are used with Exchange Server
- How Exchange Server works

You'll also need to know how to use the Exchange System Manager. These topics are all covered in this chapter.

Understanding Exchange Server Organizations

Exchange Server combines a fairly complex administrative model with an equally complex messaging architecture. Understanding how the administrative model and the messaging architecture are used and integrated isn't easy, so let's begin with a look at how Exchange environments are organized.

The root of an Exchange environment is an *organization*. It's the starting point for the Exchange hierarchy. The boundaries of the Exchange organization define the boundaries of your Exchange environment. In other words, the Exchange information store doesn't provide information on users or servers outside the organization—unless you specifically tell Exchange Server about these entities.

An Exchange organization can serve several offices and business functions. Typically, each office or business function that it supports has its own server that runs Exchange Server. For example, if your company has offices in Seattle, Portland, and San Francisco, you'll probably have at least one server running

Exchange Server at each location. To serve a large user base or high-volume messaging needs, you might also have separate servers providing Simple Mail Transfer Protocol (SMTP), Post Office Protocol (POP3), Hypertext Transfer Protocol (HTTP), and other messaging services. All these servers can be a part of the same Exchange organization.

When you installed Exchange Server, you were given the opportunity to join an existing organization or create a new organization. The organization name you assign or join is permanently associated with the Exchange server. Once designated, you *cannot* change it. As Figure 4-1 shows, you can view the current organization name in Exchange System Manager. Here, the organization name is First Organization.

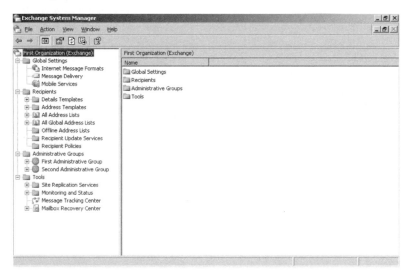

Figure 4-1. *The organization is the root of the Exchange environment, and you view it in Exchange System Manager.*

Under the organization node you'll find the key components that make up the organization. These components include the following:

- Global Settings
- Recipients
- Administrative Groups (which can contain Servers, Routing Groups, and Folders)
- Routing Groups

The following sections examine each of these Exchange components and explain how they fit into the organization. If you don't see administrative groups or routing groups, don't worry. We'll discuss how you enable and use these features later in this chapter.

Global Settings

Global settings apply to all servers and recipients in an organization. The three most common global settings that you'll work with are as follows:

- **Internet Message Formats** These global settings define the acceptable Internet message formats for the organization, as well as the way you can use message formats. The settings that you can define include default message encoding, default character sets, and default Multipurpose Internet Mail Extensions (MIME) extension mapping. MIME is the standard used for messages with several parts.

- **Message Delivery** These global settings define how and when messages are delivered. The settings that you can define include the default postmaster account name, the default quotas, and the default message filters. Message filters allow you to discard messages from specific senders and to redirect messages based on who the sender is.

- **Mobile Services** These global settings define the mobile services Exchange provides and whether wireless synchronization and browsing are permitted. Any wireless domains serviced by Exchange can also be defined here.

You'll find detailed instruction on managing global settings in Chapter 13, "Managing Microsoft Exchange Server 2003 Organizations."

Recipients

A *recipient* is an entity that can receive Exchange mail. Recipients include users, contacts, groups, and other resources. You refer to recipients as either mailbox-enabled or mail-enabled. *Mailbox-enabled recipients* (users) have mailboxes for sending and receiving e-mail messages. *Mail-enabled recipients* (contacts, groups, and public folders) have e-mail addresses but no mailboxes. Thus, mail-enabled recipients can receive messages but can't send them.

In addition to users, contacts, groups, and public folders, Exchange Server 2003 adds two types of recipients: InetOrgPerson and query-based distribution groups. Basically, an InetOrgPerson represents a user account that was imported from non-Microsoft Lightweight Directory Access Protocol (LDAP) or X.500 directory services, and a query-based distribution group is a type of distribution group you can use to build a list of recipients whenever a mail addressed to the group is received rather than having a fixed member list. Like users, InetOrgPersons can be mailbox-enabled and because InetOrgPersons are essentially users, I won't always differentiate between the two—I only do this when I am pointing out specific differences.

To manage recipients in your organization, you need to know these key concepts:

- **How recipient policies are used** Recipient policies define the technique Exchange uses to create addresses for SMTP, Exchange Server, X.400, and so forth. For example, you can set a policy for SMTP that creates e-mail addresses by combining an e-mail alias with @adatum.com. Thus, during setup of an account for William Stanek, the e-mail alias williams is combined with @adatum.com to create the e-mail address williams@adatum.com.

- **How address lists are used** You use address lists to organize recipients and resources, making it easier to find recipients and resources that you want to use, along with their related information. During setup, Exchange creates a number of default address lists. The most commonly used default address list is the global address list, which lists all the recipients in the organization. You can create custom address lists as well.

- **How address templates are used** Templates define the appearance of recipient information in the address book. When you install Exchange Server, default templates are set up for users, groups, contacts, public folders, search dialog boxes, and the mailbox agent. By modifying the appropriate template, you can change the appearance of recipient information in the address book.

Administrative Groups

Administrative groups define the logical structure of an Exchange organization. You use administrative groups to help you organize directory objects and efficiently manage Exchange resources. Administrative groups are best suited to large organizations or those with offices in several locations. In a small- or medium-sized company, you might not need to use administrative groups at all.

Using and Enabling Administrative Groups

Another way to think of administrative groups is as logical containers into which you can place directory objects and Exchange resources. For example, you could create administrative groups named Engineering, Marketing, and Administration. Within these groups, you could then define routing groups, policies, servers, public folder trees, and other objects for each department.

When you install Exchange Server, administrative group support is disabled by default. This is done primarily to simplify the Exchange management process. In System Manager, the lack of the Administrative Groups node tells you that administrative group support has been disabled. You can enable support for administrative groups by completing the following steps:

1. In System Manager, right-click the organization container, and then select Properties.
2. On the General tab of the Properties dialog box, select Display Administrative Groups.

3. When you click OK and then restart System Manager, Exchange Server enables administrative groups and configures them for the current operations mode.

Administrative Groups in Mixed-Mode and Native-Mode Operations

How you manage administrative groups depends on the operations mode in use. Exchange Server has two operations modes:

- **Mixed mode**   When operating in mixed mode, Exchange Server 2003 can support pre-Exchange Server 2000 installations.

- **Native mode**   When operating in native mode, Exchange Server 2003 supports only Exchange 2000 Server and Exchange Server 2003 installations.

Using Mixed-Mode Operations   By default, when you install Exchange Server, the operations mode is set to mixed. The mixed-mode configuration provides for interoperability with Microsoft Exchange 5.0 and Microsoft Exchange 5.5 but limits the capabilities of Exchange Server 2003. These limitations directly affect the way administrative groups are used and effectively force Exchange Server 2003 to handle administrative groups in the same way that Exchange 5.5 handles sites.

When running in mixed-mode operations, Exchange Server operates as follows:

- When Exchange Server 2003 coexists with Exchange 5.0 or Exchange 5.5, Exchange Server 2003 uses the site concept to define both administration and routing. This limitation means that each administrative group has only one functional routing group even if you create additional routing groups.

- You can't move mailboxes from a server in one administrative group to a server in another administrative group. This limitation reduces your flexibility in managing mailboxes.

Additional limitations apply if Exchange Server is installed in an Exchange 5.5 site. These additional limitations are as follows:

- Some System Manager commands don't apply to Exchange 5.5. Because of this, you can't use these commands to manipulate an Exchange 5.5 server.

- Exchange 5.5 directory service objects are replicated into Active Directory directory service with read-only properties. This means you can't edit these properties through Active Directory. You need to use the Exchange Administrator tool for this, which can be installed with Exchange Server.

- InetOrgPerson and query-based distribution groups are available only in Microsoft Windows Server 2003 domains and when Exchange is running in native mode. Further, to use query-based distribution groups all servers must be using at least Exchange 2000 with Service Pack 3.

Enabling and Using Native-Mode Operations When operating in native mode, Exchange Server isn't subject to these limitations. You can enable routing group support and create additional routing groups as necessary. It also means that Exchange Server won't be able to work with Exchange 5.0 or Exchange 5.5 sites that are part of the same organization, and it is as if the Exchange 5.0 and Exchange 5.5 servers no longer exist in the organization.

You can view and change the operations mode by completing the following steps:

1. In System Manager, right-click the Organization node, and then select Properties.

2. On the General tab of the Properties dialog box, the Operation Mode field displays the current operation mode as either Mixed Mode or Native Mode (see Figure 4-2).

3. To change the operation mode from mixed to native, click Change Mode. Confirm the action by clicking Yes. Once you change to native mode, you can't change back to mixed mode.

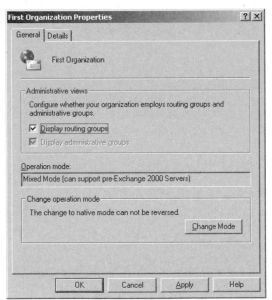

Figure 4-2. *The General tab of the organization's Properties dialog box displays the current operation mode. Be aware that once you change to native mode, you can't change back to mixed mode.*

Routing Groups

You use routing groups in advanced Exchange installations to control message connectivity and communication channels for groups of Exchange servers. When you install the first Exchange server in an organization, the server is added to the default routing group. You have no control over this routing group in mixed-mode operations. Additional servers installed in the Exchange organization are added to this same routing group by default and the message connectivity and communication among these servers is configured automatically.

If you have a single group of servers that have no special communication needs, you don't need to create additional routing groups. Normally, you use multiple routing groups when you need to connect branch offices or other geographically separated locations and when the following are true:

* You don't have high-bandwidth connections among these locations.

* You have special connectivity requirements, such as the need to control precisely how and when Exchange data is transferred among these locations.

Once a server is connected to a particular routing group, you *can't* move it to another routing group without reinstalling Exchange Server. Because of this, you should plan the messaging topology for your organization very carefully. Message transfer and communication within routing groups is handled directly with a *target server*. Message transfer and communication among routing groups is handled by a *bridgehead server*.

A bridgehead server is the point of entry and exit for all message traffic among routing groups. Bridgehead servers also handle the link state information, which is used to determine optimal routing paths. You must designate a bridgehead server in each routing group. To communicate, bridgehead servers use an Exchange Server Routing Group Connector, which provides the direct connection among routing groups. You use one Routing Group Connector to connect two routing groups.

You can enable support for routing groups by completing the following steps:

1. In System Manager, right-click the organization container, and then select Properties.

2. On the General tab of the Properties dialog box, select Display Routing Groups.

3. When you click OK, Exchange enables routing groups and configures them for the current operations mode.

Data Storage in Exchange Server

Exchange Server stores information in two places:

- Active Directory data store
- Exchange Server information store

Working with the Active Directory Data Store

The Active Directory data store contains all directory information for recipients as well as other important directory resources. Domain controllers maintain the data store in a file called Ntds.dit. The location of this file is set when Active Directory is installed and must be on an NTFS (NT file system) drive formatted for use with Windows Server 2003. You can also save directory data separately from the main data store. This is true for some public data, such as logon scripts.

Two key concepts to focus on when looking at Active Directory are multimaster replication and global catalog servers.

Using Multimaster Replication

Domain controllers replicate most changes to the data store by using multimaster replication, which allows any domain controller to process directory changes and replicate those changes to other domain controllers. Replication is handled automatically for key data types, including the following:

- **Domain data** Contains information about objects within a domain, such as users, groups, and contacts.
- **Configuration data** Describes the topology of the directory and includes a list of important domain information.
- **Schema data** Describes all objects and data types that can be stored in the data store.

Using Global Catalogs

Active Directory information is also made available through global catalogs. You use global catalogs for information searches and in some cases domain logon. A domain controller designated as a global catalog stores a full replica of all objects in the data store (for its host domain).

By default, the first domain controller installed in a domain is designated as the global catalog. Consequently, if there is only one domain controller in the domain, the domain controller and the global catalog are on the same server. Otherwise, the global catalog is on the domain controller configured as such.

Information searches are one of the key uses of the global catalog. Searches in the global catalog are very efficient and can resolve most queries locally, thus reducing the network load and allowing for quicker responses. With Exchange, the global catalog can be used to execute LDAP queries for query-based distribution groups. Here, the members of the distribution group are based on the results of the query sent to the global catalog server rather than being fixed.

Why use LDAP queries instead of a fixed member list? The idea is to reduce administrative overheard by being able to dynamically determine what the members of a distribution group should be. Query-based distribution is most efficient when the member list is relatively small (fewer than 25 members). If there are potentially hundreds or thousands of members, however, query-based distribution is very inefficient and might require a great deal of processing to complete.

Here's how distributed queries work:

1. When e-mail is received that is addressed to the group, the Exchange categorizer (a transport component) sends the predefined LDAP query to the global catalog server for the domain.

2. The global catalog server executes the query and returns the resulting address set.

3. The Exchange categorizer then uses the address list to generate the recipient list and deliver the message. If the categorizer is unable to generate the list for any reason, such as because the list is incomplete or an error was returned, the categorizer might start the process over from the beginning.

Note To make the process more efficient, large organizations can use a dedicated expansion server. Here, LDAP queries are routed to the expansion server. The expansion server processes the query and returns the results.

Working with the Exchange Server Information Store

The Exchange information store contains mailbox and public folder data. To make the information store more manageable, Exchange Server 2003 allows you to organize the information store into multiple databases. You can then manage these databases individually or in logical groupings called *storage groups*.

Exchange Server uses transactions to control changes in storage groups. As with traditional databases, these transactions are recorded in a transaction log. Changes are then committed or rolled back based on the success of the transaction. In the case of failure, you can use the transaction log to restore the database. The facility that manages transactions is the Microsoft Exchange Information Store service (Store.exe).

When working with storage groups and Exchange Server 2003 Standard Edition, you should keep the following in mind:

- Each Exchange server can have up to two storage groups (with one of the storage groups, called the recovery storage group, being reserved for database recovery operations).

- A single storage group can have up to two databases with a maximum size per database of 16 gigabytes. Thus, the maximum number of databases that a single standard server can have is 4 (with 2 reserved for the recovery storage group).

When working with storage groups and Exchange Server 2003 Enterprise Edition, you should keep the following in mind:

- Each Exchange server can have up to five storage groups (with one of the storage groups, called the recovery storage group, being reserved for database recovery operations).

- A single storage group can have up to five databases with a maximum size per database of 16 terabytes (limited only by hardware). Thus, the maximum number of databases that a single enterprise server can have is 25 (with five reserved for the recovery storage group).

Key concepts to focus on when looking at the Exchange information store and storage groups are the following:

- Exchange Database formats
- Single-instance message storage
- Files associated with storage groups

What Exchange Server Database Formats Are Available?

Exchange servers store databases in two files: a rich-text file with the .edb file extension and a streaming Internet content file with the .stm file extension. The .edb file contains message text and the .stm file contains attachments to these messages.

Because attachments are written in native format, there is no need to convert attachments to Exchange format (as was done in previous versions of Exchange). Exchange Server performs much better when reading and writing attachments in native format.

Two types of databases are available:

- **Private store databases**   contain mailboxes
- **Public store databases**   Contain public folders

What Is Single-Instance Message Storage?

Exchange Server uses single-instance message storage on a per-database basis. With this technique, a message that's sent to multiple mailboxes is

- Stored once if all the mailboxes are in the same database.
- Copied once to each database that contains a target mailbox.

Additionally, if the databases are in different storage groups, Exchange Server writes the message to each database as well as the transaction log set for each storage group. Thus, a message written to three databases that are in two different storage groups would use five times the disk space as a message written to a single database in a single storage group. To see this, consider the following example:

A 2-MB message is sent to all company employees. The mailboxes for these employees are in private stores A and B in storage group 1 and in private store

C in storage group 2. Exchange Server writes the message to the transaction log in storage groups 1 and 2 and then writes to the private storage databases A, B, and C. Storing the original 2-MB messages thus requires 10 MB of disk space.

Note Needing 10 MB of disk space to store a 2-MB message might sound like an awful lot of space, but remember the hidden savings. That 2-MB message might have been sent to 1000 employees, and without single-instance message storage, Exchange Server would use a whopping 2 GB of disk space.

What Files Are Associated with Storage Groups?

Each storage group on Exchange Server has several files associated with it. These files are as follows:

- **Edb.chk** A check file containing recovered file fragments
- **Edb.log** A transaction log file for the storage group
- **Res1.log** A reserved log file for the storage group
- **Res2.log** A reserved log file for the storage group
- **Tmp.edb** A temporary workspace for processing transactions
- *Dbname*.edb Rich-text database files for individual databases
- *Dbname*.stm Streaming Internet content files for individual databases

To create a new storage group with a private or public store, you'll need about 50 MB of free disk space. The files required by the storage group use a minimum of 23 MB of disk space. Although the total disk space used is about 23 MB, you'll need the extra space during creation and for read/write operations.

Using and Managing Exchange Server Services

Each Exchange server in the organization relies on a set of services for routing messages, processing transactions, replicating data, and much more. To manage Exchange services, you'll use the Services node in the Computer Management console, which you start by completing the following steps:

1. Choose Start, Programs or All Programs, Administrative Tools, and then select Computer Management. Or in the Administrative Tools folder, select Computer Management.

2. To connect to a remote exchange server, right-click the Computer Management entry in the console tree, and then select Connect To Another Computer from the shortcut menu. You can now choose the Exchange server for which you want to manage services.

3. Expand the Services And Applications node by clicking the plus sign (+) next to it, and then choose Services.

Figure 4-3 shows the Services view in the Computer Management console. The key fields of this window are used as follows:

- **Name** The name of the service.
- **Description** A short description of the service and its purpose.
- **Status** The status of the service as started, paused, or stopped. (Stopped is indicated by a blank entry.)
- **Startup Type** The startup setting for the service.

 Note Automatic services are started at bootup. Manual services are started by users or other services. Disabled services are turned off and can't be started.

- **Log On As** The account the service logs on as. The default in most cases is the local system account.

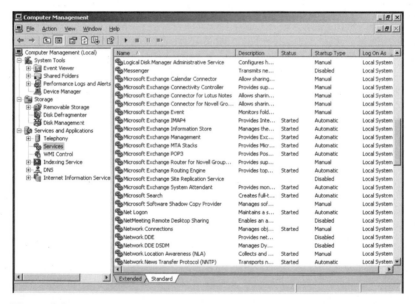

Figure 4-3. *Use the Services node of the Computer Management console to manage Exchange Server services.*

Using Core Exchange Server Services

Table 4-1 provides a summary of the services essential to normal Exchange operations. Note that the services that are available on a particular Exchange server depend on its configuration. Still, there is a core set of services that you'll find on most Exchange servers.

Table 4-1.   Core Exchange Server Services

Name	Description
ASP.NET State Service	Provides services for managing client sessions when using HTTP and remote procedure call (RPC) over HTTP, and other Internet Information Services (IIS) functions.
Distributed Transaction Coordinator	Coordinates transactions that are distributed across multiple databases, message queues, and file systems.
Event Log	Logs event informational, warning, and error messages issued by Exchange Server and other applications.
HTTP SSL	Provides services for secure transfer of data using HTTP and RPC over HTTP.
IIS Admin Service	Allows you to administer the Exchange HTTP virtual server in the IIS snap-in.
Microsoft Exchange Event	Monitors folders and generates events for Exchange 5.5 applications.
Microsoft Exchange IMAP4	Provides Microsoft Exchange services for Internet Message Access Protocol (IMAP4).
Microsoft Exchange Information Store	Manages Microsoft Exchange information storage.
Microsoft Exchange Management	Provides Windows Management Instrumentation (WMI) information for Exchange.
Microsoft Exchange MTA Stacks	Provides Microsoft Exchange X.400 services using Message Transfer Agent (MTA) stacks.
Microsoft Exchange POP3	Provides Microsoft Exchange POP3 services.
Microsoft Exchange Routing Engine	Processes Microsoft Exchange message routing and link state information.
Microsoft Exchange Site Replication Service	Replicates Exchange information within the organization.
Microsoft Exchange System Attendant	Monitors Microsoft Exchange and provides essential services.
Network News Transfer Protocol (NNTP)	Transports newsgroup messages across the network.
Simple Mail Transfer Protocol (SMTP)	Transports e-mail across the network.
World Wide Web Publishing Service	Provides HTTP services for Microsoft Exchange Server and IIS.

Security Alert It is important to note that on a new Exchange Server 2003 installation, some services are disabled initially for security reasons. Specifically, you'll find that the Microsoft Exchange POP3, Microsoft Exchange IMAP4, Microsoft Exchange Site Replication Service and Network News Transfer Protocol services are disabled. If you use these services with Exchange, you'll need to enable them for automatic startup and then start them using the techniques discussed in the section of this chapter entitled, "Using and Managing Exchange Server Services."

Starting, Stopping, and Pausing Exchange Server Services

As an administrator, you'll often have to start, stop, or pause Exchange services. You manage Exchange services through the Computer Management console or through System Manager.

To start, stop, or pause services in the Computer Management console, follow these steps:

1. To connect to a remote exchange server, right-click the Computer Management entry in the console tree, and then select Connect To Another Computer from the shortcut menu. You can now choose the Exchange server for which you want to manage services.

2. Expand the Services And Applications node by clicking the plus sign (+) next to it, and then choose Services.

3. Right-click the service you want to manipulate, and then select Start, Stop, or Pause as appropriate. You can also choose Restart to have Windows stop and then start the service after a brief pause. Also, if you pause a service, you can use the Resume option to resume normal operation.

 Tip When services that are set to start automatically fail, the status is listed as blank and you'll usually receive notification in a pop-up window. Service failures can also be logged to the system's event logs. In Windows Server 2003, you can configure actions to handle service failure automatically. For example, you could have Windows Server 2003 attempt to restart the service for you. See the section of this chapter entitled "Configuring Service Recovery" for details.

Several of the Exchange services are used to manage the Exchange virtual servers. These services are as follows:

- Microsoft Exchange IMAP4 for the IMAP4 virtual server
- Microsoft Exchange POP3 for the POP3 virtual server
- Network News Transfer Protocol (NNTP) for the NNTP virtual server
- Simple Mail Transfer Protocol (SMTP) for the SMTP virtual server

If you start, stop, or pause these services in the Computer Management console, you're managing the related virtual server as well. You can also use System Manager to perform these tasks. To do that, complete the following steps:

1. In System Manager, access the Servers node within the administrative or routing group you want to manage. Typically, you would expand Administrative Groups, First Administrative Group, and then the Servers node.

2. In the console tree, select the Exchange server you want to manage, and then double-click Protocols. You should now see a list of protocols installed on the server.

3. The Protocol folder stores related virtual servers. For example, the IMAP4 folder stores the Default IMAP4 virtual server and any other IMAP4 virtual servers you've created.

4. Right-click the virtual server you want to start, stop, or pause, and then select Start, Stop, or Pause as appropriate from the shortcut menu.

Configuring Service Startup

Essential Exchange services are configured to start automatically and normally shouldn't be configured with another startup option. That said, if you're troubleshooting a problem, you might want a service to start manually. You might also want to disable a service so that its related virtual servers don't start. For example, if you move the POP3 virtual servers to a new server for load balancing, you might want to disable the Microsoft Exchange POP3 service on the original Exchange server. In this way, the POP3 service isn't used, but it could be turned on if necessary (without having to reinstall POP3 support).

You configure service startup by completing the following steps:

1. In the Computer Management console, connect to the Exchange server for which you want to manage services.

2. Expand the Services And Applications node by clicking the plus sign (+) next to it, and then choose Services.

3. Right-click the service you want to configure, and then choose Properties.

4. On the General tab, use the Startup Type selection list to choose a startup option, as shown in Figure 4-4. Select Automatic to start services at bootup. Select Manual to allow services to be started manually. Select Disabled to turn off services.

5. Click OK.

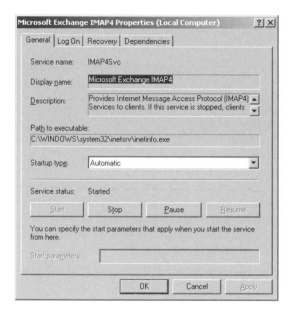

Figure 4-4. *For troubleshooting, you might want to change the service startup option in the Properties dialog box.*

Configuring Service Recovery

You can configure Windows services to take specific actions when a service fails. For example, you could attempt to restart the service or reboot the server. To configure recovery options for a service, follow these steps:

1. In the Computer Management console, connect to the computer for which you want to manage services.

2. Expand the Services And Applications node by clicking the plus sign (+) next to it, and then choose Services.

3. Right-click the service you want to configure, and then choose Properties.

4. Select the Recovery tab, as shown in Figure 4-5. You can now configure recovery options for the first, second, and subsequent recovery attempts. The available options are as follows:

    - Take No Action
    - Restart The Service
    - Run A File
    - Restart The Computer

5. Configure other options based on your previously selected recovery options. If you elected to restart the service, you'll need to specify the restart delay. After stopping the service, Windows Server 2003 waits for the specified delay period before trying to start the service. In most cases a delay of one to two minutes should be sufficient.

6. Click OK.

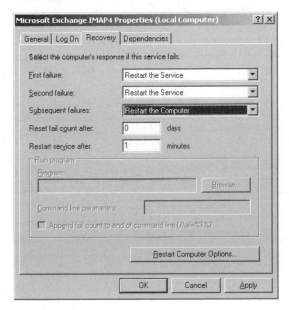

Figure 4-5. *By using the Recovery tab in the Properties dialog box, you can configure services to automatically recover in case of failure.*

When you configure recovery options for critical services, you might want to try to restart the service on the first and second attempts and then reboot the server on the third attempt.

Chapter 5
User and Contact Administration

One of your primary tasks as a Microsoft Exchange administrator is to manage user accounts and contacts. User accounts enable individual users to log on to the network and access network resources. In Active Directory, users are represented by User and InetOrgPerson objects. User and InetOrgPerson are the only Active Directory objects that can have Exchange mailboxes associated with them. Contacts, on the other hand, are people that you or others in your organization want to get in touch with. Contacts can have street addresses, phone numbers, fax numbers, and e-mail addresses associated with them. Unlike user accounts, contacts don't have network logon privileges.

Understanding Users and Contacts

In Active Directory, users are represented as objects that can be mailbox-enabled or mail-enabled. A *mailbox-enabled* user account has an Exchange mailbox associated with it. Mailboxes are private storage areas for sending and receiving mail. A user's display name is the name Exchange represents in the Global Address List and in the From field of e-mail messages.

Another important identifier for mailbox-enabled user accounts is the Exchange alias. The alias is the name that Exchange associates with the account for mail addressing. When your mail client is configured to use Exchange Server, you can type the alias or display name in the To, Cc, or Bcc fields of an e-mail message and have Exchange Server resolve the alias or name to the actual e-mail address.

Although most Microsoft Windows user accounts are mailbox-enabled, user accounts don't have to have mailboxes associated with them. You can create user accounts without assigning a mailbox. You can also create user accounts that are *mail-enabled* rather than mailbox-enabled, which means that the account has an off-site e-mail address associated with it but doesn't have an actual mailbox. Mail-enabled users have Exchange aliases and display names that Exchange Server can resolve to actual e-mail addresses. Internal users can send mail to the mail-enabled user account using the Exchange display name or alias, and the mail will be directed to the external address. Users outside the organization, however, can't use the Exchange alias to send mail to the user.

It's not always easy to decide when to create a mailbox for a user. To help you out, consider the following scenario:

1. You've been notified that two new users, Elizabeth and Joe, will need access to the domain.

2. Elizabeth is a full-time employee who starts on Tuesday. She'll work on-site and needs to be able to send and receive mail. People in the company need to be able to send mail directly to her.

3. Joe, on the other hand, is a consultant who is coming in to help out temporarily. His agency maintains his mailbox, and he doesn't want to have to check mail in two places. However, people in the company need to be able to contact him, and he wants to ensure that his external address is available.

4. You create a mailbox-enabled user account for Elizabeth. Afterward, you create a mail-enabled user account for Joe, ensuring that his Exchange information refers to his external e-mail address.

Mail-enabled users are one of several types of custom recipients that you can create in Exchange Server. Another type of custom recipient is a *mail-enabled contact*. You mail-enable a contact by specifying the external e-mail address that can be used to send e-mail to that contact.

Understanding the Basics of E-Mail Routing

Exchange uses e-mail addresses to route messages to mail servers inside and outside the organization. When routing messages internally, Exchange uses mail connectors to route messages to other Exchange servers, as well as to other types of mail servers that your company might use. The default connector, Exchange Routing Group Connector, provides a direct connection among Exchange servers in an organization. Simple Mail Transfer Protocol (SMTP) is the default transport for the Routing Group Connector. You can also configure X.400 as the transport among Exchange servers. Other connectors are available as well, including the following:

- Connector for Lotus Notes
- Connector for Novell GroupWise

You can use these connectors to connect Exchange with non-Exchange mail servers in an organization. When routing messages outside the company, Exchange uses mail gateways to transfer messages. The default gateway is SMTP.

When you create mail-enabled users or contacts, you must specify the type of address for the user or contact. When you create mailbox-enabled user accounts, Exchange automatically generates default e-mail addresses for SMTP and X.400.

The SMTP address is used for message routing to external systems. The X.400 e-mail address is used when you've specifically configured an X.400 connector to connect two routing groups and when Exchange can't resolve the distin-guished name for the account. Distinguished names are account identifiers that Exchange Server uses to locate Active Directory objects.

Keep in mind that if you've configured Exchange connectors, e-mail addresses for these connectors are generated as well. For details on Exchange organiza-tions and mail connectors, see Chapter 13, "Managing Microsoft Exchange Server 2003 Organizations."

Working with Active Directory Users And Computers

Active Directory Users And Computers is the primary administration tool for managing users and contacts. You use this utility to do the following:

* Create mailbox-enabled user accounts
* Create mail-enabled user accounts
* Manage directory contacts
* Manage mail-enabled contacts

Running Active Directory Users And Computers

You can start Active Directory Users And Computers by selecting its related option on the Microsoft Exchange menu. Click Start, choose Programs or All Pro-grams, choose Microsoft Exchange, and then select Active Directory Users And Computers. If the Exchange tools aren't available, you'll need to install them as described in Chapter 1, "Overview of Microsoft Exchange Server 2003 Adminis-tration," in the section "Exchange Server Administration Tools."

Tip   To provide quick access to Active Directory Users And Comput-ers, click Start, choose Programs or All Programs, choose Microsoft Exchange, right-click Active Directory Users And Computers, and then select Pin To Start Menu. This makes Active Directory Users And Com-puters directly accessible from the Start menu.

Using Active Directory Users And Computers

Normally, Active Directory Users And Computers works with the domain to which your computer is currently connected. As shown in Figure 5-1, you can access computer and user objects in the current domain through the console tree. However, if you can't find a domain controller, or the domain you want to work with isn't displayed, you might need to connect to a domain controller in the current domain in a different domain. Other high-level tasks you might want to perform with Active Directory Users And Computers are viewing advanced options and searching for objects.

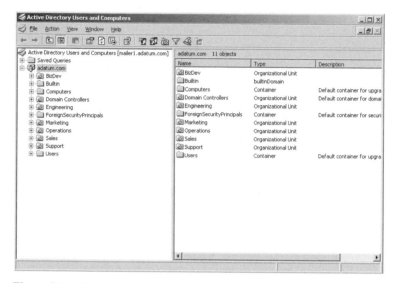

Figure 5-1. *Using Active Directory Users And Computers.*

When you access a domain in Active Directory Users And Computers, you'll note that the following standard set of folders is available:

- **Built-In** Shows built-in user groups.
- **Computers** The default container for computer accounts.
- **Domain Controllers** The default container for domain controllers.
- **ForeignSecurityPrincipals** Provides information on objects from trusted external domains. Normally, foreign security principals are created when an object from an external domain is added to a group in the current domain.
- **Saved Queries** Provides quick access to Active Directory queries you've saved.
- **Users** The default container for users.

You can also add folders for organizational units. An *organizational unit* is a subgroup of domains that often mirrors the business or functional structure of the company. For example, you could create organizational units called BizDev, Engineering, Marketing, Operations, Sales, and Support.

When you access a folder in Active Directory Users And Computers, you'll see a list of the users and groups the folder contains. Users and groups are listed by name, type, and description. You'll probably also want to display e-mail addresses, Exchange aliases, and Exchange mailbox stores associated with users. To do this, follow these steps:

1. In Active Directory Users And Computers, click View, Add/Remove Columns.

2. In the Add/Remove Columns dialog box, double click E-Mail Address, Exchange Alias, and Exchange Mailbox Store in the Available Columns list. This adds these fields to the Displayed Columns list.

3. In the Available Columns list, select Description and click Move Down three times. This places the description at the end of the list.

4. When you click OK, the new columns you've added are displayed in Active Directory Users And Computers. From now on, the additional columns should be displayed whenever you start Active Directory Users And Computers as well.

Connecting to a Domain Controller

Connecting to a domain controller serves several purposes. If you start Active Directory Users And Computers and no objects are available, you can connect to a domain controller to access user, group, and computer objects in the current domain. You might also want to connect to a domain controller when you suspect replication isn't working properly and you want to inspect the objects on a specific controller. Once you're connected, you'd look for discrepancies in recently updated objects.

To connect to a domain controller, follow these steps:

1. In the console tree, right-click Active Directory Users And Computers. Then select Connect To Domain Controller.

2. You'll see the current domain and domain controller you're working with in the Connect To Domain Controller dialog box shown in Figure 5-2.

Figure 5-2. *In the Connect To Domain Controller dialog box, select the domain controller you want to work with.*

3. Available controllers in the domain are listed in the Select An Available Domain Controller list box. The default selection is Any Writable Domain Controller. If you select this option, you'll connect to the domain controller that responds to your request first. Otherwise, choose a specific domain controller to connect to. Click OK.

Connecting to a Different Domain

In Active Directory Users And Computers you can work with any domain in the forest, provided you have access permissions. You connect to a domain by completing these steps:

1. In the console tree, right-click Active Directory Users And Computers. Then select Connect To Domain.

2. The current (or default) domain is displayed in the Connect To Domain dialog box. Type a new domain name, and then click OK. Or you can click Browse, and then select a domain in the Browse For Domain dialog box.

Searching for Existing Users and Contacts

Active Directory Users And Computers has a built-in search feature that allows you to find users, contacts, and other directory objects. You can easily search the current domain, a specific domain, or the entire directory.

You search for directory objects by completing the following steps:

1. In the console tree, right-click the current domain or a specific container that you want to search. Select Find. This opens the Find Users, Contacts, And Groups dialog box shown in Figure 5-3.

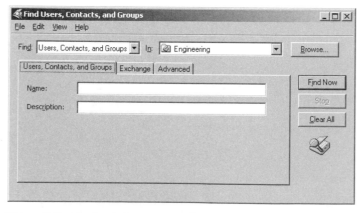

Figure 5-3. *Find existing users and contacts in Active Directory using the Find Users, Contacts, And Groups dialog box.*

2. Select Users, Contacts, And Groups, and then use the In drop-down list to choose the location to search. If you right-clicked a container such as Users, this container is selected by default. To search all the objects in the directory, select Entire Directory.

3. In the Name field, enter the name of the object you're looking for, and then click the Exchange tab. Select Show Only Exchange Recipients.

4. If you'd like to limit the search to specific types of recipients, select the related check boxes. For example, if you want to search only for users with mailboxes, select Users With Exchange Mailbox.

5. After you've typed your search parameters, click Find Now. Any matching entries are displayed in the Find view (see Figure 5-4). Double-click an object to view or modify its property settings. Right-click the object to display a shortcut menu that you can use to manage the object.

Figure 5-4. *Matching recipients are displayed in the lower portion of the Find Users, Contacts, And Groups dialog box and can be managed by right-clicking an entry.*

Managing User Accounts and Mail Features

The sections that follow examine techniques that you employ to manage user accounts and the Exchange features of those accounts.

Creating Mailbox-Enabled and Mail-Enabled User Accounts

You need to create a user account for each user who wants to use network resources. The following sections explain how to create domain user accounts that are either mailbox-enabled or mail-enabled. If the user needs to send and receive e-mail, you'll need to create a mailbox-enabled account. Otherwise, you can create a mail-enabled account.

Understanding Logon Names and Passwords

Before you create a domain user account, you should think for a moment about the new account's logon name and password. All domain user accounts are identified with a logon name. This logon name can be (but doesn't have to be) the same as the user's e-mail address. In Windows domains, logon names have two parts:

- **User name** The account's text label
- **User domain** The domain where the user account exists

For the user williams whose account is created in adatum.com, the full logon name for Windows is williams@adatum.com.

User accounts can also have passwords and public certificates associated with them. *Passwords* are authentication strings for an account. *Public certificates* combine a public and private key to identify a user. You log on with a password interactively. You log on with a public certificate using a smart card and a smart card reader.

Although Windows displays user names to describe privileges and permissions, the key identifiers for accounts are security identifiers (SIDs). SIDs are unique identifiers that are generated when accounts are created. SIDs consist of the domain's security ID prefix and a unique relative ID. Windows uses these identifiers to track accounts independently from user names. SIDs serve many purposes; the two most important are to allow you to easily change user names and to allow you to delete accounts without worrying that someone could gain access to resources simply by re-creating an account.

When you change a user name, you tell Windows to map a particular SID to a new name. When you delete an account, you tell Windows that a particular SID is no longer valid. Afterward, even if you create an account with the same user name, the new account won't have the same privileges and permissions as the previous one because the new account will have a new SID.

Creating Domain User Accounts with and without Mailboxes

Generally, there are two ways to create new domain accounts:

- **Create a completely new user account**   Right-click the container in which you want to place the user account, point to New, and then select User. This opens the New Object-User Wizard shown in Figure 5-5. When you create a new account, the default system settings are used.

Figure 5-5. *Configure the user display and logon names using the New Object-User dialog box.*

- **Base the new account on an existing account**   In Active Directory Users And Computers, right-click the user account you want to copy, and then select Copy. This starts the Copy Object-User Wizard, which is essentially the same as the New User dialog box. However, when you create a copy of an account, the new account gets most of its environment settings from the existing account. The properties that are retained include: group account memberships, profile settings, dial-in privileges, account expiration date, log on hours and permitted logon workstations.

Once the New Object-User or Copy Object-User Wizard is started, you can create the user account by completing the following steps:

1. As shown in Figure 5-5, the first wizard page lets you configure the user display name and logon name. Type the user's first and last name in the fields provided. The first and last names are used to create the Full Name, which is the user's display name.

2. As necessary, make changes to the Full Name field. For example, you might want to type the name in LastName FirstName MiddleInitial format or in FirstName MiddleInitial LastName format. The Full Name must be 64 characters or fewer.

3. In the User Logon Name field, type the user's logon name. Use the drop-down list to select the domain with which the account is to be associated. This sets the fully qualified logon name.

4. The first 20 characters of the logon name are used to set the pre-Windows 2000 logon name, which must be unique in the domain. If necessary, change the pre-Windows 2000 logon name.

5. Click Next. Configure the user's password using the wizard page shown in Figure 5-6. The options for this dialog box are used as follows:

Figure 5-6. *Configure the user's password.*

- **Password** The password for the account. This password should follow the conventions of your password policy.

- **Confirm Password** A field that ensures that you assign the account password correctly. Simply re-enter the password to confirm it.

- **User Must Change Password At Next Logon** If this check box is selected, the user must change the password at logon. This check box is selected by default for all new users.

- **User Cannot Change Password** If this check box is selected, the user can't change the password.

- **Password Never Expires** If this check box is selected, the password for this account never expires. This setting overrides the domain account policy. Generally, it isn't a good idea to set a password so it doesn't expire because it is considered to be less secure, and security is always important.

- **Account Is Disabled** If this check box is selected, the account is disabled and can't be used. Use this check box to temporarily prevent anyone from using an account.

6. Click Next. If you've properly installed the Exchange extensions on the computer that you're running, you'll be able to select whether the account should have a mailbox. If the user shouldn't have a mailbox, clear the Create An Exchange Mailbox check box, and then skip Steps 7 and 8.

7. As shown in Figure 5-7, the Exchange alias is set to the logon name by default. You can change this value by entering a new alias. The Exchange alias is used to set the user's e-mail address.

Note   Technically, the default value for the Exchange alias is set to the pre-Windows 2000 logon name, which is normally the same as the user logon name. However, if you change the pre-Windows 2000 logon name, the default Exchange alias will be set to the value you enter.

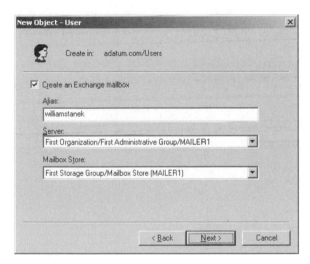

Figure 5-7. *Configure the user's Exchange mailbox.*

8. If multiple Exchange servers are configured with an Information Store, use the Server drop-down list to specify the server on which the mailbox should be stored. Also, if several mailbox stores are configured, use the Mailbox Store drop-down list to specify the mailbox store that should be used.

9. Click Next and then click Finish to create the account. If you created a mailbox-enabled account, SMTP, X.400, and connector-related e-mail addresses are configured automatically. Later on, you can add, change, and remove these addresses. You can also add additional addresses of the same type. For example, if Cindy Johnson is the company's human resources administrator, she might have two SMTP addresses: cindyj@adatum.com and resumes@adatum.com.

Note If you've configured Exchange connectors, default addresses are generated for these connectors as well. Connectors available with Exchange 2000 include Connector for Lotus Notes and Connector for Novell GroupWise.

10. Creating the user account isn't the final step. Next, you might want to do the following:

- Add detailed contact information for the user, such as business phone number and title.
- Add the user to security and distribution groups.
- Associate additional e-mail addresses with the account.
- Enable or disable Exchange features for the account.
- Modify the user's default delivery options, storage limits, and restrictions on the account.

Setting Contact Information for User Accounts

You can set contact information for a user account by completing the following steps:

1. In Active Directory Users And Computers, double-click the user name. This opens the account's Properties dialog box.
2. Click the General tab. Use the following fields to set general contact information:

- **First Name, Initials, Last Name** Sets the user's full name.
- **Display Name** Sets the user's display name as seen in logon sessions and in Active Directory.
- **Description** Sets a description of the user.
- **Office** Sets the user's office location.
- **Telephone Number** Sets the user's primary business telephone number. If the user has other business telephone numbers that you want to track, click Other, and then use the Phone Number (Others) dialog box to enter additional phone numbers.
- **E-Mail** Sets the user's business e-mail address.
- **Web Page** Sets the URL of the user's home page, which can be on the Internet or the company intranet. If the user has other Web pages that you want to track, click Other, and then use the Web Page Address (Others) dialog box to enter additional Web page addresses.

 Tip You must fill in the E-Mail and Web Page fields if you want to use the Send Mail and Open Home Page features in Active Directory Users And Computers.

3. Click the Address tab, shown in Figure 5-8. Use the fields provided to set the user's business address or home address. Normally, you'll want to enter the user's business address. This way, you can track the business locations and mailing addresses of users at various offices.

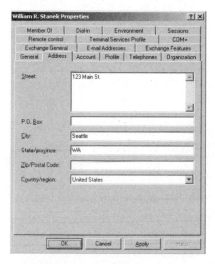

Figure 5-8. *Use the Address tab to set the user's business or home address.*

Note You need to consider privacy issues before entering private information such as home addresses and home phone numbers for users. Discuss the matter with your human resources and legal departments. You might also want to get user consent before releasing home addresses.

4. Click the Telephones tab. As appropriate, type the primary telephone numbers that should be used to contact the user:
   - Home Telephone
   - Pager
   - Mobile
   - FAX
   - IP Phone

5. You can configure other numbers for each type of telephone number. Click the associated Others button, and then use the dialog box provided to enter additional contact numbers.

6. Click the Organization tab. As appropriate, type the user's title, department, and company.

7. To specify the user's manager, click Change, and then in the Select User Or Contact dialog box, select the user's manager. When you specify a manager, the user shows up as a direct report in the manager's account.

8. Click Apply or OK to apply the changes.

Changing a User's Exchange Server Alias and Display Name

Each mailbox-enabled user account has an Exchange alias, first name, last name, and display name associated with it. The Exchange alias determines the SMTP and X.400 e-mail addresses. The logon name is the default SMTP alias. The display name determines the X.400 address.

Whenever you change the naming information, new e-mail addresses can be generated and set as the default addresses for SMTP, X.400, and Exchange connectors you've configured. The previous e-mail addresses for the account aren't deleted. Instead, these e-mail addresses remain as alternatives to the defaults. To learn how to change or delete these additional e-mail addresses, see the section of this chapter entitled "Adding, Changing, and Removing E-Mail Addresses."

To change the Exchange alias and display name on a user account, complete the following steps:

1. In Active Directory Users And Computers, double-click the user name. This opens the account's Properties dialog box.

2. Click the General tab, and then use the following fields to modify the current name:

   - **First Name, Initials, Last Name**   Sets the user's full name

   - **Display Name**   Sets the user's display name as seen in logon sessions and in Active Directory

3. Click the Exchange General tab, and then in the Alias field, enter the new Exchange alias.

4. Click OK.

Adding, Changing, and Removing E-Mail Addresses

When you create a mailbox-enabled user account, default e-mail addresses are created for SMTP, X.400, and any connectors you've configured. Any time you update the user's display name or Exchange alias, new default e-mail addresses can be created. However, the old addresses aren't deleted. They remain as alternative e-mail addresses for the account.

To add, change, or remove an e-mail address, follow these steps:

1. Open the Properties dialog box for the account by double-clicking the user name in Active Directory Users And Computers. Then click the E-Mail Addresses tab.

2. To add a new e-mail address, click New. In the New E-Mail Address dialog box, select the type of e-mail address and then click OK. Complete the Properties dialog box and then click OK again.

Tip   Use SMTP as the address type for standard Internet e-mail addresses. For details on how to use other types of e-mail addresses, see Chapter 13, "Managing Microsoft Exchange Server 2003 Organizations.

3. To change an existing e-mail address, double-click the address entry and modify the settings in the Properties dialog box. Click OK.
4. To delete an e-mail address, select it, and then click Remove. Click Yes when prompted to confirm the deletion.

Note   You can't delete the default SMTP address. Exchange Server uses the SMTP address to send and receive messages.

Setting a Default Reply-To Address

Each e-mail address type has one default reply address. To change the default reply address, follow these steps:

1. Open the Properties dialog box for the account by double-clicking the user name in Active Directory Users And Computers. Then click the E-Mail Addresses tab.
2. Current default e-mail addresses are highlighted with bold text. E-mail addresses that aren't highlighted are used only as alternative addresses for delivering messages to the current mailbox.
3. To change the current default settings, select an e-mail address that isn't highlighted and then click Set As Primary.

Enabling and Disabling Exchange Server Mail

Mail-enabled users and contacts are defined as custom recipients in Exchange Server. They have an Exchange alias and an external e-mail address. You can mail-enable a user or contact by completing the following steps:

1. In Active Directory Users And Computers, right-click the related entry, and then select Exchange Tasks to start the Exchange Task Wizard.
2. If a Welcome page is displayed, click Next. You can skip the Welcome page in the future by selecting Do Not Show This Welcome Page Again.
3. Under Available Tasks, select Establish E-Mail Addresses and then click Next.
4. Enter an Exchange Alias for the user or contact, and then click Modify.
5. You'll see the New E-Mail Address dialog box. Select the type of e-mail address and then click OK.

6. Complete the Properties dialog box for the e-mail address, and then click OK again.

7. On the Exchange Task Wizard page, click Next and then click Finish.

Later, if you want to delete the Exchange alias and remove any e-mail addresses that might be associated with the user or contact, follow these steps:

1. In Active Directory Users And Computers, right-click the related entry, and then select Exchange Tasks to start the Exchange Task Wizard.

2. If a Welcome page is displayed, click Next. You can skip the Welcome page in the future by selecting Do Not Show This Welcome Page Again.

3. Under Available Tasks, select Delete E-Mail Addresses and then click Next.

4. Click Next and then click Finish.

Creating a User Account to Receive Mail and Forward Off-Site

Custom recipients, such as mail-enabled users and contacts, don't normally receive mail from users outside the organization because a custom recipient doesn't have an e-mail address that resolves to a specific mailbox in your organization. At times, though, you might want external users, applications, or mail systems to be able to send mail to an address within your organization and then have Exchange forward this mail to an external mailbox.

 Tip In my organization I've created forwarding mailboxes for pager alerts. This simple solution lets managers (and monitoring systems) within the organization quickly and easily send text pages to IT personnel. Here, I've set up mail-enabled contacts for each pager e-mail address, such as 8085551212@adatum.com, and then created a mailbox that forwards e-mail to the custom recipient. Generally, the display name of the mail-enabled contact is in the form Alert *User Name*, such as Alert William Stanek. The display name and e-mail address for the mailbox are in the form Z *LastName* and *AE-MailAddress@myorg.com*, such as Z Stanek and AWilliamS@adatum.com, respectively. Afterward, I hide the mailbox so that it isn't displayed in the global address list or in other address lists so users can see only the Alert William Stanek mailbox.

To create a user account to receive mail and forward off-site, follow these steps:

1. In Active Directory Users And Computers, create a contact for the user. Name the contact X – *User Name*, such as X – William Stanek. Be sure to establish an external e-mail address for the contact that refers to the user's Internet address.

2. Create a user account in the domain. Name the account with the appropriate display name, such as William Stanek. Be sure to create an Exchange mailbox for the account but don't grant any special permission to the account.

You might want to restrict the account so that the user can't log on to any servers in the domain.

3. Open the Properties dialog box for the user account by double-clicking the user name in Active Directory Users And Computers. Click the Exchange General tab.

4. Click Delivery Options.

5. In the Delivery Options dialog box, click Forward To, and then click Modify.

6. In the Select Recipient dialog box, select the mail-enabled contact you created earlier, and then click OK. You can now use the user account to forward mail to the external mailbox.

Changing a User's Wireless Service and Protocol Options

When you create user accounts with mailboxes, global settings determine the wireless services and protocols that are available. You can change these settings for individual users at any time by completing the following steps:

1. In Active Directory Users And Computers, double-click the related entry, and then click the Exchange Features tab. As shown in Figure 5-9, configure the following wireless services and protocols for the user:

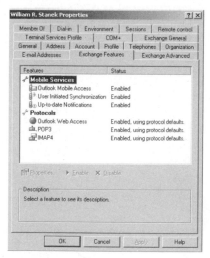

Figure 5-9. *You change wireless service and protocol options for users through the Exchange Task Wizard.*

- **Outlook Mobile Access**   Allows the user to browse the mailbox using a wireless device.

- **User Initiated Synchronization**   Allows the user to synchronize the mailbox with wireless devices.

- **Up-To-Date Notifications** Ensures the data on a wireless device is always up to date. This option can only be enabled when User Initiated Synchronization is also enabled.
- **Outlook Web Access** Permits the user to access the mailbox with a Web browser.
- **POP3** Permits the user to access the mailbox with a POP3 e-mail client.
- **IMAP4** Permits the user to access the mailbox with an IMAP4 e-mail client.

2. Select an option, then click Enable or Disable as appropriate to change the status. If you want to change the properties of a protocol, select the protocol and then click Properties.

3. Click OK.

Renaming User Accounts

In Active Directory Users And Computers, you can rename a user account by completing the following steps:

1. Right-click the account name and then choose Rename. Enter the new account name when prompted.

2. When you rename a user account, you give the account a new label. Changing the name doesn't affect the SID, which is used to identify, track, and handle accounts independently from user names.

 Note Marriage is a common reason for changing the name of user accounts. For example, if Judy Lew (JUDYL) gets married, she might want her user name to be changed to Judy Kaethler (JUDYK). When you change the user name from JUDYL to JUDYK, all associated privileges and permissions will reflect the name change. Thus, if you view the permissions on a file that JUDYL had access to, JUDYK will now have access (and JUDYL will no longer be listed).

Deleting User Accounts and Contacts

Deleting an account permanently removes the account. Once you delete an account, you can't create an account with the same name and the same permissions as the original account because the SID for the new account won't match the SID for the old account. That doesn't mean that once you delete an account, you can never again create an account with that same name. For example, a person might leave the company only to return a short while later. You can create an account using the same naming convention as before, but you'll have to redefine the permissions for that account.

Because deleting built-in accounts could have far-reaching effects on the domain, Windows doesn't let you delete built-in user accounts. You *could* remove other types of accounts by selecting them and pressing the Del key, or by right-clicking and selecting Delete. You'll see the prompt shown in Figure 5-10. If you'd like to delete the user's e-mail address and mark the mailbox for deletion, click Yes. If you click No, Windows won't delete the account.

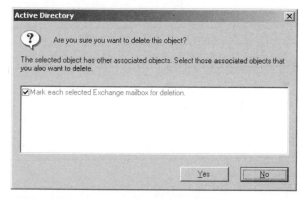

Figure 5-10. *Deleting a user's account deletes the user's e-mail address and marks the associated mailbox for deletion. Confirm the action by clicking Yes.*

Note Because Exchange security is based on domain authentication, you can't have a mailbox without an account. If you still need the mailbox for an account you want to delete, you should disable the account instead of deleting it. Disabling the account prevents the user from logging on, but you can still access the mailbox if you need to. To disable an account, right-click the account in Active Directory Users And Computers, and then select Disable Account.

Managing Contacts

Contacts represent people with whom you or others in your organization want to get in touch. Contacts can have directory information associated with them, but they don't have network logon privileges.

Creating Standard and Mail-Enabled Contacts

The only difference between a standard contact and a mail-enabled contact is the presence of e-mail addresses. A mail-enabled contact has one or more e-mail addresses associated with it; a standard contact doesn't. When a contact has an e-mail address, you can list the contact in the Global Address List or other address lists. This allows users to send messages to the contact.

You can create a standard or mail-enabled contact by completing the following steps:

1. Start Active Directory Users And Computers by selecting its related option on the Microsoft Exchange menu.

2. Right-click the container in which you want to place the contact, choose New, and then choose Contact. This opens the New Object-Contact dialog box, shown in Figure 5-11.

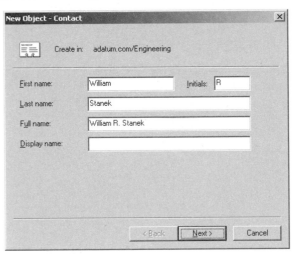

Figure 5-11. *Enter the contact's first, last, full, and display names.*

3. Enter the contact's first name, initials, and last name. The contact's full name is filled in automatically. The full name is displayed in Active Directory Users And Computers, and it's also the name that users can search for in the directory.

4. The display name is displayed in the Global Address List and other address lists created for the organization. The display name is also used when addressing e-mail messages to the contact. If the contact should have a display name that's different from the full name, enter the display name.

5. Click Next. If the contact shouldn't be mail-enabled, clear the Create An Exchange E-Mail Address check box, and then skip Steps 6 and 7.

6. Enter an Exchange alias for the contact, and then click Modify. You'll see the New E-Mail Address dialog box.

7. Select the type of e-mail address, and then click OK. Complete the Properties dialog box, and then click OK again.

8. Click Next, and then click Finish. Active Directory Users And Computers creates the new contact.

Setting Additional Directory Information for Contacts

You can set additional directory information for a contact by completing the following steps:

1. Double-click the contact's name in Active Directory Users And Computers. This opens a Properties dialog box.

2. Use the General tab to set general contact information, including the following:

   - **First Name, Initials, Last Name**   Sets the contact's full name
   - **Display Name**   Sets the contact's display name as seen in address lists
   - **Description**   Sets a description of the contact
   - **Office**   Sets the contact's office location
   - **Telephone Number**   Sets the contact's primary business telephone number
   - **E-Mail**   Sets the contact's business e-mail address
   - **Web Page**   Sets the Uniform Resource Locator (URL) of the contact's home page

3. Click the Address tab, and then use the fields provided to set the contact's business address.

4. Click the Telephones tab. As appropriate, type the primary telephone numbers for the contact. You can configure other numbers for each type of telephone number. Click the associated Others button, and then use the dialog box provided to enter additional contact numbers.

5. Click the Organization tab. As appropriate, type the contact's title, department, and company.

6. To specify the contact's manager, click Change, and then in the Select User Or Contact dialog box, select the user's manager. When you specify a manager, the user shows up as a direct report in the manager's account.

7. Click Apply or OK to apply the changes.

Changing E-Mail Addresses Associated with Contacts

When you create a new mail-enabled contact, you set the default e-mail address identifier and type as well as a default Exchange alias. You can change these identifiers by completing the following steps:

1. Double-click the contact name in Active Directory Users And Computers. This opens the account's Properties dialog box.

2. Click the Exchange General tab.

3. If desired, enter an Exchange alias for the contact, and then click Modify. If the contact already has an associated e-mail address, specify whether you want to create a new address or modify the existing address. Click OK.

4. When you modify an existing address, you'll see a Properties dialog box. Make the necessary changes and then click OK.

5. When you create a new address, you'll see the New E-Mail Address dialog box. Here, select the type of e-mail address and then click OK. Complete the Properties dialog box, and then click OK again.

6. Contacts also have default addresses for SMTP, X.400, and other connectors you've configured. You can change these through the E-Mail Addresses tab.

Chapter 6

Mailbox Administration

The difference between a good Microsoft Exchange administrator and a great one is the attention he or she pays to mailbox administration. Mailboxes are private storage places for sending and receiving mail, and they are created as part of private mailbox stores in Exchange. When you create user accounts, including those for InetOrgPersons, you have the option of creating mailboxes for those accounts. You can also add mailboxes to existing user accounts as necessary.

Mailboxes have many properties that control mail delivery, permissions, and storage limits. You can configure most mailbox settings on a per-mailbox basis. However, some settings cannot be changed without moving mailboxes to a different mailbox store or changing the settings of the mailbox store itself. For example, the storage location on the Exchange file system, the default public folder store for the mailbox, and the default offline address book are set on a per-mailbox-store basis. Keep this in mind when performing capacity planning and when deciding which storage group and mailbox store to use for a particular mailbox.

Managing Mailboxes: The Essentials

You often need to manage mailboxes the way you do user accounts. Some of the management tasks are fairly intuitive and others aren't. If you have questions, be sure to read the sections that follow.

Tip For all of the procedures in this section, you can select multiple users for whom you want to manage mailboxes. To select multiple users individually, hold down the Ctrl key and then click each user account that you want to select. To select a sequence of accounts, hold down the Shift key, select the first user account, and then click the last user account.

Adding Mailboxes to Existing User Accounts

You don't have to create an Exchange mailbox when you create a user account. If a user needs a mailbox later, you can create the mailbox by completing the following steps:

1. In Active Directory Users And Computers, right-click the user's name, and then select Exchange Tasks to start the Exchange Task Wizard. You can select multiple user accounts as well; if you do this, the Exchange alias for each user will be set to that user's logon name and cannot be changed.

2. If a Welcome page is displayed, click Next. You can skip the Welcome page in the future by selecting Do Not Show This Welcome Page Again.

3. Under Available Tasks, select Create Mailbox, and then click Next.

4. The Create Mailbox wizard page, shown in Figure 6-1, is displayed.

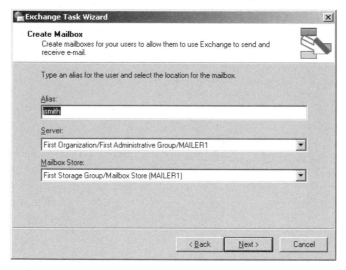

Figure 6-1. *All user accounts can have mailboxes associated with them. If you don't create a mailbox initially, you can do so later.*

5. The Exchange alias is set to the logon name by default. You can change this value by entering a new alias as long as you do not have multiple accounts selected.

6. If multiple Exchange servers are configured with an Information Store, use the Server drop-down list to specify the server on which the mailbox should be stored.

Caution In Exchange mixed-mode operations, mailboxes can't be moved from a server in one administrative group to a server in another administrative group. In addition, although you can move mailboxes to different Exchange servers, these servers must be in the same routing group. You can't move mailboxes among routing groups (regardless of the Exchange operations mode).

7. If multiple mailbox stores are configured, use the Mailbox Store drop-down list to specify the mailbox store that should be used.

8. Click Next and then click Finish.

Viewing Current Mailbox Size and Message Count

You can use Exchange System Manager to view the current mailbox size and message count by completing these steps:

1. In Exchange System Manager, access the Servers node within the administrative or routing group you want to manage. Typically, you would expand Administrative Groups, First Administrative Group, and then the Servers node.

2. In the left pane (the console tree), select the Exchange server you want to manage. You should now see a list of storage groups that are available on the server.

3. Mailboxes are stored in the mailbox store associated with a storage group. Expand the storage groups and mailbox stores until you see the Mailboxes node you want to work with. For example, you could expand First Storage Group and Technology Mailbox Store, and then select the Mailboxes node.

4. The right pane should now display a summary list of mailboxes that are stored in the selected mailbox store.

Moving Mailboxes to a New Server or Storage Group

To balance the server load or manage drive space, you can move mailboxes to another server or storage group. When you move mailboxes from one server to another or even to a different storage group on the same sever, keep in mind that the Exchange policies of the new mailbox store may be different from the old one. Because of this, consider the following issues before you move mailboxes to a new server or storage group:

- **General policy** Changes to watch out for include those for the default public folder store, the offline address book, and message settings. As a result, the users whose mailboxes you move could lose or gain access to public folders. They might have a different offline address book, which might have different entries and that will also have to be downloaded in its entirety the first time the user's mail client connects to Exchange after the move. Message settings for mailbox stores control message archiving, support for Secure/Multipurpose Internet Mail Extensions (S/MIME) signatures, and the font used to display plaintext messages.

- **Database policy** Changes to watch out for pertain to the maintenance interval and automatic mounting. If Exchange performs maintenance when these users are accessing their mail, they might have slower response times. If the mailbox store is configured so that it isn't mounted at startup, restarting the Exchange services could result in the users not being able to access their mailboxes.

- **Limits** Changes to watch out for pertain to storage limits and deletion settings. Users might be prohibited from sending and receiving mail if the user's mailbox exceeds the storage limits of the new mailbox store. Users might notice that deleted items stay in their Deleted Items folder longer or are deleted sooner than expected if the Keep Deleted Items setting is different.

 Note To learn more about these Exchange policies, see Chapter 8, "Implementing Directory Security and Microsoft Exchange Server 2003 Policies."

You move mailboxes by completing these steps:

1. Right-click the user name in Active Directory Users And Computers, and then select Exchange Tasks to start the Exchange Task Wizard. You can select multiple user accounts as well.

2. If a Welcome wizard page is displayed, click Next.

3. Under Available Tasks, select Move Mailbox, and then click Next.

4. Use the Server drop-down list to specify the server on which the mailbox should be stored. Use the Mailbox Store drop-down list to specify the mailbox store that should be used.

5. Click Next, and then click Finish. Exchange Server attempts to move the mailbox. If a problem occurs, you'll see an Error dialog box that lets you retry or cancel the operation.

 Note In Exchange mixed-mode operations, you can't move mailboxes from a server in one administrative group to a server in another administrative group. You can't move mailboxes among routing groups regardless of operations mode. To move mailboxes among servers, the servers must be in the same routing group.

Removing Mailboxes from User Accounts

Removing a mailbox from a user account deletes any e-mail addresses associated with the account and marks the primary mailbox for deletion. The mailbox is then deleted according to the retention period set on the account or on the mailbox store. For more information on deleted item retention, see the section of this chapter entitled, "Setting Deleted Item Retention Time on Individual Mailboxes."

You can remove a mailbox from a user account by completing the following steps:

1. Right-click the user name in Active Directory Users And Computers, and then select Exchange Tasks to start the Exchange Task Wizard. You can select multiple user accounts as well.
2. If a Welcome wizard page is displayed, click Next.
3. Under Available Tasks, select Delete Mailbox, and then click Next.
4. Click Next, and then click Finish.

Configuring Mailbox Delivery Restrictions, Permissions, and Storage Limits

Mailbox properties are used to set delivery restrictions, permissions, and storage limits. To change these configuration settings for mailboxes, follow the techniques discussed in this section.

Setting Message Size Restrictions on Delivery To and From Individual Mailboxes

You can set delivery restrictions on mailboxes using two techniques:

- **Globally** By creating default delivery restrictions for all mailboxes. Global restrictions are applied when the user account is created and they are updated when you define new global delivery restrictions.

- **Individually** By setting per-user delivery restrictions. You set per-user delivery restrictions individually for each user account, and they override the global default settings.

You'll learn how to set global delivery restrictions in Chapter 13, "Managing Microsoft Exchange Server 2003 Organizations." See the section of that chapter entitled "Setting Default Delivery Restrictions for the Organization."

You set individual delivery restrictions by completing the following steps:

1. Open the Properties dialog box for the mailbox-enabled user account by double-clicking the user name in Active Directory Users And Computers.

2. On the Exchange General tab, click Delivery Restrictions. As shown in Figure 6-2, you can now set the following send and receive restrictions:

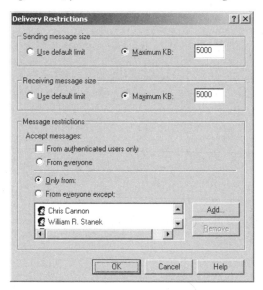

Figure 6-2. *You can apply individual delivery restrictions on a per-user basis.*

- **Sending Message Size** Sets a limit on the size of messages the user can send. If an outgoing message exceeds the limit, the message isn't sent and the user receives a nondelivery report (NDR).

- **Receiving Message Size** Sets a limit on the size of messages the user can receive. If an incoming message exceeds the limit, the message isn't delivered and the sender receives an NDR.

3. Click OK. The restrictions that you set override the global default settings.

Setting Send and Receive Restrictions for Contacts

You set message send and receive restrictions for contacts in the same way that you set these restrictions for users. Follow the steps listed in the section of this chapter entitled "Setting Message/Acceptance Restrictions on Individual Mailboxes."

Setting Message Acceptance Restrictions on Individual Mailboxes

By default, user mailboxes are configured to accept messages from anyone. To override this behavior, you can specify that only messages from the listed users, contacts, or groups should be accepted, or that messages from all e-mail addresses except the users, contacts, or groups listed should be accepted.

You can also specify that only authenticated users, meaning users who have logged on to the Exchange system or the domain, can be accepted.

You set message acceptance restrictions by completing the following steps:

1. Open the Properties dialog box for the mailbox-enabled user account by double-clicking the user name in Active Directory Users And Computers.

2. On the Exchange General tab, click Delivery Restrictions to display the Delivery Restrictions dialog box shown previously in Figure 6-2.

3. If you want to ensure that messages are accepted only from authenticated users, select the From Authenticated Users Only check box.

4. To specify that only messages from the listed users, contacts, or groups should be accepted, select the Only From option.

5. To specify that messages from all e-mail addresses except the users, contacts, or groups listed should be accepted, select the From Everyone Except option.

6. Click Add to add recipients to the inclusion or exclusion list. This displays the Select Recipient dialog box shown in Figure 6-3. Type the object names that you want to select, making sure to separate each name with a semicolon.

Tip For the object name, you can use the object's display name, such as William Stanek, or logon name, such as WilliamS. If you want to specify recipients in other domains, enter the name following the format *DomainName\ObjectName* or *ObjectName@DomainName*, such as Adatum\WilliamS or WilliamS@Adatum.

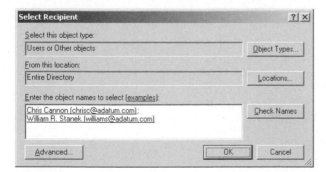

Figure 6-3. *Specify the valid recipients for the inclusion or exclusion list. Recipients can include users, contacts, and distribution groups.*

7. Click Check Names. If a name is not found, correct the object name you provided and then click OK. If multiple names are found, select the name or names that you want to use and then click OK.

8. When you click OK to close the Select Recipient dialog box, the recipients you've selected are added to the inclusion or exclusion list. Click OK twice to complete the task.

Setting Message Acceptance Restrictions for Contacts

You set message size and receive restrictions for contacts in the same way that you set these restrictions for users. Follow the steps listed in the section of this chapter entitled "Setting Message/Acceptance Restrictions on Individual Mailboxes."

Permitting Others to Access a Mailbox

Occasionally, users will need to access someone else's mailbox, and in certain situations you should allow them to. For example, if John is Susan's manager and Susan is going on vacation, John might need access to her mailbox while she's away. Another situation in which someone might need access to another mailbox is when you've set up special-purpose mailboxes, such as a mailbox for Webmaster@domain.com or a mailbox for Info@domain.com.

Granting someone the right to access a mailbox also gives that person the right to view the mailbox and send messages on behalf of the mailbox owner. You can grant or revoke access by completing the following steps:

1. Open the Properties dialog box for the mailbox-enabled user account by double-clicking the user name in Active Directory Users And Computers.

2. On the Exchange General tab, click Delivery Options. The Grant This Permission To list box shows any users that currently have access permissions. You can now do the following:

   - **Grant access**   To grant the authority to access the mailbox, click Add and then use the Select Recipient dialog box to choose the user or users who should have access to the mailbox.

   - **Revoke access**   To revoke the authority to access the mailbox, select an existing user name in the Grant This Permission To list box, and then click Remove.

3. Click OK.

 Note   Another way to grant access permissions to mailboxes is to do so through Outlook. Using Outlook, you have more granular control over permissions. You can allow a user to log on as the mailbox owner, delegate mailbox access, and grant various levels of access. For more information on this issue, see the sections of Chapter 2 entitled, "Accessing Multiple Exchange Server Mailboxes" and "Granting Permission to Access Folders Without Delegating Access."

Forwarding E-Mail to a New Address

Any messages sent to a user's mailbox can be forwarded to another recipient. This recipient could be another user or a mail-enabled contact. You can also specify that messages should be delivered to both the forwarding address and the current mailbox.

To configure mail forwarding, follow these steps:

1. Open the Properties dialog box for the mailbox-enabled user account by double-clicking the user name in Active Directory Users And Computers.

2. On the Exchange General tab, click Delivery Options. To remove forwarding, in the Forwarding Address panel, choose None.

3. To add forwarding, choose Forward To, and then click Modify. Use the Select Recipient dialog box to choose the alternate recipient. If the mail should go to both the alternate recipient and the current mailbox owner, select the Deliver Messages To Both Forwarding Address And Mailbox check box (see Figure 6-4).

Figure 6-4. *Using the Delivery Options dialog box, you can specify alternate recipients for mailboxes and deliver mail to the current mailbox as well.*

4. Click OK.

Setting Storage Restrictions on an Individual Mailbox

You can set storage restrictions on multiple mailboxes using global settings for each mailbox store or on individual mailboxes using per-user restrictions. Global restrictions are applied when you create the user account and are reapplied when you define new global storage restrictions. Per-user storage restrictions are set individually for each user account and override the global default settings.

Note Storage restrictions apply only to mailboxes stored on the server. Storage restrictions don't apply to personal folders. Personal folders are stored on the user's computer.

You'll learn how to set global storage restrictions in Chapter 10, "Mailbox and Public Folder Store Administration," See the section of that chapter entitled "Setting Mailbox Store Limits."

You set individual storage restrictions by completing the following steps:

1. Open the Properties dialog box for the mailbox-enabled user account by double-clicking the user name in Active Directory Users And Computers.

2. On the Exchange General tab, click Storage Limits. This displays the Storage Limits dialog box shown in Figure 6-5.

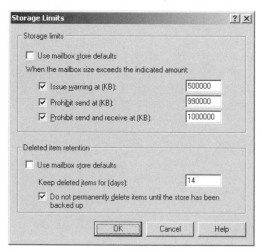

Figure 6-5. *Using the Storage Limits dialog box, you can specify storage limits and deleted item retention on a per-user basis when necessary.*

3. To set mailbox storage limits, in the Storage Limits panel, clear the Use Mailbox Store Defaults check box. Then set one or more of the following storage limits:

   • **Issue Warning At (KB)**   This limit specifies the size, in kilobytes, that a mailbox can reach before a warning is issued to the user. The warning tells the user to clean out the mailbox.

   • **Prohibit Send At (KB)**   This limit specifies the size, in kilobytes, that a mailbox can reach before the user is prohibited from sending any new mail. The restriction ends when the user clears out the mailbox and the mailbox size is under the limit.

   • **Prohibit Send And Receive At (KB)**   This limit specifies the size, in kilobytes, that a mailbox can reach before the user is prohibited from sending and receiving mail. The restriction ends when the user clears out the mailbox and the mailbox size is under the limit.

Caution Prohibiting send and receive might cause the user to lose e-mail. When a user sends a message to a user who is prohibited from receiving messages, an NDR is generated and delivered to the sender. The original recipient never sees the e-mail. Because of this, you should rarely prohibit send and receive.

4. Click OK.

Setting Deleted Item Retention Time on Individual Mailboxes

When a user deletes a message in Microsoft Office Outlook 2003, the message is placed in the Deleted Items folder. The message remains in the Deleted Items folder until the user deletes it manually or allows Outlook to clear out the Deleted Items folder. With personal folders, the message is then permanently deleted and you can't restore it. With server-based mailboxes, the message isn't actually deleted from the Exchange Information Store. Instead, the message is marked as hidden and kept for a specified period of time called the *deleted item retention period*.

Default retention settings are configured for each mailbox store in the organization. You can change these settings, as described in the section of Chapter 10, "Mailbox and Public Folder Store Administration," entitled "Setting Deleted Item Retention," or override the settings on a per-user basis by completing these steps:

1. Open the Properties dialog box for the mailbox-enabled user account by double-clicking the user name in Active Directory Users And Computers.

2. On the Exchange General tab, click Storage Limits. This displays the Storage Limits dialog box shown previously in Figure 6-5.

3. In the Deleted Item Retention panel, clear the Use Mailbox Store Defaults check box.

4. In the Keep Deleted Items For (Days) text field, enter the number of days to retain deleted items. An average retention period is 14 days. If you set the retention period to 0, messages aren't retained and can't be recovered.

5. You can also specify that deleted messages should not be permanently removed until the mailbox store has been backed up. This option ensures that the deleted items are archived into at least one backup set.

6. Click OK.

Real World Deleted item retention is very convenient because it allows the administrator the chance to salvage accidentally deleted e-mail without restoring a user's mailbox from backup. I strongly recommend that you enable this setting either in the mailbox store or for individual mailboxes, and configure the retention period accordingly.

Managing Advanced Mailbox Settings

Several key properties of mailboxes are considered to be advanced settings that should only be set as necessary. These settings include mailbox rights, Internet Locator Service (ILS) settings, and custom attributes. To view or work with these and other advanced settings, you use the Exchange Advanced tab shown in Figure 6-6.

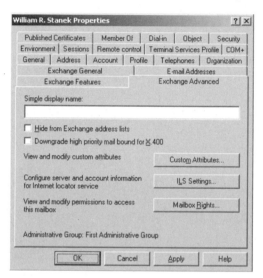

Figure 6-6. *Select View, Advanced Features to display the Exchange Advanced tab.*

 Note With Exchange 2003, the Exchange Advanced tab and its settings are available regardless of whether Advanced Features is enabled. If future security settings change this, however, you may have to select View, Advanced Features to access the Exchange Advanced tab.

Setting Alternate Mailbox Display Names for Multilanguage Environments

In some cases the full display name for a mailbox won't be available for display. This can happen when multiple language versions of the Exchange snap-in are installed on the network or when multiple language packs are installed on a system. Here, the system cannot interpret some or all of the characters in the display name, and as a result doesn't show the display name. To correct this problem, you can set an alternate display name using a different character set. For example, you could use Cyrillic or Kanji characters instead of standard ANSI characters.

You can set an alternate display name for a mailbox by following these steps:

1. Open the Properties dialog box for the mailbox-enabled user account by double-clicking the user name in Active Directory Users And Computers.

2. On the Exchange Advanced tab, type the alternate display name in the Simple Display Name field and then click OK.

Hiding Mailboxes from Address Lists

Occasionally you might want to hide a mailbox so that it doesn't appear in the global address list or other address lists. One reason for doing this is if you have administrative mailboxes that are only used for special purposes. To hide a mailbox from the address lists, follow these steps:

1. Open the Properties dialog box for the mailbox-enabled user account by double-clicking the user name in Active Directory Users And Computers.

2. On the Exchange Advanced tab, select Hide From Exchange Address Lists and then click OK.

Defining Custom Mailbox Attributes for Address Lists

Address lists, like the global address list, make it easier for users and administrators to find Exchange resources, including users, contacts, distribution groups, and public folders that are available. The fields available for Exchange resources are based on the type of resource. If you want to add additional values that should be displayed or searchable in address lists, such as an employee identification number, you can assign these values as custom attributes.

Exchange provides 15 custom attributes, labeled extensionAttribute1, extensionAttribute2, and so on, through extensionAttribute15. You can assign a value to a custom attribute by completing the following steps:

1. Open the Properties dialog box for the mailbox-enabled user account by double-clicking the user name in Active Directory Users And Computers.

2. On the Exchange Advanced tab, click Custom Attributes. This displays the Exchange Custom Attributes dialog box.

3. Double-click the attribute you want to define. This displays the Custom Attributes dialog box shown in Figure 6-7.

Figure 6-7. *You can define up to 15 custom attributes for mailboxes.*

4. Enter the attribute value in the field provided and then click OK. Define the custom attribute as a string of standard characters. If you want, you can include the name of the attribute you are defining as well as the value. However, that might make it more difficult to perform searches based on the field value.

5. Click OK twice.

Configuring ILS Settings for NetMeeting

Microsoft NetMeeting allows users to collaborate during meetings using audio, video, and a shared whiteboard. If your organization uses NetMeeting, you might want users to be able to contact each other and set up meetings through Exchange. To make this possible, you'll need to configure the ILS for user and contact mailboxes, specifying the ILS server and account that is to be used for NetMeeting.

You can specify the ILS settings by completing the following steps:

1. Open the Properties dialog box for the mailbox-enabled user account by double-clicking the user name in Active Directory Users And Computers.

2. On the Exchange Advanced tab, click ILS Settings. This displays the Exchange Internet Locator Service dialog box as shown in Figure 6-8.

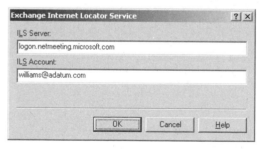

Figure 6-8. *Specify the ILS server and account to be used for NetMeeting.*

3. In the ILS Server field, enter the fully qualified domain name (FQDN) or Internet Protocol (IP) address of the ILS server to which the user or contact connects, such as logon.netmeeting.microsoft.com.

4. In the ILS Account field, enter the ILS account for the user, such as Williams@adatum.com.

5. Click OK twice.

Setting Advanced Mailbox Rights and Permissions

In Chapter 2, "Managing Microsoft Exchange Server 2003 Clients," in the sections "Accessing Multiple Exchange Server Mailboxes" and "Granting Permission to Access Folders Without Delegating Access," I discussed how you could configure access to mailboxes through Outlook. Access to mailboxes can also be configured through mailbox rights in Active Directory Users And Computers.

Mailbox rights let you assign various access rights on a per-mailbox basis. By default, the user account associated with a particular mailbox, through the special identity SELF, has full mailbox access and read permission. These access rights allow the user to access his or her mailbox, and to read, send, change, and delete mail. The Administrator user and the Administrators group are listed as the owners of mailboxes, which allows administrators to manage mailbox settings, view mailbox summary information, and delete mailboxes.

Mailbox rights that you can assign include the following:

- **Delete Mailbox Storage**   Allows a user to delete the mailbox from the information store. This mailbox right is given only to administrators by default.

- **Read Permissions**   Allows a user to read mail in the mailbox. If you assigned only this right to a user, the user could read another user's mail but not send, change, or delete messages.

- **Change Permissions**   Allows a user to delete or modify items in the mailbox.

- **Take Ownership**   Allows a user to take ownership of a mailbox. By default, the Administrator user and the Administrators group are the owners of mailboxes.

- **Full Mailbox Access**   Allows a user to access a mailbox; to create, read, and delete items in the mailbox; and to send messages from the mailbox.

To add or remove mailbox access rights, follow these steps:

1. Open the Properties dialog box for the mailbox-enabled user account by double-clicking the user name in Active Directory Users And Computers.

2. On the Exchange Advanced tab, click Mailbox Rights. This displays the Permissions For dialog box shown in Figure 6-9.

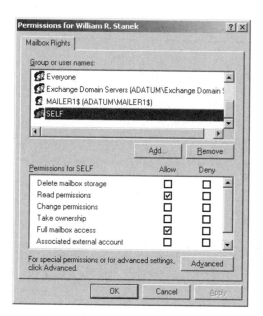

Figure 6-9. *Use the Permissions For dialog box to configure mailbox rights.*

3. Users or groups with access rights are listed in the Group Or User Names list box. You can change permissions for these users or groups by doing the following:

   • Select the user or group you want to change.

   • Use the Permissions list to grant or deny access rights.

   • Inherited permissions are dimmed. Override inherited permissions by selecting the opposite permissions.

4. To set access rights for additional users or groups, click Add. Then use Select Users, Computers, Or Groups to add users or groups. Afterward, use the Permissions area to allow or deny permissions. Repeat for other users or groups.

5. Click OK twice when you are finished.

Chapter 7

Working with Groups, Lists, and Templates

Groups, lists, and templates are extremely important in Microsoft Exchange Server 2003 administration. Careful planning of your organization's groups, address lists, and address templates can save you countless hours in the long run. Unfortunately, most administrators don't have a solid understanding of these subjects, and the few who do spend most of their time on other duties. To save yourself time and frustration, study the concepts discussed in this chapter and then use the step-by-step procedures to implement the groups, lists, and templates for your organization.

Using Security and Distribution Groups

You use groups to grant permissions to similar types of users, to simplify account administration, and to make it easier to contact multiple users. For example, you can send a message addressed to a group, and the message will go to all the users in that group. Thus, instead of having to enter 20 different e-mail addresses in the message header, you enter one e-mail address for all of the group members.

Group Types, Scope, and Identifiers

Microsoft Windows defines several different types of groups, and each of these groups can have a unique scope. In Active Directory domains, you use three group types:

- **Security**   Groups that you use to control access to network resources. You can also use user-defined security groups to distribute e-mail.
- **Standard Distribution**   Groups that have fixed membership and that you use only as e-mail distribution lists. You can't use them to control access to network resources.
- **Query-Based Distribution**   Groups for which membership is determined based on a Lightweight Directory Access Protocol (LDAP) query and that you use only as e-mail distribution lists. The LDAP query is used to build the list of members whenever messages are sent to the group.

Note Local groups are available only on local computers, and they aren't discussed here. Additionally, query-based distribution groups are only available when Exchange is running in native mode.

Security and standard distribution groups can have different scopes—*domain local, built-in local, global,* and *universal*—so that they are valid in different areas.

- You use domain local groups to grant permissions within a single domain. Members of domain local groups can include elements only from the domain in which they are defined.

- Built-in local groups are a special group scope that has domain local permissions. For the sake of simplicity, they are often referred to as domain local groups. Built-in local groups differ from other groups in that you can't create or delete them.

- You use global groups to grant permissions to elements in any domain in the domain tree or forest. Members of global groups can include elements only from the domain in which they are defined. You can't use predefined global groups.

- You use universal groups to grant permissions on a wide scale throughout a domain tree or forest. Members of global groups include elements from any domain in the domain tree or forest.

 Tip You only create security groups with universal scope when Windows is operating in native mode. Note also that the operations mode for Windows is different from the operations mode for Exchange Server 2003. Windows operations mode supports or restricts backward compatibility with pre–Windows 2000 computers. Exchange Server 2003 operations mode supports or restricts backward compatibility with pre–Exchange 2000 servers. For more detailed information on Windows operations and groups, I recommend reading Chapters 6 through 10 of *Microsoft Windows Server 2003 Administrator's Pocket Consultant* (Microsoft Press, 2003).

When you work with security and standard distribution groups, there are many things you can and can't do based on the group's scope. A summary of these items is shown in Table 7-1. Keep in mind that contacts can be members of groups as well.

Table 7-1. Understanding Group Scope

Scope	Windows Native-Mode Membership	Windows Mixed-Mode Membership	Group Membership
Domain Local Scope	Accounts, global groups, and universal groups from any domain; domain local groups from the same domain only.	Accounts and global groups from any domain.	Can be put into other domain local groups and assigned permissions only in the same domain.

Table 7-1.   Understanding Group Scope

Scope	Windows Native-Mode Membership	Windows Mixed-Mode Membership	Group Membership
Global Scope	Only accounts from the same domain and global groups from the same domain.	Only accounts from the same domain.	Can be put into other groups and assigned permissions in any domain.
Universal Scope	Accounts from any domain as well as groups from any domain, regardless of scope.	Can't be created in mixed-mode domains.	Can be put into other groups and assigned permissions in any domain.

When you work with query-based distribution groups, keep in mind that this feature is only available when Exchange is running in native mode and all Exchange servers in the enterprise are using at least Exchange 2000 with Service Pack 3. Query-based distribution groups do not have a specific local, global, or universal scope. Here, the membership could include only members of the local domain or it could include users and groups from other domains, domain trees or forests, and scope is determined by the container associated with the group when it is created.

More specifically, the associated container defines the root of the search hierarchy and the LDAP query filters to recipients in and below the specified container. For example, if the container associated with the group is adatum.com, the query filter is applied to all recipients in this domain. If the container associated with the organizational unit is Engineering, the query filter is applied to all recipients in or below this container.

As it does with user accounts, Windows uses unique security identifiers (SIDs) to track groups. This means that you can't delete a group, re-create it, and then expect all the permissions and privileges to remain the same. The new group will have a new SID, and all the permissions and privileges of the old group will be lost.

When to Use Security and Standard Distribution Groups

Exchange Server 2003 changes the rules about how you can use groups. Previously, you could use only distribution groups to distribute e-mail. Now, you can use both security and distribution groups to distribute e-mail and, as a result, you might need to rethink how and when you use groups.

Rather than duplicating your existing security group structure with distribution groups that have the same purpose, you might want to selectively mail-enable your security groups. For example, if you have a security group called Marketing, you don't need to create a MarketingDistList distribution group. Instead, you could enable Exchange mail on the original security group.

You can mail-enable built-in and predefined groups as well. Some of the groups you might want to consider mail-enabling include the following:

- Account Operators
- Backup Operators
- Domain Admins
- Domain Users
- Print Operators
- Server Operators

You might also want to mail-enable security groups that you previously defined. Then, if existing distribution groups serve the same purpose, you can delete the distribution groups.

When to Use Domain Local, Global, and Universal Groups

Domain local, global, and universal groups give you numerous options for configuring groups. Although these group scopes are designed to simplify administration, poor planning can make these group scopes your worst administration nightmare. Ideally, you'll use group scopes to help you create group hierarchies that are similar to your organization's structure and that reflect the responsibilities of particular groups of users.

The best uses for domain local, global, and universal groups are as follows:

- Groups with domain local scope have the smallest extent. Use groups with domain local scope to distribute mail to users within a specific department or office and to help you manage access to resources such as shared folders and printers. Typically, you add user accounts, global groups, and universal groups as members of domain local groups.

- Use groups with global scope to help you manage e-mail distribution, user accounts, and computer accounts in a particular domain. Then you can grant access permissions to a resource by making the group with global scope a member of the group with domain local scope.

- Groups with universal scope have the largest extent. Use groups with universal scope to consolidate groups that span domains. Normally, you do this by adding global groups as members.

 Tip If your organization doesn't have two or more domains, you don't really need to use universal groups. Instead, build your group structure with domain local and global groups. If you ever bring another domain into your domain tree or forest, you can easily extend the group hierarchy with universal groups.

When to Use Query-Based Distribution Groups

It's a fact of life that over time users will move to different departments, leave the company, or accept different responsibilities. With standard distribution groups, you'll spend a lot of time managing group membership when these types of changes occur—and that's where query-based distribution groups come into the picture. With query-based distribution groups, there isn't a fixed group membership and you don't have to add or remove users from groups. Instead, group membership is determined by the results of an LDAP query sent to your organization's global catalog (or dedicated expansion) server whenever mail is sent to the distribution group.

When the member list returned in the results is relatively small (fewer than 25 members), you'll get the most benefit from query-based distribution. If there are potentially hundreds or thousands of members, however, query-based distribution is very inefficient and could require a great deal of processing to complete. You can shift the processing requirements from the global catalog server to a dedicated expansion server (a server whose only task is to expand the LDAP queries). However, it could still take several minutes to resolve and expand large distribution lists.

One other thing to note about query-based distribution is that you can only associate one specific query with each distribution group. For example, you could create separate groups for each department in the organization. You could have groups called QD-Accounting, QD-BizDev, QD-Engineering, QD-Marketing, QD-Operations, QD-Sales, and SQ-Support. You could in turn create a standard distribution group or a query-based distribution group called AllEmployees that contains these groups as members—thereby establishing a distribution group hierarchy.

When using multiple parameters with query-based distribution, keep in mind that multiple parameters typically work as logical AND operations. For example, if you create a query with a parameter that matches all BizDev employees and a parameter that matches all Marketing employees, the query results will not contain a list of all BizDev and Marketing employees. Rather, the results will contain a list only of employees who are members of both BizDev and Marketing. In this case, you get the expected results by creating a query-based distribution group for all BizDev employees, another query-based distribution group for all Marketing employees, and a final group that has as members the other two distribution groups.

Working with Security and Standard Distribution Groups

As you set out to work with groups, you'll find that there are tasks specific to each type of group as well as tasks that can be performed with any type of group. Because of this, I've divided the group management discussion into three sections. In this section, you'll learn about the typical tasks you perform with security and standard distribution groups. The next section discusses tasks you'll perform only with query-based distribution groups. The third section discusses general management tasks.

The tool to use when you want to work with groups is Active Directory Users And Computers. Be sure to start this snap-in from the Microsoft Exchange menu.

 Note If you don't have a Microsoft Exchange menu on your computer, follow the steps discussed in Chapter 1, "Overview of Microsoft Exchange Server 2003 Administration," in the section "Exchange Server Administration Tools." This ensures you are using the Exchange Server 2003 version of System Manager and Active Directory Users And Computers.

Creating Security and Standard Distribution Groups

You use groups to manage permissions and to distribute e-mail. As you set out to create groups, remember that you create groups for similar types of users. Consequently, the types of groups you might want to create include the following:

- **Groups for departments within the organization** Generally, users who work in the same department need access to similar resources and should be a part of the same e-mail distribution lists.

- **Groups for roles within the organization** You can also organize groups according to the users' roles within the organization. For example, you could use a group called Executives to send e-mail to all the members of the executive team and a group called Managers to send e-mail to all managers and executives in the organization.

- **Groups for users of specific projects** Often, users working on a major project need a way to send e-mail to all the members of the team. To solve this problem, you can create a group specifically for the project.

You can create a security or distribution group by completing the following steps:

1. Start Active Directory Users And Computers. Right-click the container in which you want to place the group, point to New, and then select Group. This opens the New Object – Group dialog box shown in Figure 7-1.

2. Type a name for the group. Group names aren't case-sensitive and can be up to 64 characters long.

3. The first 20 characters of the group name are used to set the pre–Windows 2000 group name. This group name must be unique in the domain. If necessary, change the pre–Windows 2000 group name.

Figure 7-1. *Use the New Object – Group dialog box to create security and distribution groups.*

4. Select a group scope—either Domain Local, Global, or Universal. If you are unsure which scope to use, the recommended scope is Universal. You can't change the group scope when you're operating in Windows mixed mode. When you're operating in Windows native mode, keep the following in mind:

- You can convert a domain local group to universal scope, provided it doesn't have as its member another group having domain local scope.

- You can convert a global group to universal scope, provided it's not a member of any other group having global scope.

- You can't convert a universal group to any other group scope.

Note You can create universal security groups only when the Windows operations mode is set to native. The Windows operations mode is different from the Exchange Server 2003 operations mode.

5. Select a group type—either Security or Distribution.

6. Click Next. If you've properly installed the Exchange extensions on the computer that you're running, you'll be able to choose whether the group should have an e-mail address. If the group shouldn't have an e-mail address, clear the Create An Exchange E-Mail Address check box, and then skip Step 7. Otherwise, ensure Create An Exchange E-Mail Address is selected.

7. Like users, groups have an Exchange alias. The Exchange alias is set to the group name by default. You can change this value by entering a new alias. The Exchange alias is used to set the group's e-mail address.

8. Mail for the group is routed through the specified administrative group. As necessary, use the Associated Administrative Group selection list to change the default setting.

9. Click Next, and then click Finish to create the group. If you created an Exchange e-mail address for the group, e-mail addresses are configured automatically for Simple Mail Transfer Protocol (SMTP), X.400, and other Exchange connectors you've configured. Exchange Server uses the SMTP address for receiving messages.

10. Creating the group isn't the final step. Afterward, you might want to do the following:

   - Add members to the group.
   - Make the group a member of other groups.
   - Assign a manager as a point of contact for the group.
   - Set message size restrictions for messages mailed to the group.
   - Limit users who can send to the group.
   - Change or remove default e-mail addresses.
   - Add additional e-mail addresses.

Assigning and Removing Membership for Individual Users, Groups, and Contacts

All users, groups, and contacts can be members of other groups. You control the membership of these elements at the object level or at the group level. To manage membership at the object level, complete the following steps:

1. In Active Directory Users And Computers, double-click the user, contact, or group entry. This opens a Properties dialog box.

2. Click the Member Of tab. To make the object a member of a group, click Add. This opens the Select Groups dialog box. You can now choose groups that the currently selected object should be a member of.

3. To remove the object from a group, select a group, and then click Remove.

4. When you're finished, click OK.

Adding and Removing Group Members

Another way to manage group membership is to use the group's Properties dialog box to add or remove multiple objects. To do this, follow these steps:

1. In Active Directory Users And Computers, double-click the group entry. This opens the object's Properties dialog box.

2. Click the Members tab. To add objects to the group, click Add. This opens the Select Users, Contacts, Computers, Or Groups dialog box. You can now choose objects that should be members of this currently selected group.

3. To remove members from a group, select an object, and then click Remove.

4. When you're finished, click OK.

Enabling and Disabling a Group's Exchange Server Mail

You use mail-enabled groups to distribute e-mail to multiple users, contacts, and even to other groups. They have an Exchange alias and one or more e-mail addresses associated with them. You can mail-enable a group by completing the following steps:

1. In Active Directory Users And Computers, right-click the group name, and then select Exchange Tasks to start the Exchange Task Wizard.

2. If a Welcome wizard page is displayed, click Next. You can skip the Welcome page in the future by selecting Do Not Show This Welcome Page Again.

3. Under Available Tasks, select Establish An E-Mail Address, and then click Next.

4. Type an Exchange alias for the group, and then click Finish.

5. New e-mail addresses are generated and set as the default addresses for SMTP, X.400, and other Exchange mail connectors you've configured.

Later, if you want to delete the Exchange alias and remove any e-mail addresses that might be associated with the group, follow these steps:

1. In Active Directory Users And Computers, right-click the group name, and then select Exchange Tasks to start the Exchange Task Wizard.

2. If a Welcome wizard page is displayed, click Next.

3. Under Available Tasks, select Delete E-Mail Addresses, and then click Next.

4. Click Finish. All e-mail addresses associated with the group are deleted.

Working with Query-Based Distribution Groups

Just as there are tasks only for security and standard distribution groups, there are also tasks only for query-based distribution groups. These tasks are discussed in this section. As before, the tool to use when you want to work with groups is Active Directory Users And Computers. Be sure to start this snap-in from the Microsoft Exchange menu.

Creating Query-Based Distribution Groups

With query-based distribution groups, group membership is determined by the results of an LDAP query. As long as Exchange is running in native mode, you can create a query-based distribution group and define the query parameters, by completing the following steps:

1. Start Active Directory Users And Computers. Right-click the container in which you want to place the group, point to New, and then select Query-Based

Distribution Group. This opens the New Object – Query-Based Distribution Group dialog box shown in Figure 7-2.

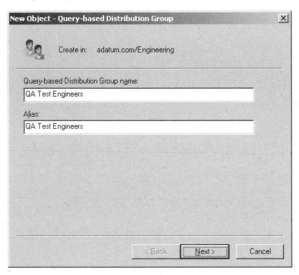

Figure 7-2. *Use the New Object – Query-Based Distribution Group dialog box to create query-based distribution groups.*

2. Type a name for the group. Group names aren't case-sensitive and can be up to 64 characters long.

3. Like users, groups have an Exchange alias. The Exchange alias is set to the group name by default. You can change this value by entering a new alias. The Exchange alias is used to set the group's e-mail address.

4. The container in which you create the group defines the scope of the query. This means the LDAP query you define for the group filters to recipients in and below the specified container. The default container, displayed in the Apply Filter To list box, is the one you right-clicked to create the group. To specify a different container for limiting the query scope, click Change and then use the Choose A Container dialog box to select a container. In most cases, you'll want to select the domain container.

5. Click Customize Filter and then click Customize. This displays the Find Exchange Recipients dialog box shown in Figure 7-3.

6. Select Entire Directory in the In drop-down list and then click Browse. Use the Browse For Container dialog box to choose the container you want to work with.

7. On the General tab, select the specific types of recipients you want to search for. For example, if you want to search only for users with mailboxes, select Users With Exchange Mailbox and clear the other check boxes.

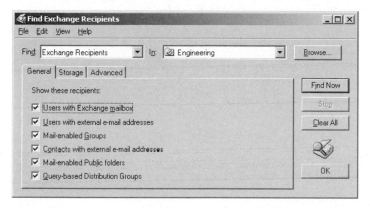

Figure 7-3. *Use the Find Exchange Recipients dialog box to customize the LDAP query parameters.*

8. If you want to limit the search to a specific Exchange server or mailbox store, click the Storage tab. Select Mailboxes On This Server or Mailboxes In This Mailbox Store as appropriate and then type the server or mailbox store name in the field provided. Click Browse to search for the resource you want to use.

9. On the Advanced tab, click Field, point to the type of object you want to work with, such as User, and then select a filter parameter. Next, use the Condition list to specify a match condition, such as Is (Exactly). After you enter an associated condition value, click Add to add the filter parameter to the Condition List. Repeat this step to define other filter parameters.

10. Click OK to close the Find Exchange Recipients dialog box. Afterward, click Next and then click Finish to create the group. E-mail addresses are configured automatically for SMTP, X.400, and other Exchange connectors you've configured. Exchange Server uses the SMTP address for receiving messages.

11. Creating the group isn't the final step. Afterward, you might want to do the following:

   • Preview the group to confirm its membership and determine how long it takes to return the query results.

   • Assign a manager as a point of contact for the group.

   • Set message size restrictions for messages mailed to the group.

   • Limit users who can send to the group.

   • Change or remove default e-mail addresses.

   • Add additional e-mail addresses.

Previewing Query-Based Distribution Group Membership

You can preview a query-based distribution group to confirm its membership and determine how long it takes to return the query results.

- In some cases, you might find that the membership isn't what you expected. If this happens, you'll need to change the query filters as discussed in the next section.

- In other cases, you might find that it takes too long to execute the query and return the results. If this happens, you might want to rethink the query parameters. You might want to create several query groups.

To preview query-based distribution group membership, follow these steps:

1. Start Active Directory Users And Computers. Double-click the group you want to work with and then click the Preview tab.

2. As shown in Figure 7-4, the Preview pane shows the group members and the LDAP Filter pane shows the LDAP query.

3. Click Start to determine how long it takes to execute the query and return results.

4. Click OK to close the Properties dialog box.

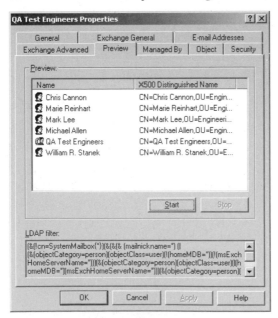

Figure 7-4. *Preview the group to confirm its membership is as expected and determine how long it takes to run the query.*

Changing Query Filters

You can change the LDAP query used with a query-based distribution group by completing the following steps:

1. Start Active Directory Users And Computers. Double-click the group you want to work with to display its Properties dialog box.

2. On the General tab, the Filter pane is used to set the query parameters. If you created a custom filter, you can click Customize to display the Find Exchange Recipients dialog box and then use the options of the General, Storage, and Advanced tabs to change the existing query parameters or define new ones.

3. Click OK twice when you are finished and then preview the group membership to confirm that the changes produce the expected results.

Other Essential Tasks for Managing Groups

Previous sections covered tasks that were specific to a type of group. As an Exchange administrator, you'll find that there are many additional group management tasks that you'll need to perform. These essential tasks are discussed in this section.

Changing a Group's Exchange Server Alias

Each mail-enabled group has an Exchange alias and one or more e-mail addresses associated with it. Whenever you change a group's naming information, new e-mail addresses can be generated and set as the default addresses for SMTP, X.400, and other Exchange mail connectors you've configured. These e-mail addresses are used as alternatives to e-mail addresses previously assigned to the group. To learn how to change or delete these additional e-mail addresses, see the section of this chapter entitled "Changing, Adding or Deleting a Group's E-Mail Addresses."

To change the group's Exchange alias, complete the following steps:

1. In Active Directory Users And Computers, double-click the group name. This opens the group's Properties dialog box.

2. Click the Exchange General tab, and then in the Alias field, type a new Exchange alias.

3. Click OK.

Changing, Adding, or Deleting a Group's E-Mail Addresses

When you create a mail-enabled group, default e-mail addresses are created for SMTP, X.400, and other Exchange connectors you've configured. Any time you update the group's Exchange alias, new default e-mail addresses can be created. The old addresses aren't deleted, however; they remain as alternative e-mail addresses for the group.

To change, add or delete a group's e-mail addresses, follow these steps:

1. Open the Properties dialog box for the group by double-clicking the group name in Active Directory Users And Computers. Then click the E-Mail Addresses tab.

2. To create a new e-mail address, click New. In the New E-Mail Address dialog box, select the type of e-mail address, and then click OK. Complete the Properties dialog box, and then click OK again.

3. To change an existing e-mail address, double-click the address entry, and then modify the settings in the Properties dialog box. Click OK.

4. To delete an e-mail address, select it, and then click Remove. To confirm the deletion, click Yes when prompted.

 Note Exchange Server uses the SMTP address to send and receive messages. You can't delete the default SMTP address, but you can rename it.

Hiding Groups from Exchange Address Lists

By default, any mail-enabled security group or other distribution group that you create is shown in Exchange address lists such as the global address list. If you want to hide a group from the address lists, follow these steps:

1. Start Active Directory Users And Computers.

2. Double-click the group you want to work with to display its Properties dialog box.

3. On the Exchange Advanced tab, select Hide Group From Exchange Address Lists.

4. Click OK.

 Note When you hide a group it isn't listed in Exchange address lists. If a user knows the name of a group, he or she can still use it in the mail client. To prevent users from sending to a group, you must set message restrictions as discussed in the section of this chapter entitled "Setting Usage Restrictions on Groups."

Hiding and Displaying Group Membership

Hiding group membership is different than hiding the group itself. By default, users can view the membership of two types of groups: security groups that are mail-enabled and standard distribution groups. You can prevent viewing the group membership if necessary. To do so, follow these steps:

1. In Active Directory Users And Computers, right-click the group name, and then select Exchange Tasks to start the Exchange Task Wizard.

2. If a Welcome wizard page is displayed, click Next.

3. Under Available Tasks, select Hide Membership and then click Next.

4. Click Next again and then click Finish.

5. If you later decide that you want users to be able to view group membership, repeat this process but this time select Unhide Membership.

Note Membership of query-based distribution groups is not displayed in global address lists because it is generated only when mail is sent to the group. Users will be able to view the membership of other types of groups, however, unless a group's permissions are specifically configured otherwise.

Setting Usage Restrictions on Groups

Groups are great resources for users in an organization. They let users send mail quickly and easily to other users in their department, business unit, or office. However, if you aren't careful, people outside the organization can use groups as well. Would your boss like it if spammers sent unsolicited e-mail messages to company employees through your distribution lists? Probably not—and you'd probably be sitting in the hot seat, which would be uncomfortable, to say the least.

To prevent unauthorized use of mail-enabled groups, you can specify that only certain users or members of a particular group can send messages to the group. For example, if you created a group called AllEmployees, of which all company employees were members, you could specify that only the members of AllEmployees could send messages to the group. You do this by specifying that only messages from AllEmployees are acceptable.

To prevent mass spamming of other groups, you could set the same restriction. For example, if you have a group called Technology, you could specify that only members of AllEmployees can send messages to that group.

Real World If you have users who telecommute or send e-mail from home using a personal account, you might be wondering how these users can send mail once a restriction is in place. What I've done in the past is create a group called OffsiteEmailUsers, and then added this as a group that can send mail to my mail-enabled groups. The OffsiteEmailUsers group contains separate mail-enabled contacts for each authorized off-site e-mail address.

Another way to prevent unauthorized use of mail-enabled groups is to specify that only mail from authenticated users is accepted. An authenticated user is any user accessing the system through a logon process. It does not include anonymous users or guests and is not used to assign permissions. If you use this option, keep in mind that off-site users will need to log on to Exchange before they can send mail to restricted groups, and this might present a problem for users who are at home or on the road.

You can set or remove usage restrictions by completing the following steps:

1. Open the Properties dialog box for the mailbox-enabled group by double-clicking the group name in Active Directory Users And Computers.

2. Click the Exchange General tab. As shown in Figure 7-5, you can now set the following restrictions:

   - **No Limit** Specifies that messages of any size can be sent to the group.

   - **Maximum (KB)** Sets a limit on the size of messages that can be sent to the group. If a message exceeds the limit, the message isn't sent and the sender receives a nondelivery report (NDR).

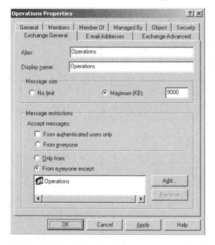

Figure 7-5. *Use the Properties dialog box to set message usage restrictions.*

   - **From Authenticated Users Only** Specifies that messages are accepted from only authenticated users.

   - **From Everyone** The default setting that specifies that messages are accepted from anyone, including Internet addresses external to the organization.

   - **Only From** Specifies that only messages from the listed users, contacts, or groups should be accepted. Click Add to add additional users, contacts, and groups to the list. Click Remove to remove users, contacts, and groups from the list.

- **From Everyone Except** Specifies that all e-mail addresses except those from the listed users, contacts, or groups should be accepted. Click Add to add additional users, contacts, and groups to the list. Click Remove to remove users, contacts, and groups from the list.

3. When you're finished setting or removing restrictions, click OK.

Note Setting usage restrictions on mail-enabled groups is a good idea in most circumstances.

Setting Out-of-Office and Delivery Report Options for Groups

By default, distribution groups are configured so that delivery reports are sent to the person who sent the mail message. You can change this so that delivery reports are sent to the group owner or not sent at all. You can also specify out-of-office messages that are returned in response to messages from the sender. To set these options, complete the following steps:

1. Start Active Directory Users And Computers, and then select Advanced Features from the View menu.

2. Double-click the group you want to work with and then in the properties dialog box, select the Exchange Advanced tab.

3. If you want out-of-office messages to be delivered to the sender, select Send Out-Of-Office Messages To Originator.

4. If you want to stop sending delivery reports, select Do Not Send Delivery Reports. You also have the option of sending delivery reports to the group owner and the message originator. Click OK.

Renaming Groups

In Active Directory Users And Computers, you can rename a group by completing the following steps:

1. Right-click the group name, and then choose Rename. Type the new group name, and then press Enter.

2. You'll see the Rename Group dialog box with the new group name highlighted. Press Tab and type a new pre–Windows 2000 group name.

3. Click OK.

When you rename a group, you give the group a new label. Changing the name doesn't affect the SID, which is used to identify, track, and handle permissions independently from group names. It also doesn't affect the exchange alias or the e-mail addresses that may be associated with the group.

Deleting Groups

Deleting a group removes it permanently. Once you delete a group, you can't create a group with the same name and automatically restore the permissions that the original group was assigned because the SID for the new group won't match the SID for the old group. You can reuse group names, but remember that you'll have to re-create all permissions settings.

Windows doesn't let you delete built-in groups. You could remove other types of groups by selecting them and pressing the Del key, or by right-clicking and selecting Delete. When prompted, click Yes to delete the group. If you click No, Windows will not delete the group.

Managing Online Address Lists

Address lists help administrators organize and manage Exchange recipients. You can use address lists to organize recipients by department, business unit, location, type, and other criteria. The default address lists that Exchange Server creates and any new address lists that you create are available to the user community. Users can navigate these address lists to find recipients to whom they want to send messages.

Using Default Address Lists

During setup, Exchange Server creates a number of default address lists, including the following:

- **Default Global Address List**   Lists all mail-enabled users, contacts, and groups in the organization.
- **Default Offline Address List**   Provides an address list for viewing offline that contains information on all mail-enabled users, contacts, and groups in the organization.
- **All Contacts**   Lists all mail-enabled contacts in the organization.
- **All Users**   Lists all mail-enabled users in the organization.
- **All Groups**   Lists all mail-enabled groups in the organization.
- **Public Folders**   Lists all public folders in the organization.

The most commonly used address lists are the global address list and the offline address list.

Creating New Address Lists

You can create new address lists to accommodate your organization's special needs. For example, if your organization has offices in Seattle, Portland, and San Francisco, you might want to create separate address lists for each office.

To create an address list that users can select in their Microsoft Office Outlook 2003 mail client, follow these steps:

1. Start System Manager, and then in the left pane (console tree), click the plus sign (+) next to the Recipients node. Next, right-click the All Address Lists node.

2. On the shortcut menu, point to New, and then select Address List.

3. Type a name for the address list. The name should describe the types of recipients that are viewed through the list. For example, if you're creating a list for recipients in the Boston office, you could call the list Boston E-Mail Addresses.

4. Click Filter Rules to select membership criteria. On the General tab, select the check boxes for the users, groups, and contacts that should appear in the address list. If you want to show only users with mailboxes, select Users With Exchange Mailbox.

5. As shown in Figure 7-6, you use the options on the Advanced tab to limit the address list to users, groups, and contacts that meet the criteria you set. Advanced options let you set very specific criteria for list members. For example, if you wanted to limit the address list to users in Boston, you would click Field, point to User, and then select City. Next, you would select Condition Is (Exactly), and type the value **Boston**. To complete the process, click Add.

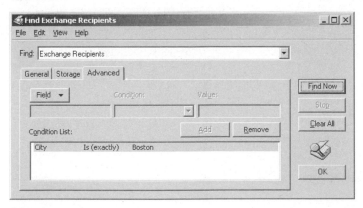

Figure 7-6. *Use the Advanced tab to limit the address list membership based on criteria you set.*

6. To edit an entry after you create it, double-click it, set new values, and then click Add.

7. Once you've set all the filters for the list, click OK. Users will be able to use the new address list the next time they start Outlook.

Configuring Clients to Use Address Lists

Address books are available to clients who are configured for corporate or workgroup use. To set the address lists used by the client, complete these steps:

1. In Outlook 2003, select Address Book from the Tools menu.
2. In the Address Book dialog box, select Options from the Tools menu, and then set the following options to configure how address lists are used:

   - **Show This Address List First** Sets the address book that the user sees first whenever he or she works with the Address Book.
   - **Keep Personal Addresses In** Specifies the default address book for storing new addresses.
   - **When Sending Mail, Check Names Using These Address Lists In The Following Order** Sets the order in which address books are searched when you send a message or click Check Names. Use the up and down arrows to change the list order.

3. Click OK.

 Tip When checking names, you'll usually want the Global Address List (GAL) to be listed before the user's own contacts or other types of address lists. This is important because users will often put internal mailboxes in their personal address lists. The danger of doing this without first resolving names against the GAL is that although the display name might be identical, the *properties* of a mailbox might change. When changes occur, the entry in the user's address book is no longer valid and any mail sent will bounce back to the sender with an NDR. To correct this, the user should either remove that mailbox from his or her personal address list and add it based on the current entry in the GAL, or change the check names resolution order to use the GAL before any personal lists.

Updating Address List Configuration and Membership Throughout the Domain

Exchange Server doesn't replicate changes to address lists throughout the domain immediately. Instead, the changes are replicated during the normal replication cycle, which means that some servers might temporarily have outdated address list information. Rather than waiting for replication, you can manually update address list configuration, availability, and membership throughout the domain. To do this, follow these steps:

1. Start System Manager, and then in the left pane (the console tree), click the plus sign (+) next to the Recipients node. Then select Recipient Update Services.
2. Current Recipient Update services should now be displayed in the right pane. Typically, you'll have an enterprise configuration and one or more additional configurations for additional domains in the domain forest.

3. To update the address list configuration information in the entire domain forest, right-click Recipient Update Service (Enterprise Configuration), and then select Update Now.

4. To update the address list availability and membership for a specific domain, right-click the related service, and then select Update Now. For example, if you wanted to update address lists in the Technology domain, you'd right-click Recipient Update Service (Technology), and then select Update Now.

Rebuilding Address List Membership and Configuration

In a large enterprise, address list membership and configuration can get out of sync when you make lots of changes. To resynchronize the address list, follow these steps:

1. Start System Manager, and then in the left pane (the console tree), click the plus sign (+) next to the Recipients node. Then select Recipient Update Services.

2. Current Recipient Update services should now be displayed in the right pane. Typically, you'll have an enterprise configuration and one or more additional configurations for additional domains in the domain forest.

3. Because you want to rebuild address list membership and configuration for a specific domain, right-click the related domain service, and then select Rebuild. When prompted to confirm the action, click Yes.

4. Rebuilding address lists can take a long time. Be patient. Users will use the updates the next time they start Outlook.

Editing Address Lists

Although you can't change the properties of default address lists, you can change the properties of address lists that you create. To do this, complete the following steps:

1. Start System Manager, and then in the left pane (the console tree), click the plus sign (+) next to the Recipients node. Next, click the plus sign (+) next to the All Address Lists node.

2. Right-click the user-defined address list that you want to modify, and then choose Properties.

3. In the Properties dialog box click Modify. You can now set a new filter for the address list.

4. Select the Users, Groups, and Contacts check boxes as appropriate to specify the types of recipients that should appear in the address list. If you want to show only users with mailboxes, select Users With Exchange Mailbox.

5. Use the options on the Advanced tab to limit the address list to users, groups, and contacts that meet the criteria you set.

6. To edit an entry after you create it, double-click it, set new values, and then click Add.

7. Once you've set all the filters for the list, click OK. Users can use the modified address list the next time they start Outlook.

Renaming and Deleting Address Lists

Although System Manager will let you rename and delete default address lists, you really shouldn't do this. Instead, you should rename or delete only user-defined address lists.

- **Renaming address lists**   To rename an address list, in System Manager, right-click its entry, and then select Rename. Type in a new name and then press Enter.

- **Deleting address lists**   To delete an address list, in System Manager, right-click its entry, and then select Delete. When prompted to confirm the action, click Yes.

Managing Offline Address Lists

You configure offline address lists differently than online address lists. To use an offline address list, the client must be configured to have a local copy of the server mailbox, or use personal folders. Controlling how e-mail is delivered was discussed in Chapter 2, "Managing Microsoft Exchange Server 2003 Clients," in the section entitled "Managing Delivery and Processing of E-Mail Messages."

Configuring Clients to Use an Offline Address List

Offline address lists are available only when users are working offline. You can configure how clients use offline address lists by completing the following steps:

1. Start Outlook 2003. Click Tools, Send/Receive and then select Download Address Book. This displays the Offline Address Book dialog box.

2. Select Download Changes Since Last Send/Receive to download only items that have changed since the last time you synchronized the address list. Clear this check box to download the entire contents of your address book.

3. Specify the information to Download as:

   - **Full Details**   Select this option to download the address book with all address information details. Full details are necessary if the user needs to encrypt messages when using remote mail.

   - **No Details**   Select this option to download the address book without address information details. This reduces the download time for the address book.

4. If multiple address books are available, use the Choose Address Book drop-down list to specify which address book to download.

5. Click OK.

Assigning a Time to Rebuild an Offline Address List

By default, offline address lists are rebuilt daily at 10:00 P.M. You can change the time when the rebuild occurs by completing these steps:

1. Start System Manager, and then in the left pane (the console tree), click the plus sign (+) next to the Recipients node. Next, select the Offline Address Lists node.

2. Right-click the address list you want to work with, and then select Properties.

3. Use the Update Interval drop-down list to set the rebuild time. The available options are as follows:

   - Run Daily At 2:00 A.M.
   - Run Daily At 3:00 A.M.
   - Run Daily At 4:00 A.M.
   - Run Daily At 5:00 A.M.
   - Never Run
   - Use Custom Schedule

Tip If you select Use Custom Schedule, click Customize to define your own rebuild schedule.

4. Select Exchange 4.0 and 5.0 compatibility if you wish to share this address list with users on previous versions of Exchange Server.

5. Click OK.

Rebuilding Offline Address Lists Manually

Normally, offline address lists are rebuilt at a specified time each day, such as 11:00 P.M. You can also rebuild offline address books manually. To do this, complete the following steps:

1. Start System Manager, and then in the left pane (the console tree), click the plus sign (+) next to the Recipients node. Next, select the Offline Address Lists node.

2. Right-click the address list you want to work with, and then select Rebuild. When prompted to confirm the action, click Yes.

3. Rebuilding address lists can take a long time. Be patient. Users will see the updates the next time they start Outlook.

Setting the Default Offline Address List

Although you can create many offline address lists, clients download only one. This address list is called the *default offline address list*, and you can set it by completing these steps:

1. Start System Manager, and then in the left pane (the console tree), click the plus sign (+) next to the Recipients node. Next, select the Offline Address Lists node.

2. In the right pane, you should see a list of the offline address lists that are currently available. The current default list has the prefix Default in its name.

3. If there are multiple offline address lists available, you can assign a new default by right-clicking an address list and then selecting Set As New Default.

4. Users will use the new default offline address list the next time they start Outlook.

Changing Offline Address List Properties

The offline address list is based on other address lists that you've created in the organization. You can modify the lists that are used to create the offline address list by completing the following steps:

1. Start System Manager, and then in the left pane (the console tree), click the plus sign (+) next to the Recipients node. Next, select the Offline Address Lists node.

2. Right-click the offline address list that you want to modify, and then choose Properties.

3. To make additional address lists a part of the master offline address list, click Add, and then select the lists you want to use.

4. If you no longer want an address list to be a part of the offline address list, select the address list, and then click Remove.

5. Click OK.

Changing the Offline Address List Server

In a large organization in which lots of users are configured to use offline folders, managing and maintaining offline address lists can put a heavy burden on Exchange Server. To balance the load, you might want to designate a server other than the primary Exchange server to manage and propagate offline address lists.

You can change the offline address list server by completing these steps:

1. Start System Manager, and then in the left pane (the console tree), click the plus sign (+) next to the Recipients node. Next, select the Offline Address Lists node.

2. Right-click the offline address list that you want to modify, and then choose Properties.

3. The current offline address book server is listed in the Offline Address List Server field. To use a different server, click Browse, and then in the Select Exchange Server dialog box, choose a different server.

Customizing Address Templates

Have users ever asked you if you could change the fields in the Address Book for users, groups, or contacts? Chances are they have, and you probably said you couldn't. Well, you *can* customize the graphical interface for address book recipients, and the way you do it is to modify Exchange Server's address templates.

Using Address Templates

Address templates specify how recipient information appears in the Address Book. This graphical interface is unique for each type of recipient, including users, contacts, groups, and public folders. There are also templates for the address book Search dialog box and the mailbox agent.

Each template has a predefined set of controls that describe its interface. These controls are as follows:

- **Label**   Creates a text label in the template
- **Edit**   Creates single-line text fields or multiline text boxes
- **Page Break**   Specifies where a tab begins and where to set the text for the tab
- **Group Box**   Creates a panel that groups together a set of controls
- **Check Box**   Adds a check box with a text label
- **List Box**   Adds a list box with optional scroll bars
- **Multi-Valued List Box**   Adds a list box that can accept and display multiple values
- **Multi-Valued Drop-Down**   Adds a drop-down list with multiple values

Each control has a specific horizontal (X) position and a specific vertical (Y) position in a dialog box. The control also has a specific width and height. The X, Y, width, and height values are set in screen pixels.

By modifying the controls within a template, you can change the way information is presented in the Address Book view. To learn how you can modify templates, see Figures 7-7 and 7-8. Figure 7-7 shows the default Address Book view for users. Figure 7-8 shows a modified Address Book view for users that is streamlined and simplified.

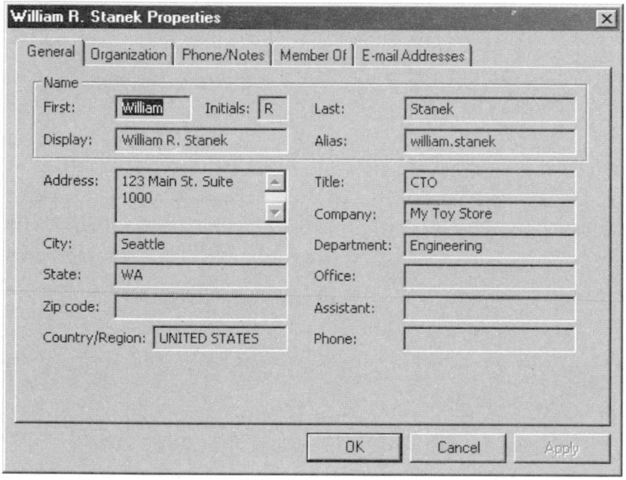

Figure 7-7. *The original Address Book view for users.*

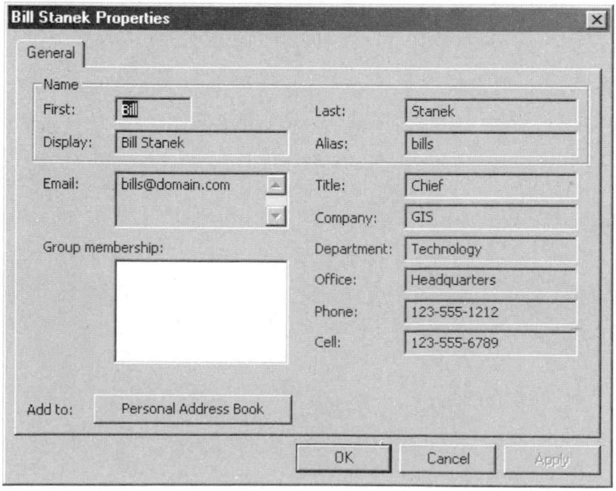

Figure 7-8. *A modified Address Book that combines fields from multiple tabs to create a view with a single tab.*

Modifying Address Book Templates

Modifying address book templates creates a custom view of the template that is available to all users in the organization. As you create the view, you'll have the opportunity to preview it so that you can check for mistakes. If you make a mistake, don't worry. You can restore the original template at any time.

Modify address book templates by completing these steps:

1. Start System Manager, and then in the left pane (the console tree), click the plus sign (+) next to the Recipients node. Next, click the plus sign (+) next to the Address Templates node, and then select the template language you want to work with. For example, if you want to modify English language templates, select English.

2. You should see the available templates in the right pane. Double-click the template you want to modify.

3. Click the Templates tab. System Manager will read all the values defined in the template and the Active Directory attributes that are available for the related object. When System Manager is finished reading attributes, you'll see the complete set of controls available for the template (see Figure 7-9).

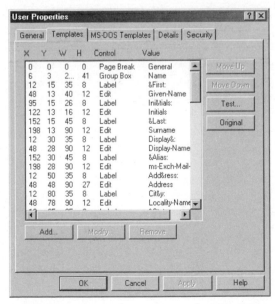

Figure 7-9. *The Templates tab lists all the controls that are assigned to the template.*

4. Click Test to preview the existing template. Study the template's configuration before you continue.

5. To add a new control to the template, click Add, and then choose a control type. Next, set the properties for the control, and then click OK. Click Test to check the modified view.

 Tip Use Page Break controls to add new tabs. The value for a particular Page Break control sets the name of the tab. Each control following the Page Break and preceding the next Page Break is on that tab.

6. To update the settings of an existing control, select the control on the Templates tab, and then click Modify. After you modify the control's properties, click OK. Click Test to check the modified view.

7. To remove a control from the address book view, select the control in the Templates tab, and then click Remove.

8. Repeat Steps 5 through 7 until the template is customized to your liking. If necessary, use the Move Up and Move Down buttons to modify the position of controls in the scrolling list. If you need to restore the original view, click Original and then confirm the action when prompted.

9. When you're finished, close the Properties dialog box by clicking OK. Then rebuild the address lists as discussed in the section of this chapter entitled "Rebuilding Address List Membership and Configuration."

Restoring the Original Address Book Templates

When you modify address book templates, the original template files aren't overwritten and you can restore the original templates if you need to. Simply complete the following steps:

1. Start System Manager, and then in the left pane (the console tree), click the plus sign (+) next to the Recipients node. Next, click the plus sign (+) next to the Address Templates node, and then select the template language you want to work with.

2. You should see the available templates in the right pane. Double-click the template you want to restore.

3. Click the Templates tab. System Manager will go out and read all the values defined in the template and the Active Directory attributes that are available for the related object.

4. Restore the original view by clicking Original. When prompted, confirm the action by clicking Yes.

5. Close the Properties dialog box by clicking OK.

6. Repeat Steps 2 through 5 for other templates that you need to restore. Then rebuild the address lists in the manner described in the section of this chapter entitled "Rebuilding Address List Membership and Configuration."

Chapter 8

Implementing Directory Security and Microsoft Exchange Server 2003 Policies

In this chapter, you'll learn how to implement directory security and Microsoft Exchange Server 2003 policies. In Active Directory, you manage security by using permissions. Users, contacts, and groups all have permissions assigned to them. These permissions control the resources that users, contacts, and groups can access. They also control the actions that users, contacts, and groups can perform.

Exchange policies are useful administration tools as well. With policies, you can specify management rules for Exchange systems and Exchange recipients. *System policies* help you manage servers and information stores. *Recipient policies* help you manage e-mail addressing and mailbox messages.

Controlling Exchange Server Administration and Usage

Users, contacts, and groups are represented in Active Directory as objects. These objects have many attributes that determine how the objects are used. The most important attributes are the permissions assigned to the object. Permissions grant or deny access to objects and resources. For example, you can grant a user the right to create public folders but deny that same user the right to view the status of the information store.

Permissions assigned to an object can be applied directly to the object or they can be inherited from another object. Generally, objects inherit permissions from *parent objects*. A parent object is an object that is above an object in the object hierarchy. In Exchange Server 2003, permissions are inherited through the organizational hierarchy. The root of the hierarchy is the *Organization node*. All other nodes in the tree inherit the Exchange permissions of this node. For example, the permissions on an administrative group folder are inherited from the Organization node.

You can override inheritance. One way to do this is to assign permissions directly to the object. Another way is to specify that the object shouldn't inherit permissions.

Assigning Exchange Server Permissions to Users and Groups

Several security groups have access to and can work with Exchange Server. These groups are Domain Admins, Enterprise Admins, Exchange Domain Servers, Exchange Enterprise Servers, and Everyone.

Domain Admins

Domain Admins are the designated administrators of a domain. Members of this global group can manage user accounts, contacts, groups, mailboxes, and computers. They can also manage messaging features, delivery restrictions, and storage limits. Nevertheless, they are subject to some restrictions in Exchange Server, and they don't have full control over Exchange Server. If a user needs to be an administrator of a local domain and manage Exchange Server, all you need to do is make that user a member of the Domain Admins group. By default, this group is a member of the Administrators group on the Exchange server and its only member is the local user, Administrator.

Enterprise Admins

Enterprise Admins are the designated administrators of the enterprise. Members of this global group can manage objects in any domain in the domain tree or forest. They have full control over Exchange Server and aren't subject to any restrictions. This means that unlike Domain Admins, Enterprise Admins can delete child objects and entire trees in Exchange Server. If a user needs full access to the enterprise and to Exchange Server, make that user a member of the Enterprise Admins group. By default, this group is a member of the Administrators group and its only member is the local user, Administrator.

Exchange Domain Servers

The Exchange Domain Servers group also has a special purpose. Members of this group can manage mail interchange and queues. By default, all computers running Exchange Server 2003 are members of this group, and you shouldn't change this setup. This domain global group is in turn a member of the domain local group Exchange Enterprise Servers.

Exchange Enterprise Servers

Exchange Enterprise Servers is a domain local group that you can use to grant special permissions to all Exchange servers throughout the domain forest. By default, the group has Exchange Domain Servers as its only member.

Everyone

The final group that has Exchange permissions is Everyone. Everyone is a special group whose members are implicitly assigned. Its members include all interactive, network, dial-up, and authenticated users. By default, members of this group can create top-level public folders, subfolders within public folders, and named properties in the information store.

Understanding Exchange Server Permissions

Active Directory objects are assigned a set of permissions. These permissions are standard Microsoft Windows permissions, object-specific permissions, and extended permissions.

Table 8-1 summarizes the most common object permissions. Keep in mind that some permissions are generalized. For example, with Read *Property* and Write *Property*, *Property* is a placeholder for the actual property name.

Table 8-1.   Common Permissions for Active Directory Objects

Permission	Description
Full Control	Permits reading, writing, modifying, and deleting
List Object	Permits listing the object
List Contents	Permits viewing object contents
Read *Property*	Permits reading a particular property of an object
Write *Property*	Permits writing to a particular property of an object
Read Properties	Permits reading properties of an object
Write Properties	Permits writing to properties of an object
Read Permissions	Permits reading object permissions
Change Permissions	Permits changing object permissions
Create Children	Permits creating child objects
Delete Children	Permits deleting child objects
Delete Tree	Permits deleting the object and its child objects
Take Ownership	Permits taking ownership of the object
Validate Write To ...	Permits a particular type of validated write
Extended Write To ...	Permits a particular type of extended write
All Validated Writes	Permits all types of validated writes
All Extended Writes	Permits all extended writes
Create Object	Permits creating a specific object type
Delete Object	Permits deleting a specific object type
Create All Child Objects	Permits creating all child objects
Delete All Child Objects	Permits deleting all child objects
Change Password	Permits changing passwords for the object
Delete	Permits deleting an object

(continued)

Table 8-1. **Common Permissions for Active Directory Objects** *(continued)*

Permission	Description
Receive As	Permits receiving as the object
Reset Password	Permits resetting passwords for the object
Send As	Permits sending as the object
Add/Remove Self	Permits adding and removing object as a member

Table 8-2 summarizes Exchange-specific permissions. You use these extended permissions to control Exchange administration and use. If you want to learn more about other types of permissions, I recommend that you read Chapter 14 of *Microsoft Windows Server 2003 Administrator's Pocket Consultant* (Microsoft Press, 2003).

Table 8-2. **Extended Permissions for Exchange Server**

Permission	Description
Administer Information Store	Permits administration of the Information Store.
Create Named Properties In The Information Store	Permits creation of named properties in the Information Store.
Create Public Folder	Permits creation of a public folder under a top-level folder.
Create Top-Level Public Folder	Permits creation of a top-level public folder.
Full Store Access	Permits full access to the Information Store.
Mail-Enable Public Folder	Permits mail-enabling a public folder.
Modify Public Folder ACL	Permits modification of the access control list (ACL) on a public folder.
Modify Public Folder Admin ACL	Permits modification of the admin ACL on a public folder.
Modify Public Folder Deleted Item Retention	Permits modification of the deleted item retention period.
Modify Public Folder Expiry	Permits modification of a public folder's expiration date.
Modify Public Folder Quotas	Permits modification of a quota on a public folder.
Modify Public Folder Replica List	Permits modification of the replication list for a public folder.
Open Mail Send Queue	Permits opening the Mail Send queue and message queuing. The Exchange Servers group must have this permission.
Read Metabase Properties	Permits reading the properties of the metabase.
View Information Store Status	Permits viewing the status of the Information Store.

Viewing Exchange Server Permissions

Permissions are inherited from the Organization node by default. You can change this behavior when you set server permissions. To view security permissions for Exchange Server, complete the following steps:

1. Start System Manager, and then right-click the root or leaf-level node you want to work with.

2. Select Properties from the shortcut menu, and then in the Properties dialog box, click the Security tab, shown in Figure 8-1.

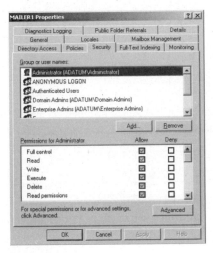

Figure 8-1. *Use the Security tab to configure object permissions.*

Note If the Properties option isn't available, you're trying to work with a nonroot or nonleaf node, such as the Recipients, Administrative Groups, or Servers nodes. Expand the node by clicking the plus sign (+), and then select a lower-level node. Note also that for some nodes, you view and assign permissions through the Exchange Administration Delegation Wizard. For details, see the section of this chapter entitled "Delegating Exchange Server Permissions."

3. In the Group Or User Names list box, select the object for which you want to view permissions. The permissions for the object are then displayed in the Permissions list box. If the permissions are shaded, it means they are inherited from a parent object.

Setting Exchange Server Permissions

You can control the administration and use of Exchange Server in several ways:

- **Globally for an entire organization** Set the permissions at the organization level. Through inheritance, these permissions are then applied to all objects in the Exchange organization.

- **For each server** Set the permissions individually for each server in the Exchange organization. Through inheritance, these permissions are then applied to all child nodes on the applicable server.

- **For each storage group** Set the permissions at the storage group level. Through inheritance, these permissions are then applied to all mailbox and public folder stores within the storage group.

- **For an individual node** Set the permissions on an individual node and disallow auditing inheritance for child nodes.

To set permissions for Exchange Server, follow these steps:

1. Start System Manager, and then right-click the root or leaf-level node you want to work with.

2. Select Properties from the shortcut menu, and then click the Security tab in the Properties dialog box, shown previously in Figure 8-1.

3. Users or groups that already have access to the Exchange node are listed in the Group Or User Names list box. You can change permissions for these users and groups by selecting the user or group you want to change, and then using the Permissions list box to grant or deny access permissions.

 Note Inherited permissions are shown in gray. Override inherited permissions by selecting the opposite permission.

4. To set access permissions for additional users, computers, or groups, click Add. This displays the Select Users, Computers, Or Groups dialog box, shown in Figure 8-2.

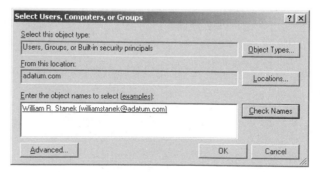

Figure 8-2. *Use the Select Users, Computers, Or Groups dialog box to select users, computers, or groups that should be granted or denied access.*

5. Use the Select Users, Computers, Or Groups dialog box to select the users, computers, or groups for which you want to set access permissions. To access account names from other domains, click Locations. You should see a list that shows the current domain, trusted domains, and other resources that you can access. Select Entire Directory to view all the account names in the folder.

6. In the Group Or User Names list box, select the user, computer, or group you want to configure, and then use the fields in the Permissions area to allow or deny permissions. Repeat for other users, computers, or groups.

7. Click OK when you're finished.

Overriding and Restoring Object Inheritance

To override or stop inheriting permissions from a parent object, follow these steps:

1. Start System Manager, and then right-click the root or leaf-level node you want to work with.

2. Select Properties from the shortcut menu, and then click the Security tab in the Properties dialog box.

3. Click Advanced to display the Advanced Security Settings dialog box.

4. Select or clear the Allow Inheritable Permissions From The Parent To Propagate To This Object And All Child Objects check box.

5. Click OK twice.

Delegating Exchange Server Permissions

At times, you might need to delegate control of Exchange Server without making a user a member of the Domain Admins or Enterprise Admins groups. For example, you might want a technical manager to be able to manage Exchange mailboxes, or you might want your boss to be able to view Exchange settings but not be able to modify settings. The tool you use to delegate control of Exchange Server is the Exchange Administration Delegation Wizard.

Working With the Exchange Administration Delegation Wizard

You use the Exchange Administration Delegation Wizard to delegate administrative permissions at the organization level or the administrative group level. The level of permissions you set is determined by where you start the wizard. If you start the wizard from the organization level, the groups or users that you specify will have administrative permissions throughout the organization. If you start the wizard from the administrative group level, the groups or users that you specify will have administrative permissions for that specific administrative group.

To simplify administration, you should always assign permissions to a group rather than to individual users. In this way, you grant permissions to additional users simply by making them members of the appropriate group, and you revoke permissions by removing the users from the group.

The Exchange Administration Delegation Wizard lets you assign any of the following administrative permissions to users and groups:

- **Exchange Full Administrator** Allows users or groups to fully administer Exchange system information and modify permissions. Grant this role to users who need to configure and control access to Exchange Server.

- **Exchange Administrator** Allows users or groups to fully administer Exchange system information but not to control access or modify permissions. Grant this role to users or groups who are responsible for the day-to-day administration of Exchange Server.

- **Exchange View Only Administrator** Allows users or groups to view Exchange configuration information. Grant this role to users or groups that need to view Exchange configuration settings but are not authorized to make changes.

 Note The Exchange Administration Delegation Wizard controls access to Exchange Server 2003. It doesn't give a user administrative access to the local machine. If Exchange administrators need to manage services or access the registry or file system on the server itself, you will need to make them local machine administrators for each Exchange Server they need to manage. For example, full administrators should be members of the local machine's Administrators group.

When setting permissions at the organization level, users and groups you delegate control to have the permissions shown in Table 8-3.

Table 8-3. Delegating Permissions at the Organization Level

Permission Type	Object	Permissions Granted	Do Permissions Apply to Subcontainers?
Full Administrator	Organization	All except Send As and Receive As permissions	Yes
Full Administrator	Exchange Container	Full Control	Yes
Administrator	Organization	All except Send As and Receive As permissions	Yes
Administrator	Exchange Container	All except Change permissions	Yes
View Only Administrator	Organization	View Information Store Status	Yes
View Only Administrator	Exchange Container	Read, List Object, List Contents	Yes

When setting permissions at the administrative group level, users and groups you delegate control to have the permissions shown in Table 8-4.

Table 8-4.   Delegating Permissions at the Administrative Group Level

Permission Type	Object	Permissions Granted	Do Permissions Apply to Subcontainers?
Full Administrator	Organization	Read, List Object, List Contents	Yes
Full Administrator	Administrative Group	All except Send As and Receive As	Yes
Full Administrator	Exchange Container	Read, List Object, List Contents	No
Full Administrator	Connectors	All except Change permissions	Yes
Full Administrator	Offline Address Lists	Write	Yes
Administrator	Organization	Read, List Object, List Contents	Yes
Administrator	Administrative Group	All permissions except Change, Send As, and Receive As	Yes
Administrator	Exchange Container	Read, List Object, List Contents	No
Administrator	Offline Address Lists	Write	Yes
View Only Administrator	Organization	Read, List Object, List Contents	No
View Only Administrator	Administrative Group	Read, List Object, List Contents, View Information Store Status	Yes
View Only Administrator	Exchange Containers	Read, List Object, List Content	Yes (Limited)

Using the Exchange Administration Delegation Wizard

You use the Exchange Administration Delegation Wizard to set permissions by completing the following steps:

1. After starting System Manager, right-click the organization or administrative group for which you want to delegate administrative permissions, and then click Delegate Control. This starts the Exchange Administration Delegation Wizard.

2. Click Next.

3. In Users Or Groups, click Add to grant a new user or group administrative permissions. The Delegate Control dialog box is displayed.

4. Click Browse. Select the group or user to which you want to grant administrative permissions, and then click OK.

5. In the Delegate Control dialog box, use Role to choose the administrative role. The options are as follows:
   - Exchange Full Administrator
   - Exchange Administrator
   - Exchange View Only Administrator

6. Click OK. Repeat Steps 3 through 5 to delegate control to other users or groups.

7. Click Next, and then click Finish to complete the procedure.

Auditing Exchange Server Usage

Auditing lets you track what's happening with Exchange Server. You can use auditing to collect information related to information store usage, creation of public folders, and much more. Any time an action that you've configured for auditing occurs, this action is written to the system's security log, where it's stored for your review. You can access the security log from Event Viewer.

Before you can configure auditing for Exchange, you must enable auditing in the domain through Group Policy. Once you enable auditing, you can configure individual Exchange servers in the domain to collect the information you want to track. You'll need to be logged on using an account that's a member of the Administrators group, or be granted the Manage Auditing And Security Log right in Group Policy.

Enabling Auditing in the Domain

You enable auditing in the domain through Group Policy. You can think of group policies as sets of rules that help you manage resources. You can apply group policies to domains, organizational units within domains, and individual systems. Policies that apply to individual systems are referred to as *local group policies* and are stored only on the local system. Other group policies are linked as objects in Active Directory.

You can enable Exchange auditing by completing the following steps:

1. Start Active Directory Users And Computers. In the console root, right-click the domain node, and then select Properties from the shortcut menu.

 Note The following steps explain how to enable auditing for an Active Directory domain. If you want a more detailed explanation of group policies and how they work, read Chapter 4 of *Microsoft Windows Server 2003 Administrator's Pocket Consultant* (Microsoft Press, 2003).

2. In the Properties dialog box, click the Group Policy tab. Edit the default policy by selecting Default Domain Policy and then clicking Edit.

3. As shown in Figure 8-3, access the Audit Policy node by working your way down through the console tree. Expand Computer Configuration, Windows Settings, Security Settings, and Local Policies. Then select Audit Policy.

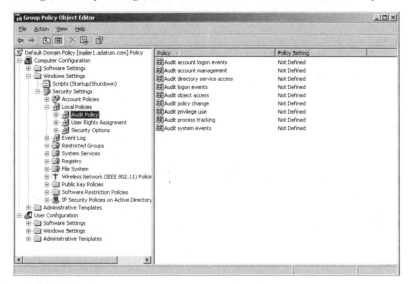

Figure 8-3. *Use the Audit Policy node in Group Policy to enable auditing.*

4. You should now see the following auditing options:

- **Audit Account Logon Events**   Tracks events related to user logon and logoff.

- **Audit Account Management**   Tracks account management by means of Active Directory Users And Computers. Events are generated any time user, computer, or group accounts are created, modified, or deleted.

- **Audit Directory Service Access**   Tracks access to Active Directory. Events are generated any time users or computers access the directory.

- **Audit Logon Events**   Tracks events related to user logon, user logoff, and remote connections to network systems.

- **Audit Object Access**   Tracks system resource usage for mailboxes, information stores, and other types of objects.

- **Audit Policy Change**   Tracks changes to user rights, auditing, and trust relationships.

- **Audit Privilege Use**   Tracks the use of user rights and privileges, such as the right to create public folders.
- **Audit Process Tracking**   Tracks system processes and the resources they use.
- **Audit System Events**   Tracks system startup, shutdown, and restart, as well as actions that affect system security or the security log.

5. To configure an auditing policy, double-click its entry, or right-click the entry, and then select Security. This opens a Properties dialog box for the policy.

6. Select Define These Policy Settings, and then select either the Success or Failure check box, or both. Success logs successful events, such as successful logon attempts. Failure logs failed events, such as failed logon attempts.

7. Repeat Steps 5 and 6 to enable other auditing policies. The policy changes won't be applied until the next time you start the Exchange server.

Starting to Log Auditable Events

To ensure the security and integrity of Exchange Server, you should set auditing policies. Auditing policies specify the actions that should be recorded in the security log. As with permissions, the auditing policies you apply are inherited by child objects in Exchange Server. Knowing this, you can configure auditing at several levels:

- **Globally**   To apply auditing policies for all of Exchange Server, set the policies at the organization level. Through object inheritance, these policies are then applied globally. Be careful, though; too many global policies can cause excessive logging, which slows the performance of Exchange Server.

- **Per server**   To apply auditing policies on a per-server basis, set the policies individually on each server in the Exchange organization. Through inheritance, these policies are then applied to all subnodes on the applicable server. Again, you should try to limit the types of actions that you audit. If you don't, you might reduce the quality of performance of Exchange Server.

- **Per storage group**   To apply auditing policies to a particular storage group, set the policies at the storage group level. Through inheritance, these policies are then applied to all mailbox and public folder stores within the storage group.

- **Per object**   To apply auditing settings to a single node or object, set the policies on a specific node. Disallow auditing inheritance for child nodes as necessary.

With this in mind, you can start logging for Exchange server by completing the following steps:

1. In System Manager, right-click the node you want to work with, and then select Properties from the shortcut menu. Click the Security tab, and then click Advanced.

2. In the Access Security Settings dialog box, click the Auditing tab. To inherit auditing settings from a parent object, make sure that the Allow Inheritable Permissions From The Parent To Propagate To This Object And All Child Objects check box is selected.

3. Use the Auditing Entries list box to select the users, groups, or computers for which you want to audit actions. To remove an account, select the account in the list box, and then click Remove.

4. To add specific objects, click Add, and then use the Select User, Computer, Or Group dialog box to select an object name to add. When you click OK, you'll see the Auditing Entry For dialog box (see Figure 8-4).

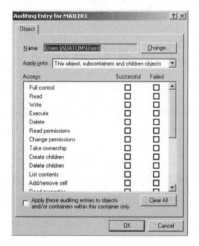

Figure 8-4. *Use the Auditing Entry For dialog box to set auditing entries for users, computers, and groups.*

5. Use the Apply Onto drop-down list to specify where objects are audited.

6. Select either the Successful or Failed check box, or both, for each of the events you want to audit. Successful logs successful events, such as successful file reads. Failed logs failed events, such as failed file deletions. The events you can audit are the same as the permissions listed in Tables 8-1 and 8-2.

7. Click OK when you're finished. Repeat this process to audit other users, groups, or computers.

Exchange Server Recipient Policies

Auditing policies are only one type of policy that you can apply directly to Exchange Server. Another type of policy is a *recipient policy*. E-mail address recipient policies control e-mail address generation in the organization, and you also use them to establish new default e-mail addresses on a global basis. Mailbox Manager recipient policies help you track and control mailbox usage.

Understanding E-mail Address Recipient Policies

You can apply e-mail address recipient policies to all mail-enabled objects, including users, groups, contacts, and public folders. The first e-mail address recipient policy created in the organization is set as the default.

The default policy establishes how default e-mail addresses are generated for X.400, Simple Mail Transfer Protocol (SMTP), and whatever other gateways might be installed in your Exchange organization. The default policy applies to all mail-enabled objects in the organization. By modifying the default policy, you can update the default e-mail addressing throughout the organization. Your updates can either override the existing e-mail addresses or be added as the primary addresses (with the current defaults set as secondary addresses).

You can create additional e-mail address recipient policies as well. Through filters, you can apply these additional policies to specific types of objects and to objects matching specific filter parameters. Here are some examples:

- By filtering for specific objects, you could create different recipient policies for users, groups, and contacts. Here, you might have user, group, and contact policies.

- By filtering objects based on the department or division field, you could create recipient policies for each business unit in your organization. Here, you might have marketing, administration, and business development policies.

- By filtering objects based on the city and state, you could create recipient policies for each office in your organization. Here, you might have Seattle, New York, and San Francisco policies.

In an organization in which many e-mail address recipient policies are in effect, only one policy is applied to a particular object. To determine which of the policies is applied to an object, Exchange Server checks the policy's priority. Exchange Server applies a recipient policy with a higher priority before a recipient policy with a lower priority.

The default recipient policy is set to the lowest priority. This means that the default policy is applied only when no other policy is available for a particular object.

When you create a new e-mail address recipient policy, the policy is applied based on the update interval of the Recipient Update Service running under the System Attendant. By default, the update interval is set to Always Run, which means that new policies are applied immediately. In a busy organization, however, continuous updating of e-mail addresses could degrade Exchange performance. That's why you can set the update interval to a different value. To determine or change the update interval, see the section of this chapter entitled "Scheduling E-mail Address Recipient Policy Updates."

Creating E-mail Address Recipient Policies

You use recipient policies to generate e-mail addresses for users, groups, contacts, and other mail-enabled objects in the organization. If your organization doesn't have a default recipient policy, the first policy you create is set as the default. You can't change some parameters of default policies. For example, you can't set filters on the default policy.

The default policy applies to all mail-enabled objects, and you can't change this behavior. Each additional policy that you create is fully customizable. You can set a name for the policy and add one or more filters.

You create an e-mail address recipient policy by completing the following steps:

1. In System Manager, expand the Recipients node, and then select Recipient Policies. In the right pane, you should see a list of current policies.

2. Right-click Recipient Policies, point to New, and then click Recipient Policy.

3. In the New Policy dialog box, select the E-Mail Addresses check box and then click OK.

4. In the Name field, type a name for the recipient policy. Use a descriptive name that makes it easy to determine how the policy is used and to which objects the policy applies.

5. Click Modify to display the Find Exchange Recipient dialog box. You can now select the recipient types that you want the new policy to apply to by selecting Show Only These Recipients, and then selecting the Users, Groups, and Contacts check boxes as appropriate.

6. As shown in Figure 8-5, use the options on the Advanced tab to set filters for the policy. These filters are based on object type. For example, if you wanted to filter users by division, you would click Field, point to User, and then select Division. Next, you would select a condition. The available conditions are Starts With, Ends With, Is (Exactly), Is Not, Present, and Not Present. You would then create the filter by clicking Add. To specify additional filters, you would repeat this process.

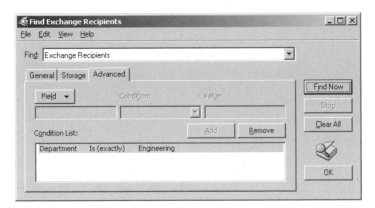

Figure 8-5. *Use the Advanced tab to set filters on individual objects.*

7. Click OK when you finish defining filters. The filter should now be displayed in the Filter Rules field of the General tab. If you made a mistake, you can edit the filter by clicking Modify again.

8. Click OK to create the policy. The policy is applied according to the schedule for the applicable Recipient Update Service. To determine or change the update interval, see the section of this chapter entitled "Scheduling E-mail Address Recipient Policy Updates."

9. As necessary, modify the default e-mail addresses assigned, as described in "Modifying E-mail Address Recipient Policies and Generating New E-mail Addresses" next.

Modifying E-mail Address Recipient Policies and Generating New E-mail Addresses

Once you create e-mail address recipient policies, they aren't etched in stone. You can change their properties at any time. The changes you make might cause Exchange Server to generate new e-mail addresses for recipients.

To modify a recipient policy, complete the following steps:

1. In System Manager, expand the Recipients node, and then select Recipient Policies.

2. In the right pane, you should see a list of current policies. Double-click the policy you want to modify.

3. If you want to rename the policy, type a new name for the policy in the Name field.

4. If you want to modify the way the policy is applied, click Modify, and then follow Steps 4 through 6 in the section of this chapter entitled "Creating E-mail Address Recipient Policies."

5. Click the E-Mail Addresses (Policy) tab, as shown in Figure 8-6. You can now reconfigure the default e-mail address generation rules for the members of the recipient policy. Current rules are displayed in the Generation Rules list. You can now do the following:

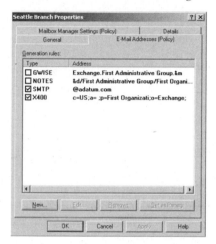

Figure 8-6. *Use the E-Mail Addresses (Policy) tab to specify how e-mail addresses should be generated.*

- **Create a new rule**   Click New. In the New E-Mail Address dialog box, select the type of e-mail address, and then click OK. Complete the Properties dialog box, and then click OK again.

- **Change an existing rule**   Double-click the e-mail address entry, and then modify the settings in the Properties dialog box. Click OK.

- **Delete a rule**   Select a rule, and then click Remove. Click Yes when prompted to confirm the deletion.

- **Set a primary e-mail address**   When several e-mail addresses are defined for a particular gateway, you can specify a primary e-mail address. Simply select the address you want to use as the primary one, and then click Set As Primary Address.

6. If you want the new e-mail addresses defined in the policy to become the primary addresses, and the current primary addresses to become alternative addresses, choose each new address in turn, and then select Set As Primary.

7. Click OK to apply the changes. If you modified the recipient membership or changed e-mail address settings, you'll see a prompt asking if you want to update all the corresponding recipient e-mail addresses. Click Yes to allow Exchange Server to generate new e-mail addresses based on the policy you've set.

Creating Exceptions to E-mail Address Recipient Policies

The Recipient Update Service is responsible for applying recipient policies. When you create new policies, the Recipient Update Service running under the System Attendant applies these policies. A policy is applied only once—unless you modify a policy and cause Exchange Server to generate new e-mail addresses.

If you want to create exceptions to recipient policies, wait until the Recipient Update Service has applied the policies. Then complete the following steps:

1. Start Active Directory Users And Computers, and then access the node that contains the recipients you want to work with.

2. Double-click the recipient object you want to exclude from the recipient policy, and then, in the Properties dialog box, click the E-Mail Address tab. Now modify the e-mail address settings for the object that you selected:

   • **Add a new e-mail address** Click New. In the New E-Mail Address dialog box, select the type of e-mail address, and then click OK. Complete the Properties dialog box, and then click OK again.

   • **Change an existing e-mail address** Double-click the address entry, and then modify the settings in the Properties dialog box. Click OK.

   • **Delete an e-mail address** Select the address you want to delete, and then click Remove. Click Yes when prompted to confirm the deletion.

3. Click OK when you're finished, and then repeat this procedure for other recipients for whom you want to create policy exceptions.

Scheduling E-mail Address Recipient Policy Updates

The Recipient Update Service is responsible for making updates to e-mail addresses, and it does this based on recipient policy changes. These updates are made at a specific interval that is defined for the service. You can view the update interval and modify it as necessary by completing the following steps:

1. Start System Manager, and then in the left pane (the console tree), click the plus sign (+) next to the Recipients node. Then select Recipient Update Services.

2. You should now see the available Recipient Update Services in the right pane. You'll have an enterprise configuration service and one or more additional services for additional domains in the domain forest.

3. Right-click the service you want to work with, select Properties, and then use the Properties dialog box to view the service's configuration settings.

4. Use Update Interval to choose a new update interval. The following options are available:

- Always Run
- Run Every Hour
- Run Every 2 Hours
- Run Every 4 Hours
- Never Run
- Use Custom Schedule

Tip If you want to set a custom schedule, choose Use Custom Schedule, and then click Customize. You can then set times when the service should make updates using the Schedule dialog box shown in Figure 8-7. In this dialog box, you can set the detail of the view to be hourly or every 15 minutes. Each hour or 15-minute interval of the day or night is a field that you can turn on and off. Intervals where updates should occur are filled in with a dark bar—you can think of these intervals as being turned on. Intervals where updates shouldn't occur are blank—you can think of these intervals as being turned off. To change the setting for an interval, click it to toggle its mode (either on or off).

5. Click OK to apply the changes.

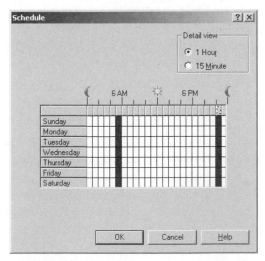

Figure 8-7. *In a busy Exchange organization, you might want to set a specific schedule for updates. If so, use the Schedule dialog box to define the update schedule.*

Forcing E-mail Address Recipient Policy Updates

Normally, the Recipient Update Service updates e-mail addresses at a specific interval. If necessary, you can manually start an update by completing the following steps:

1. Start System Manager and then, in the left pane (the console tree), click the plus sign (+) next to the Recipients node, and then select Recipient Update Services.

2. You should now see the available Recipient Update Services in the right pane. You'll have an enterprise configuration service and one or more additional services for additional domains in the domain forest.

3. Right-click the service you want to work with, and then select Update Now.

Rebuilding the Default E-mail Addresses

In some rare circumstances, the changes you've made to recipient policies might not be applied properly. If you think there's a problem, you can rebuild the default e-mail addresses for recipients. To do that, follow these steps:

1. Start System Manager and then, in the left pane (the console tree), click the plus sign (+) next to the Recipients node and then select Recipient Update Services.

2. You should now see the available Recipient Update Services in the right pane. You will have an enterprise configuration service and one or more additional services for additional domains in the domain forest.

3. Right-click the service you want to work with, and then select Rebuild. When prompted to confirm the action, click Yes.

 Caution The process of rebuilding e-mail addresses can take several hours. If you cancel the process before it's completed by either stopping the service or rebooting the Exchange server, you'll need to rebuild the addresses again.

Understanding Mailbox Manager Recipient Policies

Mailbox Manager is designed to help manage user mailboxes so that users experience fewer problems. Mailbox Manager does this by helping you as an administrator keep track of mailbox usage. You can also notify users when their mailboxes have messages that should be cleaned up or you can take action to clean up mailboxes by moving or deleting messages.

When activated, Mailbox Manager processes messages according to which folder the messages are stored in, and you can configure different settings for each type of folder. By default, items in folders older than 30 days and larger than

1 MB (1024 KB) are processed by Mailbox Manager and you have the following message processing options:

- **Generate Report Only**   Generates a report that is delivered to designated administrators. You can send either a summary report or a detailed report.

- **Move To Deleted Items Folder**   Moves items that exceed the age and size limits to the Deleted Items folder. The items will be purged from this folder based on the deletion settings for the mailbox store in which the mailbox is located or the individual settings for the user's mailbox.

- **Move To System Cleanup Folders**   Moves items that exceed the age and size limits to the System Cleanup folders. Items in the folder are marked for cleanup at the next cleanup interval, which can happen automatically or when the user chooses.

- **Delete Immediately**   Deletes the items permanently. The items are not copied to the Deleted Items folder.

Caution   You'll rarely, if ever, want to delete items immediately, and I don't recommend using this option unless you've planned carefully. For example, one scenario in which you might want to delete items immediately is if you are using Mailbox Manager only to process items in the Deleted Items and System Cleanup folders. The caution here, however, is that another administrator might not understand how you've configured mailbox management and they might add other folders to the processing list without understanding the implications of the Delete Immediately setting.

You can apply Mailbox Manager recipient policies to all mailbox-enabled objects. Unlike e-mail address recipient policy, Exchange doesn't create a default Mailbox Manager recipient policy and mailbox management isn't activated. Activating Mailbox Manager is a two-part process:

1. Create and configure a Mailbox Manager recipient policy.

2. Specify when and how mailbox management occurs.

As with an e-mail address recipient policy, you can create multiple Mailbox Manager policies and you can use filters to custom tailor the list of mailboxes that are affected by the various policies. For example, you could create different Mailbox Manager policies for executives, managers, and users. Or you could create policies for each business unit in your organization, such as Customer Service, Marketing, Administration, and Engineering. Keep in mind that regardless of whether a mailbox matches multiple filter criteria, only one Mailbox Manager policy is applied to a particular object, as determined by the priority of the policy.

Creating Mailbox Manager Recipient Policies

Mailbox Manager can be a great tool. Not only can you notify administrators of mailboxes that need cleaning up, but you can also take action by notifying users about messages that they should clean up, and moving or removing messages automatically. However, you should manage this feature carefully.

Remember, the key reasons for cleaning up mailboxes are to reduce mailbox size, reduce mailbox clutter, and eliminate potential problems. By reducing the size of the mailbox, you save disk space either on the server or on the user's computer (and sometimes in both locations). By reducing mailbox clutter, you make it easier for users to find current information and reduce distraction. Less size and clutter also mean that the mailbox is easier to manage and that it is less likely for the mailbox to get corrupted.

You create a Mailbox Manager recipient policy by completing the following steps:

1. In System Manager, expand the Recipients node, and then select Recipient Policies. In the right pane, you should see a list of current policies.

2. Right-click Recipient Policies, point to New, and then click Recipient Policy.

3. In the New Policy dialog box, select the Mailbox Manager Settings check box and then click OK.

4. In the Name field, type a name for the recipient policy. Use a descriptive name that makes it easy to determine how the policy is used and to which objects the policy applies.

5. Display the Find Exchange Recipient dialog box by clicking Modify. You can now select the recipient types that you want the new policy to apply to. Do this by selecting Show Only These Recipients, and then selecting the Users, Groups, and Contacts check boxes as appropriate.

6. Use the options on the Advanced tab to set filters for the policy.

7. Click OK when you finish defining filters. The filter should now be displayed on the General tab in the Filter Rules field. If you made a mistake, you can edit the filter by clicking Modify again.

8. Click the Mailbox Manager Settings (Policy) tab shown in Figure 8-8.

9. Use When Processing A Mailbox to specify when processing should occur. The options are as follows:

   - Generate Report Only
   - Move To Deleted Items Folder
   - Move To System Cleanup Folders
   - Delete Immediately

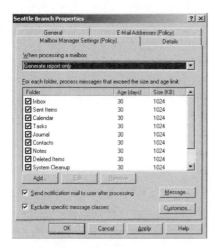

Figure 8-8. *Use the Mailbox Manager Settings (Policy) tab to specify when and how mailboxes are managed.*

10. By default, items in folders older than 30 days *and* larger than 1 MB (1024 KB) are processed by Mailbox Manager. By clearing or selecting the following folders, you can enable or disable their processing:

- **Inbox** The primary mailbox folder for users. In most cases, you'll want to ensure that 3 or more months of incoming mail messages are saved regardless of message size. With this in mind, you might want to use an age restriction of 90 days or more.

- **Sent Items** Used to save copies of outgoing mail messages. In most cases, you'll want to ensure that 2 to 3 months of outgoing mail are saved regardless of message size. With this in mind, you might want to use an age restriction of 60 to 90 days.

- **Calendar** Used to schedule and track appointments, events, and meetings. Many users, especially managers and executives, like to keep 6 months or more of calendar information. Most calendar items don't have large attachments, and I don't recommend using Mailbox Manager to clear out calendar items.

- **Tasks** Used to create and track to-do items. Most task items are very small in size.

- **Journal** Used to create and track journal entries.

- **Contacts** Used to create and track personal and business contacts. Because contacts are essential to business, I don't recommend using Mailbox Manager to clear out contacts.

- **Notes** Used to create and track notes, including sticky notes.

- **Deleted Items** Used to save temporary copies of messages that have been deleted from the Inbox or other folders.

- **System Cleanup** A system folder used by the operating system.
- **All Other Mail Folders** The catch-all option that allows you to specify what happens to other types of mail folders.

11. Age and message size limits are set on a per-folder basis. If you want to change the settings, double-click the folder entry in the Folder list to display the Folder Retention Settings dialog box shown in Figure 8-9. You can then do the following:

- Use the Age Limit (Days) field to specify the age that must be exceeded to potentially trigger processing. If you set the age limit to zero or clear the Age Limit check box, you eliminate the age limit for processing.

- Use the Message Size (KB) field to specify the message size that must be exceeded to potentially trigger processing. If you set the message size limit to zero or clear the Message Size check box, you eliminate the message size requirement for processing.

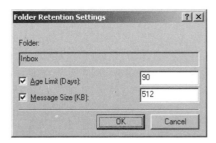

Figure 8-9. *You can change the age and message size limits for each folder as necessary.*

12. If you want to send e-mail to users about processing of their mailbox, choose Send Notification Mail To User After Processing and then click Message. After you use the Notification Message dialog box to specify the text of the message to send, click OK.

13. Click OK to create the policy. The policy is applied according to the mailbox management settings of the Exchange server. To determine or change the processing interval, see the next section, "Configuring Mailbox Management and Reporting."

Configuring Mailbox Management and Reporting

After you create Mailbox Manager policies, you can configure the mailbox management process by specifying the run schedule, the type of reporting to use (if any), and the administrator who should receive reports. You configure mailbox management and reporting by completing the following steps:

1. Start System Manager. Under the Administrative Group node, click the plus sign (+) next to the administrative group you want to work with and then click the plus sign (+) for the Servers node.

2. Right-click the server you want to configure for mailbox management and then select Properties.

3. Select the Mailbox Management tab, as shown in Figure 8-10.

Figure 8-10. *After you configure Mailbox Manager policies, specify how mailbox management should be handled on a per-server basis.*

4. Use Start Mailbox Management Process to set the mailbox management schedule. The following are the available options:

   * Never Run
   * Run Friday At Midnight
   * Run Saturday At Midnight
   * Run Sunday At Midnight
   * Use Custom Schedule

Note   If you want to set a custom schedule, choose Use Custom Schedule, and then click Customize. You can now set times when mailbox management should occur.

5. Use Reporting to specify the type of reports that should be sent to administrators. The options are as follows:

- None
- Send Summary Report To Administrator
- Send Detail Report To Administrator

6. Click Browse. Use the Select Recipient dialog box to specify the administrator that should receive mailbox management reports. Only one user account can be specified.

7. Click OK.

Running Mailbox Manager Manually

You can run the Mailbox Manager process manually at any time by right-clicking the server you want to work with and selecting Start Mailbox Management Process. In most cases, you'll only want to do this when the server workload is low, such as before or after normal business hours.

Setting the Priority of Recipient Policies

As stated previously, only one recipient policy is applied to a recipient. This policy is the highest priority policy with filter conditions that match the properties of the recipient.

Priorities are assigned to recipient policies according to their position in the Recipient Policies list. In System Manager, you can view the current position and priority of a policy by expanding the Recipients node and then selecting Recipient Policies.

The default recipient policy has the lowest priority, and you can't change this priority. You can, however, change the priority of other policies by right-clicking the policy in the Recipient Policies node, pointing to All Tasks, and then selecting Move Up or Move Down as appropriate. Changing the priority of policies might cause the Recipient Update Service to generate new e-mail addresses.

Deleting Recipient Policies

You can delete any recipient policies that you create by right-clicking the policy, selecting Delete, and then confirming the action when prompted.

For e-mail address recipient policies, the Address List service updates the e-mail addresses for the affected recipients as necessary. If for some reason these updates don't occur, you can manually start an update as described in the section of this chapter entitled "Forcing E-mail Address Recipient Policy Updates."

 Note You can't delete the default e-mail address recipient policy. This policy is mandatory.

Exchange Server System Policies

Exchange Server supports three types of system policies: server, mailbox store, and public folder store. These policies control settings for Exchange servers and information stores.

Using System Policies

You configure system policies through a set of property pages. With mailbox store policies, you can use the General, Database, and Limits property pages to configure a policy. With public store policies, you can use the General, Database, Replication, and Limits property pages to configure a policy. With server policies, you can use only the General property page to configure a policy.

The properties pages are used as follows:

- **General**   Sets general-purpose options for the policy
- **Database**   Sets storage group membership, Exchange database names, and maintenance schedules
- **Replication**   Sets the replication interval and message size limits
- **Limits**   Sets the deleted item retention interval and storage limits

When you create a policy, you don't have to use all of the available property pages. Instead, you select only the property pages you want to use. Later, if you want to add or remove property pages, you can do so by changing the property page availability. The property pages are displayed in the Properties dialog box for the policy as tabs.

You don't manage system policies in the same way that you manage recipient policies. Instead of creating a policy and relying on a service to implement it, you must take charge of each step of the creation and implementation process. For most system policies, the creation and implementation process works like this:

1. You create a server, mailbox store, or public store policy.
2. You specify the servers or stores to which the policy should apply by adding items to the policy.
3. You enforce the policy by applying it.

You can create multiple policies of a particular type, and you can apply all of these policies to the same objects. For example, you could create separate mailbox store policies to apply database, replication, and messaging controls. You could then apply these policies to the same mailbox store.

If two policies conflict, you'll be notified of the conflict when you create the policy, and you'll have the opportunity to remove the item from the conflicting policy. If you don't rectify the conflict, you won't be able to add the item to the policy. To see how this would work, consider the following scenario.

You create a policy that sets a storage limit on all mailbox stores in the Exchange organization, and then create a new policy that removes the storage limit on the

Technology mailbox store. You're notified that a conflict exists and you're given the opportunity to remove the Technology mailbox store from the first policy.

As you work with these policies, you'll note that you could use other techniques to set some of the options. For example, you can set deleted item retention these ways:

- Through the properties of individual mailboxes
- Through the Mailbox Store Properties dialog box
- Through mailbox store policies

The differences among these techniques are ones of scope and manageability. With mailbox properties, you're setting per-mailbox limits that affect a single mailbox. With mailbox store properties, you're setting limits on individual mailbox stores, which can affect multiple mailboxes. With mailbox store policies, you're setting limits on one or more mailbox stores and all of the related mailboxes.

Policy settings also take precedence, and in some cases they disallow configuring options at other levels. For example, if you set a deleted item retention period in a mailbox store policy, you can't edit the deleted item retention period in an affected mailbox store. You can override the policy settings only on individual mailboxes.

Creating Server Policies

Server policies set message tracking and logging rules for Exchange servers in an organization. Message tracking allows you to track messages sent within the organization, messages received from external mail servers, and messages coming from or going to foreign mail systems. With message tracking enabled, you can track system messages, e-mail messages, and public folder postings.

There are many reasons for using message tracking. You can use message tracking to do the following:

- Track a message's path from originator to recipient.
- Search for messages sent by specific users.
- Search for messages received by specific users.
- Confirm receipt of messages.
- Monitor the organization for inappropriate messages.

To create a server policy, complete the following steps:

1. Start System Manager. Under the Administrative Group node, click the plus sign (+) next to the administrative group you want to edit. Right-click the System Policies node, and point to New. Then click Server Policy.

 Tip If no System Policies node is listed, right-click the administrative group in which you want to create the policy, point to New, and then select System Policy Container.

2. In the New Policy dialog box, select the General check box, and then click OK. You'll see a Properties dialog box.

3. Type a descriptive name for the policy.

4. As shown in Figure 8-11, you configure the server policy options using the General (Policy) tab. Policies you can set include these:

   - **Enable Subject Logging And Display** Logs all subject fields for messages processed by the server.

   - **Enable Message Tracking** Tracks all messages processed by Exchange Server.

   - **Remove Log Files** Removes all log files older than the value set in the Remove Files That Are Older Than (Days) field. The valid range is from 1 to 99 days.

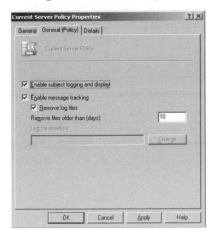

Figure 8-11. *Configure server policy options using the General (Policy) tab.*

5. Click OK to create the policy. Keep in mind that you can't modify settings that are inherited from server policies, and they appear disabled in the Server Properties dialog box.

6. Add items to the policy and then apply the policy, as discussed in the sections of this chapter entitled "Adding Items to a System Policy" and "Applying a System Policy."

Creating Mailbox Store Policies

Mailbox store policies set storage limits, deleted-item retention intervals, and maintenance rules for mailbox stores in the Exchange organization. You can't modify settings that are inherited from mailbox store policies, and they appear disabled in the Mailbox Store Properties dialog box.

You create a mailbox store policy by completing the following steps:

1. Start System Manager. Under the Administrative Group node, click the plus sign (+) next to the administrative group you want to edit. Right-click the System Policies node, point to New, and then click Mailbox Store Policy. If no System Policies node is listed, right-click the administrative group in which you want to create the policy, point to New, and then select System Policy Container.

2. In the New Policy dialog box, select the property pages you want to use in the policy. The available options are General, Database, Limits, and Full-Text Indexing.

3. When you click OK, you'll see a Properties dialog box.

4. Type a descriptive name for the policy.

5. As shown in Figure 8-12, use the General (Policy) tab to set default messaging options. The only mandatory setting is the default public store. All other settings are optional. The available options are as follows:

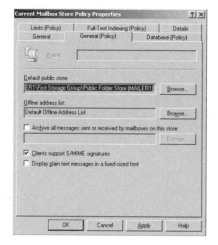

Figure 8-12. *For mailbox store policies, set general messaging options using the General (Policy) tab.*

- **Default Public Store** Shows the default public store for the mailbox store. To set this value, click the corresponding Browse button, select a public store to use, and then click OK.

- **Offline Address List** Shows the default offline address list for the mailbox store. To set this value, click the corresponding Browse button, select an offline address list to use, and then click OK.

- **Archive All Messages Sent Or Received By Mailboxes On This Store** Select this check box if you wish to enable archiving for messages sent or received on this store.

- **Clients Support S/MIME Signatures**   Select this check box if mail clients use Secure/Multipurpose Internet Mail Extensions (S/MIME).

- **Display Plain Text Messages In A Fixed-Sized Font**   Select this check box to convert the text of incoming Internet messages to a fixed-width font such as Courier.

6. In the Database (Policy) tab, use Run Maintenance During This Time to select a maintenance schedule for the affected mailbox stores. The available options are as follows:

- Run Daily From 11:00 P.M. To 3:00 A.M.

- Run Daily From Midnight To 4:00 A.M.

- Run Daily From 1:00 A.M. To 5:00 A.M.

- Run Daily From 2:00 A.M. To 6:00 A.M.

- Use Custom Schedule

Note   If you want to set a custom schedule, choose Use Custom Schedule, and then click Customize. You can then set times when maintenance should occur.

7. As shown in Figure 8-13, you use the Limits (Policy) tab to set deleted item retention and storage limits. These settings are then enforced through the policy. The available options are as follows:

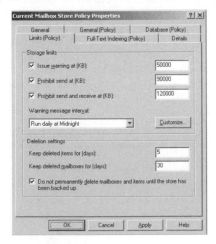

Figure 8-13. *Set deleted item retention and storage limits using the Limits (Policy) tab.*

- **Issue Warning At (KB)**   Sets the size, in kilobytes, that a mailbox can reach before a warning is issued to the user. The warning tells the user to clean out the mailbox.

- **Prohibit Send At (KB)**   Sets the size, in kilobytes, that a mailbox can reach before the user is prohibited from sending any new mail. The restriction ends when the user clears out the mailbox and the total mailbox size is under the limit.

- **Prohibit Send And Receive At (KB)**   Sets the size, in kilobytes, that a mailbox can reach before the user is prohibited from sending and receiving mail. The restriction ends when the user clears out the mailbox and the total mailbox size is under the limit. Use this option sparingly because users over this quota won't be able to receive new mail; messages intended for them will be returned to the sender.

- **Warning Message Interval**   Determines the time interval when warning messages are set. Select a specific time (Daily At Midnight, Daily At 1:00 A.M., or Daily At 2:00 A.M.) or use a custom schedule.

- **Keep Deleted Items For (Days)**   Enter the number of days to retain deleted items. If you set the retention period to 0, messages aren't retained and can't be recovered.

- **Do Not Permanently Delete Mailboxes And Items Until The Store Has Been Backed Up**   Select this check box to ensure that deleted items are archived into at least one backup set.

Tip   You should set deleted mailbox retention through the properties of individual mailbox stores. This feature is invaluable to Exchange administrators because it enables users to recover deleted items without requiring an administrator to restore the Exchange database from tape. Because the restore and extraction process of Exchange data can be arduous, this is a setting that you should enable across the enterprise, based on your service-level agreement with the user community. In most cases, users will quickly realize it if they click Delete too soon on a piece of e-mail. Therefore, it's common to set this interval to 2 weeks.

8. Click OK to create the policy.

9. Add items to the policy and then apply the policy, as discussed in the sections of this chapter entitled "Adding Items to a System Policy" and "Applying a System Policy."

Creating Public Store Policies

Public store policies set rules for storage limits, deleted item retention, replication, and maintenance of public stores in an Exchange organization. You can't modify settings that are inherited from public store policies, and they appear disabled in the Public Store Properties dialog box.

You can create a public store policy by completing the following steps:

1. Start System Manager. Under the Administrative Group node, click the plus sign (+) next to the administrative group you want to edit. Right-click the System Policies node, point to New, and then click Public Store Policy. If no System Policies node is listed, right-click the administrative group in which you want to create the policy, point to New, and then select System Policy Container.

2. In the Policy Manager dialog box, select the property pages you want to use in the policy. The available options are General, Database, Replication, Limits, and Full-Text Indexing.

3. When you click OK, you'll see a Properties dialog box.

4. Type a descriptive name for the policy.

5. Use the General (Policy) tab to set default messaging options. The available options are as follows:

   - **Clients Support S/MIME Signatures** Select this check box if mail clients use S/MIME.

   - **Display Plain Text Messages In A Fixed-Sized Font** Select this option to convert the text of incoming Internet messages to a fixed-width font such as Courier.

6. On the Database (Policy) tab, use Run Maintenance During This Time to select a maintenance schedule for the affected public stores. The available options are as follows:

   - Run Daily From 11:00 P.M. To 3:00 A.M.
   - Run Daily From Midnight To 4:00 A.M.
   - Run Daily From 1:00 A.M. To 5:00 A.M.
   - Run Daily From 2:00 A.M. To 6:00 A.M.
   - Use Custom Schedule

Note If you want to set a custom schedule, choose Use Custom Schedule, and then click Customize. You can now set times when maintenance should occur.

7. As shown in Figure 8-14, use the Limits (Policy) tab to set deleted item retention, storage limits, and folder aging. These settings are then enforced through the policy. The available options are the following:

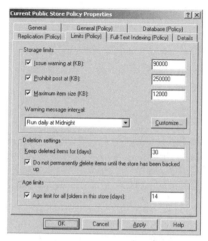

Figure 8-14. *With public stores, you can manage deleted items, storage limits, and folder aging by using policies.*

- **Issue Warning At (KB)** Sets the size, in kilobytes, of the data that a user can store in the public store before a warning is issued to the user. The warning tells the user to clean out the public store.

- **Prohibit Post At (KB)** Sets the size, in kilobytes, of how large a folder can grow before no more posts can be added.

- **Maximum Item Size (KB)** Sets the size, in kilobytes, of the largest message that can be posted to the folder.

- **Warning Message Interval** Determines when over-limit messages are set. Select a specific time (Daily At Midnight, Daily At 1:00 AM, or Daily At 2:00 AM) or use a custom schedule.

- **Keep Deleted Items For (Days)** Enter the number of days to retain deleted items. If you set the retention period to 0, messages and files aren't retained and can't be recovered.

- **Do Not Permanently Delete Items Until The Store Has Been Backed Up** Select this check box to ensure that deleted items are archived into at least one backup set.

- **Age Limit For All Folders In This Store (Days)** Sets the number of days items can remain in the public store. Items over the age limit are deleted.

8. As Figure 8-15 shows, you use the Replication (Policy) tab to set replication intervals and limits for public stores. The available options are as follows:

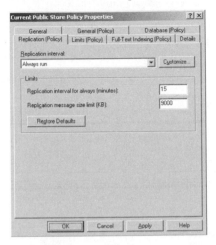

Figure 8-15. *Set replication options using the Replication (Policy) tab.*

- **Replication Interval** Determines when changes to public folders are replicated. Select a specific time (Always Run, Run Every Hour, Run Every 2 Hours, Run Every 4 Hours, or Never Run) or use a custom schedule.

- **Replication Interval For Always (Minutes)** Sets the interval, in minutes, used when you select Always Run as the replication option.

- **Replication Message Size Limit (KB)** Sets the size limit, in kilobytes, for messages that are replicated. Messages over the size limit aren't replicated.

9. Click OK to create the policy.

10. Add items to the policy and then apply the policy, as discussed in the sections of this chapter entitled "Adding Items to a System Policy" and "Applying a System Policy."

Implementing System Policies

Once you create system policies, you'll need to add items and apply the policy to the Exchange organization. The following sections explain these procedures.

Adding Items to a System Policy

You can add items to a system policy by completing these steps:

1. In System Manager, access the System Policies node under the organization or administrative group node.

2. Right-click the policy you want to work with, and then choose Add Server, Add Public Store, or Add Mailbox Store as appropriate. This displays the Select Item To Place Under The Control Of This Policy dialog box.

3. Select an item in the Name list box and then click Add. Repeat this step for each item you want to place under the control of the selected policy.

4. Click OK. You'll see a prompt asking you to confirm that you want to add the items to the policy. Click Yes.

5. If one or more of the items are under the control of another policy, you'll see individual prompts asking if you want to remove the object from the control of the other policy. Answer Yes to each prompt.

Removing Items from a System Policy

To remove items from a system policy, follow these steps:

1. In System Manager, access the System Policies node under the organization or administrative group node, and then double-click the policy you want to work with.

2. In the right pane, you should see a list of items under the control of the policy. Right-click the item you want to remove, point to All Tasks, and then choose Remove From Policy.

Applying a System Policy

You normally apply system policies during the maintenance cycle for a server or information store. However, you can apply policies immediately by completing the following steps:

1. In System Manager, access the System Policies node under the specific administrative group node where you want to apply this policy.

2. Right-click the policy you want to apply, and then choose Apply Now.

Modifying System Policies

When you make changes to system policies, you normally want these changes to be applied immediately. With this in mind, you should modify system policies by completing the following steps:

1. In System Manager, access the System Policies node under the specific administrative group node where you want to edit this policy.

2. Right-click the policy you want to work with and then choose Properties. Use the Properties dialog box to make changes to the policy.

3. When you're finished, click OK to close the dialog box.

4. Right-click the policy, and then choose Apply Now to implement the changes.

Deleting System Policies

You can delete system policies by completing the following steps:

1. In System Manager, access the System Policies node under the specific administrative group node from which you want to remove this policy.

2. Right-click the policy you want to work with, and then choose Delete. Confirm the deletion by clicking Yes.

Instead of deleting a system policy, you might want to disable it by removing all the items that are under its control. If you ever need to reapply the policy, you can simply add items instead of to re-creating the entire policy.

Part III

Microsoft Exchange Server 2003 Data Store Administration

Part III covers Microsoft Exchange Server 2003 data store administration. In Chapter 9 you'll learn how to manage Exchange data and storage groups. Chapter 10 examines the administration of mailbox and public folder stores. Chapter 11 looks at how you can use public folders. Finally, Chapter 12 explains how to back up and restore Exchange Server. You'll learn techniques that can help you reliably back up and, more important, recover Exchange Server in case of failure.

Chapter 9

Managing Microsoft Exchange Server 2003 Data and Storage Groups

As a Microsoft Exchange Server 2003 administrator, one of your most important tasks is managing the information store. Each Exchange server deployed in an organization has an information store. The information store can contain storage groups, data stores, and databases. This chapter focuses on management of storage groups and databases. You'll learn the following:

- How to enable, create, and use storage groups
- How to manage databases and their related transaction logs
- Why you might want to enable full-text indexing of Exchange databases
- How to manage indexing once it's enabled

To learn how to manage data stores, see Chapter 10, "Mailbox and Public Folder Store Administration."

Controlling the Information Store

Storage groups allow you to group databases logically, giving you the option of managing an entire storage group (with all its databases) or managing databases individually. When Exchange Server is installed, the information store has a single storage group called First Storage Group. You can create additional storage groups as needed. Exchange Server 2003 Enterprise Edition is the most flexible. With the enterprise edition, you can create up to four additional storage groups as needed for a maximum of five storage groups per server (with one of the storage groups, called the recovery storage group, being reserved for database recovery operations).

Using Storage Groups and Databases

On the surface, storage groups and databases seem to be the most fundamental Exchange Server components. Yet, as you dig deeper, the reasons for creating additional storage groups and databases become clear. You use storage groups as containers for mailbox and public folder stores. You create mailbox and public folder stores within storage groups, and each storage group can have multipledata stores.

An Exchange database is associated with each data store. You use Exchange databases to ease the administration burden that comes with managing large installations. For example, instead of having a single 100-GB database for the entire organization, you can create five 20-GB databases that you can manage more easily.

When you install a new Exchange server in an organization, two data stores are created automatically: a default mailbox store and a default public folder store. Two database files are associated with the default mailbox store:

- **Priv1.edb** A rich-text database file containing message headers, message text, and standard attachments

- **Priv1.stm** A streaming Internet content file containing audio, video, and other media that are formatted as streams of Multipurpose Internet Mail Extension Extensions (MIME) data

The default public folder store has two key files associated with it as well:

- **Pub1.edb** A rich-text database file containing message headers, message text, and standard attachments

- **Pub1.stm** A streaming Internet content file containing audio, video, and other media that are formatted as streams of MIME data

All Exchange databases have .edb and .stm files associated with them. When you create a mailbox or public folder store, you can specify the names for these files. By default, the .edb and .stm file names are the same as the name of the data store. For example, if you create a mailbox store called Administration and don't change the default .edb and .stm file names, these files are called Administration.edb and Administration.stm, respectively.

Storage groups have files associated with them as well. These files can be placed into two categories: transaction log files and system files. Transaction log files include the following:

- **E##.log** The primary transaction log file for the storage group, where ## represents the storage group prefix. The first storage group has the prefix E00, meaning its primary log file is named E00.log; the second has the prefix E01, meaning its primary log is named E01.log; and so on.

- **E#######.log** Secondary transaction log files for the storage group, where each # represents a digit. The first and second digits in the transaction log file name are the prefix for the related storage group. The remaining digits are numbered sequentially. This means the first log file for the first storage group is named E0000001.log.

- **Res1.log** A reserved log file for the storage group. The reserve logs are 5 MB each, and they act as a buffer to allow Exchange Server to continue writing transactions when the disk drive is out of space. These files are important because they buy you time to free up disk space without interrupting service. They should never be deleted.

- **Res2.log** A reserved log file for the storage group.

System files include the following:

- **E##.chk** A check file containing recovered file fragment, where ## represents the storage group prefix

- **Tmp.edb** A temporary workspace for processing transactions

Note In this section, I've listed the standard Exchange files. Depending on the state of Exchange Server, you might see other files as well. For example, sequentially numbered files with the .stf file extension are used when writing message attachments into the database. You'll see files with the name 1.stf, 2.stf, and so on. When Exchange Server is creating a new log file, you'll see a file called Edbtmp.log. This file is the template from which Exchange Server creates log files.

The many files associated with storage groups and databases provide granular control over Exchange Server, and if you configure the data files properly, they can help you scale your Exchange organization efficiently while ensuring optimal performance. To see how, consider the scenarios listed in Table 9-1, which outline some ways that small, medium, and large organizations could configure Exchange Server based on performance needs.

Note The scenarios outlined in Table 9-1 don't take into account the use of virtual servers. Virtual servers also provide a way to balance Exchange Server loads and improve performance. For more information on virtual servers and how you can use them to grow an organization, see Part IV, "Microsoft Exchange Server 2003 and Group Administration."

Table 9-1. Configuring Exchange Data Files for Small, Medium, and Large Organizations

Organization Size	Performance Needs	Storage Groups	Recommendation
Small	Low	1	Place all data files on the same drive. Consider using redundant array of independent disks (RAID) 1 or RAID 5 to protect the data.
	High	1	Place all databases on a single drive. Place all transaction logs and system files on a different drive. Consider using RAID 5 for databases and RAID 1 for transaction logs.
Medium	Low	1	Place all databases on a single drive, using RAID 5 to protect the drive in case of failure. Place all transaction logs and system files on a different drive, using RAID 1 to protect the drive in case of failure.
	High	1; multiple	Place all databases on a single drive, using RAID 5 to protect the drive in case of failure. Place all transaction logs on a different drive, using RAID 1 to protect the drive in case of failure. Place all system files on a third drive.
Large	Low	Multiple	Organize data according to storage groups, placing all the data for each storage group on separate drives. Use RAID 1 or RAID 5 to protect the drives.
	Moderate	Multiple	Each storage group should have its own database drive. Use RAID 5 to protect the database drives in case of failure. Place transaction logs and system files for each storage group on different drives, using RAID 1 to protect the drives in case of failure.
	High	Multiple	Each database should have its own drive. Use RAID 5 to protect the drive in case of failure. Place the transaction logs for each storage group on separate drives, using RAID 1 to protect the drive in case of failure. Place system files for each storage group on separate drives.

You can use storage groups to manage Exchange Server 2003 backup and recovery more effectively as well. When you perform backup operations on Exchange Server, you can back up each storage group separately. If you have a problem with Exchange Server, you can restore a specific storage group to resolve the problem instead of having to restore all the Exchange data. Log files are also useful in recovery. Each transaction in a log file is marked with a database instance ID, which enables you to recover individual databases within a single storage group as well.

Creating Storage Groups

You can create a storage group by completing the following steps:

1. In System Manager, access the Servers node within the administrative or routing group you want to manage. Typically, you would expand Administrative Groups, then First Administrative Group, and then the Servers node.

2. In the left pane (the console tree), right-click the Exchange server you want to manage, and then select New, Storage Group from the shortcut menu. You should now see the Properties dialog box shown in Figure 9-1.

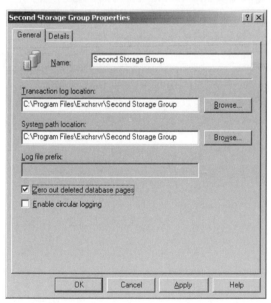

Figure 9-1. *Use the Properties dialog box to name the storage group and determine where its files are stored.*

3. In the Name field, type a descriptive name for the storage group. If you want to follow the default naming convention, name each storage group in sequence, as in First Storage Group, Second Storage Group, Third Storage Group, and so on.

4. Click Browse to the right of the Transaction Log Location field, and then select a location for the transaction logs. You can't store files for additional storage groups in the same directory in which you have an existing storage group.

 Tip Each storage group has its own set of transaction logs. These logs are used to perform transactional processing within Exchange Server. To improve performance, you could place each set of transaction logs on a physically separate drive, and the number of transaction log drives should equal the number of storage groups you're using. For example, if a server uses two storage groups, the server should have two transaction log drives. To protect transaction log drives against failure, you should mirror them as well. RAID 1 (disk mirroring) is recommended over RAID 5 (disk striping with parity) because you'll have better write performance with RAID 1 in most instances—and the transaction log drives are written too frequently on busy servers.

5. Click Browse to the right of the System Path Location field and then select a location for the system files that the storage group will use.

6. Click OK to create the storage group. You can now add mailbox and public folder stores to the storage group.

Changing Transaction Log Location and System Path

As discussed earlier, the transaction log location and system path have an important role in managing Exchange Server performance. The transaction log location determines where primary, secondary, and reserved log files are stored. The system path determines where check files are stored and where temporary transactions are processed.

You can change the transaction log location and system path for an existing storage group by completing the following steps:

1. In System Manager, click the plus sign (+) next to the Exchange server you want to manage. Typically, you would expand Administrative Groups, then First Administrative Group, and then the Servers node.

2. You should see a list of storage groups that are available on the server. Right-click the storage group you want to change, and then select Properties from the shortcut menu. You should now see the Properties dialog box shown in Figure 9-2.

3. Click Browse to the right of the Transaction Log Location field, and then select a new location for the storage group's transaction logs.

4. Click Browse to the right of the System Path Location field, and then select a new location for the storage group's system files. The folder location must already exist. If the folder location doesn't exist, you'll need to create it in Windows Explorer or by clicking New Folder in the Browse window. If you don't place the system files on a separate drive, you should place them on the same drive as the transaction logs.

5. Click OK.

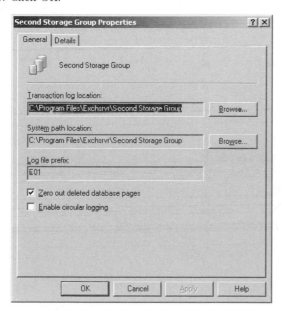

Figure 9-2. *Use the Properties dialog box to modify the storage group's properties.*

Zeroing Out Deleted Database Pages

Databases read and write information in pages. Each time Exchange Server needs to increase the size of a database, it does so by creating new data pages and then filling those pages with information. Zeroing out deleted database pages (rather than removing them) allows Exchange Server to reuse previously created data pages. By zeroing out deleted pages, you can realize a slight performance enhancement in an environment in which old data is frequently being deleted and new data is frequently being stored in the database.

You control the zeroing out of database pages at the storage group level. Each storage group can have a different policy for zeroing out deleted database pages. To enable or disable zeroing out of database pages, complete the following steps:

1. In System Manager, click the plus sign (+) next to the Exchange server you want to manage. Typically, you would expand Administrative Groups, then First Administrative Group, and then the Servers node.
2. Right-click the storage group you want to change, and then select Properties from the shortcut menu.
3. Select or clear the Zero Out Deleted Database Pages check box as appropriate, and then click OK.

Enabling and Disabling Circular Logging

Circular logging allows Exchange Server to overwrite transaction log files after the data they contain has been committed to the database. Overwriting old transactions reduces the disk space requirements for Exchange Server, yet makes it impossible to recover Exchange Server up to the last transaction. If circular logging is enabled, you can recover Exchange Server only up to the last full backup.

You control circular logging at the storage group level, which allows each storage group to have a different policy for logging. To enable or disable circular logging, complete the following steps:

1. In System Manager, click the plus sign (+) next to the Exchange server you want to manage. Typically, you would expand Administrative Groups, then First Administrative Group, and then the Servers node.
2. Right-click the storage group you want to change, and then select Properties from the shortcut menu.
3. Select or clear the Enable Circular Logging check box as appropriate, and then click OK.

 Caution If you enable circular logging, you are limiting your recovery options for Exchange Server. As mentioned previously, you will only be able to recover Exchange Server up to the last full backup. Thus, you won't be able to successfully apply changes contained in differential or incremental backups that were created after the last full backup.

Renaming Storage Groups

Renaming storage groups is simple. Right-click the storage group, select Rename from the shortcut menu, and then enter a new name for the storage group. What you don't see are the repercussions of renaming, and this is what you need to be aware of.

All objects in Active Directory are located by a unique identifier that uses the directory namespace and works through each element in the directory hierarchy to a particular object. When you change the name of a storage group, you change the namespace for all the objects in that storage group, which includes databases, data stores, mailboxes, and more. Thus, the simple act of renaming a storage group has a definite impact on Exchange Server.

Deleting Storage Groups

Before attempting to delete a storage group, you must delete or move the data stores it contains. Exchange Server allows you to delete storage groups only when they are empty (that is, only when they contain no data stores).

Once the storage group is empty, right-click the storage group and then select Delete from the shortcut menu to remove it. When prompted, confirm the action by clicking Yes.

Content Indexing

Content Indexing is a built-in Exchange feature. Every Exchange server in your organization supports and uses some type of indexing. To manage indexing more effectively, use the techniques discussed in this section.

Understanding Indexing

Content indexing enables fast searches and lookups through server-stored mailboxes and public folders. Exchange Server supports two types of indexing:

- Standard indexing
- Full-text indexing

The Exchange Server storage engine automatically implements and manages standard indexing. Standard indexing is used with searches for common key fields such as message subjects. Users take advantage of standard indexing every time they use the Find feature in Microsoft Office Outlook. With server-based mail folders, standard indexing is used to quickly search To, Cc, and Subject fields. With public folders, standard indexing is used to quickly search From and Subject fields.

As you probably know, users can perform advanced searches in Outlook as well. In Outlook, all they need to do is select the Advanced Find option from the Tools menu, enter their advanced search parameters, and then click Find Now. When Exchange Server receives an advanced query without full-text indexing, Exchange Server searches through every message in every folder. This means that as Exchange mailboxes and public folders grow, so does the time it takes to complete an advanced search. With standard searching, Exchange Server is unable to search through message attachments.

With full-text indexing, Exchange Server builds an index of all searchable text in a particular mailbox or public folder store before users try to search. The index can then be updated or rebuilt at a predefined interval. Then when users perform advanced searches, they can quickly find any text within a document or attachment.

 Note Full-text indexes work only with server-based data. If users have personal folders, Exchange Server doesn't index the data in these folders.

The drawback of full-text indexing is that it's resource-intensive. As with any database, creating and maintaining indexes requires CPU time and system memory, which can affect Exchange performance. Full-text indexes also use disk space. A newly created index uses approximately 20 percent of the total size of the Exchange database. This means that a 1-GB database would have an index of about 200 MB.

Each time you update an index, the file space that the index uses increases. Don't worry; only changes in the database are stored in the index updates. This means that the additional disk space usage is incremental. For example, if the original 1-GB database grew by 50 MB, the index would use about 210 MB of disk space (200 MB for the original index and 10 MB for the update).

As an administrator, you have fairly granular control over indexing. You set the maintenance schedule and determine the indexing priority. By scheduling maintenance during off-peak hours, you can reduce the impact on operations. By lowering the indexing priority, you can restrict the level of system resource usage.

Setting Indexing Priority for an Information Store

System resources, such as CPU time and memory, are used every time Exchange Server builds, updates, or re-creates an index. The level of resource usage is completely configurable and is determined by the indexing priority set for the server's information store. There is a direct trade-off between the indexing priority and the time it takes to complete an index. The higher the priority, the more system resources are used and the less time is required for creating an index. The lower the priority, the fewer system resources are used and the more time is required for creating an index.

Each Exchange server has its own indexing priority setting. You can view or change the indexing priority by completing the following steps:

1. In System Manager, access the Servers node within the administrative or routing group you want to manage. Typically, you would expand Administrative Groups, then First Administrative Group, and then the Servers node.

2. Right-click the Exchange server you want to manage, and then select Properties from the shortcut menu.

3. As shown in Figure 9-3, use the System Resource Usage drop-down list on the Full-Text Indexing tab to set the indexing priority. The available values are as follows:

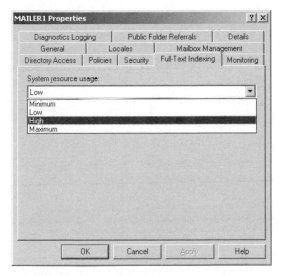

Figure 9-3. *Use the Full-Text Indexing tab to control the amount of system resource usage required for indexing.*

- **Minimum**   Sets the indexing priority to its lowest value, which has the least impact on system resources. The downside is that this setting requires the most time to index and reindex content.

- **Low**   Sets the indexing priority to low. This reduces the impact on system resources while maintaining a fairly adequate indexing speed.

- **High**   Sets the indexing priority to high, which has modest impact on system resources while achieving good indexing speed. This setting is the default.

- **Maximum**   Sets the indexing priority to its highest value. Although this greatly increases the impact on system resources, Exchange Server is able to index and reindex content in much less time.

4. Click OK.

Creating Full-Text Indexes

You can create full-text indexes for both mailbox stores and public folder stores. With mailbox stores, the full-text index is based on all text in message bodies and message attachments. With public folders, the full-text index is based on all text in postings and attachments to postings. Data in personal folders isn't included in the full-text index generated by Exchange Server.

You can create a full-text index for a mailbox or public folder store by completing the following steps:

1. In System Manager, work your way down to the storage group that contains the mailbox or public folder store you want to work with. Typically, you would do this by expanding the server node and then the storage group node.

2. Right-click the mailbox or public folder store that you want to index, and then select Create Full-Text Index from the shortcut menu.

3. Type the folder location for the index files. If the folder location doesn't exist, Exchange Server will create the folder.

4. When you click OK, Exchange Server creates the index. The index will be about one-fifth of the size of the original data store, so you'll need to use a folder on a drive with plenty of free space.

 Tip By default, Exchange Server will not update or rebuild the full-text index. You'll need to do this manually or set a maintenance schedule. For better performance, you might want to use a separate drive for storing your indexes.

Updating and Rebuilding Indexes Manually

You can update or rebuild an index manually at any time. Exchange Server updates an index by making note of any changes to the data store and then indexing those changes. Exchange Server rebuilds an index by re-creating it. This means that Exchange Server takes a new snapshot of the database and uses this snapshot to build the index from scratch.

To manually update or rebuild an index, follow these steps:

1. In System Manager, work your way down to the storage group that contains the mailbox or public folder store you want to work with. Typically, you would do this by expanding the server node and then the storage group node.

2. Right-click the mailbox or public folder store that you want to work with.

3. To update an existing index, select Start Incremental Population. (This option is also available on the All Tasks shortcut menu.) Confirm the action by clicking Yes.

4. To rebuild an index, select Start Full Population. (This option is also available on the All Tasks shortcut menu.) Confirm the action by clicking Yes.

Pausing, Resuming, and Stopping Indexing

During the updating or rebuilding process, you can pause or stop the indexing. A key reason to pause the process is to allow Exchange Server to perform other tasks. A key reason to stop indexing is to postpone the update or rebuild.

You can pause and then resume in-process indexing by completing the following steps:

1. In System Manager, work your way down to the storage group that contains the mailbox or public folder store you want to work with. Typically, you would do this by expanding the server node and then the storage group node.

2. Right-click a mailbox or public folder store that is actively being indexed and select Pause Population. (This option is also available on the All Tasks shortcut menu.)

3. When you're ready to resume indexing the population, right-click the mailbox or public folder store, and then select Resume Population.

To stop in-process indexing, complete these steps:

1. In System Manager, work your way down to the storage group that contains the mailbox or public folder store you want to work with. Typically, you would do this by expanding the server node and then the storage group node.

2. Right-click a mailbox or public folder store that is in the process of full-text indexing, and select Stop Population. (This option is also available on the All Tasks shortcut menu.)

3. Confirm the action by clicking Yes.

Scheduling Index Updating and Allowing Index Searching

You can configure Exchange Server to automatically update full-text indexes and to allow clients, such as Outlook users, to search the indexes. You configure these processes separately for each data store by completing these steps:

1. In System Manager, work your way down to the storage group that contains the mailbox or public folder store you want to work with. Typically, you would do this by expanding the server node and then the storage group node.

2. Right-click a mailbox or public folder store that you want to configure and then select Properties. In the Properties dialog box, click the Full-Text Indexing tab, as shown in Figure 9-4.

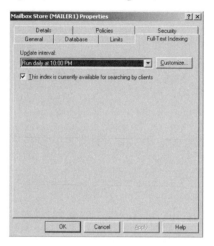

Figure 9-4. *Use the Full-Text Indexing tab to schedule index updating and rebuilding to occur at a specific time or according to a custom schedule.*

3. Use the Update Interval drop-down list to choose how often the indexes should be updated.

   • Usually, you will want to update the index daily at a specific time rather than updating the index every hour or continuously as changes are made. With this in mind, you could select one of the run daily options, such as Run Daily At 1:00 AM.

   • If you want to set a custom schedule, click Customize. You can then use the Schedule dialog box to set the times when Exchange Server should make updates. In this dialog box, you can set the detail of the view to be in hourly or 15-minute intervals. Each hour or 15-minute interval of the day or night is a field that you can turn on and off. Intervals where updates should occur are filled in with a dark bar—you can think of these intervals as being turned on. Intervals where updates shouldn't occur are blank—you can think of these intervals as being turned off. To change the setting for an interval, click it to toggle its mode (either on or off).

4. Select the This Index Is Currently Available For Searching By Clients check box, and then click OK.

Enabling and Disabling Client Access to Indexes

If you've configured full-text indexing and users are still unable to search on text in a data store, you might have a corrupt index. In this case, you might want to disable the index, rebuild it during off-peak hours, and then make the index available to users again. You can do this by completing the following steps:

1. In System Manager, work your way down to the storage group that contains the mailbox or public folder store you want to work with. Typically, you would do this by expanding the server node and then the storage group node.

2. Right-click a mailbox or public folder store that you want to configure, and then select Properties. In the Properties dialog box, click the Full-Text Indexing tab.

3. Set the Update Interval selection menu to Never Run.

4. Clear the This Index Is Currently Available For Searching By Clients check box.

5. Click OK. After the index is rebuilt, restore the data store properties to their original settings.

Checking Indexing Statistics

Exchange Server 2003 tracks fairly detailed information on each full-text index. You can access and use this information by completing the following steps:

1. In System Manager, work your way down to the storage group that contains the mailbox or public folder store you want to work with. Typically, you would do this by expanding the server node and then the storage group node.

2. Click the plus sign (+) next to the mailbox or public folder store on which you want to view indexing statistics, and then select the Full-Text Indexing node.

3. In the right pane, you should see the following indexing statistics:

    - **Index State**   The full-text indexing status for the data store. States you could see include: Idle (the data store isn't being indexed), Crawling (Exchange Server is actively indexing the data store), and Paused (the indexing has been paused by an administrator).

    - **Number Of Documents Indexed**   The total number of documents indexed.

    - **Index Size (MB)**   The size of the index in megabytes.

Tip If the number of documents indexed or the index size seems inaccurate, you might have a corrupt index. To resolve this, rebuild the index.

- **Last Build Time** The date and time stamp for the last manual or automatic build of the index. If no index exists, you'll see the message "There is no full-text index for this store." If the index is newly created and hasn't been updated or rebuilt, you'll see the message "This catalog was never built."
- **Index Name** The name of the index. You'll find a folder with this name at the location specified by Index Location. All index files within this folder begin with this identifier as well.
- **Index Location** The folder location of the index files.

Changing the Index File Location

Once you've started full-text indexing, Exchange Server doesn't allow you to change the index file location. A workaround is to stop indexing, delete the full-text index on the data store, and then re-create the index in a new location.

Deleting Indexes and Stopping Indexing Permanently

To delete indexes and stop data store indexing, complete the following steps:

1. In System Manager, work your way down to the storage group that contains the mailbox or public folder store you want to work with. Typically, you would do this by expanding the server node and then the storage group node.

2. Right-click a mailbox or public folder store that is currently being indexed, and select Delete Full-Text Index. (This option is also available on the All Tasks shortcut menu.)

3. Confirm the action by clicking Yes.

When you delete the full-text index for a data store, you remove the index catalog files and stop indexing. No scheduled updates or rebuilds will be made afterward.

Chapter 10

Mailbox and Public Folder Store Administration

Data stores are containers for information. Microsoft Exchange Server 2003 uses two types of data stores: *mailbox stores*, which store a server's mailboxes, and *public folder stores*, which store a server's public folders. The information in a particular data store isn't exclusive to either mailboxes or public folders. Exchange Server maintains related information within data stores as well. Within mailbox stores, you'll find information about Exchange logons and mailbox usage. Within public folder stores, you'll find information about Exchange logons, public folder instances, and replication. Mailbox and public folder stores also maintain information about full-text indexing. Understanding how to manage data stores and the information they contain is the subject of this chapter.

Using Mailbox Stores

Each Exchange server installed in the organization has an information store. The information store can hold multiple storage groups, and you can create multiple mailbox stores within those storage groups. Each mailbox store has database files associated with it. These files are stored in a location that you specify when you create or modify the mailbox store.

Understanding Mailbox Stores

Mailboxes are the delivery location for messages coming into an organization. Mailboxes contain messages, message attachments, and other types of information that the user might have placed in the mailbox. Mailboxes are in turn stored in mailbox stores.

A default mailbox store is created on each Exchange server in the organization. The default mailbox store is meant to be a starting point, and most Exchange organizations can benefit from having additional mailbox stores, especially as the number of users in the organization grows. There are many reasons for creating additional mailbox stores, but the key reasons are the following:

- To provide a smaller unit of recovery in case of failure. Each mailbox store has its own database, which is backed up as part of a storage group. During recovery, you can restore the entire storage group or individual data stores within the storage group. By restoring only a specific mailbox store, you reduce the impact on the user community.

*   To impose a different set of mailbox rules on different sets of users. Each additional mailbox store can have its own property settings for maintenance, storage limits, deleted item retention, indexing, security, and policies. By placing a user's mailbox in one mailbox store instead of another, you can apply a different set of rules.

*   To optimize Exchange performance. Each mailbox store can have its own storage location. By placing the mailbox stores on different drives, you can improve the performance of Exchange Server 2003.

*   To create separate mailbox stores for different purposes. For example, you might want to create a mailbox store called General In-Out to handle all general-purpose mailboxes being used throughout the organization. These general-purpose mailboxes could be set up for Postmaster, Webmaster, Technical Support, Customer Support, and other key functions.

When you create a mailbox store, you specify the following information:

*   What the name of the store should be
*   Where the store's database files are to be located
*   When maintenance on the store should occur
*   What limitations there are on mailbox size
*   Whether deleted items and mailboxes should be retained

You must also specify which default public folder store to use. Each Exchange server in the organization has a default public folder store that refers to the All Public Folders tree. The All Public Folders tree is the only public folder tree accessible to Messaging Application Programming Interface (MAPI) clients, such as Microsoft Outlook 2003, as well as to Microsoft Windows applications and browsers. You can use the organization's default (which I call the public root store) or specify that an alternative public folder store be used as the default. The disadvantage of using an alternative public folder store is that it isn't accessible to MAPI clients.

Creating Mailbox Stores

You can create a mailbox store by completing the following steps:

1. In System Manager, select the Exchange server you want to manage.
2. Right-click the storage group to which you want to add the mailbox store, point to New, and then click Mailbox Store.
3. You should now see the Properties dialog box shown in Figure 10-1. In the Name field, type a name for the mailbox store.

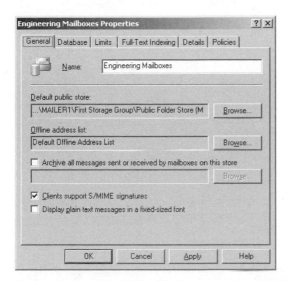

Figure 10-1. *Set the messaging properties for the new mailbox store on the General tab.*

4. Click the Database tab, as shown in Figure 10-2. You'll see the default location for the Exchange database and the Exchange streaming database. If you want to change the location of the database files, use the Browse buttons to the right of the related fields to set new file locations.

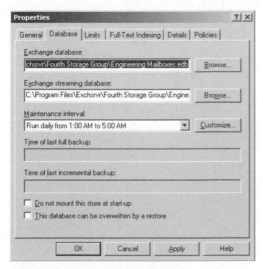

Figure 10-2. *Use the Database tab to set database file and maintenance options for the mailbox store.*

5. Changes made to Exchange database files can cause the files to become inconsistent over time. To correct problems that might arise, Exchange Server runs maintenance tasks on the database daily from 1:00 A.M. to 5:00 A.M. by default. If necessary, click Customize and use the Schedule grid to choose a different maintenance time.

6. Click the Limits tab, as shown in Figure 10-3. Use the following options to set storage limits and deleted item retention:

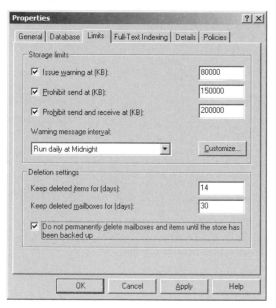

Figure 10-3. *Use the Limits tab to set storage limits and deleted item retention for individual mailboxes and entire mailbox stores.*

- **Issue Warning At (KB)** Sets the size limit, in kilobytes, that a mailbox can reach before a warning is issued to the user. The warning tells the user to clear out the mailbox.

- **Prohibit Send At (KB)** Sets the size limit, in kilobytes, that a mailbox can reach before the user is prohibited from sending any new mail. The restriction ends when the user clears out the mailbox and the total mailbox size is under the limit.

- **Prohibit Send And Receive At (KB)** Sets the size limit, in kilobytes, that a mailbox can reach before the user is prohibited from sending and receiving mail. The restriction ends when the user clears out the mailbox and the total mailbox size is under the limit.

Caution Prohibiting send and receive might cause users to lose e-mail. When a user sends a message to a user who is prohibited from receiving messages, a nondelivery report (NDR) is generated and delivered to the sender. The recipient never sees the e-mail. Because of this, you should prohibit send and receive only in very rare circumstances.

- **Warning Message Interval** Sets the interval for sending warning messages to users whose mailboxes exceed the designated limits. The default interval is daily at midnight.

- **Keep Deleted Items For (Days)** Sets the number of days to retain deleted items. An average retention period is 14 days. If you set the retention period to 0, deleted messages aren't retained, and you can't recover them.

- **Keep Deleted Mailboxes For (Days)** Sets the number of days to retain deleted mailboxes. The default setting is 30 days. You'll want to keep most deleted mailboxes for at least 7 days to allow the administrators to extract any data that might be needed. If you set the retention period to 0, deleted mailboxes aren't retained, and you can't recover them.

- **Do Not Permanently Delete Mailboxes And Items Until The Store Has Been Backed Up** Ensures that deleted mailboxes and items are archived into at least one backup set before they are removed.

7. Click OK. Exchange Server creates the new mailbox store. When prompted, click Yes to mount the store. By mounting the store, you make it available for use.

Setting the Default Public Store, Offline Address List, and Other Messaging Options

Mailbox stores have different types of information associated with them, including a default public store and a default offline address list. You set these and other messaging options for mailbox stores using the General tab of the related Properties dialog box. To view this dialog box and update the messaging options, follow these steps:

1. In System Manager, right-click the mailbox store and then select Properties. You should see the Properties dialog box with the General tab selected by default.

Note If you can't update the fields on the General tab, it means that a policy has been applied to the mailbox store. You must directly edit or remove the policy and then make the necessary changes.

2. The Default Public Store field shows the full path to the public folder store that the mailbox store is using. If you've created additional public folder trees or made changes to the public folder stores, you might want to change the default public folder store as well. In this case, click Browse, select the public folder store that points to the public folder tree that you want to use, and then click OK.

Caution   The public folder tree used by default is the one that points to the All Public Folders tree. The All Public Folders tree is the only public folder tree accessible to MAPI clients such as Outlook 2000. If you specify an alternative public folder tree, the tree you specify might not be accessible to some users.

3. The Offline Address List field shows the offline address list for the mailbox store. Offline address lists contain information on mail-enabled users, contacts, and groups in the organization and are used when users aren't connected to the network. If you've created additional address lists beyond the global default, you can specify one of these additional address lists as the default for the mailbox store. Click Browse, select the address list you want to use, and then click OK.

4. You can create archives for all messages sent to a mailbox store. The archive is stored in a designated container (mailbox), which can belong to an end user. To start the archive process, select Archive All Messages Sent Or Received By Mailboxes On This Store and then click the related Browse button. Then select the container in which the archive should be created and click OK.

Tip   For a general-purpose mailbox store, archiving messages makes a lot of sense. You can then maintain the message archives for historical tracking and for later reference. For mailbox stores being used by end users, archiving messages usually isn't a good choice. Few users want their day-to-day messages to be archived where they could be searched and scrutinized.

5. The next two options have to do with the preferences of users whose mailboxes are placed in the mailbox store. If the users have clients that support Secure/Multipurpose Internet Mail Extensions (S/MIME), select Clients Support S/MIME Signatures. If the users prefer to see plain-text messages in a fixed-width font such as Courier, select Display Plain Text Messages In A Fixed-Sized Font.

6. Click OK to apply the changes.

Setting Mailbox Store Limits

Mailbox store limits are designed to control the amount of information that users can store in their mailboxes. Users who exceed the designated limits might receive warning messages and might be subject to certain restrictions, such as the inability to send messages.

To view or set limits on a mailbox store, right-click the mailbox store in System Manager and then select Properties. You'll see a Properties dialog box. Use the options on the Limits tab to set mailbox store limits as described in Step 6 of the section of this chapter entitled "Creating Mailbox Stores."

Setting Deleted Item Retention

Deleted item retention is designed to ensure that messages and mailboxes that might be needed in the future aren't permanently deleted. If retention is turned on, you can retain deleted messages and mailboxes for a specified period of time before they are permanently deleted and nonrecoverable.

An average retention period for messages is about 14 days, and the minimum retention period for mailboxes should be 7 days. In most cases you'll want deleted messages to be maintained for 5 to 7 days and deleted mailboxes to be maintained for 3 to 4 weeks. A 5- to 7-day interval is used for messages because users usually realize that they shouldn't have deleted a message within a few days. A 3- to 4-week interval is used for mailboxes because several weeks can (and often do) pass before users realize that they need a deleted mailbox. To understand why, consider the following scenario.

Sally leaves the company. A coworker gives the go-ahead to delete Sally's user account and mailbox. Three weeks later, Sally's boss realizes that she was the only person who received and archived the monthly reports e-mailed from corporate headquarters. The only way to get reports for previous years is to recover Sally's mailbox.

To view or set deleted item retention for a mailbox store, follow these steps:

1. Right-click the mailbox store in System Manager and then select Properties.
2. In the Properties dialog box, click the Limits tab and then change the settings for Keep Deleted Items For (Days) and Keep Deleted Mailboxes For (Days).
3. You can also specify that deleted items and mailboxes shouldn't be permanently deleted until the store has been backed up.

Recovering Deleted Mailboxes

The deleted mailbox retention interval determines the number of days you have to recover deleted mailboxes. As long as you're within the interval, you can recover deleted mailboxes. To recover multiple deleted mailboxes, you'll want to use the Mailbox Recovery Center as discussed in the section of this chapter entitled, "Using Mailbox Recovery Center." The Mailbox Recovery Center also lets you export mailbox property information.

To recover a single deleted mailbox, complete the following steps:

1. In System Manager, select the Exchange server you want to manage and then click the plus sign (+) next to the storage group you want to work with.

2. You should see a list of available data stores. Click the plus sign (+) next to the mailbox store you want to work with, and then select Mailboxes.

3. Deleted mailboxes are displayed with a mailbox icon and a red X. Right-click the deleted mailbox you want to recover, and then select Reconnect.

4. Use the Select A New User For This Mailbox dialog box to select the user who should be assigned this mailbox. Click OK.

 Note Deleted mailboxes aren't marked as such immediately, and it may take 15 minutes to an hour before the mailbox is marked as deleted, during which time the mailbox is displayed normally, but you will not be able to do anything to it. In addition, you can't assign the mailbox to a user who already has a mailbox. That's why users who already have a mailbox aren't listed in the Select A New User For This Mailbox dialog box.

Deleting a User's Mailbox Permanently

You delete a user's mailbox by following the steps listed in the section of Chapter 6, "Mailbox Administration," entitled "Removing Mailboxes from User Accounts." If you've set a deleted mailbox retention interval, however, the mailbox isn't permanently deleted. To permanently delete the mailbox, either you must wait for the mailbox retention period to expire or you must manually purge the mailbox from the mailbox store.

You manually purge a mailbox from the mailbox store by completing the following steps:

1. In System Manager, select the Exchange server you want to manage and then click the plus sign (+) next to the storage group you want to work with.

2. You should see a list of available data stores. Click the plus sign (+) next to the mailbox store you want to work with and then select Mailboxes.

3. Deleted mailboxes are displayed with a mailbox icon and a red X. Right-click the deleted mailbox you want to permanently remove and then select Purge. When prompted to confirm the action, click Yes.

Recovering Deleted Items from Mailbox Stores

You can recover deleted items from mailbox stores as long as you've set a deleted item retention period for the data store from which the items were deleted and the retention period hasn't expired. If both of these are the case, you can recover deleted items from mailbox stores by completing the following steps:

1. Log on as the user who deleted the message and then start Outlook.

2. Click Deleted Items, and then select Recover Deleted Items from the Tools menu. You should now see the Recover Deleted Items From dialog box.

3. Select the items you want to recover, and then click Recover Selected Items.

Using Public Folder Stores

This section explains how to create public folder stores and set basic public folder store properties. It doesn't go into detail on managing the many facets of public folders. That topic is covered in Chapter 11, "Using and Replicating Public Folders."

Understanding Public Folder Stores

Public folders are used to share messages and files in an organization. You manage public folder stores much differently than mailbox stores. For starters, public folder stores must have a public folder tree associated with them. This public folder tree must be unique and can be assigned to a single public folder store only. Users access items that are stored in public folders through the public folder tree.

Each Exchange server in your organization has a default public folder store. I refer to this store as the public root store.

Mailbox stores should point to the public root store. If the mailbox stores don't point to it, the public folder tree will be inaccessible to a user's mail client. The reason for this is that the public root store contains the All Public Folders tree, which is the only public folder tree accessible to MAPI mail clients such as Microsoft Office Outlook 2003. Only compliant Web browsers and Windows applications can access other public folder trees.

Working with public folders and public folders stores isn't as straightforward as working with mailboxes and mailbox stores, but that doesn't mean you should avoid creating additional public folder stores. On the contrary, you'll often need additional public folder stores. The following are some leading reasons for creating additional public folder stores:

- To share files and messages pertaining to projects. For example, you could create a public folder store called Project Store. Project managers could then create folders for individual projects in the related public folder tree. Project members could share information by posting messages and files to a particular project folder.

- To share files and messages within a department or business unit. For example, you could create a public folder store called Group Store. Department managers could then create folders for each business unit and the members of these business units could share information by posting messages and files to a folder.

- To impose different sets of rules on different sets of users. Each additional public folder store can have its own property settings for maintenance, storage limits, deleted item retention, indexing, security, and policies.

- To help optimize Exchange performance. Each public folder store can have its own storage location. By placing the public folder stores on different drives, you can improve the overall performance of Exchange Server 2003.

Unlike mailbox stores, which are completely separate from one another, you can replicate public folder stores from one server to another. Replication allows users to access public data on multiple servers, which distributes the load and provides alternative data sources in case of server failure.

Creating Public Folder Stores

You can create a public folder store by completing the following steps:

1. In System Manager, select the Exchange server you want to manage.
2. Right-click the storage group to which you want to add the public folder store, point to New, and then click Public Store.
3. If a public folder tree isn't available for use, you'll see the dialog box shown in Figure 10-4. Before you can continue, you'll need to create a public folder tree as described in the section of Chapter 11 entitled "Creating Public Folder Trees."

Figure 10-4. *To create a public folder store, a public folder tree must be available for use. If one isn't available, you'll need to create it.*

4. You should now see the Properties dialog box shown in Figure 10-5. Type a name for the public folder store in the Name field.
5. Click Browse to the right of the Associated Public Folder Tree field, and then use the Select A Public Folder Tree dialog box to associate a public folder tree with the public folder store.
6. Click the Database tab. You'll see the default location for the Exchange database and the Exchange streaming database. If you want to change the location of the database files, use the Browse buttons to the right of the related fields to set new file locations.
7. Changes made to Exchange database files can cause the files to become inconsistent over time. By default, Exchange Server runs maintenance tasks against the database daily between 1:00 A.M. and 5:00 A.M. If necessary, click Customize and use the Schedule grid to choose a different maintenance schedule.

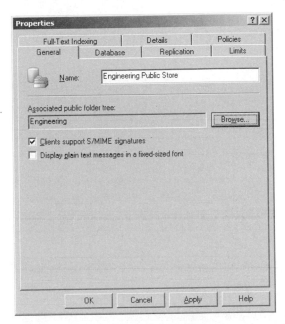

Figure 10-5. *To create a public folder store, name the store and then associate it to a public folder tree.*

8. As Figure 10-6 shows, you use the Replication tab to set replication intervals and limits for all folders in the public folder store. The available options are as follows:

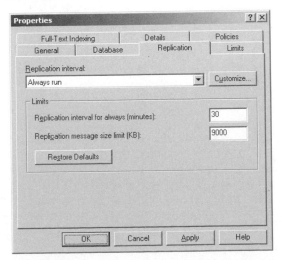

Figure 10-6. *Set replication options using the Replication tab.*

- **Replication Interval** Determines when changes to public folders are replicated. Select a specific time (Always Run, Run Every Hour, Run Every 2 Hours, Run Every 4 Hours, or Never Run) or Use Custom Schedule.

- **Replication Interval For Always (Minutes)** Sets the interval (in minutes) that's used when you select Always Run as the replication option. The default is 15 minutes.

- **Replication Message Size Limit (KB)** Sets the size limit (in kilobytes) for messages that are replicated. Messages over the size limit aren't replicated. The default size limit is 300 KB.

 Note Chapter 11, "Using and Replicating Public Folders," covers public folder replication in detail. There you'll find complete information on replication and how it works.

9. Use the Limits tab to set storage limits and deleted item retention on a per-user basis. The available options are as follows:

- **Issue Warning At (KB)** Sets the size, in kilobytes, of the data that a user can post to the public store before a warning is issued to the user. The warning tells the user to clean out the public store.

- **Prohibit Post At (KB)** Sets the maximum size, in kilobytes, of the data that a user can post to the public store. The restriction ends when the total size of the user's data is under the limit.

- **Maximum Item Size (KB)** Sets the maximum size, in kilobytes, for postings to the data store.

- **Warning Message Interval** Sets the interval for sending warning messages to users whose total data size exceeds the designated limits. The default interval is daily at midnight.

- **Keep Deleted Items For (Days)** Sets the number of days to retain deleted items. An average retention period is 14 days. If you set the retention period to 0, deleted postings aren't retained, and you can't recover them.

- **Do Not Permanently Delete Items Until The Store Has Been Backed Up** Ensures that deleted items are archived into at least one backup set before they are removed.

- **Age Limit For All Folders In This Store (Days)** Sets the number of days to retain postings in the store. Postings older than the limit are automatically deleted.

 Caution If you set an age limit, be sure that all users who post to the public folder know about it. Otherwise, they'll be surprised when data is removed, and they could lose important work.

10. Click OK. Exchange Server creates the new public folder store. When prompted, click Yes to mount the store. By mounting the store, you make it available for use.

Setting Public Store Limits

Public store limits are designed to control the amount of information that users can post to public folders. As with mailbox stores, users who exceed the designated limits might receive warning messages and might be subject to certain restrictions, such as the inability to post messages.

To view or set limits on a public folder store, right-click the public folder store in System Manager, and then select Properties. Use the options on the Limits tab to set the limits as described in Step 9 of the section of this chapter entitled "Creating Public Folder Stores."

Setting Age Limits and Deleted Item Retention

Because public folders help users share messages, documents, and ideas, they're an important part of any Exchange organization. Over time, however, public folders can become cluttered, which reduces their usefulness. To reduce the clutter, you can set an age limit on items that are posted to public folders. Items that reach the age limit expire and are permanently removed from the public folder.

When you set the age limit, keep in mind the type of information stored in the related public folders. For example, if you have a public store for general discussion and file sharing, you might want the age limit to be a few weeks. However, if you have a public store for projects, you might want the age limit to extend throughout the life of the project, which could be months or years.

The age limit and the deleted item retention are two separate values. Deleted item retention is designed to ensure that postings and documents that could be needed in the future aren't permanently deleted. When retention is turned on, deleted items are retained for a specified period of time before they are permanently deleted and made nonrecoverable.

The age limit applies to deleted items as well. If a deleted item reaches the age limit, it's permanently deleted along with other items that have reached their age limit.

To set the age limit and deleted item retention for a public folder store, follow these steps:

1. Right-click the public folder store in System Manager and then select Properties.

2. In the Properties dialog box, click the Limits tab and then change the settings for Keep Deleted Items For (Days) and Age Limit For All Folders In This Store.

3. You might also want to specify that deleted items shouldn't be permanently deleted until the store has been backed up.

Recovering Deleted Items from Public Folder Stores

You can recover deleted items from public folder stores as long as you've set a deleted item retention period for the public folder store from which the items were deleted and the retention period for this data store hasn't expired. If both of these conditions are met, you can recover deleted items by completing the following steps:

1. Log on to the domain using either an account with administrative privileges in the domain or an account with full control over the public folder from which you need to recover items.

2. After starting Outlook, access the Public Folders node and then select the public folder from which you need to recover an item.

3. Select Recover Deleted Items from the Tools menu. You should now see the Recover Deleted Items From dialog box.

4. Select the items you want to recover and then click Recover Selected Items.

Managing Data Stores

Now that you know how to create and use data stores, let's look at some general techniques you'll use to manage data stores.

Viewing and Understanding Logons

The information store tracks logons to mailbox and public folder stores. You can use this information to view a wide range of activity in the data store.

To view logon information, follow these steps:

1. In System Manager, select the Exchange server you want to manage and then click the plus sign (+) next to the storage group you want to work with.

2. You should see a list of available data stores. Click the plus sign (+) next to the data store you want to examine and then select Logons.

3. As Figure 10-7 shows, information about all logons to the store is displayed in the Details pane. The default view provides basic logon information such as the user name, the related Windows account, the logon time, the last access time, and the client version.

To get more detailed logon information, you can customize the logon view. Right-click Logons, point to View, and then click Add/Remove Columns. Next, use the Add/Remove Columns dialog box to add or remove columns from the view. Table 10-1 provides a summary of the available columns. Use the extra information provided to help you track logons and related data store activity.

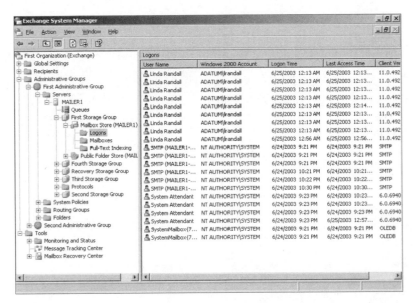

Figure 10-7. *The Logons node provides summary information for all logon activity in the data store.*

Table 10-1.   Understanding the Column Headings in the Logon Details

Column Name	Description
Adapter Speed	The speed of the network adapter with which the user connected in Mbps, such as 100000 for 100 Mbps connection.
Client IP Address	The IP address of the client, such as 192.168.1.202.
Client Mode	The connection mode used by the client. Access mode zero (0) is used for the system attendant and access mode 2 is used for access with an e-mail client, such as Outlook 2003.
Client Name	The DNS name of the computer used to connect to Exchange, such as gandolf.adatum.com.
Client Version	The version of the client that was used to log on.
Code Page	The code page that the client was using, such as 1252.
Folder Ops	The total number of folder operations performed in the last 60 seconds. Operations tracked include opening, closing, and renaming folders.
Full Mailbox Directory Name	The complete path string for the user's mailbox in Active Directory.
Full User Directory Name	The complete path string for the related user object in Active Directory.

(continued)

Table 10-1. **Understanding the Column Headings in the Logon Details** *(continued)*

Column Name	Description
Host Address	The server host used with the connection. IIS-HTTPDAV means the user connected using Outlook Web Access, ie they made a WebDAV connection over HTTP to IIS.
Last Access Time	The date and time the user last accessed the mailbox store.
Latency	The delay between when a request is made and the time it's received in milliseconds. Generally speaking the latency experienced by the user is out of your hands. However, a high degree of latency could explain why e-mail seems slow for the user.
Locale ID	The locale ID for the language the client is using.
Logon Time	The date and time that the user last logged on.
MAC Address	The machine address of the user's computer.
Messaging Ops	The total number of messaging operations performed in the last 60 seconds. Operations tracked include opening, closing, and deleting messages.
Open Attachments	The total number of open attachments.
Open Folders	The total number of open folders.
Open Messages	The total number of open messages.
Other Ops	The total number of miscellaneous operations performed in the last 60 seconds.
Progress Ops	The total number of progress operations performed in the last 60 seconds. Progress operations tell users how long it takes to complete a task.
RPC Calls Succeeded	The number of remote procedure calls that succeeded.
Stream Ops	The total number of stream operations performed in the last 60 seconds. Operations tracked include changing and deleting attachments.
Table Ops	The total number of table operations performed in the last 60 seconds. Operations tracked include displaying folder contents and expanding public folder tree views.
Total Ops	The total number of operations performed in the last 60 seconds.
Transfer Ops	The total number of transfer operations performed in the last 60 seconds. Operations tracked include copying and moving messages.
User Name	The full name of the user who last logged on, such as William R. Stanek.
Windows 2000 Account	The Windows account name of the user who last logged on, such as DEV\williams.

Typically, you'll use custom views to help you understand the level of activity in a particular data store. Generally, you're most interested in seeing this information:

- Who accessed the store
- Which IP addresses were used
- The last access time
- How many messages and attachments are open
- The total number of operations performed in the last 60 seconds

A custom view to provide this information would include these columns:

- User Name
- Client IP/Client Name
- Last Access Time
- Open Messages
- Open Attachments
- Open Folders
- Total Ops

Viewing and Understanding Mailbox Summaries

Just as you can view information about logons, you can also view information about mailboxes. The available information tells you the following:

- How many messages are stored in a mailbox
- How much space the mailbox is using
- Whether the mailbox has deleted items that are being retained
- How long items have been deleted
- Whether the mailbox is subject to storage limits
- Who the last user to log on to the mailbox was

You can view mailbox summaries by completing the following steps:

1. In System Manager, select the Exchange server you want to manage and then click the plus sign (+) next to the storage group you want to work with.

2. You should see a list of available data stores. Click the plus sign (+) next to the mailbox store you want to examine and then select Mailboxes.

3. As Figure 10-8 shows, mailbox summaries should now be displayed in the Details pane. The default view provides basic mailbox information such as the mailbox name, the last user account to log on to the mailbox, the mailbox size, and the total number of items in the mailbox.

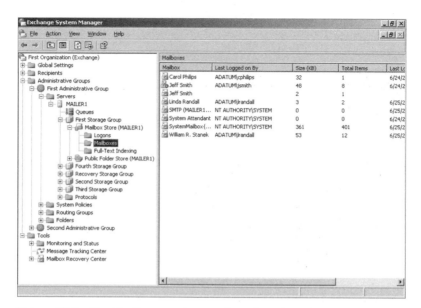

Figure 10-8. *The Mailboxes node provides information that can help you track mailbox usage.*

To get more detailed mailbox information, you can customize the mailbox view. Right-click Mailboxes, point to View, and then click Add/Remove Columns. Next, use the Add/Remove Columns dialog box to add or remove columns from the view. Table 10-2 provides a summary of the available columns. Use the extra information provided to help you track mailbox activity.

Table 10-2.   Understanding the Column Headings in the Mailbox Details

Column Name	Description
Deleted Items (KB)	The total amount of disk space, in kilobytes, occupied by deleted items that are being retained for the mailbox
Disconnect Time	The date and time at which Exchange Server detected the deletion of the user account for this mailbox
Full Mailbox Directory Name	The complete Active Directory path string for the specified mailbox
Last Logged On By	The account name of the user who last logged on to the mailbox
Last Logoff Time	The time that a user last logged off this mailbox
Last Logon Time	The time that a user last logged on to this mailbox

Table 10-2.   Understanding the Column Headings in the Mailbox Details

Column Name	Description
Mailbox	The mailbox name
Size (KB)	The total amount of disk space, in kilobytes, that a mailbox occupies
Storage Limits	Specifies whether a mailbox is subject to storage limits
Total Associ-ated Messages	Total number of system messages, views, rules, and so on, associated with the mailbox.
Total Items	Total number of messages, files, and postings that are stored in the mailbox.

Mounting and Dismounting Data Stores

You can access only data stores that are mounted. If a store isn't mounted, the store isn't available for use. This means that an administrator has probably dismounted the store or that the drive on which the store is located isn't online.

Real World   Dismounted stores could also point to problems with the database files used by the store. During startup, Exchange Server 2003 obtains a list of database files registered in Active Directory and then checks for the database files before mounting each store. If files are missing or corrupted, Exchange Server 2003 will not be able to mount the store. Exchange Server 2003 then generates an error and logs it in the application event log on the Exchange server. The most common error is Event ID 9547. An example of this error follows:

```
The Active Directory indicates that the database file
D:\Exchsrvr\mdbdata\Marketing.edb exists for the Microsoft
Exchange Database /o=My Organization/ou=First Administra
tive Group/cn=Configuration/cn=Servers/cn=MAILER2/
cn=Marketing, however no such files exist on the disk.
```

This error tells you that the Exchange database (Marketing.edb) is registered in Active Directory but Exchange Server 2003 is unable to find the file on the disk. When Exchange Server 2003 attempts to start the corrupted mailbox store, you'll see an additional error as well. The most common error is Event ID 9519. An example of this error follows:

```
Error 0xfffffb4d starting database First Storage
Group\Marketing on the Microsoft Exchange Information
Store.
```

This error tells you that Exchange Server 2003 couldn't start the Marketing database. To recover the mailbox store, you must restore the database files as discussed in Chapter 12, "Backing Up and Restoring Microsoft Exchange Server 2003," under "Recovering Exchange Server." If you are unable to restore the database files, you can re-create the store structures in System Manager by mounting the store. When you mount the store, Exchange Server 2003 creates new database files and as a result, all the data in the store is lost and cannot be recovered. Exchange Server 2003 displays a warning before mounting the store and re-creating the database files. Click Yes only when you are absolutely certain that you cannot recover the database.

Checking the Mount Status of Data Stores

To determine whether a store is mounted, follow these steps:

1. In System Manager, select the Exchange server you want to manage and then click the plus sign (+) next to the storage group you want to work with.

2. You should see a list of available data stores in the Details pane. The icon to the right of the data store name indicates the mount status. If the icon shows a red down arrow, the store isn't mounted.

Dismounting Data Stores

You should rarely dismount an active data store, but if you need to do so, follow these steps:

1. In System Manager, select the Exchange server you want to manage and then click the plus sign (+) next to the storage group you want to work with.

2. You should see a list of available data stores in the Details pane. The icon to the right of the data store name indicates the mount status. If the icon shows a red down arrow, the store is already dismounted.

3. Right-click the store you want to dismount, select Dismount Store, and then confirm the action by clicking Yes. Exchange Server dismounts the store. Users accessing the store will no longer be able to work with their server-based folders.

Mounting Data Stores

If you've dismounted a data store to perform maintenance or recovery, you can remount the store by completing the following steps:

1. In System Manager, select the Exchange server you want to manage and then click the plus sign (+) next to the storage group you want to work with.

2. You should see a list of available data stores in the Details pane. The icon to the right of the data store name indicates the mount status.

3. You should see a red down arrow indicating that the store isn't mounted. If so, right-click the store and then select Mount Store.

4. If Exchange Server is able to mount the store, you'll see a dialog box confirming that the store has been mounted. Click OK.

5. The new store isn't accessible to users that are currently logged on to Exchange server. Users need to exit and then restart Outlook before they can access the newly mounted store.

Specifying Whether a Store Should Be Automatically Mounted

Normally, Exchange Server automatically mounts stores on startup. You can, however, change this behavior. For example, if you're recovering Exchange server from a complete failure, you might not want to mount data stores until you've completed recovery. In this case you can disable automatic mounting of data stores.

To enable or disable automatic mounting of a data store, complete the following steps:

1. In System Manager, select the Exchange server you want to manage and then click the plus sign (+) next to the storage group you want to work with.

2. Right-click the data store you want to work with and then select Properties.

3. Click the Database tab in the Properties dialog box.

4. To ensure that a data store isn't mounted on startup, select the Do Not Mount This Store At Start-Up check box.

5. To mount the data store on startup, clear the Do Not Mount This Store At Start-Up check box.

6. Click OK.

Setting the Maintenance Interval

You should run maintenance routines against data stores on a daily basis. The maintenance routines organize the data store, clear out extra space, and perform other essential housekeeping tasks. By default, Exchange Server runs maintenance tasks daily from 1:00 A.M. to 5:00 A.M. If this conflicts with other activities on the Exchange server, you can change the maintenance schedule by following these steps:

1. In System Manager, select the Exchange server you want to manage and then click the plus sign (+) next to the storage group you want to work with.

2. Right-click the store you want to work with and then select Properties.

3. Click the Database tab in the Properties dialog box, and then use the Maintenance Interval drop-down menu to set a new maintenance time. Select a time (such as Run Daily From 11:00 P.M. To 3:00 A.M.) or Use Custom Schedule.

4. Click OK.

Tip If you want to set a custom schedule, choose Use Custom Schedule and then click Customize. You can now set the times when maintenance should occur.

Checking and Removing Applied Policies

You use mailbox and public folder policies to control settings for groups of data stores. When a policy applies to a property, the property is unavailable and you're unable to change its value in the data store's Properties dialog box. The only way you can change a policy-controlled property is to do the following:

- Edit the related policy.
- Remove the policy from the data store.

To determine whether a policy applies to a data store, follow these steps:

1. In System Manager, select the Exchange server you want to manage and then click the plus sign (+) next to the storage group you want to work with.
2. Right-click the store you want to work with and then select Properties.
3. Any policies that affect the data store are listed on the Policies tab. You can modify or delete the policy by following the techniques discussed in the sections of Chapter 8, "Implementing Directory Security and Microsoft Exchange Server 2003 Policies," entitled "Modifying System Policies" and "Deleting System Policies."

Renaming Data Stores

To rename a data store, follow these steps:

1. In System Manager, select the Exchange server you want to manage and then click the plus sign (+) next to the storage group you want to work with.
2. Right-click the data store, select Rename from the shortcut menu, and then type a new name for the storage group.

 Note All objects in Active Directory are located by a unique identifier. This identifier uses the directory namespace and works through each element in the directory hierarchy to a particular object. When you change the name of a data store, you change the namespace for all the objects in the data store.

Deleting Data Stores

Deleting a data store removes the data store and all the public folders or mailboxes it contains. Before you delete a data store, make sure that you no longer need the items it contains. If they are necessary, you should move them to a new data store. You move mailboxes as described in the section of Chapter 6, "Mailbox Administration," entitled "Moving Mailboxes to a New Server or Storage Group." You move public folders as described in the section of Chapter 11 entitled "Renaming, Copying, and Moving Public Folder Trees."

Once you've moved items that you might need, you can delete the data store by completing the following steps:

1. In System Manager, select the Exchange server you want to manage and then click the plus sign (+) next to the storage group you want to work with.

2. Right-click the data store you want to delete and then select Delete from the shortcut menu.

3. When prompted, confirm the action by clicking Yes.

Using Mailbox Recovery Center

Earlier in the chapter, I discussed how to recover an individual mailbox. Deleted, disconnected, or otherwise unavailable mailboxes can also be recovered using Mailbox Recovery Center. The advantage to using Mailbox Recovery Center is that you can perform recovery operations on multiple mailboxes at one time rather than recovering mailboxes individually. Mailbox Recovery Center also lets you export mailbox data. You can export mailbox properties to an Active Directory container, and you can export mailbox data to a file.

You'll find Mailbox Recovery Center under the Tools node in System Manager. Expand the Tools node and then click Mailbox Recovery Center. Before you can recover mailboxes, you must add the mailbox stores that you want to work with to the Mailbox Recovery Center's details view. You'll then be able to export mailbox property information or associate users with disconnected mailboxes so that you can make them available by reconnecting them. When you are finished working with the mailbox stores, you should remove them from the Mailbox Recovery Center. This ensures the mailbox stores aren't locked for recovery and are restored to normal operation status.

Adding Mailbox Stores to Mailbox Recovery Center

You must add the mailbox stores that you want to work with to the recovery center's details view. To do this, complete the following steps:

1. In System Manager, right-click Mailbox Recovery Center and then select Add Mailbox Store. Keep in mind that any mailbox store already added to Mailbox Recovery Center won't be available.

2. In the Add Mailbox Store(s) dialog box, type the name of the mailbox store you want to work with, such as Engineering Mailbox Store. You can enter multiple mailbox store names by separating each name with a semicolon. Click Check Names.

   - If multiple matching names are found, you'll see the Multiple Names Found dialog box shown in Figure 10-9. Select the mailbox store you want to work with. Press Shift or Ctrl to select multiple stores. Click OK to close the Multiple Names Found dialog box.

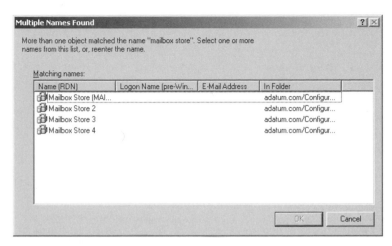

Figure 10-9. *If multiple mailbox stores match the name you entered, you'll be able to select the store or stores you want to work with. You can use Shift or Ctrl to select multiple stores.*

- If a matching name isn't found, you'll see the Name Not Found dialog box shown in Figure 10-10. Retype the mailbox store name and then click OK. If this doesn't work, you might need to change the directory location you are working with. Click Locations and then use the Locations dialog box to browse for the location to use.

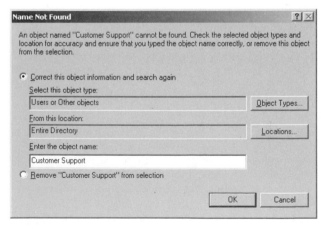

Figure 10-10. *If the mailbox store isn't found, try reentering the mailbox store name. If that doesn't work, check the directory location you are working with.*

3. Click OK to close the Add Mailbox Store(s) dialog box and add the selected mailbox stores to the recovery center. You can now export mailbox data, or associate users with disconnected mailboxes so that you can make them available by reconnecting them.

Working with Mailbox Recovery Center

Once you've added one or more mailbox stores to the recovery center, you'll see an overview of any deleted or disconnected mailboxes those mailbox stores contain as shown in Figure 10-11. The default view provides basic mailbox information, such as the mailbox name, the associated mailbox store, the full mailbox directory name, the date and time when the mailbox was disconnected, and the mailbox size.

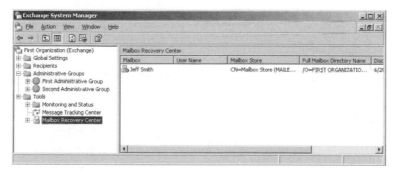

Figure 10-11. *Once you add mailbox stores, any deleted or disconnected mailboxes are listed in the Mailbox Recovery Center Details pane.*

To get more detailed recovery information, you can customize the view. Right-click Mailbox Recovery Center, point to View, and then click Add/Remove Columns. Next, use the Add/Remove Columns dialog box to add or remove columns from the view. Table 10-3 provides a summary of the available columns. Use the extra information provided to help you recover mailboxes.

Table 10-3.   Understanding the Column Headings in the Mailbox Recovery Center Details Pane

Column Name	Description
Deleted Items (KB)	The total amount of disk space, in kilobytes, occupied by deleted items that are being retained for the mailbox
Disconnect Time	The date and time at which Exchange Server detected the deletion of the user account for this mailbox
Full Mailbox Directory Name	The full directory path for the mailbox in the Active Directory data store
Last Logged On By	The account name of the user who last logged on to the mailbox
Last Logoff Time	The time that a user last logged off this mailbox

(continued)

Table 10-3. Understanding the Column Headings in the Mailbox Recovery Center Details Pane *(continued)*

Column Name	Description
Last Logon Time	The time that a user last logged on to this mailbox
Mailbox	The mailbox name
Mailbox GUID	The globally unique identifier (GUID) of the mailbox in Active Directory
Mailbox Store	The mailbox store that contains the deleted mailbox
Size (KB)	The total amount of disk space, in kilobytes, that a mailbox occupies
Storage Limits	Specifies whether a mailbox is subject to storage limits
Total Associated Messages	Total number of system messages, views, rules, and so on, associated with the mailbox
Total Items	Total number of messages, files, and postings that are stored in the mailbox

Exporting Mailbox Recovery Data

Mailbox Recovery Center lets you export mailbox recovery data, which includes information about the user account previously or currently associated with the mailbox. You can use that user account information to confirm mailbox associations. To recover mailbox data, follow these steps:

1. In System Manager, select the Mailbox Recovery Center node and then in the Details pane, right-click the mailbox you want to work with and select Export. You can select multiple mailboxes using Shift or Ctrl to select the mailboxes you want to work with and then right-clicking.

2. When the Exchange Mailbox Export Wizard starts, click Next.

3. Choose the Active Directory properties for the related user objects that you want to export (if any) and then click Next. The available properties include the following:

   - **userAccountControl**   The account control identifier
   - **MsExchUserAccountControl**   The Exchange account control identifier
   - **DisplayName**   The display name for the user account
   - **ObjectClass**   The object class, such as user
   - **SAMAccountName**   The System Account Manager (SAM) name associated with the mailbox. This is also referred to as the pre–Windows 2000 user logon name.

 Note   You don't have to export the data to Active Directory. In fact, if you aren't going to use the data in Active Directory, I don't recommend exporting it. Clear the property selections before continuing.

4. Click Browse and then use the Choose A Container dialog box to select the Active Directory container for the exported properties. Click OK and then click Next.

5. Specify the name of the export file for the mailbox data. The mailbox data is stored as an LDiff file with the extension .ldf. Click Browse to use the Export File dialog box to find a save location.

Note The LDiff file is stored as plain text and can be viewed with any standard text editor, including Notepad. If you open the file, you'll find that the information is easy to read and interpret.

6. If you want to append the data to an existing file without overwriting it, choose Append The Next Definitions. Otherwise, click Replace Existing Content.

7. Click Next and then click Finish.

Associating Users and Reconnecting Mailboxes

Recovering a disconnected mailbox is a multipart process. First you need to associate a user account with the mailbox by finding user accounts that are the best match for the mailbox. Matches are made using the mailbox properties, primarily, the SAM account name and the display name. When a user account is matched to a mailbox, there will be an entry in the User Name field. This entry specifies the Active Directory path for the related user object.

After you match the mailbox to a user account, you can attempt to reconnect the mailbox. Reconnecting the mailbox creates an association between the mailbox and the specified user account and makes the mailbox available for use. If there are problems reconnecting the mailbox, you can attempt to resolve and trouble-shoot any conflicts.

To associate users with mailboxes and then reconnect them, follow these steps:

1. In System Manager, select the Mailbox Recovery Center node and then in the Details pane, right-click the mailbox you want to work with and then select Find Match. You can select multiple mailboxes using Shift or Ctrl to select the mailboxes you want to work with and then right-clicking.

2. When the Exchange Mailbox Matching Wizard starts, click Next to show the results of the matching tasks. Note any conflicts that are detected and whether the matching operations complete successfully and then click Finish.

3. Select the mailboxes where the matching operation completed successfully, right-click, and then choose Reconnect to start the Exchange Mailbox Reconnect Wizard.

4. Click Next. Note the operations that will be performed and then click Next again.

5. Note the status of the operation and then click Finish. The reconnect operation should complete successfully and the red X for the mailboxes should no longer be displayed. If any conflicts or errors occurred during this procedure, you can attempt to resolve them as discussed in the section of this chapter entitled "Resolving Matching and Reconnection Conflicts."

Resolving Matching and Reconnection Conflicts

When you are attempting to match and reconnect mailboxes, the most common reason for a conflict is that there is no user account to match to the mailbox. This happens if the user account has been deleted. In this case, you can create a new account for the user in Active Directory Users And Computers, or associate the mailbox with a different user account using the Exchange Mailbox Conflict Resolution Wizard. If an error occurred while reconnecting a matched mailbox, you can also use the wizard to attempt to resolve the problem.

To resolve matching and reconnection conflicts, follow these steps:

1. In System Manager, select the Mailbox Recovery Center node and then in the Details pane, select any mailboxes for which conflicts occurred. Right-click and then choose Resolve Conflicts to start the Exchange Mailbox Conflict Resolution Wizard.

2. Click Next to see a list of user accounts that are possible matches. Select the account to use and then click Next. If the user account you want to use isn't shown, click Browse and then use the Select A Matching User For This Mailbox dialog box to choose a user account to associate with a particular mailbox.

3. Click Next and then click Finish.

 Note You won't be able to match a mailbox for a user that already has a mailbox. If you try, you'll get a warning that says "An object with the following name cannot be found." This is the same error you get when there is no match.

Removing Mailbox Stores from Mailbox Recovery Center

When you are finished working with the mailbox stores, you should remove them from Mailbox Recovery Center. This ensures the mailbox stores aren't locked for recovery and are restored to normal operation status. To remove mailbox stores from Mailbox Recovery Center, complete the following steps:

1. In System Manager, right-click Mailbox Recovery Center and then select Remove Mailbox Store.

2. In the Remove Mailbox Store(s) dialog box, type the name of the mailbox store you want to remove from the recovery center. You can enter multiple mailbox store names by separating each name with a semicolon. Click Check Names.

- If multiple matching names are found, you'll see the Multiple Names Found dialog box and be able to select the specific stores to remove.

- If a matching name isn't found, you'll see the Name Not Found dialog box and be able to retype the mailbox store name or change the directory location you are working with.

3. Click OK to close the Remove Mailbox Store(s) dialog box and remove the selected mailbox stores from the recovery center.

Chapter 11

Using and Replicating Public Folders

Public folders are one of the most underused and least understood aspects of Microsoft Exchange Server. Administrators often avoid using public folders because they think they're difficult to configure and impossible to manage, but nothing could be further from the truth. Public folders add great value to any Exchange organization, especially if users need to collaborate on projects or day-to-day tasks.

If you want to learn to use and replicate public folders, this chapter shows you how. Unleashing the power of public folders is what it's all about.

Making Sense of Public Folders and Public Folder Trees

Public folders are used to share files and messages within an organization. To maintain security, each public folder can have very specific usage rules. For example, you could create public folders called CompanyWide, Marketing, and Engineering. Whereas the CompanyWide folder would be accessible to all users, the Marketing folder would be accessible only to users in the marketing department and the Engineering folder would be accessible only to users in the engineering department.

Public folders are stored in a hierarchical structure referred to as a *public folder tree*. There is a direct correspondence between public folder trees and public folder stores. You can't create a public folder store without first creating a public folder tree, and users can access public folder trees only when they're part of a public folder store. The only public folder tree accessible to Messaging Application Programming Interface (MAPI) clients, such as Microsoft Office Outlook 2003, is the default public folder tree. You can access other public folder trees in compliant Web browsers and Microsoft Windows applications. You can also access public folders through the Exchange Information Store.

You can replicate public folders to multiple Exchange servers. These copies of folders, called *replicas*, provide redundancy in case of server failure and help to distribute the user load. All replicas of a public folder are equal. There is no master replica. This means that you can directly modify replicas of public folders. Folder changes are replicated automatically to other servers.

Public folder trees define the structure of an organization's public folders. Each tree has its own hierarchy, which you can make accessible to users based on criteria you set. Whereas public folder trees are replicated to all Exchange servers in the organization, folder contents are replicated only to designated servers that host replicas of public folder data. Two types of public folder trees are used with Exchange Server 2003:

- **Default** This tree, referred to as the MAPI Clients tree in System Manager, is the only tree accessible to MAPI clients. Each Exchange server in the organization has a default public folder store that points to this tree. In System Manager, the default name for this tree is Public Folders. In Outlook, you access this tree through the All Public Folders node.

- **Alternate** Alternate trees provide additional public folder hierarchies for the Exchange organization but are accessible only to compliant Web browsers and Windows applications. In System Manager, alternate trees are referred to as General Purpose trees. One way to access alternate trees is to use Microsoft Outlook Web Access.

Web browsers and other applications can remotely access public folder trees using Web Distributed Authoring and Versioning (WebDAV). Another way to access a public folder is to use the Exchange Information Store. The next section of this chapter explains how to access public folders using WebDAV and the Exchange Information Store.

Accessing Public Folders

Exchange Server 2003 makes it possible to access public folders just about anywhere. You can do the following:

- Access public folders through e-mail clients.
- Access public folders on the Web or the corporate intranet.
- Access public folders through the Information Store.

The following sections explain each of these techniques.

Accessing Public Folders in E-Mail Clients

You can access public folders from just about any e-mail client, provided the client is MAPI compliant. The recommended client is Outlook 2003. When Outlook 2003 is configured for Exchange Server, users have direct access to the Public Folders tree but not to alternate trees. When Outlook 2003 is configured for Internet-only use, users can access public folders only when their client is configured for IMAP.

If Outlook is configured properly, users can access public folders by completing the following steps:

1. Start Outlook 2003. If the Folder List isn't displayed, click Go, and then select Folder List.

2. In the Folder List, expand Public Folders and then expand All Public Folders to get a complete view of the available top-level folders. A top-level folder is simply a folder at the next level below the tree root.

Note Chapter 2, "Managing Microsoft Exchange Server 2003 Clients," discusses techniques you can use to configure Outlook. Refer to the section of that chapter entitled "Configuring Mail Support for Outlook 2003 and Outlook Express."

Accessing Public Folders from the Web

You use WebDAV to access public folders over the World Wide Web and the corporate intranet. WebDav is an extension to the Hypertext Transfer Protocol (HTTP). Using HTTP and WebDav, clients can create and manage public folders and the items they contain. One way to do this is to access a public folder through an HTTP virtual server hosted by Exchange Server 2003. Simply type the folder's Uniform Resource Locator (URL) into the browser's Address or Location field.

To access the public folder tree in a browser, type the URL **http://*servername*/public**, where *servername* is a placeholder for the HTTP virtual server hosted by Exchange Server 2003 and **public** is the default name of the Public Folders Web share. You can access alternate public folder trees through their Web share as well.

Exchange Server 2003 automatically configures Web sharing and access controls. You can check the configuration by completing the following steps:

1. In System Manager, expand the node for the Exchange server you want to manage and then expand the Protocols node for this server.

2. Expand HTTP and then expand Exchange Virtual Server.

3. You should now see a list of Web shares for the Exchange virtual server. Right-click Public, and then select Properties from the shortcut menu.

4. Click the Access tab, as shown in Figure 11-1. You can now check the access and application permissions for the share. By default, Exchange Server grants certain access permissions. To allow reading, writing, and directory browsing, you should make sure that these permissions are granted as well. The default permissions granted to the folder are the following:
   - Read
   - Write
   - Script Source Access
   - Directory Browsing

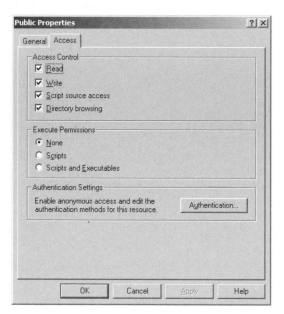

Figure 11-1. *Use the Access tab to check the configuration of the shared folder. If other administrators inadvertently changed settings, you should change the settings back to the defaults used by Exchange Server.*

5. Because all application permissions are denied, Application Permissions should be set to None.

Real World Most problems with Web sharing of public folders can be traced to individuals who inadvertently change the access settings. If you restore the original settings, users should regain access to the public folder. Note that only Exchange Server can initialize Web sharing for public folders. If Exchange Server isn't sharing public folders correctly, you might have incorrectly configured Microsoft Internet Information Services (IIS) or Outlook Web Access. For details on working with IIS and HTTP virtual servers, see Chapter 16, "Managing HTTP Virtual Servers for Web and Mobile Access Users."

Accessing Public Folders through the Information Store

Another way to access a public folder is to use the Exchange Information Store. The network path for the Exchange Information Store is \\.\BackOfficeStorage and you can work with folders within the Information Store in much the same way as you work with network shares.

The BackOfficeStorage path to the Exchange Information Store has the following basic features:

- A domain folder for each available domain
- A mailbox (MBX) folder that is the root for all mailboxes on the Exchange server
- A Public Folders folder that is the root of the default public folder tree

At a command prompt, you can examine the contents of the Information Store using the DIR command. For example, if you are working in the Adatum.com domain and want to see the contents of the Public Folders folder, you could type **dir "\\.\BackOfficeStorage\Adatum.com\Public Folders"**. The quotation marks are required because of the space in the folder name.

Note   In Exchange 2000, the Information Store was accessible using the M drive. The Information Store is no longer mapped to a drive. Virus checkers, backup software, or other programs that perform file-level checks on the M drive could cause corruption of the Exchange Information Store. If users need to access public folders in the Exchange store, they should use an e-mail client or the Web.

Creating and Managing Public Folder Trees

The sections that follow discuss key creation and management tasks for public folder trees. The only type of tree that you can create, change, or delete is an alternate tree. You can't create, change, or delete the default public folder tree. The default tree is created automatically when Exchange Server 2003 is installed and it is managed by Exchange Server 2003.

Creating Public Folder Trees

When you create a new public folder tree, Exchange Server creates an object in Active Directory that represents the tree. The directory object holds the properties and attributes of the tree and must be stored in a specific container. A default container is automatically created in the Exchange organization. If you want to use a different container, you must create the container before you create the public folder tree.

You need to create additional containers for public folder trees only when you use administrative groups. With administrative groups, each group that you create after the first group can have a public folders container. To create this container, follow these steps:

1. Start System Manager. Click Start, point to Programs, point to Microsoft Exchange, and then click System Manager.

2. Expand Administrative Groups, and then expand the group you want to work with. If the group already has a Folders node, a public folder tree has already been created and you can't create another. If the group doesn't have a Folders node, right-click the group, point to New, and then choose Public Folders Container.

3. You can now create public folder trees in the container.

To create a public folder tree, follow these steps:

1. Start System Manager. Click Start, point to Programs, point to Microsoft Exchange, and then click System Manager.

2. If administrative groups are displayed, expand Administrative Groups, and then expand the group you want to work with.

3. In the left pane (the console tree), right-click Folders, point to New, and then click Public Folder Tree.

4. Type a descriptive name for the public folder tree. To make the tree easier to access in Web browsers, don't use spaces in the tree name. Some browsers don't understand spaces, and users might have to type the escape code %20 instead of a space.

5. Click OK. To make the new tree available for use, create a public folder store that uses the tree. See the section of Chapter 10, "Mailbox and Public Folder Store Administration," entitled "Creating Public Folder Stores."

Once you've created a public folder tree and added it to a public folder store, authorized users can create subfolders within the tree that can be used to meet different collaboration requirements. These additional folders can contain other folders, items, and messages.

Designating Users Who Can Make Changes to Public Folder Trees

By default, all users can create folders in the public folder tree. To change these security settings and allow only specific users or groups to make changes, you'll need to perform the following tasks:

1. Use the procedures outlined in the section of Chapter 8, "Implementing Directory Security and Microsoft Exchange Server 2003 Policies," entitled "Setting Exchange Server Permissions" to designate users and groups who can do the following:

   • Create public folders

   • Create top-level public folders

   • Create named properties in the Information Store

2. Remove security permissions for the Everyone group

3. Confirm that the changes are appropriate by testing the security controls.

Renaming, Copying, and Moving Public Folder Trees

You can manipulate public folder trees in much the same way that you can manipulate other objects. To rename a public folder tree, follow these steps:

1. In System Manager, right-click the public folder tree you want to work with.
2. Select Rename, type a new name, and then press Enter.
3. If the tree is associated with a public folder store, Exchange Server needs to update all references to the tree. Click Yes when prompted to allow the update to occur.

To copy a public folder tree, follow these steps:

1. In System Manager, right-click the public folder tree you want to work with, and then select Copy.
2. In the administrative group node in which you want to create the tree, right-click Folders, and then select Paste.
3. You'll see a prompt that says the tree isn't unique within the Exchange organization. Click OK.
4. Type a new name for the tree, and then click OK. Exchange Server creates the new tree.

To move a public folder tree, follow these steps:

1. In System Manager, right-click the public folder tree you want to work with, and then select Cut.
2. Expand a different administrative group. Right-click Folders in this group, and then select Paste.
3. Moving the tree changes the directory path to the tree and as a result, the tree might become disconnected from the store it's associated with. When you click it in System Manager, you'll see an error stating that the tree is no longer available.
4. To reconnect the tree with its store, right-click the tree, and then select Connect To. In the Select A Public Store dialog box, select the store that the tree should be connected to, and then click OK.

Deleting Public Folder Trees and Their Containers

You can delete public folder trees only when they contain no other objects and aren't associated with a public folder store. Therefore before you try to delete a public folder tree, you must delete the other objects it contains as well as the public folder store in which it's placed. Afterward, you can delete the tree in System Manager by right-clicking it and then selecting Delete. When prompted, confirm the deletion by clicking Yes.

Similarly, you can delete public folder containers only when they contain no other objects. Once you empty the container, you delete the container in System Manager by right-clicking it and then selecting Delete. When prompted, confirm the deletion by clicking Yes.

Caution You can't recover a public folder tree or container once it has been deleted. You can, however, restore the tree or container from backup. To do this, you'll need to restore the administrative group in which the tree or container was created (which might overwrite changes to other items in the administrative group). See Chapter 12, "Backing Up and Restoring Microsoft Exchange Server 2003," for more information on restoring Exchange from backup.

Creating and Working with Public Folders

The following sections examine techniques you can use to create and work with public folders within public folder trees. Keep in mind that although the Public Folders tree is accessible to MAPI clients, Windows applications, and Web browsers, other trees have limited accessibility.

Creating Public Folders in System Manager

Administrators can create public folders within public folder trees in several ways. One key way is to create the necessary folders in System Manager. To do that, complete the following steps:

1. Start System Manager. If administrative groups are enabled, expand Administrative Groups, and then expand the group you want to work with.

2. Expand Folders. Right-click the public folder tree in which you want to create the public folder, point to New, and then click Public Folder. You'll see a Properties dialog box.

3. Type a name for the public folder in the Name field, and then enter a description in the Public Folder Description field. The name you specify is used to set the e-mail address for the public folder. You can use the e-mail address to submit messages to the public folder.

4. Click the Replication tab, as shown in Figure 11-2. The Replicate Content To These Public Stores list includes the default public store for the public folder tree. To replicate the folder to other servers in the Exchange organization, click Add, select an additional public folder store to use, and then click OK. Repeat this process for other servers that should have replicas.

5. Replication message priority determines how items placed in folders are replicated. The available priorities are the following:

   • **Urgent** Messages in folders with urgent priority are replicated before messages with other priorities, which can reduce delays in updating folders. Use this priority setting judiciously. Too many folders with urgent priority can degrade performance in the Exchange organization.

   • **Normal** Messages in folders with normal priority are sent before messages with not urgent priority. This is the default replication priority.

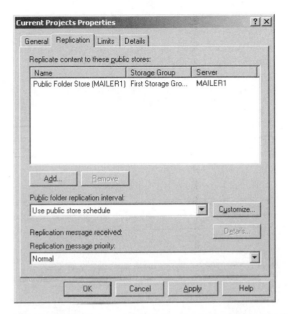

Figure 11-2. *To ensure that the folder is highly available, use the Replication tab to configure folder replication.*

- **Not Urgent** Messages in folders with this priority are sent after messages with higher priority. Use this priority when items have low importance.

6. On the Limits tab, select Use Public Store Defaults in each instance or enter specific defaults as described in the section of this chapter entitled "Setting Limits on Individual Folders."

7. Click OK. Complete, as necessary, the following tasks as explained in the section of this chapter entitled "Managing Public Folder Settings":

- Set folder, message, and Active Directory rights.
- Designate public folder administrators.
- Propagate public folder settings.

Creating Public Folders in Microsoft Outlook

Both administrators and authorized users can create public folders in Outlook. To do this, complete the following steps:

1. Start Outlook 2003. If the Folder List isn't displayed, click Go, and then select Folder List.

2. Expand Public Folders in the Folder List, and then right-click All Public Folders or the top-level folder in which you want to place the public folder.

3. Select New Folder. You'll see the Create New Folder dialog box.

4. Enter a name for the public folder, and then use the Folder Contains drop-down list box to choose the type of item you want to place in the folder.

5. Click OK. Complete, as necessary, the following tasks as explained in the section of this chapter entitled "Managing Public Folder Settings":

   * Control replication and set messaging limits.
   * Set client permissions and Active Directory rights.
   * Designate public folder administrators.
   * Propagate public folder settings.

Creating Public Folders in Internet Explorer

If a public folder tree is configured for Web sharing, administrators and authorized users can create public folders through Microsoft Internet Explorer. To do this, follow these steps:

1. In the Address field of Internet Explorer 5.0 or later, type the URL of the public folder tree, such as *http://mymailserver/public*.

2. If prompted, type your network user name and password. Click OK.

3. You should see a folder view in the browser window. Right-click Public Folders or the top-level folder in which you want to place the public folder.

4. Select New Folder. You'll see the Create New Folder-Web Page dialog box.

5. Enter a name for the public folder, and then use the Folder Contains drop-down list box to choose the type of item you want to place in the folder.

6. Click OK. Complete, as necessary, the following tasks as explained in the section of this chapter entitled "Managing Public Folder Settings":

   * Control replication and set messaging limits.
   * Set client permissions and Active Directory rights.
   * Designate public folder administrators.
   * Propagate public folder settings.

Browsing and Checking Public Folders

In Exchange Server 2003, you can quickly and easily browse, search, and check the status of public folders using System Manager. To do this, follow these steps:

1. Start System Manager. If administrative groups are enabled, expand Administrative Groups, and then expand the group you want to work with.

2. Expand Folders, and then select the public folder you want to work with.

3. As Figure 11-3 shows, the right pane provides five quick-access tabs:

   * **Details** Shows the folder name and creation date.
   * **Content** Shows the content of the public folder using Outlook Web Access, and allows you to manage the folder and its contents. Select a post to view its contents. Right-click a post to reply, flag, delete, or mark the post. Click New to create a new post.

- **Find** Use to search the public folder hierarchy for folders with specific names, permissions, replicas, and creation or modification dates.

- **Status** Shows the status of the selected public folder, including the folder size, number of items, the date and time last accessed, and the date and time the last update was received.

- **Replication** Shows the replication status for the folder, including the server from which the replica was received, the last received time, and the average transmission time.

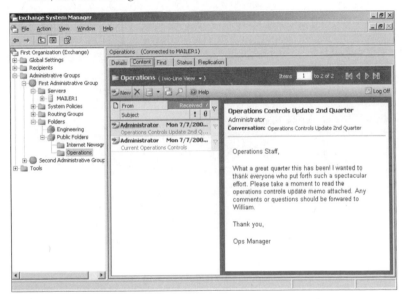

Figure 11-3. *You can use Exchange System Manager to access public folders through Outlook Web Access.*

Adding Items to Public Folders Using System Manager

Exchange administrators can post items to any public folder to which they have access using System Manager. To do this, complete these steps:

1. Start System Manager. If administrative groups are enabled, expand Administrative Groups, and then expand the group you want to work with.

2. Expand Folders. Select the public folder you want to work with and then click the Content tab.

3. Click New to display the Post dialog box.

4. Type a subject for the message, and then type your message text. Add any necessary attachments.

5. Click Post.

Adding Items to Public Folders Using Outlook and Internet Explorer

Authorized users can post items to public folders through any compliant application. Let's briefly look at how you could use Outlook, Internet Explorer, and plain old e-mail to perform this task.

In Outlook, authorized users can post items to public folders by completing these steps:

1. Start Outlook 2003. If the Folder List isn't displayed, click Go, and then select Folder List.

2. Expand Public Folders and then All Public Folders in the Folder List. Afterward, select the folder you want to use.

3. Click New or press Ctrl+Shift+S. Notice that when a public folder is selected, the New button automatically changes to public folder post mode.

4. Type a subject for the message, and then type your message text. Add any necessary attachments.

5. Click Post.

In Internet Explorer, authorized users can post items to public folders by completing the following steps:

1. In the Address field of Internet Explorer 5.0 or later, type the URL of the public folder tree, such as *http://mymailserver/public*.

2. If prompted, type your network user name and password. Click OK.

3. In the Folders view, select the folder you want to use, and then click New.

4. Type a subject for the message, and then type your message text. Add any necessary attachments.

5. Click Post.

Mail-Enabling Public Folders

Unlike previous editions of Exchange Server, public folders are not mail-enabled by default. If you want authorized users to be able to submit items using standard e-mail, you can mail-enable the public folder by right-clicking it, pointing to All Tasks and then selecting Mail Enable.

Once mail-enable the public folder, users simply address an e-mail to the public folder and the message is received as a posting. The default e-mail address is the same as the folder name (with any spaces or special characters removed). For example, if the public folder name was Operations and Adatum.com is the e-mail domain, the email address of the public folder would be operations@adatum.com.

Administrators can check the e-mail address and alias for a public folder by completing the following steps:

1. Right-click the public folder, and then select Properties. You'll see a Properties dialog box.

2. The folder's e-mail addresses are displayed on the E-Mail Addresses tab. Note the Simple Mail Transfer Protocol (SMTP) address, because this is the one most e-mail clients use.

3. The folder's e-mail alias is displayed in the Alias field of the Exchange General tab.

All public folders are mail-enabled by default. Mail-enabling allows authorized users to submit items using standard e-mail. Simply address an e-mail to the public folder and the message is received as a posting. The default e-mail address is the same as the folder name (with any spaces or special characters removed). Administrators can check the e-mail address for a public folder by completing the following steps:

1. Start System Manager. If administrative groups are enabled, expand Administrative Groups, and then expand the group you want to work with.

2. Expand Folders, and then expand the public folder tree that contains the public folder you want to examine.

3. Right-click the public folder, and then select Properties. You'll see a Properties dialog box.

4. The folder's e-mail addresses are displayed on the E-Mail Addresses tab. Note the Simple Mail Transfer Protocol (SMTP) address, because this is the one most e-mail clients use.

Searching Public Folders

You can search public folders in two key ways. You can search the public folder hierarchy for folders with specific names, permissions, replicas, and creation or modification dates. You can also search for a particular posting to a public folder using the subject, sender, and sent-to fields as search criteria.

To search the public folder hierarchy for a particular folder, complete the following steps:

1. Start System Manager. If administrative groups are enabled, expand Administrative Groups, and then expand the group you want to work with.

2. Expand Folders. Select the public folder you want to work with and then in the right pane, click the Find tab (as shown in Figure 11-4).

3. In the Name Contains field, enter the name or partial name of a public folder to search. If you leave this field blank, all subfolders of the currently selected folder are searched.

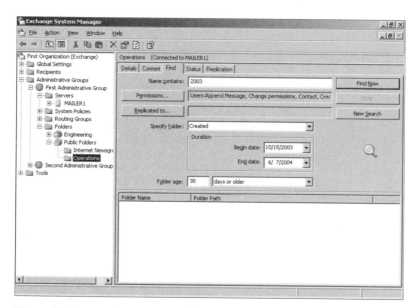

Figure 11-4. *Use the options of the Find tab to search public folders.*

4. To search for folders for which users are granted or denied permissions, click Permissions. The Select Permissions dialog box is displayed. Use the following options in this dialog box to set the permission criteria and then click OK:

   - **User**   Limits the search to a specific user or group. Click User. Enter the name of the specific user or group to search for. Click Check Names and then click OK.

   - **Granted Any Of These Permissions**   Select this option to search for folders for which users or groups are granted the designated permissions.

   - **Denied Any Of These Permissions**   Select this option to search for folders for which users or groups are denied the designated permissions.

5. To search for folders replicated to a specific server, click Replicated To. In the Select Servers dialog box, select the servers that have replicas of the folder you are looking for and that you want to search. Click OK.

6. To search folders by creation or modification dates, click the Specify Folder drop-down list and then select either Created or Modified as appropriate. Afterward, use the Begin Date and End Date drop-down lists to set the creation or modification date range to match.

7. Click Find Now to begin the search. Any matching folders are shown in the Folder Name list. Right-click a folder and select Properties to manage its properties.

To search for a particular posting rather than a particular folder, complete the following steps:

1. Start System Manager. If administrative groups are enabled, expand Administrative Groups, and then expand the group you want to work with.

2. Expand Folders. Select the public folder you want to work with and then in the right pane, click the Content tab.

3. Click Search on the Content tab toolbar to display the Search dialog box shown in Figure 11-5.

4. To search subfolders in addition to the currently selected folder, select the Search Subfolders check box.

5. To limit the search by the Subject field, type the subject keyword or words that you want to match. You can search for phrases in the subject by enclosing the words in quotation marks. To search for individual words in the subject, don't use quotation marks.

Tip   If you are limiting the search by subject, you can search for the same keywords in the message body by selecting the Also Search Message Body check box. The catch, however, is that this slows down the search process because Outlook Web Access must search the contents of every post.

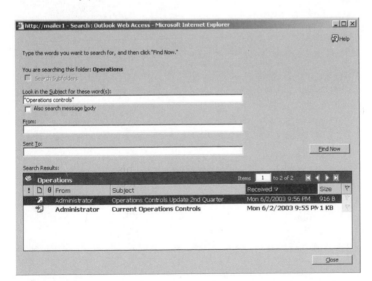

Figure 11-5. *You can also search for a particular posting rather than a particular folder.*

6. If you know the sender's name, type the name in the From field. You can enter a partial name that could potentially match multiple users, or a full name that is enclosed in quotation marks to limit the search to a specific user.

7. If you know the name of any user or group in the To or Cc fields of the post, type the name in the Sent To field. Again, you can enter a partial name that could potentially match multiple users, or a full name that is enclosed in quotation marks to limit the search to a specific user.

8. Click Find Now to begin the search. Keep in mind that Outlook Web Access looks for messages that match all the specified criteria, so if you entered more than one search parameter, this might limit the search. When Outlook Web Access completes the search, you'll see a list of all items (if any) that match your search criteria. Double-click a message to open it so you can view the message, post a reply, print the message, or delete it.

Managing Public Folder Settings

You should actively manage public folders. If you don't, you won't get optimal performance, and users might encounter problems when reading from or posting to the folders. Each folder in a public folder tree has its own settings and each time a folder is created you should review and modify the following settings:

- Replication options
- Messaging limits
- Client permissions
- Active Directory rights

You might also want to designate folder administrators and propagate the changes you've made. This section of the chapter explains these and other public folder administration tasks.

Controlling Folder Replication

Each folder in a public folder tree has its own replication settings. By default, the content of a public folder is replicated only to the default public store for the tree. You can replicate the folder to additional public stores by following these steps:

1. Start System Manager. If administrative groups are enabled, expand Administrative Groups, and then expand the group you want to work with.

2. Expand Folders, and then expand the public folder tree that contains the public folder you want to replicate.

3. Right-click the public folder, and then select Properties.

4. Click the Replication tab. The Replicate Content To These Public Stores field shows where replicas of the folders are currently being created.

5. To replicate the folder to other servers in the Exchange organization, click Add, select an additional public folder store to use, and then click OK. Repeat this step for other servers that should have replicas.

6. The replication interval determines when changes to public folders are replicated. Use the Public Folder Replication Interval selection menu to choose a replication time. You can use a custom schedule by selecting Use Custom Schedule, clicking Customize, and then creating your own custom schedule. You can use the public store's settings by selecting Use Public Store Schedule.

7. The replication priority determines how items placed in folders are replicated. The available priorities are urgent, normal, and not urgent. Messages in folders with a higher priority are replicated before messages in other folders.

8. Click OK.

Tip In most cases, you'll want to use the normal priority, which is the default. However, if a folder contains items that need to be replicated quickly throughout the organization, you might want to use the urgent priority setting. Watch out, though—too many folders with urgent priority can degrade performance in the Exchange organization.

Setting Limits on Individual Folders

In most cases you'll want to set storage limits and deleted item retention on a per-store basis rather than on individual folders. If this is the case, see the section of Chapter 10 entitled "Setting Public Store Limits." On the other hand, if you want to set a limit on an individual folder, follow these steps:

1. Start System Manager. If administrative groups are enabled, expand Administrative Groups, and then expand the group you want to work with.

2. Expand Folders, and then expand the public folder tree that contains the public folder you want to work with.

3. Right-click the public folder, and then select Properties.

4. Click the Limits tab. If you want to set storage limits on the folder, clear the Use Public Store Defaults check box in the Storage Limits panel, and then configure these options:

   - **Issue Warning At (KB)**   Sets the size, in kilobytes, of the data that a user can post to the public folder before a warning is issued to the user. The warning tells the user to clean out the public folder.

   - **Prohibit Post At (KB)**   Sets the maximum size, in kilobytes, of the data that the user can post to the public folder. The restriction ends when the total size of the user's data is under the limit.

   - **Maximum Item Size (KB)**   Sets the maximum size, in kilobytes, for postings to the public folder.

5. If you want to set deleted item retention separately for the folder, clear the Use Public Store Defaults check box in the Deletion Settings panel, and then use Keep Deleted Items For (Days) to set the number of days to retain deleted items. An average retention period is 14 days. If you set the retention period to 0, deleted postings aren't retained and you can't recover them.

6. If you want to set age limits separately for the folder, clear the Use Public Store Defaults check box in the Age Limits panel, and then use Age Limit For Replicas (Days) to set the number of days to retain postings distributed to other servers.

7. Click OK.

Setting Client Permissions

You use client permissions to specify which users can access a particular public folder. By default, all users (including those accessing the folder anonymously over the Web) have permission to access the folder and read its contents. Users who log on to the network or to Outlook Web Access have additional permissions. These permissions allow them to create subfolders, to create items in the folder, to read items in the folder, and to edit and delete items they've created.

To change permissions for anonymous and authenticated users, you need to set a new role for the special users Anonymous and Default, respectively. Initially, anonymous users have the role of Contributor and authenticated users have the role of Publishing Author. These and other client permission roles are defined as follows:

- **Owner**   Grants all permissions in the folder. Users with this role can create, read, modify, and delete all items in the folder. They can create subfolders and can change permission on folders as well.

- **Publishing Editor**   Grants permission to create, read, modify, and delete all items in the folder. Users with this role can create subfolders as well.

- **Editor**   Grants permission to create, read, modify, and delete all items in the folder.

- **Publishing Author**   Grants permission to create and read items in the folder, to modify and delete items the user created, and to create subfolders.

- **Author**   Grants permission to create and read items in the folder as well as to modify and delete items that the user created.

- **Nonediting Author**   Grants permission to create and read items in the folder.

- **Reviewer**   Grants read-only permission.

- **Contributor**   Grants permission to create items but not to view the contents of the folder.

- **None**   Grants no permission in the folder.

To set new roles for users or to modify existing client permissions, complete the following steps:

1. Start System Manager. If administrative groups are enabled, expand Administrative Groups, and then expand the group you want to work with.

2. Expand Folders, and then expand the public folder tree that contains the public folder you want to work with.

3. Right-click the public folder, and then select Properties.

4. On the Permissions tab, click Client Permissions. You'll see the Client Permissions dialog box shown in Figure 11-6.

5. The Name and Role lists display account names and their permissions on the folder. If you want to grant users permissions that are different from the default permission, click Add.

6. In the Add Users dialog box, select the name of a user who needs access to the mailbox. Then click Add to put the name in the Add Users list. Repeat this step as necessary for other users. Click OK when you're finished.

7. In the Name and Role lists, select one or more users whose permissions you want to modify. Then use the Roles selection list to assign a role or select individual permission items.

8. When you're finished granting permissions, click OK.

Figure 11-6. *Use the Client Permissions dialog box to set permissions for users and then assign a role to each user. The role controls the actions the user can perform.*

Setting Active Directory Rights and Designating Administrators

Client permissions allow users to manipulate folder contents, but they don't let users manage the permissions on the folder itself. Only administrators can set folder permissions and modify public folder properties. If you want other users to be able to set permissions, grant the users directory rights to the folder. If you want users to be able to administer a public folder as well, grant them administrative rights to the folder.

To set a folder's directory and administrative rights, follow these steps:

1. Start System Manager. If administrative groups are enabled, expand Administrative Groups, and then expand the group you want to work with.

2. Expand Folders, and then expand the public folder tree that contains the public folder you want to work with.

3. Right-click the public folder, and then select Properties.

4. On the Permissions tab, click Directory Rights, and then use the Permissions dialog box to set the folder's Active Directory permissions as described in the section of Chapter 8 entitled "Controlling Exchange Server Administration and Usage."

5. When you're finished setting directory rights, click Administrative Rights on the Permissions tab. Then use the Permissions dialog box to grant or deny administrative privileges.

6. Click OK when you're finished modifying the folder's rights.

Propagating Public Folder Settings

Any property changes you make to public folders aren't automatically applied to subfolders. You can, however, manually propagate setting changes if you need to. To do this, follow these steps:

1. Right-click the public folder for which you want to propagate settings to subfolders, point to All Tasks, and then click Propagate Settings.

2. You'll see the Propagate Folder Settings dialog box shown in Figure 11-7. Select the type of settings you want to propagate, and then click OK.

3. Exchange Server performs any necessary preparatory tasks, and then propagates the settings you've designated.

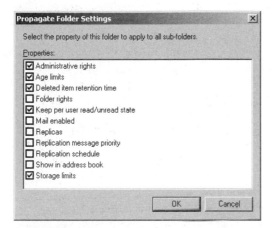

Figure 11-7. *The Propagate Folder Settings dialog box gives you complete control over the settings that are propagated to subfolders. Be sure to consider the impact of your changes before clicking OK.*

Viewing and Changing Address Settings for Public Folders

In Exchange Server 2003, public folders are not mail-enabled by default. If you mail-enable a folder (by right-clicking the folder, pointing to all tasks and then selecting Mail Enable), you'll find that the public folder has new characteristics that you can access in the folder's Properties dialog box, including:

- **An address list name** Set by default to be same as the folder name but not displayed in the Global Address List. You can set a new name with the Use This Name field found on the General tab. You can reveal the folder in the address list by clearing the Hide From Exchange Address Lists check box on the Exchange Advanced tab.

- **An Exchange Server alias** Set by default to the name of the public folder. You can view and change it using the Alias field on the Exchange General tab.

- **One or more e-mail addresses** Set by default for SMTP and X.400. Viewable and changeable in the E-Mail Addresses tab.

- **A display name** Not set by default, but you can configure it by using the Simple Display Name field on the Exchange Advanced tab.

- **Delivery options** Set by clicking Delivery Options on the Exchange General tab. Delivery options are covered in the sections of Chapter 6, "Mailbox Administration," entitled "Permitting Others to Access a Mailbox" and "Forwarding E-Mail to a New Address."

Manipulating, Renaming, and Recovering Public Folders

Because public folders are stored as objects in Active Directory, you can manipulate them using standard techniques, such as cut, copy, and paste. Follow the procedures outlined in this section to manipulate, rename, and recover public folders.

Renaming Public Folders

To rename a public folder, follow these steps:

1. In System Manager, right-click the public folder you want to rename.

2. Select Rename, type a new name, and then press Enter.

Copying and Moving Public Folders

You can copy and move public folders only within the same public folder tree. You can't copy or move a public folder to a different tree.

To create a copy of a public folder, follow these steps:

1. In System Manager, right-click the public folder you want to work with, and then select Copy.

2. Right-click the folder into which you want to copy the folder, and then select Paste.

To move a public folder to a new location in the same tree, follow these steps:

1. In System Manager, right-click the public folder you want to work with, and then select Cut.

2. Right-click the folder into which you want to move the folder, and then select Paste.

Deleting Public Folders

When you delete a public folder, you remove its contents, any subfolders it contains, and the contents of its subfolders. Before you delete a folder, however, you should ensure that any existing data the folder contains is no longer needed and make a backup of the folder contents just in case.

You delete public folders and their subfolders by completing the following steps:

1. In System Manager, right-click the public folder you want to remove, and then select Delete.

2. You'll be asked to confirm the action. Click Yes.

Recovering Public Folders

You can recover deleted folders from public folder stores, provided you've set a deleted item retention period for the public folder store from which the folders were deleted and the retention period for this data store hasn't expired. If both of these conditions are met, you can recover deleted folders by completing the following steps:

1. Log on to the domain using an account with administrative privileges in the domain or with an account with full control over the public folders you need to recover.

2. After starting Outlook, access the Public Folders node, and then select the All Public Folders node or the node that contained the public folders.

3. Select Recover Deleted Items from the Tools menu. You should now see the Recover Deleted Items From dialog box.

4. Select the folders you want to recover, and then click Recover Selected Items.

5. Each top-level folder restored by the recovery operation has "(Recovered)" appended to the folder name. After you verify the contents of the folder, you can complete the recovery operation by doing the following:

   - **Restoring the original folder name**   Right-click the folder, select Rename, type a new name, and then press Enter.

   - **Restoring the folder's e-mail addresses**   Right-click the folder, and then select Properties. In the Properties dialog box, click the E-Mail Addresses tab. Edit each e-mail address so that it's restored to its original value.

Working with Public Folder Replicas

Public folder replicas are copies of public folders that have been created through replication. You can use the replicas to check the status of replication and to perform other basic replication tasks.

Adding and Removing Replicas

To create replicas on other Exchange servers, follow the steps listed in the section of this chapter entitled "Controlling Folder Replication." Later, if you want to remove a replica of the folder, follow these steps:

1. In System Manager, right-click the public folder you want to work with, and then select Properties.

2. Click the Replication tab. The Replicate Content To These Public Stores field shows where replicas of the folders are currently being created. To stop replication to a public folder store, select the store, and then click Remove.

Viewing Public Folder Instances

The Information Store tracks all instances of a public folder. By examining these instances, you can find information about public folders, including their size and the deletion information.

To view public folder instances, follow these steps:

1. In System Manager, select the Exchange server you want to manage, and then click the plus sign (+) next to the storage group you want to work with.

2. You should see a list of available data stores. Click the plus sign (+) next to the public folder store you want to examine, and then select Public Folder Instances.

3. As Figure 11-8 shows, information about all public folder instances in the store is displayed in the Details pane. The default view provides basic logon information about the folder instance, with the most important information being the folder size and the Removed Older Than time stamp.

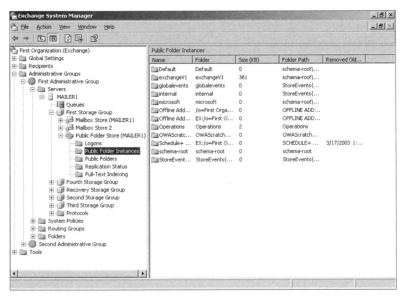

Figure 11-8. *The Public Folder Instances node provides summary information for all public folder replicas in the data store.*

Viewing and Setting Replica Properties

The age limit is the key property that affects public folder replicas. The age limit determines when (if ever) the replica is deleted. By default, there's no age limit on replicas and they're maintained as long as the folder is being copied. If you set an age limit, the replica is deleted if it isn't updated by the time the replica expires.

You can view and set the age limit for a replica by completing these steps:

1. In System Manager, select the Exchange server you want to manage, and then click the plus sign (+) next to the storage group you want to work with.

2. You should see a list of available data stores. Click the plus sign (+) next to the public folder store you want to examine, and then select Public Folder Instances.

3. Replicas are shown in the Details pane. Right-click the replica you want to examine, and then select Replica Properties.

4. The Properties dialog box displays any applicable age limits. If you want to set an age limit, select Age Limit Of This Folder On This Public Store (Days), and then enter the age limit in days.

5. Click OK.

Checking Replication Status

The replication status is the best way to keep track of public folder replication, and you'll want to periodically check the status of replication on each public folder store. To do this, access the public folder store in System Manager, and then click Replication Status. In the Details pane, you'll see the following columns:

- **Name**   The name of the affected public folder store
- **Last Received Time**   The time the last replica was received
- **Number Of Replicas**   The number of replicas received
- **Replication Status**   The status of the replication, either completed or failed

Another way to check replication status is to examine replication for individual public folders. Through this process, you can confirm that an individual folder was replicated and check the average amount of time it took to complete the replication. To check replication status for an individual public folder, select the folder you want to work with in System Manager and then click the Replication tab. You should now see the detailed replication status of the folder.

Chapter 12

Backing Up and Restoring Microsoft Exchange Server 2003

Microsoft Exchange Server 2003 is critically important to your organization. If a server crashes, you are faced with the possibility of every user on that server losing days, weeks, or even months of work. To protect Exchange Server and your users' data, you need to implement a backup and recovery plan. Backing up Exchange Server can protect against database corruption, hardware failures, accidental loss of user messages, and even natural disasters. As an administrator, it's your job to make sure that backups are performed and that backup media is stored in a secure location.

Understanding the Essentials of Exchange Server Backup and Recovery

Backing up and recovering Exchange data is a bit different than backing up other types of data, primarily because Exchange Server 2003 has different units of backup and recovery than Microsoft Windows. You not only work with files and drives, you also work with the information store and the data structures it contains. As you know from previous chapters, the information store can contain one or more storage groups and in turn, each storage group can contain one or more databases.

Backing Up Exchange Server: The Basics

To create a complete backup of an Exchange server, you must back up the following:

- Exchange configuration data, which includes the configuration settings for the Exchange organization. You take configuration settings from the Exchange directory database (Dir.edb), Active Directory, the Windows registry, and the Key Management Service database (if installed). Configuration data doesn't include any user data.

- Exchange user data, which includes Exchange mailbox store databases, public folder store databases, and transaction logs. If you want to be able to recover mailbox and public folder stores, you must back up this data. User data doesn't contain Exchange configuration settings.

- State data for the operating system, which includes essential system files needed to recover the local system. All computers have system state data, which you must back up in addition to other files to restore a complete working system.

- Folders and drives that contain Windows and Exchange files. Normally, this means backing up the root drive C, which is the special partition for Exchange Server.

Storage groups and databases are the units of backup and recovery for the information store. Storage groups are the smallest units of backup, and mailboxes are the smallest units of recovery. This means you have the following backup and recovery options for the information store:

- Backup options

  - You can back up the entire information store.

  - You can back up sets of storage groups.

  - You can back up individual storage groups.

- Recovery options

  - You can recover the entire information store.

  - You can recover sets of storage groups.

  - You can recover individual storage groups.

  - You can recover groups of databases.

  - You can recover individual databases.

  - You can recover individual mailboxes.

The ability to recover an individual database from backup is a great improvement over Microsoft Exchange 5.0 and Exchange 5.5, and there are some fundamental issues you should know about before you try to recover individual databases. These issues pertain to transactions, transaction logs, and transaction logging modes.

Exchange Server uses transactions to control database changes. You can think of a transaction as a logical unit of work that contains one or more operations that affect the information store. If all the operations in a transaction are successfully executed, Exchange Server marks the transaction as successful and permanently commits the changes. If one or more of the operations in a transaction fails to complete, Exchange Server marks the transaction as failed and removes any changes that the transaction created. The process of removing changes is referred to as *rolling back* the transaction.

Transaction logs are units of storage for transactions. Exchange Server writes each transaction to a log file and maintains the log files according to the logging mode. Exchange Server has two logging modes:

- **Standard** With standard logging, Exchange Server reserves 5 MB of disk space for the active transaction log. Transactions are committed or rolled back based on success or failure. Once the contents of the log reaches 5 MB, Exchange Server creates a new log file. Because the transaction logs are maintained until the next full backup, you can recover Exchange Server to the last transaction.

- **Circular** Circular logging works much like standard logging with one key distinction: Exchange Server overwrites transaction log files after the data they contain has been committed to the database. Overwriting old transactions reduces Exchange's disk space requirements. However, without the old transactions, you can't recover Exchange Server up to the last transaction. You can recover Exchange Server only up to the last full backup.

Note The active transaction log is named E##.log where ## is the unique identifier for the storage group. Additional transaction logs are named E######.log, where ###### is a numerical value that increases for each new log file, such as E000001.log, E000002.log, and E000003.log for logs associated with the first storage group and E010001.log, E010002.log, and E010003.log for logs associated with the second storage group.

The ability to recover mailboxes selectively from backup is an improvement over Microsoft Exchange 2000, and as with recovering databases, there are some fundamental issues you should know about before you try to recover individual mailboxes. These issues pertain to recovery storage groups.

Recovery storage groups are special types of storage groups that are reserved for recovery operations. Using a recovery storage group, you can restore mailboxes from any of the regular storage groups in an Exchange organization. You can recover individual or multiple mailboxes at the same time, provided the databases for those mailboxes are in the same storage group. You cannot, however, use recovery storage groups to restore public folder databases.

The server on which you create the recovery storage group must be in the same administrative group as the server for which you want to recover mailboxes. If you need to recover mailboxes stored on multiple Exchange servers, you don't have to create a recovery storage group on each server. Instead, you can create one recovery storage group for each administrative group.

Note Don't confuse this recovery procedure with those used with Mailbox Recovery Center. You use Mailbox Recovery Center to recover deleted, disconnected, or otherwise unavailable mailboxes, as long as those mailboxes are available for recovery from an existing mailbox store. You use the recovery storage group to recover mailboxes from a previous backup of a mailbox store.

Formulating an Exchange Server Backup and Recovery Plan

Creating a backup and recovery plan for Exchange Server 2003 requires forethought on your part. You need to plan the following:

- The number of Exchange servers to use in your organization. Do you need multiple servers to ensure high availability? Do you need multiple servers to improve performance? Do you need multiple servers because the organization spans several geographic areas?

- The number of storage groups for each Exchange server, as well as how the groups are organized. Do you create storage groups for each department or division in the organization? Do you create storage groups for different business functions? Do you create separate storage groups for public folders and other types of data?

- The number and type of databases (data stores) for each storage group. Do you create separate data stores for different departments, divisions, and business functions? Do you create separate data stores for different types of public folder data?

Once you've planned the Exchange organization, you can create a backup and recovery plan to support that organization. You'll need to figure out what data needs to be backed up, how often the data should be backed up, and more. To help you create a plan, consider the following:

- **How important is the mailbox or public folder store you're backing up?** The importance of the data can go a long way in helping you determine when and how the data store should be backed up. For critical data such as a department's mailbox store, you'll want to have redundant backup sets that extend back for several backup periods. For less important data, such as public folders for newsgroups, you won't need such an elaborate backup plan, but you'll need to back up the data regularly and ensure that you can recover the data easily.

- **How quickly do you need to recover the data?** Time is an important factor in creating a backup plan. You might need to get critical data, such as the primary mailbox store, back online swiftly. To do this, you might need to alter your backup plan. For example, you might need to create multiple mailbox stores and place them in different storage groups on different servers. You could then recover individual databases, individual storage groups, or individual servers as the situation warrants.

- **Do you have the equipment to perform backups?** If you don't have backup hardware, you can't perform backups. To perform timely backups, you might need several backup devices and several sets of backup media. Backup hardware includes tape drives, optical drives, and removable disk drives.

- **Who will be responsible for the backup and recovery plan?** Ideally, someone should be the primary contact for the Exchange backup and recovery plan. This person might also be responsible for performing the actual backup and recovery of Exchange Server.

- **What is the best time to schedule backups?**   Scheduling backups when system use is as low as possible speeds the backup process. However, because you can't always schedule backups for off-peak hours, you'll need to carefully plan when data is backed up.

- **Do you need to store backups off-site?**   Storing copies of backup tapes off-site is essential to recovering Exchange Server in the case of a natural disaster. In your off-site storage location, you should also include copies of all the software you might need to recover Exchange Server.

Choosing Backup Options

As you'll find when you work with data backup and recovery, there are many techniques for backing up data. The techniques you use depend on the type of data you're backing up, how convenient you want the recovery process to be, and more.

You can perform backups online (with Exchange services running) or offline (with Exchange services stopped). With online backups, you can archive the following:

- Exchange configuration data
- Exchange user data
- System state
- Files and folders that contain Windows and Exchange files

With offline backups, you can't archive Exchange configuration or user data. This means that you can only archive the following:

- System state
- Files and folders that contain Windows and Exchange files

Real World   With Exchange Server Enterprise Edition running on Microsoft Windows Server 2003, you have the option of using the Volume Shadow Copy Service (VSS) to perform online backups. VSS creates point-in-time snapshots of data at the beginning of the backup process. The snapshot data is then used to create the backup rather than working with the server's hard disk. This allows normal operations to continue while the backup occurs and ensures that the backup is consistent, even if the data changes while the backup is in progress. Shadow copies of Exchange data can only be made if the backup software you are using supports the Exchange VSS extensions. Although Windows Backup supports the Windows VSS extensions, allowing you to make shadow copies at the operating system level, it does not support the Exchange VSS extensions at the time of this writing. Until this is remedied, you must use third-party backup software if you want to take advantage of VSS.

The basic types of backups you'll want to perform with Exchange Server are as follows:

- **Normal/full backups** Backs up all Exchange data that has been selected, including the related data stores and the current transaction logs. A normal backup tells Exchange Server you've performed a complete backup, which allows Exchange Server to clear out the transaction logs.

- **Copy backups** Backs up all Exchange data that has been selected, including the related data stores and the current transaction logs. Unlike a normal backup, a copy backup doesn't tell Exchange Server you've performed a complete backup and, as a result, the log files aren't cleared. This allows you to perform other types of Exchange backups later.

- **Differential backups** Designed to create backup copies of all data that has changed since the last normal backup. Only transaction log files are backed up and not the actual data stores. The log files aren't cleared. To recover Exchange Server, you must apply the most recent normal backup and the most recent differential backup.

- **Incremental backups** Designed to create backups of data that has changed since the most recent normal or incremental backup. Only transaction log files are backed up and not the actual data stores. The log files are cleared once the incremental backup is completed. To recover Exchange Server, you must apply the most recent full backup and then apply each incremental backup after the full backup. You must apply transaction logs in order.

 Caution You cannot perform incremental or differential backups with circular logging enabled because circular logging allows Exchange Server to overwrite log files, which makes it impossible to reliably restore from the transaction logs.

In your backup plan you'll probably want to perform full backups on a weekly basis and supplement them with nightly differential or incremental backups. You might also want to create an extended backup set for monthly and quarterly backups that are rotated to off-site storage.

Backing Up Exchange Server

Windows provides a backup utility, called Backup, for creating backups on local and remote systems. Backup has special extensions that allow you to create online backups of Exchange Server 2003. You use Backup to do the following:

- Archive Exchange configuration and user data
- Access media pools reserved for Backup
- Access remote Exchange servers through My Network Places
- Create snapshots of the system state for backup and restore

- Schedule backups through the Task Scheduler
- Recover Exchange configuration and user data

You create backups using the Backup utility's Backup tab or the Backup Wizard. Both techniques make use of default options set for the Backup utility. You can view or change the default options by clicking Tools and then selecting Options. The account you use for backup and restore should be a member of both the Backup Operators and Server Operators groups.

Starting the Backup Utility

You can access the Backup utility in several ways:

- Select Run from the Start menu. In the Run dialog box, type **ntbackup** and then click OK.
- Select Programs or All Programs as appropriate from the Start menu, select Accessories, select System Tools, and then select Backup.

The first time you use the Backup utility, it starts in basic wizard mode. As an administrator, you'll want to use advanced mode because it gives you more options. Clear the Always Start In Wizard Mode check box and then click Advanced Mode. You should now see the main Backup Utility interface. As shown in Figure 12-1, the standard interface has four tabs that provide easy access to key features. These tabs are as follows:

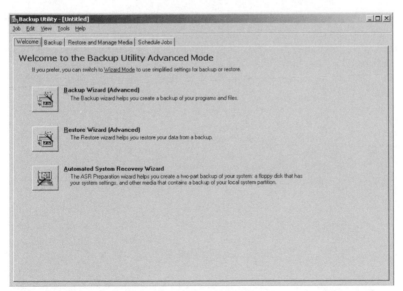

Figure 12-1. *The Windows Backup utility provides a user-friendly interface for backup and restore.*

- **Welcome** Introduces Backup and provides buttons for starting the Backup Wizard, the Restore Wizard, and the Automated System Recovery Wizard.

- **Backup** Provides the main interface for selecting data to back up. You can back up data on local and mapped network drives.

- **Restore And Manage Media** Provides the main interface for restoring archived data. You can restore data to the original location or to an alternate location anywhere on the network.

- **Schedule Jobs** Provides a month-by-month job schedule for backups. You can view executed jobs as well as jobs scheduled for future dates.

Backing Up Exchange Server with the Backup Wizard

The procedures you use to work with the Backup Wizard are similar to those you use to back up data manually. You can perform backups with Exchange Server online or offline. For online backups, verify that the Exchange System Attendant and Microsoft Information Store services are running before starting a backup. For offline backups, verify that all Exchange services are stopped before performing a backup.

You start and work with the wizard by completing the following steps:

1. Start the Backup utility in advanced mode and then click Backup Wizard on the Welcome tab. If wizard mode is enabled, click Advanced Mode and then click Backup Wizard.

2. Click Next. Select Back Up Selected Files, Drives, Or Network Data and then click Next again.

3. As shown in Figure 12-2, choose the user data you want to back up. You make selections by selecting or clearing the check boxes associated with a particular drive or folder. When you select a top-level folder, all the subfolders are selected. When you clear a check box for a top-level folder, check boxes for the related subfolders are cleared as well. Key backup options for Exchange Server are as follows:

   - To create a full backup that includes all Exchange servers in the organization, you need to select the Microsoft Information Store node of each individual server. Expand Microsoft Exchange Server, expand the node for the first server that you want to back up, and then select Microsoft Information Store. Afterward, expand the node for the next server that you want to back up, and then select Microsoft Information Store, and so on.

   - To back up specific Exchange servers, expand Microsoft Exchange Server, expand the node for the server that you want to back up, and then select Microsoft Information Store.

   - To back up all user databases on a specific Exchange server, expand Microsoft Exchange Server, expand the node for the server that you want to back up, and then select Microsoft Information Store.

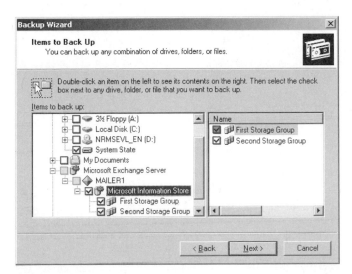

Figure 12-2. *Choose the Exchange data to back up.*

- To back up individual databases on an Exchange server, expand Microsoft Exchange Server, expand a server, expand Information Store, expand the storage group you want to work with, and then select the database to use.

- To back up all databases used by Exchange 5.5 users, expand Microsoft Exchange Server and then select Microsoft Site Replication Service.

- To back up individual databases used by Exchange 5.5 users, expand Microsoft Exchange Server, expand a server, expand Microsoft Site Replication Service, and then select a storage group.

4. If you want to back up configuration data, choose additional items. Key options are as follows:

- To back up Exchange Server 2003 and Windows settings, select all hard disk drives where Windows and Exchange Server are installed. Normally, this means backing up the root drive C and the drives used by Exchange Server.

- To back up the Windows registry and Active Directory settings, expand My Computer and then select System State. System State includes essential system files needed to recover the local system. All computers have system state data, which you must back up in addition to other files to restore a complete working system.

- To back up Key Management Services data, expand Microsoft Exchange Server, expand all servers running this service, and then select Key Management Service wherever applicable. You must also back up the system state data, which contains public keys for users in the organization.

5. Click Next, and then select the Backup Media Type. Choose File if you want to back up to a file. Choose a storage device if you want to back up files and folders to a tape or removable disk.

6. Select the backup file or media you want to use. If you're backing up to a file, select a location from those available or click Browse to specify a file location and name. If you're backing up to a tape or removable disk, choose the tape or disk you want to use. Afterward, type a name for the backup you are creating, such as Exchange Backup January 2004.

 Note When you write backups to a file, the backup file normally has the .bkf file extension. You can use another file extension if you want. Note also that you use Removable Storage to manage tapes and removable disks.

7. Click Next. Click Advanced if you want to override default options or schedule the backup to be run as a job. Then follow Steps 8 through 11. Otherwise, skip to Step 12.

8. Select the type of backup to perform. The available types are Normal, Copy, Differential, Incremental, and Daily. Click Next.

9. You can now set the following options for verification and compression and then click Next:

   • **Verify Data After Backup** Instructs Backup to verify data after the backup procedure is completed. If selected, every file on the backup tape is compared to the original file. Verifying data can protect against write errors or failures, but requires more time than a backup without verification.

   • **Use Hardware Compression, If Available** Allows Backup to compress data as it's written to the storage device. The option is available only if the device supports hardware compression and only compatible drives can read the compressed information, which might mean that only a drive from the same manufacturer can recover the data.

10. Set options for copying data to the designated file, tape, or removable disk. To add the backup after existing data, select Append This Backup To The Existing Backups. To overwrite existing data, select Replace The Existing Backups. If you're overwriting data, you can specify that only the owner and an administrator can access the archive file by selecting Allow Only The Owner And Administrator Access. Click Next.

11. Determine when the backup will run. Select Now to run the backup now and then click Next. Select Later to schedule the backup for a specific date. If you want to schedule the backup for a later date, type a job name, click Set Schedule, and then set a run schedule. When you click Next, you'll have

to enter an account name and password to add it to the schedule. This account must have Backup Operator privileges or be a member of a group that has Backup Operator privileges.

12. Click Finish to start the backup. You can cancel the backup by clicking Cancel in the Set Information and Backup Progress dialog boxes. When the backup is completed, click Close to complete the process or click Report to view the backup log.

Note Backup selection scripts and backup logs are stored in %Userprofile%\Local Settings\Application Data\Microsoft\WindowsNT\ NTBackup\Data. Backup selection scripts are saved with the .bks extension. Backup logs are saved with the .log extension. You can view these files with any standard text editor, such as Notepad.

Backing Up Exchange Server Manually

You don't have to use a wizard to back up Exchange Server 2003. You can configure backups manually by completing the following steps:

1. You can perform backups with Exchange Server online or offline, provided that you keep in mind the following:

   • You can perform online backups only when key Exchange services are running. Verify that the Exchange System Attendant and Microsoft Information Store services are running before starting a backup.

   • You can perform offline backups only when all Exchange services are stopped. Verify that all Exchange services are stopped before starting a backup.

2. Start Backup. If wizard mode is enabled, click Advanced Mode and then click the Backup tab shown in Figure 12-3. Otherwise, just click the Backup tab.

3. Clear any existing selections on the Backup tab by selecting New from the Job menu and clicking Yes when prompted.

4. Choose the items you want to back up by selecting or clearing the check boxes associated with a particular drive or folder. When you select a top-level folder, all the subfolders are selected. When you clear a check box for a top-level folder, check boxes for the related subfolders are cleared as well. Key backup options for Exchange Server are as follows:

   • To create a full backup that includes all Exchange servers in the organization, you need to select the Microsoft Information Store node of each individual server. Expand Microsoft Exchange Server, expand the node for the first server that you want to back up, and then select Microsoft Information Store. Afterward, expand the node for the next server that you want to back up, select Microsoft Information Store, and so on.

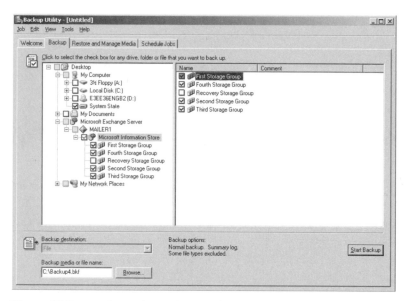

Figure 12-3. *Use the Backup tab to configure backups by hand, and then click Start Backup.*

- To back up specific Exchange servers, expand Microsoft Exchange Server, expand the node for the server that you want to back up, and then select Microsoft Information Store.

- To back up all user databases on a specific Exchange server, expand Microsoft Exchange Server, expand the node for the server that you want to back up, and then select Microsoft Information Store.

- To back up individual databases on an Exchange server, expand Microsoft Exchange Server, expand a server, expand Information Store, expand the storage group you want to work with, and then select the database to back up.

- To back up all databases used by Exchange 5.5 users, expand Microsoft Exchange Server, and then select Microsoft Site Replication Service.

- To back up individual databases used by Exchange 5.5 users, expand Microsoft Exchange Server, expand a server, expand Microsoft Site Replication Service, and then select a storage group.

5. If you want to back up configuration data, choose additional items. The key options are as follows:

- To back up Exchange Server 2003 and Windows settings, select all hard disk drives where Windows and Exchange Server are installed. Normally, this means backing up the root drive C and the drives used by Exchange Server.

- To back up the Windows registry and Active Directory settings, expand My Computer and then select System State. System State includes essential system files needed to recover the local system. All computers have system state data, which you must back up in addition to other files to restore a complete working system.

- To back up Key Management Services data, expand Microsoft Exchange Server, expand all servers running this service, and then select Key Management Service wherever applicable. You must also back up the system state data, which contains public keys for users in the organization.

6. Use the Backup Destination drop-down list to choose the media type for the backup. Choose File if you want to back up to a file. Choose a storage device if you want to back up files and folders to a tape or removable disk.

Note   When you write backups to a file, the backup file normally has the .bkf file extension. You can use another file extension if you want. Note also that you use Removable Storage to manage tapes and removable disks.

7. In Backup Media Or File Name, select the backup file or media you want to use. If you're backing up to a file, type a path and file name for the backup file or click Browse to find a file. If you're backing up to a tape or removable disk, choose the tape or disk you want to use.

8. Click Start Backup. This displays the Backup Job Information dialog box shown in Figure 12-4. You use the options in this dialog box as follows:

   - **Backup Description**   Sets the backup label, which applies to the current backup only

   - **Append This Backup To The Media**   Adds the backup after existing data

   - **Replace The Data On The Media With This Backup**   Overwrites existing data

   - **If The Media Is Overwritten, Use This Label To Identify The Media**   Sets the media label, which is changed only when you're writing to a blank tape or overwriting existing data

9. Click Advanced if you want to override the default options. The advanced options are as follows:

   - **Backup Data That Is In Remote Storage**   Archives placeholder files for Remote Storage with the backup. This ensures that you can recover an entire file system with necessary Remote Storage references intact.

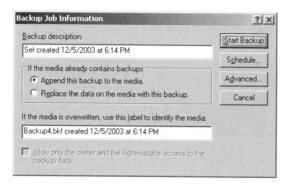

Figure 12-4. *Use the Backup Job Information dialog box to configure backup options and information as necessary, and then click Start Backup.*

- **Verify Data After Backup** Instructs Backup to verify data after the backup procedure is completed. If selected, every file on the backup tape is compared to the original file. Verifying data can protect against write errors or failures.

- **If Possible, Compress Backup Data To Save Space** Allows Backup to compress data as it's written to the storage device. This option is available only if the device supports hardware compression, and only compatible drives can read the compressed information, which might mean that only a drive from the same manufacturer can recover the data.

- **Automatically Backup System Protected Files With The System State** Backs up all the system files in the %SystemRoot% folder, in addition to the boot files that are included with the system state data.

- **Backup Type** The type of backup to perform. The available types are Normal, Copy, Differential, Incremental, and Daily.

10. Click Schedule if you want to schedule the backup for a later date. When prompted to save the backup settings, click Yes. Next, type a name for the backup selection script and then click Save. In the Scheduled Job Options dialog box, type a job name, click Properties, and then set a run schedule. Skip the remaining steps.

 Note Backup selection scripts and backup logs are stored in %Userprofile%\Local Settings\Application Data\Microsoft\WindowsNT\ NTBackup\Data. Backup selection scripts are saved with the .bks extension. Backup logs are saved with the .log extension. You can view these files with any standard text editor, such as Notepad.

11. Click Finish to start the backup operation. You can cancel the backup by clicking Cancel in the Set Information and Backup Progress dialog boxes.

12. When the backup is completed, click Close to complete the process or click Report to view the backup log.

Recovering Exchange Server

With the Windows Backup utility, you can restore Exchange Server 2003 using the Restore Wizard or the Restore tab within the Backup program. You can perform recovery on individual databases and storage groups or on all databases on a particular server. The recovery procedure you use depends on the types of backups you have available.

If you use normal backups and differential backups, you can recover an Exchange database or storage group to the point of failure by completing the following steps:

1. Restore the most recent normal (full) backup as described in the sections of this chapter entitled "Recovering Exchange Server with the Restore Wizard" or "Recovering Exchange Server Manually." Don't set the Last Backup Set option, and don't mount the database after restore.

2. Restore the most recent differential backup as described in the sections of this chapter entitled "Recovering Exchange Server with the Restore Wizard" or "Recovering Exchange Server Manually." Be sure to set the Last Backup Set option and mount the database after restore. This starts the log file replay after the restore completes.

3. Check the related mailbox and public folder stores to make sure that the data recovery was successful.

If you use normal backups and incremental backups, you can recover an Exchange database or storage group to the point of failure by completing the following steps:

1. Restore the most recent normal (full) backup as described in the sections of this chapter entitled "Recovering Exchange Server with the Restore Wizard" or "Recovering Exchange Server Manually." Don't set the Last Backup Set option, and don't mount the database after restore.

2. Apply each incremental backup in order. Restore the first incremental backup created after the normal backup, then the second, and so on, as described in the sections of this chapter entitled "Recovering Exchange Server with the Restore Wizard" or "Recovering Exchange Server Manually."

3. When restoring the last incremental backup, be sure to set the Last Backup Set option and mount the database after restore. This starts the log file replay after the restore completes.

4. Check the related mailbox and public folder stores to make sure that the data recovery was successful.

Recovering Exchange Server with the Restore Wizard

To recover Exchange Server 2003 with the Restore Wizard, follow these steps:

1. Restore system and configuration data before restoring the user data by following these instructions:

   - When restoring configuration data, stop all services being used by Exchange Server as well as Internet Information Services (IIS) services—IIS Admin, Network News Transport Protocol (NNTP), Simple Mail Transfer Protocol (SMTP), and World Wide Web Publishing Service. Exit Exchange System Manager. Restart the Microsoft Exchange Information Store service.

   - When restoring user data, dismount the affected data stores before starting the recovery operation. During recovery, Exchange services are stopped temporarily.

   - When recovering an entire server, make sure that you restore drives, system state data, Exchange configuration data, and Exchange user data.

2. Start the Backup utility in advanced mode and then click Restore Wizard on the Welcome tab. If wizard mode is enabled, click Advanced Mode and then click Restore Wizard.

3. As shown in Figure 12-5, you can now choose the data you want to restore. The left view displays files organized by volume. The right view displays media sets. If the media set you want to work with isn't shown or there is no media information, click Browse, and then type the path to the catalog for the backup.

   - To recover Exchange data, select the Information Store storage groups you want to restore. Each storage group must be selected individually. If you want to restore an individual mailbox store or the log files for a storage group, expand the storage group node and then select the mailbox store and log file nodes as appropriate.

   - To recover regular file data, select the check box next to any drive, folder, or file that you want to restore. You can't restore regular file data and Exchange data in the same operation. You need to restore each in turn and probably want to start with the regular file data.

   - To restore system state data, select the System State check box and boxes for other data you want to restore. If you're restoring to the original location, the current system state is replaced by the system state data you're restoring. If you restore to an alternate location, only the registry, system volume, and system boot files are restored. You can restore system state data only on a local system.

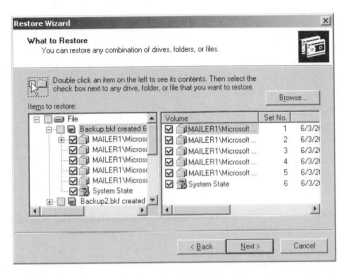

Figure 12-5. *In the Restore Wizard, select the Exchange data to restore.*

Tip By default, Active Directory and other replicated data, such as
Sysvol, aren't restored on domain controllers. This information is
instead replicated to the domain controller after you restart it, which
prevents accidentally overwriting essential domain information.

4. Click Next. In the Restore To field, type the name of the computer on which
   you want to restore files, such as Mailer1, or click Browse to search for the
   computer.

5. In Temporary Location For Log And Patch Files, enter the folder path for a
   temporary restore location, such as C:\Temp.

6. If this is the last backup set you need to recover, select Last Backup Set and
   Mount Database After Restore.

7. Click Next. If they're available, you can choose to restore security and system files using the following options:

   - **Restore Security Settings** Restores security settings for Exchange
     data, files, and folders on NTFS volumes.

   - **Restore Junction Points, Not The Folder And File Data They
     Reference** Restores network drive mappings but doesn't restore
     the actual data to the mapped network drive. Essentially, you're
     restoring the folder that references the network drive.

   - **When Restoring Replicated Data Sets, Mark The Restored Data
     As The Primary Data For All Replicas** Useful if you're restoring
     replicated data and want the restored data to be published to sub-
     scribers. If you don't choose this option, the data might not be

replicated because it will appear older than existing data on the subscribers.

8. Click Next, and then click Finish. If prompted, type the path and name of the backup set to use. You can cancel the backup by clicking Cancel in the Operation Status and Restore Progress dialog boxes.

9. When the restore is completed, click Close to complete the process or click Report to view a backup log containing information about the restore operation.

Always check the related mailbox and public folder stores to make sure that the data recovery was successful.

Recovering Exchange Server Manually

You don't have to use the Restore Wizard to recover Exchange Server 2003. You can recover Exchange data manually by completing the following steps:

1. Restore system and configuration data before restoring the user data by following these instructions:

   * When restoring configuration data, stop all services being used by Exchange Server as well as IIS services (IIS Admin, NNTP, SMTP, and World Wide Web Publishing Service). Exit Exchange System Manager. Restart the Microsoft Exchange Information Store service.

   * When restoring user data, dismount the affected data stores before starting the recovery operation. During recovery, Exchange services are stopped temporarily.

   * When recovering an entire server, make sure that you restore drives, system state data, Exchange configuration data, and Exchange user data.

2. Start Backup. If wizard mode is enabled, click Advanced Mode and then click the Restore And Manage Media tab. Otherwise, just click the Restore And Manage Media tab.

3. Choose the data you want to restore, as shown in Figure 12-6. The left view displays files organized by volume. The right view displays media sets. If the media set you want to work with isn't shown or there is no media information, right-click File in the left pane and then select Catalog File. You can then type the path to the catalog for the backup.

   * To recover Exchange data, select the Information Store storage groups you want to restore. Each storage group must be selected individually. If you want to restore an individual mailbox store or the log files for a storage group, expand the storage group node and then select the mailbox store and log file nodes as appropriate.

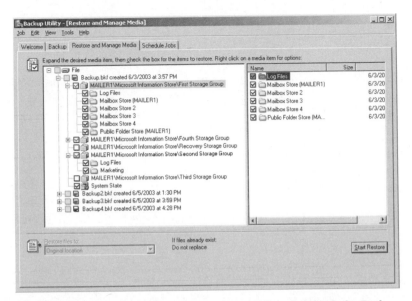

Figure 12-6. *Using the Restore And Manage Media tab, specify the Exchange data to restore.*

- To recover regular file data, select the check box next to any drive, folder, or file that you want to restore. You can't restore regular file data and Exchange data in the same operation. You need to restore each in turn and probably want to start with the regular file data.

- To restore system state data, select the System State check box and check boxes for other data you want to restore. If you're restoring to the original location, the current system state is replaced by the system state data you're restoring. If you restore to an alternate location, only the registry, Sysvol, and system boot files are restored. You can restore system state data only on a local system.

Tip By default, Active Directory and other replicated data, such as Sysvol, aren't restored on domain controllers. Instead, this information is replicated to the domain controller after you restart it, which prevents accidentally overwriting essential domain information.

4. Use the Restore Files To drop-down list to choose the restore location. The options are as follows:

- **Original Location** Restores data to the folder or files it was in when it was backed up.

- **Alternate Location** Restores data to a folder that you designate, preserving the directory structure. After you select this option, enter the folder path to use or click Browse to select the folder path.

- **Single Folder** Restores all files to a single folder without preserving the directory structure. After you select this option, enter the folder path to use or click Browse to select the folder path.

5. Specify how you want to restore files. Click Tools, and then select Options. This displays the Options dialog box with the Restore folder selected. The available options are as follows:

- **Do Not Replace The Files On My Computer (Recommended)** Select this option if you don't want to copy over existing files.

- **Replace The File On Disk Only If The File On Disk Is Older** Select this option to replace older files on disk with newer files from the backup.

- **Always Replace The File On My Computer** Select this option to replace all files on disk with files from the backup.

6. Click Start Restore. This displays the Restoring Database Store dialog box.

7. In the Restore To field, type the name of the computer on which you want to restore files, such as Mailer1, or click Browse to search for the computer.

8. In Temporary Location For Log And Patch Files, enter the folder path for a temporary restore location, such as C:\Temp.

9. If this is the last backup set you need to recover, select Last Backup Set and Mount Database After Restore.

10. Click OK to start the restore operation. If prompted, enter the path and name of the backup set to use. You can cancel the backup by clicking Cancel in the Operation Status and Restore Progress dialog boxes.

11. When the restore is completed, click Close to complete the process or click Report to view a backup log containing information about the restore operation.

Always check the related mailbox and public folder stores to make sure that the data recovery was successful.

Restoring Mailboxes Selectively from Backup

You use recovery storage groups to restore mailboxes selectively from any of the regular storage groups in an Exchange organization. The process of using a recovery storage group to restore mailbox data works like this:

1. Create a recovery storage group in the administrative group that contains the server or servers for which you want to restore mailboxes.

2. Add the databases you want to recover to the recovery storage group, keeping in mind that the databases must be from the same storage group.

3. Use a backup utility, such as Windows Backup, to restore the mailbox databases and then mount the recovery database in the recovery storage group

you previously created. Mailboxes in the recovery storage group are disconnected and are not accessible to users.

4. Use the Microsoft Exchange Mailbox Merge Wizard to select the mailboxes to restore and restore them to the original mailbox store database. The wizard copies data from the mailboxes in the recovery databases and merges it with data in the corresponding mailboxes in the specified database.

5. When you are finished using the recovery storage group, dismount the recovery databases. By dismounting the recovery databases, you allow normal recovery operations of Exchange server to resume.

Although restoring mailboxes from backups is a lengthy process, it is the best way to selectively recover mailboxes from backup. Keep in mind that you don't have to use recovery storage groups to recover all the mailboxes in a given mailbox database. In this case, you simply restore the entire mailbox database.

Step 1: Creating and Using Recovery Storage Groups

Regardless of whether you are using Exchange Server 2003 Standard Edition or Exchange Server 2003 Enterprise Edition, each Exchange server in your organization can have a recovery storage group. If you need to recover mailboxes stored on multiple Exchange servers, you don't have to create a recovery storage group on each server. Instead, you can create one recovery storage group for each administrative group in your Exchange organization.

Before you create a recovery storage group, plan carefully for the additional storage requirements. During the recovery process, two types of files are created:

- **Transaction**   Transaction files, stored in the transaction log location, are given the file prefix R00 by default. These files are created when you mount the recovery database. You'll find a transaction checkpoint file that contains recovered file fragments (R00.chk), a temporary log file that is used as temporary workspace for processing transactions (R00tmp.log), and a transaction log file that is the primary transaction log file for the recovery group. The total space required for transaction files is at least as much as that of the databases for which you plan to restore mailboxes.

- **System**   System files, stored in the system path location, include the rich-text database (.edb) file, the streaming Internet content (.stm) file, and log files for mailbox store databases. These files are created when you restore and then mount the recovery database. The total space required for system files is the same as that of the original mailbox store database and logs files.

To create a recovery storage group, follow these steps:

1. In System Manager, expand the Servers node. Right-click the server you want to work with, point to New, and then select Recovery Storage Group. Remember, the recovery storage group must be in the same administrative group as the server for which you want to recover mailboxes.

2. You should now see the Properties dialog box shown in Figure 12-7. In the Name field, type a name for the recovery storage group.

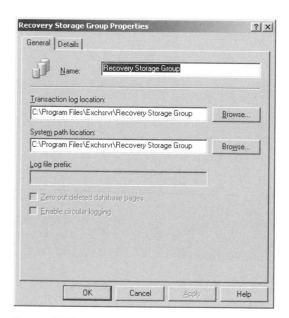

Figure 12-7. *Set the properties for the new recovery storage group on the General tab.*

3. You'll see the default location for the transaction log and the system path. If you want to change the location of these files, use the Browse buttons to the right of the related fields to set new file locations.

> **Caution** You don't want to overwrite existing files. The transaction log and system file locations you use must be different than the location of the original files.

4. Click OK to create the recovery storage group. Although you can right-click the associated node in System Manager and select Properties to view the settings, you cannot change the settings. This means the system path and transaction log location are fixed, and the only way to change the settings is to delete the recovery storage group and then re-create it.

Step 2: Adding Databases to Recover

After you create the recovery storage group, you can add the databases containing mailboxes you need to restore. When you add databases to the recovery storage group, you are marking the databases for recovery. While in the recovery state, any restore operation on the database is written to the recovery storage group rather than to the Exchange Information Store.

To specify the database to recover, complete the following steps:

1. In System Manager, right-click Recovery Storage Group and then select Add Database To Recover. The Select Database To Recover dialog box is displayed, as shown in Figure 12-8. Select the database you want to use and then click OK.

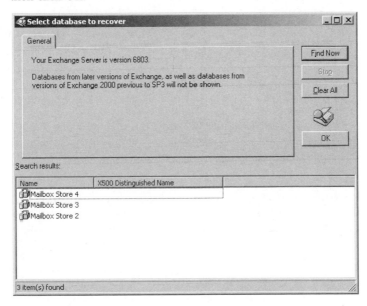

Figure 12-8. *All the databases in the storage groups you've restored are available to recover; select the one you want to use and then click OK.*

2. The Properties dialog box for the database you selected is displayed. Confirm that this is the database you want to use and then click OK.

3. To add more databases to the recovery storage group, repeat Steps 1 and 2. Keep in mind that all the databases must be from the same storage group.

Step 3: Restoring and Mounting the Recovery Databases

Once you mark databases for recovery, you should restore them using Windows Backup, making sure to apply the last full (normal) backup and any subsequent differential or incremental backups as necessary. When the restore operation is complete, you can mount the database to the recovery storage group. To do this, complete the following steps:

1. Start Windows Backup. If wizard mode is enabled, click Advanced Mode and then click the Restore tab. Otherwise, just click the Restore tab.

2. Expand the backup media containing the last full backup of the Exchange server Information Store and then select the storage group that contains the

databases you want to work with. If you want to restore an individual mailbox store, expand the storage group node and then select the mailbox store and any associated log files.

3. Click Start Restore. This displays the Restoring Database Store dialog box.

4. In the Restore To field, type the name of the computer on which you want to restore files, such as Mailer1, or click Browse to search for the computer.

5. In Temporary Location For Log And Patch Files, enter the folder path for a temporary restore location, such as C:\Temp.

6. If this is the last backup set you need to recover, select Last Backup Set and Mount Database After Restore.

7. Click OK to start the restore operation. When the restore is completed, click Close to complete the process. Keep in mind the databases aren't recovered to the Exchange Information Store—they are written to the recovery storage group.

 Tip If you need to apply differential or incremental backups, repeat Steps 2 through 7, making sure to select the correct backup media. With differential backups, you only need to restore the last differential backup. With incremental backups, you must restore each incremental backup sequentially, starting with the first one made after the last full (normal) backup.

8. In System Manager, expand the administrative group you want to work with and then select Recovery Storage Group.

9. In the Details pane, right-click a database and then select Mount Store. Confirm the action by clicking Yes. Repeat this step to mount any other databases to the recovery storage group.

Step 4: Selecting and Restoring Mailboxes

Now that you've recovered the databases and mounted them, you can use the Microsoft Exchange Mailbox Merge Wizard to select mailboxes and restore them. The wizard copies data from the mailboxes in the recovery databases and merges it with the existing data in the mailboxes of the original database.

Before you can use the Microsoft Exchange Mailbox Merge Wizard, you might need to install it by completing the following steps:

1. Insert the Exchange Server 2003 CD-ROM into the CD-ROM drive.

2. Start and open a command prompt and then type **xcopy d:\Support\Utils\ I386\ExMerge*.*** "*%ProgramFiles%\Exchsrvr\Bin*" where d is the drive letter of the CD-ROM drive and *%ProgramFiles%\Exchsrvr\Bin* is the path to the bin directory for Exchange Server enclosed in quotation marks.

3. The following files should be copied successfully to the bin directory:

- **ExMerge.exe** The executable for the Mailbox Merge Wizard
- **ExMerge.ini** An initialization file for the Mailbox Merge Wizard
- **ExMerge.rtf** A summary on using and working with the Mailbox Merge Wizard

Once the Microsoft Exchange Mailbox Merge Wizard is installed, you can use it to select and extract mailbox data by completing the following steps:

1. Click Start and then select Run. In the Open prompt of the Run dialog box, type the path to ExMerge.exe, which should be **%ProgramFiles%\Exchsrvr\Bin\Exmerge**, and then click OK.

2. Click Next. Select Extract Or Import (One Step Procedure) and then click Next.

3. On the Source Server wizard page shown in Figure 12-9, type the name of the server on which you created the recovery group, such as Mailer1, in the field provided.

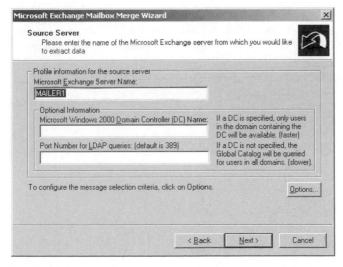

Figure 12-9. *Specify the server on which you created the recovery group and then configure additional options.*

4. Click Options to display the Data Selection Criteria dialog box. Use the options in this dialog box to specify what data to export and how data should be handled. Five tabs are provided:

   - **Data** Specify which data from the source store to use. Select User Messages And Folders to copy all user data; Associated Folder Messages to copy folder rules, folder views, and other associated messages for folders; Folder Permissions to overwrite any existing permissions with those of the source mailbox; and Items From Dumpster to copy items in the Deleted Items folder.

- **Import** Specify whether to copy, merge, or replace data. With copy, all messages in the source mailbox are copied to the target mailbox, which could result in duplicate messages in the target mailbox. With merge, the wizard checks to see if a source message exists in the target mailbox before copying it and if it does, the message isn't copied. With replace, the wizard checks to see if a source message exists in the target mailbox before copying it and if it does, the message is deleted from the target and then copied from the source mailbox.

- **Folders** Specify folders that should be processed. To specify that folders shouldn't be processed, click Modify under Ignore These Folders and then add available folders to the selected folder lists. To explicitly specify folders that should be processed, click Modify under Process Only These Folders and then add available folders to the selected folder lists.

- **Dates** Specify whether the message date is used to filter messages. By default, message dates aren't used to determine whether messages are processed. You can limit the date range by selecting Dated and then entering start and end dates in the From and To fields, respectively.

- **Message Details** Specify the exact message subjects or file name of attachments you are looking for. Multiple subjects and attachment names can be specified.

5. Click Next. On the Destination Server wizard page, type the name of the destination server in the field provided. This server should be the same as the original server, meaning the server from which the backup was made.

6. Click Next. On the Database Selection wizard page, select the recovery storage group you want to work with and then click Next again.

7. On the Mailbox Selection wizard page, select the mailboxes to recover as shown in Figure 12-10 and then click Next. You can use Shift and Ctrl to select multiple mailboxes.

8. On the Locale Selection wizard page, select the default language to use when connecting to a mailbox that has not yet been created. This controls the language used for the default folders of any mailbox that is created. Click Next.

9. On the Target Directory wizard page, click Change Folder and then use the Browse For Folder dialog box to specify a temporary folder for the mailbox PST files that need to be created. Confirm that the disk space available and required values are adequate using the fields of the Disk Space pane and then click Next.

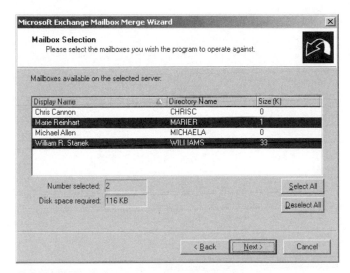

Figure 12-10. *Select the mailboxes you want to recover.*

10. To save settings and options for next time you use the wizard, click Save Settings and then click Next. Otherwise, just click Next.

11. Click Finish. The wizard exports the data into PST files and then imports the data into the designated mailboxes. If errors occur, you can check the merge log (ExMerge.log) file, which is created in the %ProgramFiles%\Exchsrvr\Bin folder, to determine what error occurred and how to correct it if necessary.

Step 5: Dismounting Recovery Databases

When you are finished using the recovery storage group, dismount the recovery databases by selecting the recovery storage group in System Manager, right-clicking the mounted database, and then selecting Dismount Store. Confirm the action by clicking Yes when prompted to continue. By dismounting the recovery database, you allow normal recovery operations of Exchange Server to resume.

As an additional step, you can delete the recovery database to remove references to it in Exchange Server. Right-click the database and then select Delete. Deleting the database does not remove the system and transaction files used by the database. You must delete these files yourself.

Part IV

Microsoft Exchange Server 2003 and Group Administration

Part IV covers advanced tasks for managing and maintaining Microsoft Exchange Server 2003 organizations. Chapter 13 provides the essentials for managing servers, administrative groups, and routing groups. In this chapter you also learn how to configure global settings for your organization. Chapter 14 explores message routing within your organization. The chapter starts with a discussion of the X.400 Message Transfer Agent and X.400 stacks and then explains how to install and use connectors for routing groups, Simple Mail Transfer Protocol (SMTP), and X.400. Chapter 15 explores ways to configure SMTP, Internet Message Access Protocol 4 (IMAP4), and Post Office Protocol 3 (POP3) virtual servers. Chapter 16 covers Hypertext Transfer Protocol (HTTP) virtual servers and access from the Web. Finally, Chapter 17 discusses Exchange Server maintenance, monitoring, and queuing.

Chapter 13

Managing Microsoft Exchange Server 2003 Organizations

This chapter discusses techniques you'll use to manage Microsoft Exchange organizations. Exchange organizations are the root of your Exchange environment, and it's at the organization level that you specify global settings and define the administrative and routing group structures you want to use. Global settings define default message conversion rules and message delivery options for all Exchange servers in your organization. Administrative groups define the logical structure of your organization; you use them primarily in large Exchange installations to simplify the management of permissions. Routing groups define the connectivity and communication channels for the organization's Exchange servers; you normally use them only when you need to connect branch offices or other geographically separated locations.

Configuring Global Settings for the Organization

You use global settings to set basic messaging rules throughout the organization. They are ideally suited to environments in which you require consistent message formatting and delivery options. Although global settings are important, you can specify many of the same configuration options at other levels in the organization. For example, instead of setting the rules on a global basis, you can set messaging rules for servers, data stores, or individual mailboxes.

It's important to make sure that global settings don't conflict with settings made elsewhere in the organization. This is why local settings always override global settings. This means you can set global values at the organization level and then override those values as necessary.

Setting Internet Message Formats

Internet message format options allow you to set rules that Simple Mail Transfer Protocol (SMTP) servers use to format outgoing messages. By default, when Messaging Application Programming Interface (MAPI) clients in the organization send messages, the message body is converted from Exchange Rich Text Format (RTF) to Multipurpose Internet Mail Extensions (MIME) and message attachments are identified with a MIME content type based on the attachment's file extension. You can change this behavior by applying new rules.

Using SMTP Policies to Apply Formatting

You enforce message formatting rules through SMTP policies. The default policy applies to all outbound mail that isn't subject to another SMTP policy. Other policies apply to a specific domain that you designate.

Assigning Default Message Formats for the Organization   You can access and modify the default SMTP policy by completing the following steps:

1. Start System Manager, and then expand Global Settings.

2. Select Internet Message Formats. In the right pane, you should see a list of the currently defined SMTP policies. The Domain column specifies the domains to which the policies apply.

3. Right-click the policy labeled Default, and then select Properties. You can now view or modify the default message formats for the organization.

 Note   If the default policy has been renamed, you can use the value in the Domain field to determine the global default. An asterisk in the Domain column indicates that the policy applies to all domains.

Assigning Message Formats on a Per Domain Basis   Occasionally, you'll need to format mail that is bound for another organization in a specific way. To do this, you'll need to create an SMTP policy for the domain by completing the following steps:

1. Start System Manager, and then expand Global Settings.

2. Right-click Internet Message Formats, point to New, and then choose Domain. This displays the Properties dialog box shown in Figure 13-1.

3. In the Name field, type a descriptive name for the SMTP policy. Then type the Domain Name System (DNS) name of the domain to which the policy will apply, such as **microsoft.com**.

4. Click the Message Format tab and then set the message encoding and character sets you want to use as described in the section of this chapter entitled "Setting Message Encoding and Character Set Usage."

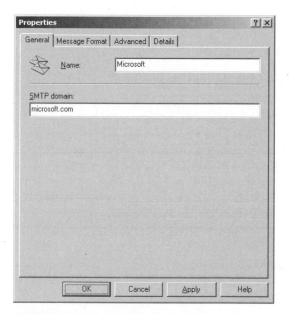

Figure 13-1. *Use the Domain Properties dialog box to create SMTP policies for individual domains.*

5. Click the Advanced tab and then set advanced formatting options as described in the section of this chapter entitled "Managing Rich-Text Formatting, Word Wrap, Autoresponses, and Display Names."

6. Click OK to create the policy. The policy is then applied to all mail being delivered to the designated domain.

Changing and Deleting Message Formatting Rules You can change or delete message formatting rules at any time. To do this, follow these steps:

1. Start System Manager, and then expand Global Settings.

2. Select Internet Message Formats. In the right pane, you should see a list of the currently defined SMTP policies. The Domain column specifies the domains to which the policies apply.

3. To edit the formatting rules for a domain, right-click the related policy, and then select Properties. You can now modify the message formatting rules for this domain.

4. To delete the formatting rules for a domain, right-click the related policy, and then select Delete. When prompted to confirm the deletion, click Yes.

Setting Message Encoding and Character Set Usage

Two key aspects of message formatting are encoding and character set usage. Message encoding rules determine the formatting for elements in the body of outbound messages. Character set usage determines which character sets are used for reading and writing messages. If users send messages with text in more than one language, the character set that's used determines how the various languages are displayed.

To set message encoding and character set usage, follow these steps:

1. Start System Manager, and then expand Global Settings.

2. Select Internet Message Formats. In the right pane, you should see a list of the currently defined SMTP policies.

3. Right-click the policy you want to edit, and then select Properties.

4. Click the Message Format tab, as shown in Figure 13-2. Exchange Server can format messages using either UUEncode or MIME. To use UUEncode, select UUEncode and then, if you wish, select Use BinHex For Macintosh to deliver messages to Macintosh clients using the native binary encoding format. To use MIME, select MIME in the Message Encoding panel, and then choose one of the following options:

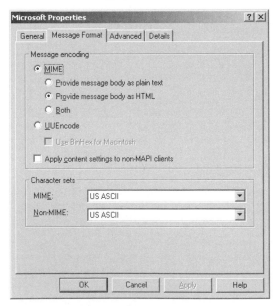

Figure 13-2. *Use the Message Format tab to change global defaults for message encoding and character set usage.*

- **Provide Message Body As Plain Text** Exchange Server converts the message body to text format and any other elements, such as graphics, are replaced with textual representations.

- **Provide Message Body As HTML** Exchange Server converts the message body to Hypertext Markup Language (HTML). This allows compliant client applications to display the message body with graphics, hypertext links, and other elements. Clients that don't support HTML, however, display the actual markup tags mixed in with the text, which can make the message difficult to read.

- **Both**   Exchange Server delivers messages with their original formatting, which can be either plain text or HTML. Use this option to allow the sender to choose the message format.

Note   Exchange Server also supports a third message encoding format called Exchange Rich Text Format that you enable through an advanced configuration setting, which I will discuss later on. Exchange Rich Text Format is displayed only when clients elect to use this format and you've set the Rich Text Format as Always Use or Determined By Individual User Settings.

5. Select the character sets to use for MIME and non-MIME messages, such as Western European (ISO-8859-1). All text in the affected outbound messages uses the character set you specify.

6. Click OK to apply the changes. Keep in mind that local settings override global settings.

Managing Rich-Text Formatting, Word Wrap, Autoresponses, and Display Names

Many advanced options are available for message formatting as well. These options control the use of Exchange Rich Text Format, word wrap, autoresponses, and display names.

To set these advanced formatting options, follow these steps:

1. Start System Manager, and then expand Global Settings.

2. Select Internet Message Formats. In the right pane you should see a list of the currently defined SMTP policies.

3. Right-click the policy you want to edit, and then select Properties. Click the Advanced tab, as shown in Figure 13-3.

4. Exchange Rich Text Format is a preferred text format for older Exchange clients. By default, individual user settings are used to determine availability of Exchange Rich Text Format. If you want to override this setting, in the Exchange Rich-Text Format panel, select Always Use or Never Use. With Always Use, all outbound messages to which this policy applies are formatted in RTF, provided that you haven't set MIME encoding to HTML on the Message Format tab. With Never Use, RTF support is disabled, and Exchange Server uses the format you set on the Message Format tab.

5. Text word wrap controls whether long lines of text are reformatted with line breaks. By default, individual user settings determine when text word wrapping occurs and the Never Use option is selected. If you want to enforce text word wrapping at a specific character position, select Use At Column and then enter a column number.

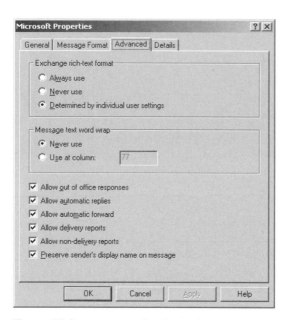

Figure 13-3. *You control rich-text formatting, word wrap, autoresponses, and display names on the Advanced tab.*

6. Use the options in the lower third of the dialog box to enable or disable autoresponses. Autoresponses are automatic messages sent in response to an inbound message. By default, all autoresponse messages are enabled. These messages are as follows:

- **Out Of Office Responses** Notifies the sender that the recipient is out of the office

- **Automatic Replies** Notifies the sender that the message was received

- **Automatic Forward** Allows Exchange Server to forward or deliver a duplicate message to a new recipient

- **Allow Delivery Reports** Allows Exchange Server to return delivery confirmation reports to the sender

- **Allow Non-Delivery Reports** Allows Exchange Server to return nondelivery confirmation reports to the sender

- **Preserve Sender's Display Name On Message** Allows both the sender's name and e-mail address to appear on outbound e-mail messages

7. The final option on the Advanced tab controls the use of display names. If you want Exchange Server to deliver messages with the display name shown in the Address Book, select Preserve Sender's Display Name On Message. Otherwise, clear this check box, and Exchange Server delivers messages using the Exchange alias.

8. Click OK to apply the changes. Keep in mind that local settings override global settings.

Associating MIME Types with Extensions

When Exchange Server sends messages to clients outside the organization, message attachments are assigned a content type based on the attachment's file extension. This content type tells the client about the contents of the attachment, such as whether it's an HTML document, a Graphics Interchange Format (GIF) image, or a Portable Document Format (PDF) file.

You can associate multiple file extensions with a single content type. For example, the MIME type text/html has two file extension mappings by default. These mappings are for the file extensions .htm and .html.

To view current MIME type-to-file extension mappings, follow these steps:

1. Start System Manager, and then expand Global Settings.

2. Right-click Internet Message Formats, and then choose Properties. This displays the Properties dialog box shown in Figure 13-4.

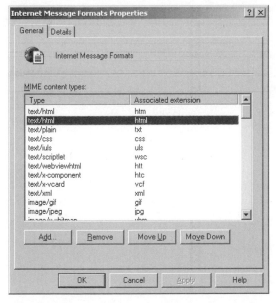

Figure 13-4. *Use the Internet Message Formats Properties dialog box to change, add, or delete MIME type-to-file extension mappings.*

To add a new MIME type-to-file extension mapping, follow these steps:

1. Start System Manager, and then expand Global Settings.

2. Right-click Internet Message Formats, and then choose Properties.

3. On the General tab, click Add.

4. In the Type field, type the MIME content type, such as **text/html**.

5. In the Associated Extension field, type the file extension to associate with the content type, such as **htm**.

6. Click OK in the Add MIME Content Type dialog box. Repeat this procedure to add other MIME content type mappings.

To edit an existing MIME type-to-file extension mapping, follow these steps:

1. Start System Manager, and then expand Global Settings.

2. Right-click Internet Message Formats, and then choose Properties.

3. Double-click the MIME content type mapping that you want to change.

4. Make changes in the MIME Type Properties dialog box, and then click OK.

To remove a MIME type-to-file extension mapping, follow these steps:

1. Start System Manager, and then expand Global Settings.

2. Right-click Internet Message Formats, and then choose Properties.

3. Select the MIME content type mapping that you want to delete, and then click Remove. When prompted to confirm the deletion, click Yes.

Setting Message Delivery Options

Message delivery options allow you to set restrictions for messages sent within, and received by, the organization's Exchange servers. A related option is the default SMTP postmaster account, which is used with nondelivery reports (NDRs). These global delivery options apply throughout the organization unless local settings override them.

Setting Default Delivery Restrictions for the Organization

Delivery restrictions control the maximum size of messages that can be sent and the maximum number of recipients to which a message can be addressed. These delivery restrictions are useful whenever you need to closely control the use of Exchange Server resources. By restricting message size, you prevent users from sending messages that might require excessive processing time when routing within the organization. By restricting the number of recipients, you prevent users from sending messages that could require hundreds or thousands of individual directory lookups and delivery connections.

To set delivery restrictions, follow these steps:

1. Start System Manager, and then expand Global Settings.

2. Right-click Message Delivery, and then choose Properties.

3. As shown in Figure 13-5, click the Defaults tab, and then use these options to set delivery restrictions:

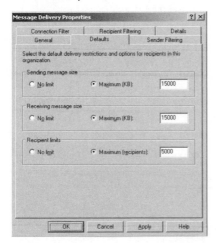

Figure 13-5. *Use the Defaults tab of the Message Delivery Properties dialog box to control the size of messages and the total number of recipients.*

- **Sending Message Size**   Controls the size of the messages that users can send. By default, the limit is set to 10240 KB. To remove the limit, select No Limit. To change the limit, select Maximum (KB) and then type a new maximum outgoing message size.

- **Receiving Message Size**   Controls the size of the messages that users can receive. By default, the limit is set to 10240 KB. To remove the limit, select No Limit. To change the limit, select Maximum (KB), and then type a new maximum incoming message size.

- **Recipient Limits**   Controls the number of recipients to which a message can be addressed. By default, the limit is set to 5000. To remove the limit, select No Limit. To change the limit, select Maximum (Recipients), and then type a new recipient limit.

4. Click OK to apply the restrictions.

Real World   A reasonable limit for incoming and outgoing messages is 15 MB (15,360 KB). A 15-MB limit allows users to attach fairly large files to messages if necessary but doesn't allow them to abuse the e-mail system. Most Microsoft PowerPoint presentations and even application executables could be sent with this restriction. Keep in mind, though, that the 15-MB limit applies to the total message size, which includes all the overhead needed by Exchange Server to format the message into sections for delivery.

Setting the Default SMTP Postmaster Account

When a message can't be delivered in the organization, the sender receives an NDR. NDRs are always sent by the organization's postmaster account. This means that the postmaster is listed in the From field of all nondelivery messages, and when users reply to a nondelivery message, the message is addressed to the postmaster by default.

The default postmaster is the Exchange Administrator account. To allow users to reach an actual person in case of problems, you should set up a separate mailbox or designate a postmaster for the organization.

To designate an existing account as the postmaster mail recipient, follow these steps:

1. Start Active Directory Users And Computers.
2. Right-click the mail-enabled user account that you would like to make the postmaster and then select Properties.
3. On the E-mail Addresses tab, click New. Afterward, in the New E-mail Address dialog box, click SMTP Address and then click OK.
4. In the E-mail Address field, type **postmaster@*domain.com*** where ***domain.com*** is the organization's default domain name.
5. Click OK.

Configuring Antispam and Message Filtering Options

Every minute users spend dealing with unsolicited commercial e-mail (called spam) or other unwanted e-mail is a minute they cannot do their work and deal with other issues. To deter spammers and other senders from whom users don't want to receive messages, you can use message filtering to block these people from sending messages to your organization. Not only can you filter messages that claim to be from a particular sender or are sent to a particular receiver, you can also establish connection filtering rules based on real-time block lists.

The sections that follow discuss sender, recipient, and connection filtering options. Configuring filtering is a two-step process:

1. Configure the sender, recipient, and connection filters that you want to use.
2. Enforce the filter rules by applying them to your organization's SMTP virtual servers.

 Real World As you configure filtering, keep in mind that Exchange Server 2003 is designed to combat the most commonly used spammer techniques, not all of them. Like the techniques of those who create viruses, the techniques of those who send spam frequently change, and you won't be able to prevent all unwanted e-mail from going through. You should, however, be able to substantially reduce the flow of spam into your organization.

Filtering Spam and Other Unwanted E-mail by Sender

Sometimes when you are filtering spam or other unwanted e-mail, you'll know specific e-mail addresses or e-mail domains from which you don't want to accept messages. In this case, you can block messages from these senders or e-mail domains by configuring sender filtering. Another sender that you probably don't want to accept messages from is a blank sender. If the sender is blank, it means the From field of the e-mail message wasn't filled in and the message is probably from a spammer.

To configure filtering according to the sender of the message, follow these steps:

1. Start System Manager, and then expand Global Settings.
2. Right-click Message Delivery, and then choose Properties. This displays the Message Delivery Properties dialog box.
3. Click the Sender Filtering tab, as shown in Figure 13-6. The Senders list box shows the current sender filters if there are any.

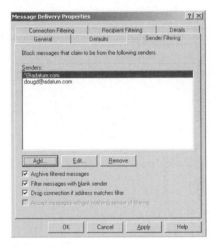

Figure 13-6. *Use the Sender Filtering tab of the Message Delivery Properties dialog box to set restrictions on addresses and domains that can send mail to your organization.*

4. You can add a sender filter by clicking Add, typing the address you'd like to filter, and then clicking OK. Addresses can be of the following formats:
   - A specific e-mail address, such as walter@microsoft.com
   - A display name enclosed in quotes, such as "Walter"
   - A group of e-mail addresses designated with the wildcard character (*), such as *@microsoft.com, to filter all e-mail addresses from microsoft.com, or *@*.microsoft.com to filter all e-mail addresses from child domains of microsoft.com.

5. You can remove a filter by selecting it, and then clicking Remove.

6. To edit a filter, double-click the filter entry, enter a new value, and then click OK.

7. You can also filter messages that don't have an e-mail address in the From field. To do this, select the Filter Messages With Blank Sender check box.

8. If you want to ensure Exchange doesn't waste processing power and other resources dealing with messages from filtered senders, select the Drop Connection If Address Matches Filter check box. With this check box selected, Exchange breaks the connection with the mail server attempting to deliver the message and doesn't archive the message or return an NDR to the sender. Click OK and skip the remaining steps.

9. If you want Exchange to archive filtered messages or return NDRs to the senders, clear the Drop Connection If Address Matches Filter check box.

10. Filtered messages are automatically deleted unless you archive them by selecting the Archive Filtered Messages check box. The filtered message archive is created in the Exchange Mailroot directory for the SMTP virtual server (which is normally located at C:\Exchsrvr\Mailroot\vsi*N* where *N* is the number of the SMTP virtual server).

11. An NDR is automatically generated for filtered messages and sent to the sender. To prevent filter notification, select the Accept Messages Without Notifying Sender Of Filtering check box.

12. Click OK.

Filtering Spam and Other Unwanted E-mail by Recipient

In any organization, you'll have users whose e-mail addresses change, perhaps because they requested it, left the company, or changed office locations. Although you might be able to forward e-mail to these users for a time, you probably won't want to forward e-mail indefinitely. At some point, you or someone else in the organization will decide it's time to delete the user's account, mailbox, or both. If the user is subscribed to mailing lists or other services that deliver automated e-mail, the automated messages continue to come in unless you manually unsubscribe the user or reply to each e-mail that you don't want to receive the messages any more. That's a measure that wastes time, but Exchange administrators often find themselves doing this. It's much easier to add the old or invalid e-mail address to a recipient filter list and specify that Exchange shouldn't accept messages for users who aren't in the Exchange Directory. Once you do this, Exchange won't attempt to deliver messages for filtered or invalid recipients, and you won't see related NDRs, either.

To configure filtering according to the message recipient, follow these steps:

1. Start System Manager, and then expand Global Settings.

2. Right-click Message Delivery, and then choose Properties. This displays the Message Delivery Properties dialog box.

3. Click the Recipient Filtering tab as shown in Figure 13-7. The Recipients list box shows the current recipient filters if there are any.

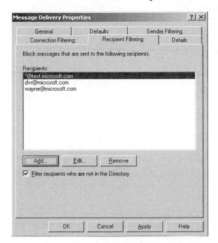

Figure 13-7. *Use the Recipient Filtering tab of the Message Delivery Properties dialog box to set restrictions for specific or invalid recipients.*

4. You can add a recipient filter by clicking Add, typing the address you'd like to filter, and then clicking OK. Addresses can refer to a specific e-mail address, such as walter@microsoft.com, or a group of e-mail addresses designated with the wildcard character (*), such as *@microsoft.com to filter all e-mail addresses from microsoft.com, or *@*.microsoft.com, to filter all e-mail addresses from child domains of microsoft.com.

5. You can remove a filter by selecting it and then clicking Remove.

6. To edit a filter, double-click the filter entry, enter a new value, and then click OK.

7. You can also filter messages that are sent to invalid recipients who don't have e-mail addresses and aren't listed in the Exchange Directory. To do this, select the Filter Recipients Who Are Not In The Directory check box.

8. Click OK.

Using Connection Filtering and Real-Time Block Lists

If you find that sender and recipient filtering isn't enough to stem the flow of spam into your organization, you might want to consider subscribing to a real-time block list service. Here's how this works:

1. You subscribe to a real-time block list service. Typically, you'll have to pay a monthly service fee. In return, the service lets you query their servers for known sources of unsolicited e-mail and known relay servers.

2. The service provides you with domains you can use for validation and a list of status codes to watch for. You configure Exchange to use the specified domains and enter connection filtering rules to match the return codes. Then you configure any exceptions for recipient e-mail addresses or sender Internet Protocol (IP) addresses.

3. Each time an incoming connection is made, Exchange performs a lookup of the source IP address in the block list domain. A "host not found" error is returned to indicate the IP address is not on the block list and that there is no match. If there is a match, the block list service returns a status code that indicates the suspected activity. For example, a status code of 127.0.0.3 might mean the IP address is from a known source of unsolicited e-mail.

4. If there is a match between the status code returned and the filtering rules you've configured, Exchange returns an error message to the user or server attempting to make the connection. The default error message says the IP address has been blocked by a connection filter rule, but you can specify a custom error message to return instead.

The sections that follow discuss creating connection filter rules, setting filter priority, defining custom error messages to return, and configuring connection filter exceptions. These are all tasks you'll perform when you work with connection filters.

Creating Connection Filter Rules

Before you get started, you'll need to know the domain of the block list service provider and you should also consider how you want to handle the status codes the provider returns. Exchange allows you to specify that any return status code is a match, that only a specific code matched to a bit mask is a match, or that any of several status codes that you designate can match.

Table 13-1 shows a list of typical status codes that might be returned by a provider service. Rather than filter all return codes, in most cases, you'll want to be as specific as possible about the types of status codes that match. This ensures that you don't accidentally filter valid e-mail. For example, based on the list of status codes of the provider, you might decide that you want to filter known sources of unsolicited e-mail and known relay servers, but not filter known sources of dial-up user accounts, which might or might not be sources of unsolicited e-mail.

Table 13-1. Typical Status Codes Returned by Block List Provider Services

Return Status Code	Code Description	Code Bit Mask	Return Status Code
127.0.0.2	Dial-up user account	0.0.0.2	127.0.0.2
127.0.0.3	Known source of unsolicited e-mail	0.0.0.3	127.0.0.3
127.0.0.4	Known relay server	0.0.0.4	127.0.0.4

Table 13-1. Typical Status Codes Returned by Block List Provider Services

Return Status Code	Code Description	Code Bit Mask	Return Status Code
127.0.0.5	Dial-up user account using a known source of unsolicited e-mail	0.0.0.5	127.0.0.5
127.0.0.6	Dial-up user account using a known relay server	0.0.0.6	127.0.0.6
127.0.0.7	Known source of unsolicited e-mail and a known relay server	0.0.0.7	127.0.0.7
127.0.0.9	Dial-up user, known source of unsolicited e-mail and known relay server	0.0.0.9	127.0.0.9

You can create connection filter rules by completing the following steps:

1. Start System Manager, and then expand Global Settings.

2. Right-click Message Delivery, and then choose Properties. This displays the Message Delivery Properties dialog box.

3. Click the Connection Filter tab. The Rule list box on the Connection Filter tab shows the current filters (if any).

4. Click Add to display the Connection Filtering Rule dialog box shown in Figure 13-8.

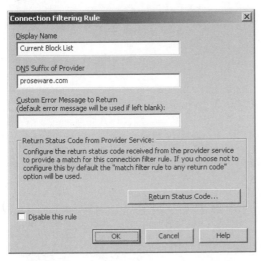

Figure 13-8. *Configure the connection rule using the Connection Filtering Rule dialog box.*

5. Type the name of the rule in the Display Name field, such as Current Block List Rule or Relay Server Filter Rule.

6. In the DNS Suffix Of Provider field, type the domain name of the block list provider service, such as proseware.com.

7. Click Return Status Code to display the dialog box shown in Figure 13-9. Select one of the following options and then click OK:

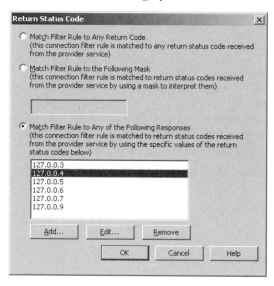

Figure 13-9. *By default any status code is matched, but you can set specific match rules as well.*

- **Match Filter Rule To Any Return Code**   Select this option to match any return code (other than an error) received from the provider service.

- **Match Filter Rule To The Following Mask**   Select this option to match a specific return code and no others received from the provider service. For example, if the return code for known relay server is 127.0.0.4 and you want to match only on this specific code, you would enter the mask 0.0.0.4.

- **Match Filter Rule To Any Of The Following Responses**   Select this option to match specific values in the return status codes. Click Add, type a return status code to match, and then click OK. Repeat as necessary for each return code you want to add.

8. Click OK to create the connection filter rule.

Setting Connection Filter Priority and Enabling Filter Rules

You can configure multiple connection filter rules. Each rule is listed in priority order and if Exchange makes a match using a particular rule, the other rules are not checked for possible matches. In addition to priority, rules also have a status as either enabled or disabled. If you disable a rule, it is ignored when looking for possible status code matches.

You can set connection filter priority and enable or disable rules by completing the following steps:

1. Start System Manager, and then expand Global Settings.

2. Right-click Message Delivery, and then choose Properties. This displays the Message Delivery Properties dialog box.

3. Select the Connection Filter tab shown in Figure 13-10. The Block List Service Configuration list box shows the current filters in priority order.

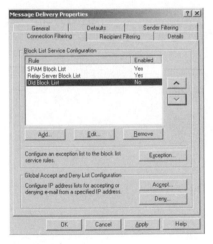

Figure 13-10. *Use the Connection Filter tab of the Message Delivery Properties dialog box to define connection filter rules and their priority.*

4. To change the priority of a rule, select it and then click the Up or Down arrow to change its order in the rule list.

5. To disable a rule, select it, and then click Edit. Next, in the Connection Filtering Rule dialog box, select Disable This Rule and then click OK.

6. Click OK to close the Message Delivery Properties dialog box.

Specifying Custom Error Messages to Return

When a match is made between the status code returned and the filtering rules you've configured, Exchange returns an error message to the user or server attempting to make the connection. The default error message says the IP address has been blocked by a connection filter rule. If you want to override the default error message, you can specify a custom error message to return on a per rule basis. The error message can contain the following substitution values:

- %0 to insert the connecting IP address
- %1 to insert the name of the connection filter rule
- %2 to insert the domain name of the block list provider service

Some examples of custom error messages include the following:

- The IP address (%1) was blocked and not allowed to connect.
- %1 was rejected by %2 as a potential source of unsolicited e-mail.

Using the substitution values, you can create a custom error message by following these steps:

1. Start System Manager, and then expand Global Settings.
2. Right-click Message Delivery, and then choose Properties. This displays the Message Delivery Properties dialog box.
3. Click the Connection Filter tab and then select the filter you want to work with.
4. Click Edit. In the Custom Error Message To Return field, type the error message to return.
5. Click OK twice.

Defining Connection Filter Exceptions and Global Accept/Deny Lists

Sometimes you'll find that an IP address, a network, or an e-mail address shows up incorrectly on a block list. The easiest way to correct this problem is to create a block list exception that specifies that the specific IP address, network, or e-mail address shouldn't be filtered.

Creating Connection Filter Exceptions for E-Mail Addresses

You can create connection filter exceptions for e-mail addresses by completing the following steps:

1. Start System Manager, and then expand Global Settings.
2. Right-click Message Delivery, and then choose Properties. This displays the Message Delivery Properties dialog box.
3. On the Connection Filter tab, click Exception to display the Block List Service Configuration Settings dialog box shown in Figure 13-11. Any current exceptions are listed in the SMTP Address list.

Figure 13-11. *Use the Block List Service Configuration Settings dialog box to configure recipients that should not be filtered.*

4. Click Add to add a filter exception. In the Add Recipient dialog box, type the e-mail address, such as abuse@adatum.com, and then click OK.

5. Select an existing e-mail address and then click Remove to delete a filter exception.

Note   Be sure that an e-mail address specified as an exception doesn't match an address on the Recipient Filtering tab. If it does, a conflict occurs, and in most cases, the e-mail address is matched against the recipient filter, meaning Exchange won't attempt to deliver messages for that e-mail address.

6. Click OK twice.

Creating Global Accept Lists for IP Addresses and Networks

Exchange will accept e-mail from any IP address or network on the global accept list. To define accept-list entries for IP addresses and networks, complete the following steps:

1. Start System Manager, and then expand Global Settings.

2. Right-click Message Delivery, and then choose Properties. This displays the Message Delivery Properties dialog box.

3. Click Accept on the Connection Filtering tab. This displays the Accept List dialog box. You'll find a list of current IP addresses and networks that are configured on the accept list in the IP Address (Mask) List.

4. Click Add to add an IP address or network to the accept list.
   - For a single IP address, select Single IP Address and then type the IP address in the field provided, such as 192.168.10.45.
   - For groups of computers, select Group Of IP Addresses and then type the subnet address, such as 192.168.0.0, and subnet mask, such as 255.255.0.0.
5. Select an existing entry and then click Remove to remove it from the accept list.
6. Click OK twice.

Creating Global Deny Lists for IP Addresses and Networks

Exchange will reject e-mail from any IP address or network on the deny list. To define deny list entries for IP addresses and networks, complete the following steps:

1. Start System Manager, and then expand Global Settings.
2. Right-click Message Delivery, and then choose Properties. This displays the Message Delivery Properties dialog box.
3. Click Deny on the Connection Filtering tab. This displays the Deny List dialog box. You'll find a list of current IP addresses and networks that are configured on the deny list in the IP Address (Mask) List.
4. Click Add to add an IP address or network to the deny list.
   - For a single IP address, select Single IP Address and then type the IP address in the field provided, such as 192.168.10.45.
   - For groups of computers, select Group Of IP Addresses and then type the subnet address, such as 192.168.0.0, and subnet mask, such as 255.255.0.0.
5. Select an existing entry and then click Remove to remove it from the deny list.
6. Click OK twice.

Applying Message Filters on SMTP Virtual Servers

Each SMTP virtual server in your organization has a different set of rules for message filters. If you want to enforce message filter rules, you must enable the sender, recipient, and connection filters you've configured separately on each SMTP virtual server.

To apply message filters on a virtual server, follow these steps:

1. Start System Manager. Double-click Servers or, if administrative groups are enabled, double-click the administrative group that contains the server you want to work with and then double-click Servers.
2. Expand the entry for the server you want to work with and then expand Protocols, SMTP.

3. Right-click the SMTP virtual server on which you want to filter messages, and then choose Properties.

4. On the General tab, click Advanced.

5. In the Advanced dialog box, select the IP address you want to filter, and then click Edit. This displays the Identification dialog box shown in Figure 13-12.

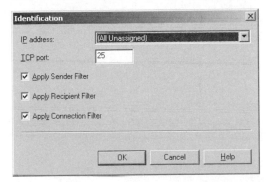

Figure 13-12. *Use the Identification dialog box to enable the filters you want to use for the selected IP address.*

6. You can now enable filter options selectively by selecting Apply Sender Filter, Apply Recipient Filter, or Apply Connection Filter. You can also enable any combination or all of the filters by selecting the filters you want to use.

7. Click OK to close the Identification dialog box. If you want to apply filters to another IP address configured on the SMTP virtual server, repeat Steps 5 and 6.

8. Click OK twice.

Managing Administrative Groups

Administrative groups define the logical structure of an Exchange organization, and you use them to help you organize and manage Exchange resources. Administrative groups are also useful in managing permissions. When you first install Exchange Server, administrative group support is disabled. However, if you followed the techniques discussed in Chapter 4, "Microsoft Exchange Server 2003 Administration Essentials," you probably enabled administrative group support. You can confirm this by looking in System Manager for an Administrative Groups node.

Administrative groups are best suited to large organizations or organizations with offices in several locations. With these types of organizations, you might want to create administrative groups for each department or office location and then use the administrative group structure to help organize related servers, routing groups, system policies, chat communities, and public folder trees—all of which you can configure on a per-administrative-group basis.

Creating Administrative Groups

When you enable administrative group support, as described in the section of Chapter 4 entitled "Using and Enabling Administrative Groups," a default administrative group called First Administrative Group is created. You can create additional administrative groups by completing the following steps:

1. In System Manager, right-click Administrative Groups, point to New, and then select Administrative Group.

2. On the General tab, type a descriptive name for the group, and then click OK.

3. Exchange Server creates the new administrative group but doesn't assign any servers to the group or create any other containers. You'll need to add these, as we'll describe in the next section.

Adding Containers to Administrative Groups

Administrative groups have containers for the following:

- Servers
- Routing groups
- System policies
- Public folder trees

Containers for servers are added to an administrative group the first time you install an Exchange server and make it a member of the group. Other containers can be added to an administrative group manually. To do this, right-click the administrative group in System Manager, point to New, and then select the container you want to create.

Each administrative group can have only one container of each type.

Controlling Access to Administrative Groups

One of the key reasons for creating administrative groups is to aid in permission management. Each administrative group can have its own security permissions, and this enables you to control who accesses a particular administrative group and the actions users can perform. You manage permissions by granting or denying access as described in the section of Chapter 8, "Implementing Directory Security and Microsoft Exchange Server 2003 Policies," entitled "Setting Exchange Server Permissions" or by delegating control at the administrative group level as described in the section of Chapter 8 entitled "Delegating Exchange Server Permissions."

Renaming and Deleting Administrative Groups

You can manage administrative groups much like any other Exchange element. To rename an administrative group, complete the following steps:

1. Start System Manager and then expand Administrative Groups.
2. Right-click the administrative group, choose Rename from the shortcut menu, and then type a new name for the administrative group.
3. Keep in mind that when you change the name of an administrative group, you change the namespace for all objects in the administrative group.

Deleting an administrative group removes the group and all its contents. Before deleting an administrative group, you should either make sure that the items it contains are no longer needed or move the items to a new administrative group. You move objects in an administrative group as described in the section of this chapter entitled "Moving and Copying Among Administrative Groups."

Once you've moved items that you might need, you can delete the administrative group by completing the following steps:

1. Start System Manager, and then expand Administrative Groups.
2. Right-click the administrative group and choose Delete from the shortcut menu.
3. When prompted, confirm the action by clicking Yes.

Moving and Copying Among Administrative Groups

You can move or copy some types of objects, such as policies and public folder trees, between administrative groups. You can copy or move objects only between containers of the same type, however.

To move an object between administrative groups, follow these steps:

1. Start System Manager, and then expand Administrative Groups. As necessary, expand the administrative groups and containers you want to work with.
2. Right-click the object you want to move, and then select Cut.
3. Right-click the target container, and then select Paste.

To copy an object between administrative groups, follow these steps:

1. Start System Manager, and then expand Administrative Groups. As necessary, expand the administrative groups and containers you want to work with.
2. Right-click the object you want to move, and then select Copy.
3. Right-click the target container, and then select Paste.

Managing Routing Groups

You use routing groups when you need to control the connectivity between geographically separated Exchange servers or when you have unreliable connections between Exchange servers in any location. For example, if your company has branch offices in Seattle and San Francisco, each office might have a separate routing group. To connect the routing groups, you must install a connector. The available connectors for communications among routing groups are the Exchange Routing Group connector, the SMTP connector, and the X.400 connector. Each has its advantages and disadvantages, which you'll learn more about in Chapter 14, "Managing Message Transfer and Routing Within the Organization."

If you have a single geographic location or have reliable, permanent connections between servers, you don't need to create additional routing groups and you don't have to install routing group connectors. Instead, you can let Exchange Server handle the necessary connections, which are configured automatically whenever you install a new Exchange server in your organization. That said, in special circumstances you might want to create multiple routing groups. For example, if you want to manage message tracking or control replication of public folders between locations, you might want to set up separate routing groups.

Creating Routing Group Containers

Routing groups aren't enabled by default in Exchange Server. Before you can create a routing group, you must enable routing group support and create a routing group container. To do this, follow these steps:

1. Right-click the organization node in System Manager, and then select Properties.
2. On the General tab of the Properties dialog box, select Display Routing Groups.
3. When you click OK, Exchange Server enables routing groups and configures them for the current operations mode.

 Note Routing groups behave differently when Exchange is in mixed mode operations. For details, see the section of Chapter 4 entitled "Understanding Exchange Server Organizations."

Creating Routing Groups

Routing group configuration is a three-part process. First, you create a routing group, then you add member servers to the routing group, and finally you connect the routing group using a messaging connector.

You create a routing group by completing the following steps:

1. Start System Manager.
2. Expand Administrative Groups and then select the administrative group in which you want to create the routing group.
3. Right-click Routing Groups, point to New, and then choose Routing Group. If the administrative group doesn't have a Routing Groups node, create it by

right-clicking the administrative group, pointing to New, and selecting Routing Groups Container.

4. On the General tab, type a descriptive name for the group, and then click OK.

5. Exchange Server creates the new routing group but doesn't assign any servers to the group or create connector links. You'll need to add these.

Moving Exchange Servers Among Routing Groups

By default, every Exchange server in your organization is a member of a routing group. The routing group assignment is normally made during the installation of Exchange Server 2003. After installation, you can move servers among routing groups to place servers with reliable connections within the same routing group. However, the servers must be in the same administrative group. You can't move servers among routing groups in different administrative groups.

You can move a server to a different routing group by completing the following steps:

1. Start System Manager. Expand Administrative Groups, and then select the administrative group that contains the routing groups you want to work with.

2. Expand Routing Groups, and then expand the routing groups you want to work with.

3. Right-click the server in the Members folder of the source routing group, and then select Cut.

4. Right-click the Members folder in the target routing group, and then select Paste.

Connecting Routing Groups

You must configure and actively manage connections between routing groups using Routing Group, SMTP, or X.400 connectors. These connectors are discussed in Chapter 14.

Designating Routing Group Masters

Each Exchange routing group has a routing group master. The master server is responsible for distributing link state information among the routing group's member servers. Only two states exist for any link: the link is either up or down. If a link is up, Exchange Server can establish a connection over the link and then use the connection to deliver mail. If a link is down, Exchange Server 2003 can't use the link and routing group servers must find an alternate route to the destination.

When a link is down, the server that identified the outage notifies the master server of the condition. The master server in turn notifies the other member servers within the routing group. The master server checks the link every 60 seconds until the link can be reestablished. Once the link is reestablished, the master server notifies the member servers that the link is up.

Normally, the routing group master is the first server installed in the routing group, but you can designate any server in the group as the master. To do this, follow these steps:

1. Start System Manager. Expand Administrative Groups, and then select the administrative group that contains the routing group you want to work with.

2. Expand Routing Groups, and then expand the routing group you want to work with.

3. In the Members folder, right-click the server you want to designate as the master server, and then select Set As Master.

Link state information helps Exchange Server 2003 determine the best route to take to deliver messages. In a well-connected Exchange organization, there should be redundant communication paths to ensure that messages can be delivered. One way to create redundant communication paths is to install multiple connectors between routing groups.

 Caution If the routing group master is unavailable, the link state information can't be updated and servers in the routing group continue using old routing information unless they discover the problem on their own through failed mail transfers. Typically, you'll see poor performance until you restore the routing group master.

Renaming and Deleting Routing Groups

You can change the name of a routing group at any time in System Manager. To do that, follow these steps:

1. Start System Manager. Expand Administrative Groups, and then select the administrative group that contains the routing group you want to work with.

2. Expand Routing Groups, right-click the routing group you want to rename, and then select Rename.

3. Type a new name for the routing group, and then press Enter.

Deleting a routing group removes the group and all its contents. Before deleting an administrative group, you must move its member servers to another routing group as described in the section of this chapter entitled "Moving Exchange Servers Among Routing Groups." Once you've moved the member servers, you can delete the routing group by completing the following steps:

1. Start System Manager. Expand Administrative Groups, and then select the administrative group that contains the routing group you want to work with.

2. Expand Routing Groups, right-click the routing group you want to remove, and then select Delete.

3. When prompted, confirm the action by clicking Yes.

Chapter 14
Managing Message Transfer and Routing Within the Organization

Every Microsoft Exchange Server 2003 administrator should have a solid understanding of message transfer and message routing. The X.400 message transfer agent handles message transfer, both within the organization and to servers outside it—unless you configure a different connector. The Message Transfer Agent (MTA) provides the necessary addressing and routing information for sending messages from one server to another; it's the functional equivalent of the Microsoft Exchange Message Transfer Agent used in previous versions of Exchange Server. The MTA relies on X.400 transfer stacks to provide additional details for message transfer. The purpose of X.400 stacks is similar to that of the Exchange virtual servers used with Simple Mail Transfer Protocol (SMTP), Post Office Protocol 3 (POP3), and Internet Message Access Protocol 4 (IMAP4).

Messaging settings for the MTA determine how connections are made, when transfer timeouts occur, and more. The MTA doesn't manage message delivery, however. Message delivery is handled by SMTP or other mail transfer protocols.

Message routing within the organization is either managed by Exchange Server itself or handled manually by the administrator. When you add an Exchange server to an organization and place it in an existing routing group, Exchange Server 2003 automatically configures the connection between the new server and other servers in the routing group. If you have multiple routing groups, however, Exchange Server 2003 doesn't configure connections between the routing groups. You must manually connect two routing groups using Exchange connectors.

Three types of Exchange connectors are available:

- Routing group connectors
- SMTP connectors
- X.400 connectors

Routing group connectors are preferred because they're the easiest to configure. For fault tolerance and load balancing, you can configure multiple connectors between routing groups. The key to load balancing is to use the same routing cost for all connectors that form the messaging link.

Configuring the X.400 Message Transfer Agent

Proper configuration of the X.400 MTA is essential to the smooth operation of Exchange Server. The MTA handles message transfers to the Internet and to servers within the organization. The values you set for the MTA become the default values for other X.400 connectors used within the organization as well. Keep in mind that the MTA isn't responsible for message delivery, which is handled by SMTP or another messaging protocol.

Setting Local MTA Credentials

The local MTA credentials set the local X.400 name and an optional password for a server. The X.400 name identifies the MTA to foreign systems, and if you don't provide an alternate name, the setting defaults to the name of the server. The X.400 password provides a password that other servers use when connecting to the X.400 agent. Use a password when you want to prevent unauthorized servers from connecting to the MTA.

You usually won't need to change the MTA credentials. However, if you want to identify the server using different credentials, you'll need to update the related settings by completing the following steps:

1. Start System Manager. If Administrative Groups are enabled, expand the administrative group in which the server you want to use is located.

2. Navigate to the X.400 container in the console tree. Expand Servers, expand the server you want to work with, and then expand Protocols.

3. Right-click X.400, and then select Properties. This displays the X.400 Properties dialog box shown in Figure 14-1.

4. The Local X.400 Name field shows the current setting for the X.400 name. Click Modify. Type a new X.400 name and then, if desired, type a password in the Password field and the Confirm Password field.

5. Click OK twice.

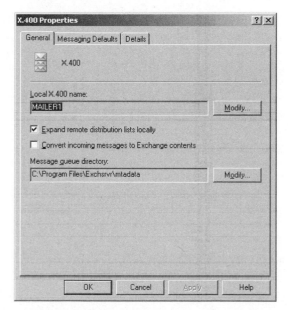

Figure 14-1. *Use the General tab of the X.400 Properties dialog box to set the local X.400 name and other message options.*

Note   The X.400 name can be up to 32 characters long. The X.400 password can be up to 64 characters long.

Expanding Remote Distribution Lists and Converting Messages

The X.400 MTA has limited control over how incoming messages are handled. You can configure whether remote distribution lists are expanded and whether incoming messages are converted to Exchange contents.

Expanding remote distribution lists makes them available to users on the local server. This is the optimal setting and it is enabled by default. Only in rare circumstances, when you want to expand lists elsewhere, should you disable this option.

Converting incoming messages changes the message addressing and contents to a form compatible with Exchange and Messaging Application Programming Interface (MAPI) clients. If you experience problems with message addressing from foreign systems, you might want to enable this option temporarily to see if this resolves the problem. Otherwise, this option is usually disabled.

To change these messaging settings, follow these steps:

1. Start System Manager. If Administrative Groups are enabled, expand the administrative group in which the server you want to use is located.
2. Navigate to the X.400 container in the console tree. Expand Servers, expand the server you want to work with, and then expand Protocols.
3. Right-click X.400, and then select Properties. This displays the X.400 Properties dialog box shown in Figure 14-1.
4. Select the Expand Remote Distribution Lists Locally check box to make remote lists available, or clear this check box to disable this option.
5. Select the Convert Incoming Messages To Exchange Contents check box to convert incoming message contents, or clear this check box to disable this option.
6. Click OK.

Setting Connection Retry Values for X.400

Connection retry values for the X.400 MTA play a key role in determining how Exchange Server connects to other servers and how messages are transferred. Retry values do not, however, control message delivery. Message delivery is controlled by the messaging protocol.

You can configure four message retry values:

* **Maximum Open Retries** Controls the maximum number of times Exchange Server tries to open a connection before failing and generating a nondelivery report (NDR). The default is 144 retries.
* **Maximum Transfer Retries** Controls the maximum number of times Exchange Server tries to transfer a message across an open connection before failing and generating an NDR. The default is two retries.
* **Open Interval** Controls the number of seconds Exchange Server waits before attempting to reopen a failed connection. The default is 600 seconds.
* **Transfer Interval** Controls the number of seconds Exchange Server waits before attempting to resend a message across an open connection. The default is 120 seconds.

Based on these values, a typical connection looks like this:

1. Exchange Server attempts to open a connection to the destination mail system. If it's unable to establish a connection, Exchange Server waits for the open interval and then tries to open a connection again, as long as the maximum retry value hasn't been reached. If the maximum retry value has been reached, Exchange Server generates an NDR that gets returned to the sender.
2. Once a connection has been established, Exchange Server attempts to transfer the message. If it's unable to transfer the message, Exchange Server waits for the transfer interval and then tries to transfer the message again—as long as the maximum retry value hasn't been reached. If the maximum retry value

has been reached, Exchange Server generates an NDR that gets returned to the sender.

To view or change connection retry values for the X.400 MTA, follow these steps:

1. Start System Manager. If Administrative Groups are enabled, expand the administrative group in which the server you want to use is located.

2. Navigate to the X.400 container in the console tree. Expand Servers, expand the server you want to work with, and then expand Protocols.

3. Right-click X.400, and then select Properties. This displays the X.400 Properties dialog box shown in Figure 14-1.

4. Click the Messaging Defaults tab. You'll see the current connection retry values. You can enter new values or click Reset Default Value to restore the default connection values.

5. Click OK.

Setting Reliable Transfer Service Values for X.400

Reliable transfer service (RTS) values for the X.400 MTA play a key role in determining how Exchange Server transfers message data. You can configure three RTS values:

- **Checkpoint Size (KB)**   Controls the amount of data Exchange Server transfers before performing a checkpoint. If the checkpoint results in an error being generated, Exchange Server restarts the message transfer from the most recent checkpoint. The default value is 30 KB.

- **Recovery Timeout (Sec)**   Controls the amount of time Exchange Server waits for a broken connection to be reestablished. If the wait exceeds the timeout value, Exchange Server restarts the message transfer. The default value is 60 seconds.

- **Window Size**   Controls the maximum number of unacknowledged checkpoints that can occur. If this value is exceeded, message transfer is suspended. The default is five.

Based on these values, a typical data transfer looks like this:

1. Exchange Server begins transferring data across an open connection. The transfer continues until a checkpoint is reached. After performing a checkpoint (and assuming an error didn't occur), Exchange Server continues the data transfer.

2. If the checkpoint is acknowledged, Exchange Server resets a counter tracking the current window size against the maximum value allowable. If the checkpoint isn't acknowledged, Exchange Server increments the tracking counter. If the value of the counter exceeds the maximum allowable window size, an error occurs.

3. If an error is generated at the checkpoint, the transfer stops and Exchange Server waits for the recovery timeout interval before restarting the message transfer from the most recent checkpoint that was acknowledged.

To view or change RTS values for the X.400 MTA, follow these steps:

1. Start System Manager. If Administrative Groups are enabled, expand the administrative group in which the server you want to use is located.

2. Navigate to the X.400 container in the console tree. Expand Servers, expand the server you want to work with, and then expand Protocols.

3. Right-click X.400, and then select Properties.

4. Click the Messaging Defaults tab, and then click Additional Values. As shown in Figure 14-2, the RTS Values panel displays the current RTS values. You can enter new values as necessary or click Reset Default Values to restore the default settings for RTS, association parameters, and transfer timeouts.

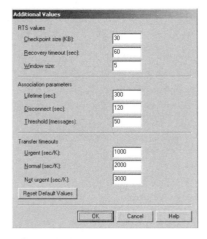

Figure 14-2. *Use the Additional Values dialog box to configure RTS values, association parameters, and transfer timeouts.*

 Tip If you have an unreliable connection, you might want to decrease the checkpoint size, which forces Exchange Server to perform checkpoints more frequently. However, you should rarely (if ever) set the checkpoint size to zero because this tells Exchange Server not to perform checkpoints and, as a result, message transfer might become unreliable.

5. Click OK.

Setting Association Parameters for X.400

Association parameters for the X.400 MTA play a key role in determining how Exchange Server handles connections once they've been established. You can configure three association parameters:

- **Lifetime (Sec)**   Controls the amount of time Exchange Server maintains an association for a remote system. A key property of the association is the identification of an open connection to a remote system. If the lifetime expires, the association is terminated but the related connection isn't broken until the disconnect period expires. The default value is 300 seconds.

- **Disconnect (Sec)**   Controls the amount of time Exchange Server waits before disconnecting a connection that no longer has an association. Typically, you want connections to remain open for a short period after the association is terminated. The default is 120 seconds.

- **Threshold (Messages)**   Controls the maximum queue size for each association. When the number of queued messages for the association exceeds this value, Exchange Server establishes a new connection and creates a new association. The default is 50 messages.

Here's how Exchange Server uses these values to handle open connections:

1. Exchange Server creates an association for each open connection to a remote system. It creates new associations as new messages enter the queue and new connections are established. It also creates new associations when the number of queued messages to any single remote server exceeds the threshold value.

2. When there are no more messages to send to a particular remote server, Exchange Server starts tracking the association lifetime. If the lifetime expires, the association is terminated but the connection remains open.

3. The open connection to the server isn't broken automatically. If a new message is queued for a server with an association that was terminated and the connection is still open, Exchange Server creates a new association and transfers the message. Otherwise, the open connection is broken when the disconnect value is reached.

You can view or change association parameters for the X.400 MTA by completing the following steps:

1. Start System Manager. If Administrative Groups are enabled, expand the administrative group in which the server you want to use is located.

2. Navigate to the X.400 container in the console tree. Expand Servers, expand the server you want to work with, and then expand Protocols.

3. Right-click X.400, and then select Properties.

4. Click the Messaging Defaults tab, and then click Additional Values. The Association Parameters panel displays the current parameters. You can enter

new values as necessary or click Reset Default Values to restore the default settings for RTS, association parameters, and transfer timeouts.

5. Click OK.

Setting Transfer Timeout for X.400

Generating lots of NDRs in a short amount of time can seriously degrade Exchange Server performance. To prevent this from happening, Exchange Server doesn't immediately generate NDRs. Instead, Exchange Server generates the NDR based on the message priority, the associated transfer timeout value, and the size of the message. The default transfer timeout values are as follows:

- **Urgent**   1000 seconds per KB
- **Normal**   2000 seconds per KB
- **Not Urgent**   3000 seconds per KB

The transfer timeouts are configured this way because messages flagged as urgent have processing precedence over normal messages, and normal messages have precedence over not-urgent messages. Because of this, urgent messages should get processed in less time than other types of messages and normal messages should get processed in less time than not urgent messages. Note also that the transfer timeout defaults have changed from previous Exchange installations. Previously, Exchange versions allowed longer transfer times for urgent messages and shorter transfer times for less important messages. You can view or change transfer timeouts for the X.400 MTA by completing the following steps:

1. Start System Manager. If Administrative Groups are enabled, expand the administrative group in which the server you want to use is located.

2. Navigate to the X.400 container in the console tree. Expand Servers, expand the server you want to work with, and then expand Protocols.

3. Right-click X.400, and then select Properties.

4. Click the Messaging Defaults tab, and then click Additional Values. The Transfer Timeouts panel displays the current parameters. You can enter new values as necessary or click Reset Default Values to restore the default settings for RTS, association parameters, and transfer timeouts.

5. Click OK.

Using Routing Group Connectors

Routing group connectors are the easiest connectors to configure and, as such, they're the preferred connectors for Exchange Server. You use a routing group connector to link two routing groups, which must be within the same organization. For those of you familiar with Exchange Server 5.0 and Exchange Server 5.5, this concept is similar to a site connector.

Understanding Routing Group Connectors

Routing group connectors establish links between routing groups using one or more designated bridgehead servers. Bridgehead servers act as communication relays for routing groups and you define them both locally and remotely.

Local bridgehead servers function as the originator of message traffic, and remote bridgehead servers function as the destination for message traffic. By default, all servers in the originating routing group act as local bridgehead servers. You can, however, select specific servers to act as bridgeheads. Selecting multiple servers as local bridgeheads provides load balancing and fault tolerance, which is essential when high availability is a concern. Selecting a single server as the local bridgehead ensures that all mail flows through the designated server, but it doesn't provide redundancy.

For the routing group connector, delivery options control when messages are sent through the connector. One of the key features is your ability to set connection schedules for all messages or specifically for standard-sized and large-sized messages. If you have a relatively fast, reliable link between the two routing groups, you probably want to set the same delivery schedule for all messages. On the other hand, if you have a relatively slow link between the two routing groups, you might want to set a separate schedule for large messages to ensure that oversized messages don't use all the available bandwidth during peak usage hours.

The routing group connector can deliver messages at many intervals. The interval you use depends on your reliability and availability needs:

- If you want message delivery to be highly reliable and the link to be highly available, you probably want to set the delivery interval to Always Run or Run Every Hour. You might also want to set a custom schedule that has an interval of every 30 minutes.

- If you want message delivery to be reliable and available but don't want message delivery to be a priority, you probably want to set the delivery interval to Run Every 2 Hours or Run Every 4 Hours.

- If the link is used to distribute message digests or public folder data infrequently, you probably want to set a specific delivery time, such as Run Daily At 11:00 P.M., Run Daily At Midnight, Run Daily At 1:00 A.M., or Run Daily At 2:00 A.M.

Installing Routing Group Connectors

You must have at least two routing groups in the organization to install a routing group connector. If you do, you can install a routing group connector by completing the following steps:

1. Start System Manager. If Administrative Groups are enabled, expand the administrative group you want to work with.

2. Expand Routing Groups, and then expand the routing group you want to use as the originator of the connection.

3. Right-click Connectors, click New, and then choose Routing Group Connector. This displays the dialog box shown in Figure 14-3.

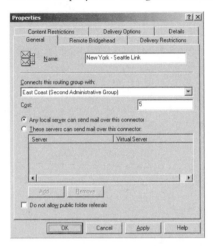

Figure 14-3. *Use the Routing Group Connector Properties dialog box to configure connectivity between two routing groups.*

4. On the General tab, type a descriptive name for the connector.

5. Choose the destination routing group by selecting it in the Connect This Routing Group With list box.

6. If you want all servers in the originating routing group to act as bridgehead servers, select Any Local Server Can Send Mail Over This Connector. Otherwise, select These Servers Can Send Mail Over This Connector, and then designate the local bridgehead servers that you want to use by clicking Add, and then selecting servers from the list provided.

7. On the Remote Bridgehead tab, click Add. You'll see a list of available routing groups and servers. In the destination routing group, select the server that you want to act as the remote bridgehead.

8. Click OK to install the connector. Later, you might want to set connector cost, delivery options, delivery restrictions, and content restrictions.

Configuring Routing Group Connector Delivery Options

To set the delivery options for an existing routing group connector, follow these steps:

1. Start System Manager. If Administrative Groups are enabled, expand the administrative group you want to work with.

2. Expand Routing Groups, and then expand the routing group you want to use as the originator of the connection.

3. Expand Connectors, right-click the routing group connector you want to configure, and then select Properties.

4. Click the Delivery Options tab, as shown in Figure 14-4. Use the Connection Time list box to specify the times when messages are sent through the connector. The available options are: Always Run, Run Daily At 11:00 P.M., Run Daily At Midnight, Run Daily At 1:00 A.M., Run Daily At 2:00 A.M., Run Every Hour, Run Every 2 Hours, Run Every 4 Hours, Never Run, and Use Custom Schedule.

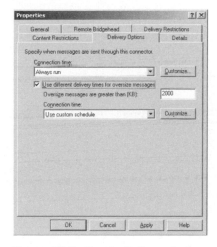

Figure 14-4. *Use the Delivery Options tab to control when messages are sent through the routing group connector.*

5. To set separate delivery options for standard and large messages, select the Use Different Delivery Times For Oversize Messages check box. For Oversize Messages Are Greater Than (KB), type the minimum size, in kilobytes, of messages you want to designate as oversized. The default is 2000 KB. Finally, use the options in the second Connection Time list box to set the delivery times for large messages.

6. Click OK.

Performing Other Routing Group Connector Tasks

You perform most other routing group connector tasks in the same way that you perform tasks for other connectors. The section of this chapter entitled "Handling Core Connector Administration Tasks" explains these common tasks.

Using SMTP Connectors

SMTP connectors are another type of Exchange connector. SMTP connectors transfer messages from local bridgehead servers to remote servers. You use SMTP connectors to connect Exchange servers, non-Exchange servers, routing groups, and organizations.

Understanding SMTP Connectors

SMTP connectors are a bit more complex than routing group connectors, but the additional settings they make available gives them definite advantages over routing group connectors. With SMTP connectors, you can encrypt message traffic sent over the link and require stricter authentication than with routing group connectors. You can transmit messages to a designated server—called a *smart host*, which then transfers the message—or you can use Domain Name System (DNS) mail exchanger (MX) records to route messages. If the other mail system supports Extended Simple Mail Transfer Protocol (ESMTP), you can enable extended options as well.

When you install an SMTP connector, you must define which local bridgehead servers the connector will use as well as the connector scope, message routing technique, and address space. SMTP virtual servers act as local bridgehead servers for SMTP connectors. This means that the virtual servers are responsible for routing the message traffic. Multiple local bridgeheads provide load balancing and fault tolerance, which is essential when high availability is a concern. A single bridgehead, on the other hand, ensures that all mail flows through a designated server, but it doesn't provide redundancy.

SMTP connectors have a specific scope that controls how the connector routes messages. You use an SMTP connector with a routing group scope to transfer messages within your organization. You can use an SMTP connector with an organizational scope to connect independent Exchange organizations, to connect Exchange servers with other SMTP-compatible servers (such as UNIX Sendmail servers), and to connect Exchange Server 2003 with earlier versions of Exchange Server.

SMTP connectors use smart hosts or DNS MX records to route mail. If you use a smart host, Exchange Server 2003 transfers messages directly to the smart host, which then sends out messages over an established link. The smart host allows you to route messages on a per domain basis. If you use DNS MX records, Exchange Server 2003 performs a DNS lookup for each address to which the connector sends mail.

When you install an SMTP connector, you must also define the address space for the connector. The address space determines when the connector is used. For example, if you want to connect two domains in the same Exchange organization—dev.microsoft.com and corp.microsoft.com—you could create the SMTP connector in dev.microsoft.com, and then add an SMTP address type for the e-mail domain corp.microsoft.com.

You can define multiple address types for a single SMTP connector. The address types can be any combination of SMTP, X.400, MS Mail, cc:Mail, Lotus Notes, and Lotus GroupWise addresses. These address types can point to different domains. Thus, you could use an SMTP connector to connect dev.microsoft.com with sales.microsoft.com, bizdev.microsoft.com, and eng.microsoft.com. You could also use an SMTP connector to connect two specific routing groups.

For load balancing and high availability, you could configure multiple SMTP connectors to handle the same address space. For example, if a large volume of traffic is routinely sent between corp.microsoft.com and support.microsoft.com, you could install two SMTP connectors to handle the message routing between these domains.

Installing SMTP Connectors

To install an SMTP connector, complete the following steps:

1. Start System Manager. If administrative groups are enabled, expand the administrative group you want to work with.

2. If available, expand Routing Groups, and then expand the routing group you want to use as the originator of the connection.

3. Right-click Connectors, click New, and then choose SMTP Connector. This displays the dialog box shown in Figure 14-5.

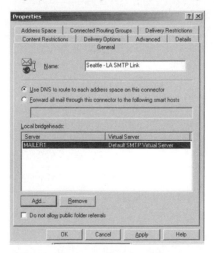

Figure 14-5. *Use the Properties dialog box to configure SMTP connectors. SMTP connectors transmit messages to a designated smart host or use DNS MX records.*

4. On the General tab, type a descriptive name for the connector.

5. To use a smart host for routing, select Forward All Mail Through This Connector To The Following Smart Hosts, and then type the fully qualified domain name or Internet Protocol (IP) address of the server through which you'd like to route messages. The SMTP connector then uses this smart host to route messages to the remote server.

 Tip You can enter multiple smart hosts as well. Separate each entry using a comma or semicolon. If you use an IP address, be sure to enclose the address in brackets, as in [192.168.12.99]. The brackets tell Exchange Server that the value is an IP address and, as a result, Exchange Server doesn't try to perform a DNS lookup on the value.

 Note The smart host setting for a connector overrides the smart host setting for the virtual servers that act as bridgeheads for the connector.

6. To use DNS MX records for routing, select Use DNS To Route To Each Address Space On This Connector. The precedence order of MX records determines which servers are used in a particular domain.

7. You must specify at least one local bridgehead server. Click Add, and then select the SMTP virtual server that you want to use as the local bridgehead server. Repeat this step if you want to use additional bridgehead servers.

8. Connector scope is set on the Address Space tab. If you're connecting two Exchange organizations, set the Connector Scope as Entire Organization, click Add on the Address Space tab, and then set the properties for the address space. Be sure to set the cost for the address space. Connector costs range from 1 to 100, with the lowest cost having the highest priority for routing. Repeat for other address types the connector should handle.

9. If you're connecting two routing groups, set the Connector Scope as Routing Group, and then click Add on the Address Space tab and set the properties for the address space. Be sure to set the cost for the address space. Connector costs range from 1 to 100, with the lowest cost having the highest priority for routing. Repeat for other address types the connector should handle. Afterward, click Add on the Connected Routing Groups tab, and then select the routing group to which you want to connect.

 Note You'll usually want to use the SMTP address type when the routing group to which you want to connect contains Exchange servers. With SMTP address types, you can enter an asterisk (*) as the domain to have the connector route messages for all domains in the routing group you're connecting.

10. If you want to allow the local server to relay messages to domains in the other organization or routing group, select Allow Messages To Be Relayed To These Domains.

11. Click OK to install the connector. Later, you might want to set delivery options, outbound security, delivery restrictions, content restrictions, and advanced controls, which I'll explain in the following sections.

Configuring Delivery Options for SMTP Connectors

SMTP connectors have delivery options that determine when messages are sent through the connector as well as whether messages are queued for remote delivery. To control when messages are sent, you set connection schedules. You can have separate schedules for standard-sized and large-sized messages. To control message queuing, you can enable or disable message queuing for remote delivery on a per user basis. From then on, when a specified user logs on to the network, Exchange Server triggers delivery of all queued messages for this user. In this way, you can more efficiently manage how messages are delivered to remote clients with temporary connections.

You configure delivery options for SMTP connectors by completing the following steps:

1. In System Manager, navigate to Connectors. Right-click the SMTP connector you want to configure, and then select Properties.

2. Click the Delivery Options tab, as shown in Figure 14-6. Use the Connection Time list box to specify the times when messages are sent through the connector.

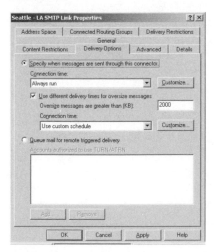

Figure 14-6. *Use the Delivery Options tab of the SMTP Connector Properties dialog box to control when messages are sent through the connector. Note that delivery options for SMTP connectors are slightly different than those of routing group connectors.*

3. To set separate delivery options for standard and large messages, select the Use Different Delivery Times For Oversize Messages check box. For Oversize Messages Are Greater Than (KB), type the minimum size, in kilobytes, of messages you want to designate as oversized. The default is 2000 KB. Finally, use the options in the second Connection Time list box to set the delivery times for large messages.

4. Message queuing is ideal for clients who connect periodically to download messages. To enable message queuing for remote users, select Queue Mail For Remote Triggered Delivery. Click Add, and then use the Select Recipient dialog box to specify users who should have this option.

5. Click OK.

Configuring Outbound Security for SMTP Connectors

By default, SMTP connectors don't authenticate connections to remote domains. This means that the connectors anonymously access remote domains to send messages. You can, however, configure an SMTP connector to pass authentication credentials to remote domains. The key reason to do this is that you require a specific level of authentication to access a remote domain or you're sending messages to a specific address in the remote domain that requires authentication.

Exchange Server 2003 supports three types of authentication:

• **Basic** Standard authentication with wide compatibility. With basic authentication, the user name and password specified are passed as cleartext to the remote domain.

• **Integrated Windows Authentication** Secure authentication for Microsoft Windows–compatible domains. With integrated Windows authentication, the user name and password are passed securely to the remote domain.

• **TLS Authentication** Encrypted authentication for servers with smart cards or X.509 certificates. Transport Layer Security (TLS) authentication is combined with basic or integrated Windows authentication.

To configure SMTP outbound security, follow these steps:

1. In System Manager, navigate to Connectors. Right-click the SMTP connector you want to configure, and then select Properties.

2. Click the Advanced tab, and then click Outbound Security. This displays the dialog box shown in Figure 14-7.

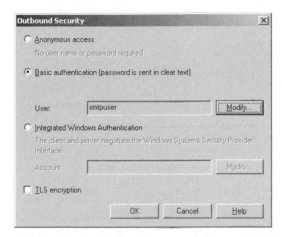

Figure 14-7. *Use the Outbound Security dialog box to set security options for outgoing messages.*

3. If you want to set standard authentication for wide compatibility, select Basic Authentication, and then click Modify. Otherwise, to set secure authentication for Windows-compatible domains, select Integrated Windows Authentication, and then click Modify. The Outbound Connection Credentials dialog box should be displayed.

4. Use the Account, Password, and Confirm Password fields to set the authentication credentials. Click OK.

5. If you want to encrypt message traffic and the destination servers in the remote domain support smart cards or X.509 certificates, select the TLS Encryption check box.

Caution   The destination servers in the remote domain must support smart cards or X.509 certificates. If they do not, all messages sent across the connector will be returned with an NDR.

6. Click OK.

Setting Advanced Controls for SMTP Connectors

Advanced options for SMTP connectors control whether Exchange Server uses standard SMTP or ESMTP, as well as how mail delivery is initiated using SMTP or ESMTP. The ESMTP standard is more efficient and secure than SMTP, but some messaging systems, particularly older ones, don't support ESMTP, and you might need to disable ESMTP support to prevent errors.

By default, SMTP connectors always try to initiate ESMTP sessions, but you can change this behavior using the HELO and EHLO start session commands. SMTP connectors initiate SMTP sessions with other mail servers by issuing the HELO start command. SMTP connectors initiate ESMTP sessions with other mail servers by issuing an EHLO start command.

By default, SMTP connectors don't force delivery of queued messages. Forced delivery is necessary when you queue mail for remote triggered delivery. Not forcing delivery causes delays as clients first wait for a connection timeout, and then have to retry the connection. Two commands control delivery of queued messages: TURN and ETRN. TURN is a command for SMTP, and ETRN is a command for ESMTP. These commands allow a mail client to ask a remote server to start processing mail queued for delivery to the client.

You can configure these advanced options by completing the following steps:

1. In System Manager, navigate to Connectors. Right-click the SMTP connector you want to configure, and then select Properties.

2. Click the Advanced tab. This displays the dialog box shown in Figure 14-8.

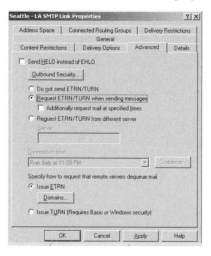

Figure 14-8. *Use the Advanced tab of the SMTP Connector Properties dialog box to configure whether the connector should use SMTP or ESMTP.*

3. The Send HELO Instead Of EHLO check box controls whether SMTP or ESMTP is used. To use SMTP, select this check box. To use ESMTP (which is the default), clear this option.

4. Configure remote triggered delivery of messages using the following options:

   • **Do Not Send ETRN/TURN**   Prevents clients from requesting that remote mail servers start processing queued mail. On the Delivery Options tab, you should ensure that Queue Mail For Remote Triggered Delivery isn't selected.

- **Request ETRN/TURN When Sending Messages** Enables remote triggered delivery of messages. If you want to automatically request messages at a specified interval, select the Additionally Request Mail At Specified Times check box and then set the interval using the Connection Time drop-down list.

Note If you request ETRN/TURN when sending messages, you must also forward all mail going through this connector using a smart host. You specify the smart host on the General tab using the field labeled Forward All Mail Through This Connector To The Following Smart Hosts.

- **Request ETRN/TURN From Different Server** Requests that messages are triggered for delivery from a server other than the one to which the messages are sent. If you select this option, you must specify the server name in the Server field. You must also set the interval for message delivery using the Connection Time drop-down list.

5. If you enabled remote triggered delivery and requested ETRN/TURN, you must specify how the requests are submitted to remote servers. Select either Issue ETRN or Issue TURN. To specify domains for which ETRN should be used, click Domains, and then add the domains.

6. Click OK.

Performing Other SMTP Connector Tasks

You perform most other SMTP connector tasks in the same way you perform tasks for other connectors. The section of this chapter entitled "Handling Core Connector Administration Tasks" explains these common tasks.

Using X.400 Connectors

In the beginning of this chapter, you learned that the X.400 MTA handles message transfer both within the organization and to servers outside it. Normally, the X.400 message transfer is handled within routing groups and not between them. You can, however, configure X.400 connectors to connect two routing groups in the same Exchange organization. The primary reason to do this is when you need to strictly control bandwidth usage between the routing groups. You can also use X.400 connectors to connect an Exchange routing group with a foreign X.400 messaging server.

The key reason for using an X.400 connector instead of another type of connector is that the X.400 connector incurs less overhead than other connectors when sending large messages. This means that sending large messages through an X.400 connector requires less bandwidth than sending the same messages through other types of connectors.

Understanding X.400 Connectors

Because X.400 connectors are more complex than other types of connectors, they're difficult to use. Unlike other connectors, X.400 connectors have several variations, including these:

- **TCP/IP X.400 connectors** Used to transfer messages over a standard TCP/IP network. Use this connector when you have a dedicated connection such as a T1 line. Because most X.400 messaging systems support TCP/IP, this is the most common type of X.400 connector used.

- **X.25 X.400 connectors** Configured to connect to an X.25 adapter on a remote mail server. With this connector, you can support standard X.25 protocols as long as an X.25 adapter is available and you know the X.121 address of the remote server.

Before you configure an X.400 connector, you must install and configure an X.400 transport stack that is the same type as the connector. The transport stack contains configuration information that the connector needs to properly transport messages. The available transport stacks include the TCP/IP X.400 stack and the X.25 X.400 stack.

Unlike other connectors, you can define only a single local and remote bridgehead server for an X.400 connector. This means you can't build fault tolerance or load balancing into the connector configuration. Instead, you need to install multiple X.400 connectors to achieve these goals.

Installing X.400 Stacks

Each X.400 connector type has a corresponding X.400 stack. Unlike mail connectors, which you install at the administrative group level, transport stacks are installed on specified Exchange servers. The server on which you install the stack processes all messages from X.400 connectors that reference the stack.

The sections that follow examine how X.400 stacks are configured.

Creating and Configuring TCP/IP X.400 Stacks

When you install a TCP/IP X.400 stack on an Exchange server, the server can process messages for one or more TCP/IP X.400 connectors configured for use in the organization. The stack works with standard TCP/IP protocols configured for use on the server. If necessary, you can create and configure multiple TCP/IP X.400 stacks. Each of these stacks can have a different configuration.

You can create a TCP/IP X.400 stack by completing the following steps:

1. Start System Manager. If administrative groups are enabled, expand the administrative group you want to work with.

2. Expand Servers, and then expand the node for the server you want to work with.

3. Expand Protocols, and then right-click X.400. Choose New, and then choose TCP/IP X.400 Service Transport Stack. This displays the dialog box shown in Figure 14-9.

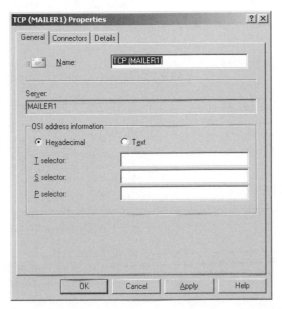

Figure 14-9. *Use the Properties dialog box to configure a TCP/IP X.400 transport stack. You must create a TCP/IP X.400 stack before you install a TCP/IP X.400 connector.*

4. On the General tab, type a descriptive name for the stack. The default is TCP (servername). You can't change this name after you create the stack.

5. If applications other than Exchange Server will use the transport stack, set OSI address information for the connector by using either hexadecimal or text characters. The T Selector field sets the transport service access point. The S Selector field sets the session service access point. The P Selector field sets the presentation service access point.

6. Click OK.

Creating and Configuring X.25 X.400 Stacks

When you install an X.25 X.400 stack on an Exchange server, the server can process messages for one or more X.25 X.400 connectors for use in the organization. The stack relies on the installation of a dedicated X.25 device. If necessary, you can create and configure multiple X.25 X.400 stacks. Each of these stacks can have a different configuration.

You can create an X.25 X.400 stack by completing the following steps:

1. Start System Manager. If administrative groups are enabled, expand the administrative group you want to work with.

2. Expand Servers, and then expand the node for the server you want to work with.

3. Expand Protocols, and then right-click X.400. Choose New, and then choose X.25 X.400 Service Transport Stack. This displays the dialog box shown in Figure 14-10.

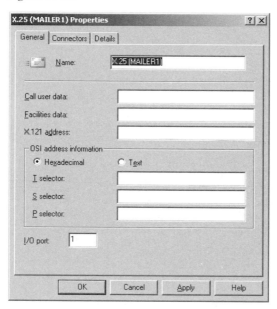

Figure 14-10. *Use the Properties dialog box to configure an X.25 X.400 stack. You must create an X.25 X.400 stack before you install an X.25 X.400 connector.*

4. On the General tab, type a descriptive name for the stack. The default is X.25 (servername). You can't change this name after you create the stack.

5. All other steps are optional, so you can click OK to create the stack or continue with the configuration, and then click OK. The primary values you can set are as follows:

- **Call User Data** Sets additional connection data for users.
- **Facilities Data** Sets X.25 provider options.
- **X.121 Address** Sets the X.121 address of the remote server. This designator is defined in the X.25 network service setup on the remote server.
- **I/O Port** Sets the X.25 adapter port number. Type a number between 0 and 255. The default port is 1. The I/O port you specify must not match the value used by any other X.25 X.400 transport stack on the same server.

6. If applications other than Exchange Server will use the transport stack, set OSI address information for the connector by using either hexadecimal or text characters. The T Selector field sets the transport service access point.

The S Selector field sets the session service access point. The P Selector field sets the presentation service access point.

7. Click OK.

Installing X.400 Connectors

Once you've created a stack for the transport you want to use, you can create one or more X.400 connectors that use the stack to transport messages to a remote host that you designate. Unlike other connectors, X.400 connectors have only one local bridgehead and one remote bridgehead. Essentially, the connector creates a direct link between a server in one routing group and a server in another routing group or organization.

Installing TCP X.400 Connectors

TCP X.400 connectors depend on TCP services being installed on both the local server and the remote server you're connecting. Once these services are installed and you've created the necessary transport stacks, you can install a TCP X.400 connector by completing the following steps:

1. Start System Manager. If administrative groups are enabled, expand the administrative group you want to work with.

2. If available, expand Routing Groups and then expand the routing group you want to use as the originator of the connection.

3. Right-click Connectors, click New, and then choose TCP X.400 Connector.

4. On the General tab, type a descriptive name for the connector, as shown in Figure 14-11.

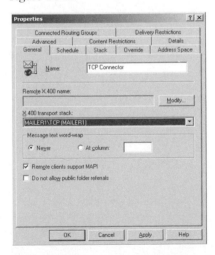

Figure 14-11. *Use the Properties dialog box to configure a TCP X.400 connector. TCP X.400 connectors operate over a designated TCP/IP transport stack.*

5. On the General tab, under Remote X.400 Name, click Modify. This displays the Remote Connection Credentials dialog box.

6. In the Remote X.400 Name field, type the name of the X.400 connector on the remote server. In most cases, the remote connector name defaults to the remote server name.

7. In both the Password and Confirm Password fields, type the password for the remote X.400 connector. Click OK.

8. On the General tab in the Properties dialog box, use the X.400 Transport Stack drop-down list to choose the X.400 transport stack that the connector should use.

9. Click the Address Space tab in the Properties dialog box.

10. If you're connecting two Exchange organizations, set the Connector Scope as Entire Organization, click Add, and then set the properties for the address space. Be sure to set the cost for the address space. Connector costs range from 1 to 100, with the lowest cost having the highest priority for routing. Repeat for other address types the connector should handle.

11. If you're connecting two routing groups, set the Connector Scope as Routing Group, click Add, and then set the properties for the address space. Be sure to set the cost for the address space. Connector costs range from 1 to 100, with the lowest cost having the highest priority for routing. Repeat for other address types the connector should handle. Afterward, click Add on the Connected Routing Groups tab and then select the routing group to which you want to connect.

12. On the Stack tab, select Remote Host Name or IP Address, and then in the Address box, type the fully qualified domain name of the remote X.400 server to which you're connecting or enter the remote server's IP address.

 Tip If you use an IP address, be sure to enclose the address in brackets, as in [192.168.12.99]. The brackets tell Exchange Server that the value is an IP address and, as a result, Exchange Server doesn't try to perform a DNS lookup on the value.

13. Click the Schedule tab, and then set the schedule for the connector. The available options are as follows:

   • **Never** Disables the connector.

   • **Always** Allows the connector to continuously transfer messages over the link.

   • **Selected Times** Allows you to set a custom schedule for the transfer of messages over the link. A custom schedule is useful when you want to control the timing of message transfers.

   • **Remote Initiated** Messages are transferred only when the remote server initiates the transfer.

14. If the remote system isn't an Exchange server, click the Advanced tab, and then clear the Allow Exchange Contents check box. If you don't clear this check box, messages are sent with e-mail addresses in domain name form and not in X.400 form, making it impossible to reply.

15. To override default X.400 settings, click the Override tab and then set connection values, RTS values, association parameters, and transfer timeouts for the connector as described in the section of this chapter entitled "Configuring the X.400 Message Transfer Agent."

16. Click OK to install the connector. Later, you might want to set delivery restrictions, content restrictions, and advanced controls.

Note   You must configure both sides of the connection before messages can be sent in both directions. If you're connecting servers in an Exchange organization or routing group, configure an X.400 connector on the designated remote server.

Installing X.25 X.400 Connectors

X.25 X.400 connectors depend on X.25 adapters being available and the existence of an X.25 transport stack. Once you've installed these items and made them available, you can install an X.25 X.400 connector by completing the following steps:

1. Start System Manager. If administrative groups are enabled, expand the administrative group you want to work with.

2. If available, expand Routing Groups, and then expand the routing group you want to use as the originator of the connection.

3. Right-click Connectors, click New, and then choose X.25 X.400 Connector.

4. On the General tab, type a descriptive name for the connector, as shown in Figure 14-12.

Tip   X.25 X.400 connectors use X.25 devices to transport messages. You need to configure the device and the X.25 transport stack before trying to install a connector.

5. On the General tab, under Remote X.400 name, click Modify. This displays the Remote Connection Credentials dialog box.

6. In the Remote X.400 Name field, type the name of the X.400 connector on the remote server. In most cases, the remote connector name defaults to the remote server name.

7. In both the Password and Confirm Password fields, type the password for the remote X.400 connector. Click OK.

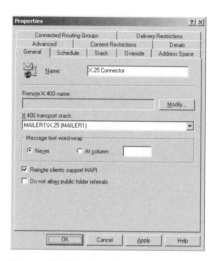

Figure 14-12. *Use the Properties dialog box to configure an X.25 X.400 connector.*

8. Use the X.400 Transport Stack drop-down list to choose the X.400 transport stack that the connector should use.

9. Click the Address Space tab to define the connector's address type and scope.

   You have two options:

   • If you're connecting two Exchange organizations, set the Connector Scope as Entire Organization, click Add on the Address Space tab, and then set the properties for the address space. Be sure to set the cost for the address space. Connector costs range from 1 to 100, with the lowest cost having the highest priority for routing. Repeat for other address types the connector should handle.

   • If you're connecting two routing groups, set the Connector Scope as Routing Group, click Add on the Address Space tab, and then set the properties for the address space. Be sure to set the cost for the address space. Connector costs range from 1 to 100, with the lowest cost having the highest priority for routing. Repeat for other address types the connector should handle. Afterward, click Add on the Connected Routing Groups tab and then select the routing group to which you want to connect.

10. On the Stack tab, use the X.121 Address field to set the X.121 address of the remote server. This designator is defined in the X.25 network service setup on the remote server. Optionally, set additional connection data for users in the Call User field and X.25 provider options in the Facilities field.

11. Click the Schedule tab and then set the schedule for the connector. The available options are as follows:

    • **Never**   Disables the connector.

    • **Always**   Allows the connector to continuously transfer messages over the link.

    • **Selected Times**   Allows you to set a custom schedule for the transfer of messages over the link. A custom schedule is useful when you want to control the timing of message transfers.

    • **Remote Initiated**   Messages are transferred only when the remote server initiates the transfer.

12. If the remote system isn't an Exchange server, click the Advanced tab, and then clear the Allow Exchange Contents check box. If you don't clear this check box, messages are sent with e-mail addresses in domain name form and not in X.400 form, making it impossible to reply.

13. To override default X.400 settings, click the Override tab, and then set connection values, RTS values, association parameters, and transfer timeouts for the connector as described in the section of this chapter entitled "Configuring the X.400 Message Transfer Agent."

14. Click OK to install the connector. Later, you might want to set delivery restrictions, content restrictions, and advanced controls.

Note   You must configure both sides of the connection before messages can be sent in both directions. If you're connecting servers in an Exchange organization or routing group, configure an X.400 connector on the designated remote server.

Setting Connection Schedules

X.400 connectors follow a very specific schedule that determines how and when they are used. You can set the connection schedule by completing the following steps:

1. Start System Manager, and then navigate to the Connectors tab.

2. Right-click the X.400 connector you want to work with and then select Properties.

3. On the Schedule tab, use the following options to set the connection schedule:

    • **Never**   Disables the connector.

    • **Always**   Allows the connector to continuously transfer messages over the link.

    • **Selected Times**   Allows you to set a custom schedule for the transfer of messages over the link. A custom schedule is useful when you want to control the timing of message transfers.

- **Remote Initiated** Messages are transferred only when the remote server initiates the transfer.
4. Click OK.

Overwriting X.400 MTA Properties

X.400 connectors automatically inherit settings from the X.400 MTA. You can override these settings on a per connector basis by completing the following steps:

1. Start System Manager, and then navigate to the Connectors tab.
2. Right-click the X.400 connector you want to work with, and then choose Properties.
3. On the Override tab, set connection values, RTS values, association parameters, and transfer timeouts for the connector as described in the section of this chapter entitled "Configuring the X.400 Message Transfer Agent."

Setting Text Wrapping and Remote Client Support for X.400 Connectors

X.400 connectors configure default options for text wrapping and remote client support. The default options aren't always optimal, and you might want to examine them.

By default, text word wrapping is disabled, which means the connector enforces no maximum line length. If you'd like message text to wrap at a specific line length, you can enable text word wrapping at a specific column position, such as 72 characters.

By default, X.400 connectors send messages in their original text formatting, which can include Rich Text Format. This setting works well with most MAPI-compliant mail applications, but not with noncompliant applications. With noncompliant applications, you usually want the connector to convert message text to ASCII text prior to delivery. To do this, disable support for remote MAPI clients.

You can control text word wrapping and MAPI client support by completing the following steps:

1. Start System Manager, and then navigate to the Connectors tab.
2. Right-click the X.400 connector you want to work with, then choose Properties.
3. The General tab should be selected.
4. Under Message Text Word-Wrap, select At Column to enable word wrap, and then type the column position in the field provided. To disable word wrap, select Never.

5. The Remote Clients Support MAPI check box controls MAPI client support. Select the check box to enable MAPI client support or clear the check box to disable MAPI client support.

6. Click OK.

Performing Other X.400 Connector Tasks

You perform most other X.400 connector tasks in the same way you perform tasks for other connectors. The next section of this chapter, "Handling Core Connector Administration Tasks," explains these common tasks.

Handling Core Connector Administration Tasks

Regardless of which type of connector you use, you'll perform a common set of administrative tasks. This section examines these tasks.

Designating Local and Remote Bridgeheads

Bridgehead servers act as the communication relays for routing groups, and you define them locally and remotely. Local bridgehead servers serve as the originator of message traffic, and remote bridgehead servers serve as the destination for message traffic. Each connector has a slightly different way of handling bridgehead servers.

With routing group connectors, you can have multiple local bridgeheads but only a single remote bridgehead, and you can designate the bridgehead servers as described in Steps 6 and 7 of the section of this chapter entitled "Installing Routing Group Connectors."

With SMTP connectors, you can have one or more local bridgehead servers. These bridgeheads are identified using the SMTP virtual servers that are available on the local server for which you're configuring the connector. You don't specifically define remote bridgehead servers, however. Instead, you designate a smart host or use DNS MX records to locate remote mail servers in a specific routing group. These mail servers then act as remote bridgehead servers. To specify bridgeheads for SMTP connectors, follow Steps 5 through 8 in the section of this chapter entitled "Installing SMTP Connectors."

With X.400 connectors, you have one local bridgehead server and one remote bridgehead server. Because of this, you can build fault tolerance and load balancing into the connector configuration only by configuring multiple connectors. You specify bridgeheads for X.400 connectors through the local and remote X.400 names you designate for the connector.

Setting Delivery Restrictions

Delivery restrictions enable you to accept or reject messages before transferring them over the connector. You accept or reject messages based on the sender's e-mail address. By default, no delivery restrictions are set and, as a result, connectors accept all messages from all senders unless configured otherwise.

To configure the connector to accept messages only from specific senders, follow these steps:

1. Start System Manager, and then navigate to the Connectors tab.
2. Right-click the connector you want to work with and then choose Properties.
3. Click the Delivery Restrictions tab, as shown in Figure 14-13.

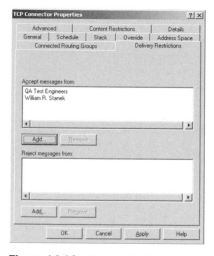

Figure 14-13. *Use the Delivery Restrictions tab to determine whether connectors accept or reject messages from particular users.*

4. Under Accept Messages From, click Add, and then use the Select Recipient dialog box to choose users, contacts, and groups from which messages can be accepted. All other senders are rejected automatically.
5. Under Reject Messages From, select any name listed, and then click Remove. Repeat this process for all other names listed under Reject Messages From.
6. Click OK.

To configure the connector to reject messages from specific senders and to accept all other messages, follow these steps:

1. Start System Manager, and then navigate to the Connectors tab.
2. Right-click the connector you want to work with and then choose Properties.
3. Click the Delivery Restrictions tab, as shown in Figure 14-13.

4. Under Reject Messages From, click Add, and then use the Select Recipient dialog box to choose users, contacts, and groups from which messages are rejected. All other senders are accepted automatically.

5. Under Accept Messages From, select any name listed, and then click Remove. Repeat this process for all other names listed under Accept Messages From.

6. Click OK.

Setting Content Restrictions

Content restrictions determine the allowed priorities, types, and sizes for messages transferred by a connector. By default, no content restrictions are set.

To set content restrictions, follow these steps:

1. Start System Manager, and then navigate to the Connectors tab.

2. Right-click the connector you want to work with and then choose Properties.

3. Click the Content Restrictions tab, as shown in Figure 14-14.

4. Use the options provided to set allowed message priorities and types. System messages include NDRs and other types of system messages. Nonsystem messages include all messages sent by users.

5. To restrict the size of messages that can be transferred by the connector, select the Only Messages Less Than (KB) check box, and then type the maximum message size in kilobytes.

6. Click OK.

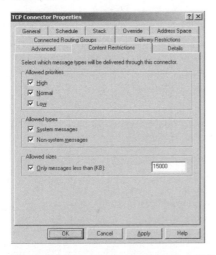

Figure 14-14. *Use the Content Restrictions tab to determine what types of messages you want a connector to transfer.*

Setting Routing Cost for Connectors

Routing cost plays a key role in optimizing message routing. When two or more connectors link the same servers or routing groups, the connector with the lowest routing cost has preference over the other connectors. If the connector with the lowest cost is unavailable for any reason, Exchange Server uses the connector with the next lowest routing cost. By having multiple connectors and setting routing costs, administrators can ensure that messages are delivered even when a primary connector fails.

You can also use routing cost to balance the messaging load over two or more servers. In this example, you configure multiple connectors with the same routing cost, which tells Exchange Server to distribute the load as evenly as possible among the connectors.

To set routing cost for a connector, follow these steps:

1. Start System Manager, and then navigate to the Connectors tab.
2. Right-click the connector you want to work with and then choose Properties.
3. For routing group connectors, you set the routing cost using the Cost field on the General tab.
4. For SMTP and X.400 connectors, each address space and connected routing group has an associated cost. You configure these costs in the Address Space and Connected Routing Groups tabs, respectively.
5. Click OK.

Setting Public Folder Referrals

Public folder referrals allow users on remote servers to access public folders on local servers. Public folder referrals are made possible through transitive affinities, which are enabled by default in Exchange Server 2003. If you don't want users in other routing groups to be able to access public folders through a connector, you'll need to disable public folder referrals. You can do this by completing the following steps:

1. Start System Manager, and then navigate to the Connectors tab.
2. Right-click the connector you want to work with and then choose Properties.
3. On the General tab, select Do Not Allow Public Folder Referrals.
4. Click OK.

Disabling and Removing Connectors

Connectors can be disabled or removed at any time. To disable a connector, follow these steps:

1. Start System Manager, and then navigate to the Connectors tab.
2. Right-click the connector you want to work with and then select Properties.

3. On the Schedule tab, select Never as the connection schedule.

4. Click OK.

To remove a connector, follow these steps:

1. Start System Manager, and then navigate to the Connectors tab.

2. Right-click the connector you want to work with and then select Delete.

3. When prompted to confirm the action, click Yes.

Note In most cases you'll want to disable a connector instead of removing it. The advantage of disabling a connector instead of removing it is that you can later enable the connector if you need to and you won't have to reconfigure its settings.

Chapter 15

Administering SMTP, IMAP4, and POP3

Microsoft Exchange Server 2003 supports Simple Mail Transfer Protocol (SMTP), Internet Message Access Protocol 4 (IMAP4), and Post Office Protocol 3 (POP3). These protocols play an important role in determining how mail is delivered and transferred both within and outside the Exchange organization.

*   SMTP is the native mail protocol for mail submission and mail transport. This means that clients use SMTP to send messages and Exchange servers use SMTP to deliver messages and message data.

*   IMAP4 is a protocol for reading mail and accessing public and private folders on remote servers. Clients can log on to an Exchange server and use IMAP4 to download message headers and then read messages individually while online.

*   POP3 is a protocol for retrieving mail on remote servers. Clients can log on to an Exchange server and then use POP3 to download their mail for offline use.

Each of these protocols has an associated virtual server. You use virtual servers to specify configuration information and control access. You can also create additional virtual servers.

The following sections examine the key tasks you'll use to manage SMTP, IMAP4, and POP3.

Working with SMTP, IMAP4, and POP3 Virtual Servers

SMTP, IMAP4, and POP3 services are hosted on separate virtual servers. A virtual server is a server process that has its own configuration information, which includes an Internet Protocol (IP) address, a port number, and authentication settings. If you installed SMTP, IMAP4, and POP3 using the default options:

*   The default SMTP virtual server is configured to use any available IP address on the server and respond on port 25. SMTP virtual servers replace and extend the Internet Mail Connector and Internet Mail Service that were used in previous versions of Exchange Server. To control outbound connections

and message delivery, you configure the default SMTP virtual server for the organization.

- The default IMAP4 virtual server is configured to use any available IP address on the server and respond on ports 143 and 993. Port 143 is used for standard communications, and port 993 is used for Secure Sockets Layer (SSL) communications. IMAP4 virtual servers allow Internet clients to download message headers and then read messages individually while online.

- The default POP3 virtual server is configured to use any available IP address on the server and respond on ports 110 and 995. Port 110 is used for standard communications, and port 995 is used for SSL communications. POP3 virtual servers allow Internet clients to download mail for offline use.

You can change the IP address and port assignment at any time. In most cases you'll want the messaging protocol to respond on a specific IP address. For SMTP, this is the IP address or addresses you've designated in the Domain Name System (DNS) mail exchanger (MX) records for the domains you're supporting through Exchange Server. For IMAP4 and POP3, this is the IP address or IP addresses associated with the fully qualified domain name (FQDN) of the Exchange servers providing these services.

Although a single Exchange server could provide SMTP, IMAP4, and POP3 services, you can install these services on separate Exchange servers. Here are some typical scenarios:

- In a moderately sized enterprise, you might want one Exchange server to handle SMTP and another to handle IMAP4 and POP3. You install Server A as the SMTP server and then update the domain's MX record so that it points to Server A. Next, you install Server B as the POP3 and IMAP4 server. Afterward, you configure Internet mail clients so that they use Server B for POP3 and IMAP4 (incoming mail) and Server A for SMTP (outgoing mail).

- In a large enterprise, you might want a different Exchange server for each protocol. You install Server A as the SMTP server and then update the domain's MX record so that it points to Server A. Next, you install Server B as the POP3 server and Server C as the IMAP4 server. Afterward, you configure POP3 clients so that they use Server B for POP3 (incoming mail) and Server A for SMTP (outgoing mail). Then you configure IMAP4 clients so that they use Server C for IMAP4 (incoming mail) and Server A for SMTP (outgoing mail).

- When mail exchange is critical to the enterprise, you might want to build fault tolerance into the Exchange organization. Typically, you do this by installing multiple Exchange servers that support each protocol. For example, to ensure fault tolerance for SMTP, you could install Server A, Server B, and Server C as SMTP servers. Then, when you create the domain's MX records, you set a priority of 10 for Server A, a priority of 20 for Server B, and a priority of 30 for Server C. In this way, any one of the servers can be offline without affecting mail submission and delivery in the organization.

A single virtual server can provide messaging services for multiple domains. You can also install multiple virtual servers of the same type. You can use additional virtual servers to help provide fault tolerance in a large enterprise or to handle messaging services for multiple domains. When you create multiple SMTP virtual servers, you must also create additional MX records for the servers.

Mastering Core SMTP, IMAP4, and POP3 Administration

Regardless of whether you're working with SMTP, IMAP4, or POP3, you'll perform a common set of administrative tasks. These tasks are examined in this section.

Starting, Stopping, and Pausing Virtual Servers

Virtual servers run under a server process, which you can start, stop, and pause much like other server processes. For example, if you're changing the configuration of a virtual server or performing other maintenance tasks, you might need to stop the virtual server, make the changes, and then restart it. When you stop a virtual server, it doesn't accept connections from users, and you can't use it to deliver or retrieve mail.

An alternative to stopping a virtual server is to pause it. Pausing a virtual server prevents new client connections, but it doesn't disconnect current connections. When you pause a POP3 or IMAP4 virtual server, active clients can continue to retrieve mail. When you pause an SMTP virtual server, active clients can continue to submit messages and the virtual server can deliver existing messages that are queued for delivery. No new connections are accepted, however.

The master process for each virtual server of a particular type is the Microsoft Windows service under which the virtual server process runs—either Simple Mail Transfer Protocol (SMTP), Microsoft Exchange IMAP4, or Microsoft Exchange POP3. Stopping the master process stops all virtual servers using the process and halts all message delivery for the service. Starting the master process restarts all virtual servers that were running when the master process was stopped.

You can start, stop, or pause a virtual server by completing the following steps:

1. Start System Manager. If administrative groups are enabled, expand the administrative group in which the server you want to use is located.

2. In the console tree, navigate to the Protocols container. Expand Servers, expand the server you want to work with, and then expand Protocols.

3. In the console tree, expand SMTP, IMAP4, or POP3, and then right-click the virtual server you want to manage. You can now do the following:

   - Select Start to start the virtual server.
   - Select Stop to stop the virtual server.
   - Select Pause to pause the virtual server.

Note The *metabase update service* is responsible for processing and replicating configuration changes. This service reads data from Active Directory and enters it into the virtual server's local metabase. Exchange Server uses the service to make configuration changes to virtual servers on remote systems without needing a permanent connection. When the service updates a remote server, it might need several minutes to read and apply the changes.

You can start, stop, or pause the master process for virtual servers by completing the following steps:

1. Start Computer Management. Click Start, Programs or All Programs as appropriate, Administrative Tools, and then Computer Management.

2. If you wish to connect to a remote server, right-click the Computer Management entry in the console tree. Choose Connect To Another Computer from the shortcut menu. You can now choose the Exchange server for which you want to manage services.

3. Expand the Services And Applications node by clicking the plus sign (+) next to it, and then choose Services. The SMTP, Microsoft Exchange IMAP4, and Microsoft Exchange POP3 services control SMTP, IMAP4, and POP3, respectively.

4. Right-click the service you want to manipulate, and then select Start, Stop, or Pause as appropriate. You can also choose Restart to have Windows stop and then start the service after a brief pause. If you pause a service, you can use the Resume option to resume normal operation.

Configuring Ports and IP Addresses Used by Virtual Servers

Each virtual server has an IP address and a Transmission Control Protocol (TCP) port configuration setting. The default IP address setting is to use any available IP address. On a multihomed server, however, you'll usually want messaging protocols to respond on a specific IP address and to do this, you need to change the default setting.

What the default port setting is depends on the messaging protocol being used and whether SSL is enabled or disabled. Table 15-1 shows the default port settings for key protocols used by Exchange Server 2003.

Table 15-1. Standard and Secure Port Settings for Messaging Protocols

Protocol	Default Port	Default Secure Port
SMTP	25	
HTTP	80	443
IMAP4	143	993

Table 15-1.   Standard and Secure Port Settings for Messaging Protocols

Protocol	Default Port	Default Secure Port
POP3	110	995
NNTP (Network News Transfer Protocol)	119	563

To change the IP address or port number for a virtual server, complete the following steps:

1. Start System Manager. If administrative groups are enabled, expand the administrative group in which the server you want to use is located.

2. In the console tree, navigate to the Protocols container. Expand Servers, expand the server you want to work with, and then expand Protocols.

3. In the console tree, expand SMTP, IMAP4, or POP3. Right-click the virtual server you want to manage, and then select Properties.

4. On the General tab, use the IP Address drop-down list to select an available IP address. Select (All Unassigned) to allow the protocol to respond on all unassigned IP addresses that are configured on the server.

Tip   If the IP address you want to use isn't listed and you want the server to respond on that IP address, you'll need to update the server's TCP/IP network configuration. For details, see "Configuring Static IP Addresses" in Chapter 16 of *Microsoft Windows Server 2003 Administrator's Pocket Consultant* (Microsoft Press, 2003).

5. On the General tab, click Advanced. As Figure 15-1 shows, the Advanced dialog box shows the current TCP port settings for the protocol. You can assign ports for individual IP addresses and for all unassigned IP addresses.

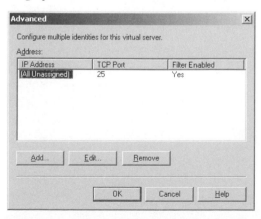

Figure 15-1.   *Use the Advanced dialog box to configure TCP ports on an individual IP address basis or for all unassigned IP addresses.*

6. Use the following options in the Advanced dialog box to modify port settings:

- **Add** Adds a TCP port on a per IP address basis or all unassigned IP address basis. Click Add, and then select the IP address you want to use.
- **Edit** Allows you to edit the TCP port settings for the currently selected entry in the Address list box.
- **Remove** Allows you to remove the TCP port settings for the currently selected entry in the Address list box.

 Note The IP address/TCP port combination must be unique on every virtual server. Multiple virtual servers can use the same port as long as the servers are configured to use different IP addresses.

7. Click OK twice.

Controlling Incoming Connections to Virtual Servers

You can control incoming connections to virtual servers in several ways. You can do the following:

- Grant or deny access using IP addresses or Internet domain names.
- Require secure incoming connections.
- Require authentication for incoming connections.
- Restrict concurrent connections and set connection time-out values.

Each of these tasks is discussed in the sections that follow.

 Note With SMTP, you can configure both incoming and outbound connections. To learn how to configure outbound connections for SMTP, see the section of this chapter entitled "Configuring Outgoing Connections."

Securing Access by IP Address, Subnet, or Domain

By default, virtual servers are accessible to all IP addresses, which presents a security risk that could allow your messaging system to be misused. To control use of a virtual server, you might want to grant or deny access by IP address, subnet, or domain.

- Granting access allows a computer to access the virtual server but doesn't necessarily allow users to submit or retrieve messages. If you require authentication, users still need to authenticate themselves.
- Denying access prevents a computer from accessing the virtual server. As a result, users of the computer can't submit or retrieve messages from the virtual server—even if they could have authenticated themselves with a user name and password.

As stated earlier, POP3 and IMAP4 virtual servers control message retrieval by remote clients and SMTP virtual servers control message delivery. Thus, if you want to block users outside the organization from sending mail, you deny access to the SMTP virtual server. If you want to block users from retrieving mail, you deny access to POP3, IMAP4, or both.

Note   You can also restrict access by e-mail address. To do this, you must set a filter and then enable the filter on the SMTP virtual server. For details, see the section of Chapter 13, "Microsoft Exchange Server 2003 and Group Administration," entitled "Configuring Antispam and Message Filtering Options."

To grant or deny access to a virtual server by IP address, subnet, or domain, follow these steps:

1. Start System Manager. If administrative groups are enabled, expand the administrative group in which the server you want to use is located.

2. In the console tree, navigate to the Protocols container. Expand Servers, expand the server you want to work with, and then expand Protocols.

3. In the console tree, expand SMTP, IMAP4, or POP3. Right-click the virtual server you want to manage, and then select Properties.

4. Click Connection on the Access tab. As shown in Figure 15-2, the Computers list shows the computers that currently have connection controls.

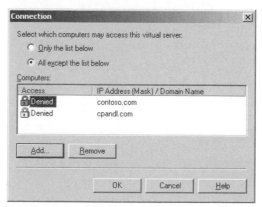

Figure 15-2. *Use the Connection dialog box to control connections by IP address, subnet, or domain.*

5. To grant access to specific computers and deny access to all others, select Only The List Below.

6. To deny access to specific computers and grant access to all others, select All Except The List Below.

7. Create the grant or deny list. Click Add, and then in the Computer dialog box, specify Single Computer, Group Of Computers, or Domain.

- For a single computer, type the IP address for the computer, such as 192.168.5.50.

- For groups of computers, type the subnet address, such as 192.168.5, and the subnet mask, such as 255.255.0.0.

- For a domain name, type the FQDN, such as eng.microsoft.com.

 Caution When you grant or deny by domain, Exchange Server must perform a reverse DNS lookup on each connection to determine whether the connection comes from the domain. These reverse lookups can severely affect Exchange Server's performance, and this performance impact increases as the number of concurrent users and connections increases.

8. If you want to remove an entry from the grant or deny list, select the related entry in the Computers list and then click Remove.

9. Click OK.

Controlling Secure Communications for Incoming Connections

By default, mail clients pass connection information and message data through an insecure connection. If corporate security is a high priority, however, your information security team might require mail clients to connect over secure communication channels. You have several options for configuring secure communications, including smart cards, SSL, and Pretty Good Privacy (PGP). In an environment in which you need to support multiple transfer protocols, such as HTTP and SMTP, SSL offers a good solution.

You configure secure SSL communications by completing the following steps:

1. Create a certificate request for the Exchange server for which you want to use secure communications. Each server (but not necessarily each virtual server) must have its own certificate.

2. Submit the certificate request to a certification authority (CA). The certification authority then issues you a certificate (usually for a fee).

3. Install the certificate on the Exchange server. Repeat Steps 1 through 3 for each Exchange server that needs to communicate over a secure channel.

4. Configure the server to require secure communications on a per virtual server basis.

Following this procedure, you could create, install, and enable a certificate for use on a virtual server by completing the following steps:

1. Start System Manager. If administrative groups are enabled, expand the administrative group in which the server you want to use is located.

2. In the console tree, navigate to the Protocols container. Expand Servers, expand the server you want to work with, and then expand Protocols.

3. In the console tree, expand SMTP, IMAP4, or POP3. Right-click the virtual server for which you want to use secure communications, and then select Properties.

4. On the Access tab, click Certificate. This starts the Web Server Certificate Wizard. Use the wizard to create a new certificate. For additional virtual servers on the same Exchange server, you'll want to assign an existing certificate.

5. Send the certificate request to your CA. When you receive the certificate back from the CA, access the Web Server Certificate Wizard from the virtual server's Properties dialog box again. Now you'll be able to process the pending request and install the certificate.

6. When you're finished installing the certificate, don't close the Properties dialog box. Instead, on the Access tab, click Communication.

7. In the Security dialog box, click Require Secure Channel. If you've also configured 128-bit security, select Require 128-Bit Encryption.

8. Click OK twice.

Note For worldwide installations, you'll want to use 40-bit encryption. The 128-bit encryption level is available only in the United States and Canada.

Restricting Incoming Connections and Setting Time-Out Values

You can control incoming connections to a virtual server in two ways. You can set a limit on the number of simultaneous connections and you can set a connection time-out value.

Virtual servers normally accept an unlimited number of connections, and in most environments this is an acceptable setting. However, when you're trying to prevent a virtual server from becoming overloaded, you might want to limit the number of simultaneous connections. Once the limit is reached, no other clients are permitted to access the server. The clients must wait until the connection load on the server decreases.

The connection time-out value determines when idle connections are disconnected. Normally, connections time out after they've been idle for 30 minutes. In most situations a 30-minute time-out value is sufficient. Still, there are times when you'll want to increase the time-out value, and this primarily relates to clients who get disconnected when downloading large files. If you discover that clients get disconnected during large downloads, the time-out value is one area to examine. You'll also want to look at the Message Transfer Agent settings as discussed in Chapter 14, "Managing Message Transfer and Routing Within the Organization."

You can modify connection limits and time-outs by completing the following steps:

1. Start System Manager. If administrative groups are enabled, expand the administrative group in which the server you want to use is located.

2. In the console tree, navigate to the Protocols container. Expand Servers, expand the server you want to work with, and then expand Protocols.

3. In the console tree, expand SMTP, IMAP4, or POP3. Right-click the virtual server that you want to work with, and select Properties. This displays the Properties dialog box, as shown in Figure 15-3.

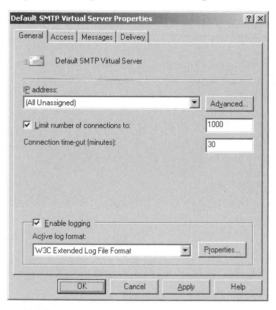

Figure 15-3. *Use the Properties dialog box to configure connection limits and time-outs. Enabling these options can help reduce server load and help troubleshoot connection problems.*

4. To remove connection limits, clear the Limit Number Of Connections To check box. To set a connection limit, select the Limit Number Of Connections To check box and then type the limit value.

5. The Connection Time-Out field controls the connection time-out. Type the new time-out value in minutes. In most cases, you'll want to use a time-out value between 30 and 90 minutes.

6. Click OK.

Viewing and Ending User Sessions

A user session is started each time a user connects to a virtual server. The session lasts for the duration of the user's connection. Each virtual server tracks user sessions separately. By viewing the current sessions, you can monitor server load and determine which users are logged on to a server and how long they have been connected. If an unauthorized user is accessing a virtual server, you can terminate the user's session, which immediately disconnects the user. You also have the option of disconnecting all users who are accessing a particular virtual server.

To view or end user sessions, complete the following steps:

1. Start System Manager. If administrative groups are enabled, expand the administrative group in which the server you want to use is located.

2. In the console tree, navigate to the Protocols container. Expand Servers, expand the server you want to work with, and then expand Protocols.

3. In the console tree, expand SMTP, IMAP4, or POP3, and then double-click the virtual server that you want to work with.

4. You should now see a node called Current Sessions. Select this node in the console tree. The details pane displays current sessions.

5. To disconnect a single user, right-click a user entry in the details pane, and then select Terminate.

6. To disconnect all users, right-click any user entry in the details pane, and then select Terminate All.

Managing SMTP Virtual Servers

SMTP virtual servers have two roles in the Exchange organization. They handle mail transport and mail submission. This means that servers use SMTP to deliver messages and clients use SMTP to submit messages. The tasks you use to manage SMTP virtual servers are examined in this section.

Creating SMTP Virtual Servers

When you first install Exchange Server 2003 in an organization, a default SMTP virtual server is created. The default SMTP virtual server is used for mail transport and mail submission.

In most cases you won't need to create an additional SMTP virtual server. However, if you're hosting multiple domains and you want to have more than one default domain, you might want to create additional SMTP virtual servers to service these domains. Another reason to create additional SMTP virtual servers is for fault tolerance. When you have several SMTP virtual servers, one of the servers can go offline without stopping message delivery in the Exchange organization.

You can create additional SMTP virtual servers by completing the following steps:

1. If you want the SMTP virtual server to use a new IP address, you must configure the IP address before installing the SMTP virtual server. For details, see "Configuring Static IP Addresses" in Chapter 16 of *Microsoft Windows Server 2003 Administrator's Pocket Consultant.*

2. Start System Manager. If administrative groups are enabled, expand the administrative group in which the server you want to use is located.

3. In the console tree, navigate to the Protocols container. Expand Servers, expand the server you want to work with, and then expand Protocols.

4. In the console tree, right-click SMTP, point to New, and then select SMTP Virtual Server. As shown in Figure 15-4, this starts the New SMTP Virtual Server Wizard.

Figure 15-4. *Use the New SMTP Virtual Server Wizard to create an additional virtual server.*

5. Type a descriptive name for the virtual server, and then click Next.

6. Use the IP Address drop-down list to select an available IP address. Choose (All Unassigned) to allow SMTP to respond on all IP addresses that are configured on the server and have not been assigned. The TCP port is mapped automatically as port 25.

Tip The IP address/TCP port combination must be unique on every virtual server. Multiple virtual servers can use the same port as long as the servers are configured to use different IP addresses.

7. Click Finish to create the virtual server. If the default startup setting for the SMTP service is set to Automatic, the new SMTP virtual server starts automatically as well.

Note If the server doesn't start automatically, you might have selected an IP address/TCP port combination that's already in use. In this case, right-click the SMTP virtual server entry and then select Properties. In the Properties dialog box, modify IP address and port settings as necessary.

8. Configure the server using the tasks outlined in this section and the earlier section entitled "Mastering Core SMTP, IMAP4, and POP3 Administration."

Managing Message Delivery for SMTP and the Exchange Server Organization

SMTP delivery options determine how mail is delivered once a connection has been established and the receiving computer has acknowledged that it's ready to receive the data transfer. This section shows you how to use the configuration options that determine how message delivery and transfer occurs.

You can set the following options to control message delivery:

- Outbound retry intervals
- Outbound and local delay notification
- Outbound and local expiration time-out values
- Message hop count
- Domain name options
- Reverse DNS lookups
- External DNS server lists

Setting Outbound Retry Intervals, Delay Notification, and Expiration Time-Out

Once a connection has been established and the receiving computer has acknowledged that it's ready to receive the data transfer, Exchange Server attempts to deliver messages queued for delivery to the computer. If a message can't be delivered on the first attempt, Exchange Server tries to send the message again after a specified time. Exchange Server keeps trying to send the message at the intervals you've specified until the expiration time-out is reached. When the time limit is reached, the message is returned to the sender with a nondelivery report (NDR). The default expiration time-out is two days.

After each failed attempt to deliver a message, Exchange Server generates a delay notification and queues it for delivery to the user who sent the message. Notification doesn't occur immediately after failure. Instead, Exchange Server sends the delay notification message only after the notification delay interval and then only if the message hasn't already been delivered. The default delay notification is 12 hours.

The way in which Exchange Server handles delay notification and expiration time-out values depends on whether the message originated within or outside the organization. Exchange Server handles messages that originate within the organization using the local delay notification and expiration time-out values. Exchange Server handles messages that originate outside the organization using the outbound delay notification and expiration time-out values.

 Tip A copy of the failed message and the NDR can be sent to your organization's postmaster or other administrator's inbox. To do this, follow the procedure outlined in the section of this chapter entitled "Managing Message Delivery for SMTP and the Exchange Server Organization."

You can view or change the retry interval, delay notification, and expiration time-out by completing the following steps:

1. Start System Manager. If administrative groups are enabled, expand the administrative group in which the server you want to use is located.

2. In the console tree, navigate to the Protocols container. Expand Servers, expand the server you want to work with, and then expand Protocols.

3. In the console tree, expand SMTP. Right-click the virtual server that you want to work with, and then select Properties. The default SMTP virtual server controls message delivery for the default domain.

4. Click the Delivery tab, as shown in Figure 15-5, and then use the following options to set the retry values:

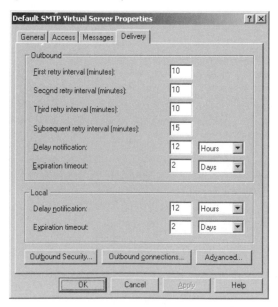

Figure 15-5. *Use the options on the Delivery tab to control message delivery in the organization.*

- **First Retry Interval (Minutes)**   Sets the amount of time to wait after the first delivery attempt. The default is 10 minutes.

- **Second Retry Interval (Minutes)**   Sets the amount of time to wait after the second delivery attempt. The default is 10 minutes after the first retry interval.

- **Third Retry Interval (Minutes)**   Sets the amount of time to wait after the third delivery attempt. The default is 10 minutes after the second retry interval.

- **Subsequent Retry Interval (Minutes)**   Sets the amount of time to wait after the fourth and subsequent delivery attempts. The default is 15 minutes.

5. Set the outbound delay notification and expiration time-out values using the Delay Notification and Expiration Timeout fields in the Outbound panel. You can set these values in minutes, hours, or days.

6. Set the local delay notification and expiration time-out values using the Delay Notification and Expiration Timeout fields in the Local panel. You can set these values in minutes, hours, or days.

7. Click OK.

Setting the Message Hop Count

Messages can be routed through many different servers before reaching their final destination. The number of servers a message passes through is called the *hop count*. As an administrator, you can control the maximum allowable hop count and you'll usually want to do this to prevent a message from being repeatedly misrouted.

The default maximum hop count is 30, which works well for most network configurations. However, if users frequently get NDRs that state that the maximum hop count was reached and the message wasn't delivered, you might want to consider increasing the maximum allowable hop count. The number of received lines in the message header determines the total hops.

Caution   Don't automatically increase the hop count without first examining the network. NDRs due to the hop count can also indicate network problems. You can run a traceroute command (tracert hostname) to the destination mail server to help determine if a misconfigured or down network is the source of the delivery problem.

You can view or set the maximum hop count by completing the following steps:

1. Start System Manager. If administrative groups are enabled, expand the administrative group in which the server you want to use is located.

2. In the console tree, navigate to the Protocols container. Expand Servers, expand the server you want to work with, and then expand Protocols.

3. In the console tree, expand SMTP. Right-click the virtual server that you want to work with, and then select Properties. The default SMTP virtual server controls message delivery for the default domain.

4. On the Delivery tab, click Advanced. This displays the Advanced Delivery dialog box.

5. If you want to change the hop count, type a new value in the Maximum Hop Count field. Valid values are between 10 and 256.

6. Click OK twice.

Setting Domain Name Options

Domain names play an important role in determining how mail is delivered in the enterprise, and you have two options for configuring domain name usage. You can set a *masquerade domain*, or you can set an FQDN for the SMTP virtual server.

A masquerade domain replaces the local domain name in any Mail From lines in the message header. Mail From information is used to determine the address for sending NDRs and doesn't replace the From lines in the message body that are displayed to mail clients. The name replacement occurs on the first hop only.

The FQDN of the Exchange server is used in mail delivery. The server must have an FQDN, and this FQDN is associated with an e-mail domain through a DNS MX record. In Exchange Server you have two options for specifying an FQDN:

- You can use the name specified on the Network Identification tab of the System utility.

- You can specify a unique FQDN for the SMTP virtual server you're configuring.

The name on the Network Identification tab is used automatically. If you change the name on this tab, the new name is used the next time the computer is rebooted. No action is required to update the FQDN for the virtual server. However, if you want to override the setting on the Network Identification tab, you can do so by specifying a unique FQDN for the SMTP virtual server.

You can set the masquerade domain name or override the default FQDN by completing the following steps:

1. Start System Manager. If administrative groups are enabled, expand the administrative group in which the server you want to use is located.

2. In the console tree, navigate to the Protocols container. Expand Servers, expand the server you want to work with, and then expand Protocols.

3. In the console tree, expand SMTP. Right-click the virtual server that you want to work with, and then select Properties. The default SMTP virtual server controls message delivery for the default domain.

4. On the Delivery tab, click Advanced. This displays the Advanced Delivery dialog box shown in Figure 15-6.

Figure 15-6. *Use the Advanced Delivery dialog box to configure the domain name options. Domain names play an important role in determining how mail is delivered.*

5. In the Masquerade Domain field, type the domain name to which you would like NDRs to be sent. This domain name replaces the default domain name in outgoing message headers.

6. If you want to override the default FQDN, type a new value in the Fully-Qualified Domain Name field. Click Check DNS to ensure that you've entered the correct value and that DNS resolution is configured properly.

7. Click OK twice.

Configuring Reverse Lookups and External DNS Servers

When you want to put extra controls on how DNS is used with a particular virtual server, you have several options. You can enable reverse DNS lookups or you can specify an explicit list of external DNS servers to use for name resolution.

With reverse lookups enabled, Exchange Server attempts to verify that the mail client's IP address matches the host and domain submitted by the client in the start session command. If the IP and DNS information match, Exchange Server passes the message through without modifying its contents. If Exchange Server can't verify the IP and DNS information, Exchange Server modifies the message header so that the key word "unverified" is inserted on the Received line of the message header.

As stated previously, reverse lookups can severely affect Exchange Server's performance, and this performance impact increases as the number of concurrent users and connections increases. Because of this, you'll want to be very cautious about enabling reverse lookups.

DNS servers are used to resolve host and domain names for message delivery. Internal DNS servers are used to resolve host and domain names within the organization, and external DNS servers are used to resolve names outside the organization. Normally, the list of DNS servers that you want to use for name resolution is configured in the TCP/IP settings for the Exchange server. If necessary, you can override these settings for external servers by defining an external DNS server list for an individual virtual server.

Once the external DNS server list is created, the SMTP virtual server uses only the servers on that list. If you want to keep using some or all of the local DNS servers, you must manually add those IP addresses to the list.

To enable reverse DNS lookups or define an external DNS server list, complete the following steps:

1. Start System Manager. If administrative groups are enabled, expand the administrative group in which the server you want to use is located.

2. In the console tree, navigate to the Protocols container. Expand Servers, expand the server you want to work with, and then expand Protocols.

3. In the console tree, expand SMTP. Right-click the virtual server that you want to work with, and then select Properties. The default SMTP virtual server controls message delivery for the default domain.

4. On the Delivery tab, click Advanced. This displays the Advanced Delivery dialog box shown previously in Figure 15-6.

5. To enable reverse lookups, select the Perform Reverse DNS Lookup On Incoming Messages check box. To disable reverse lookups, clear this check box.

6. To define an external DNS server list, click Configure. The External DNS list shows the servers that are currently configured (if any). The order of entries in the list is extremely important. The SMTP virtual server starts with the top DNS server and then goes down the list until one of the servers returns the information it needs. You use the options in the Configure dialog box as follows:

   - **Add**   Adds an entry to the external DNS server list. Click Add, type the IP address of a DNS server, and then click OK.

   - **Remove**   Removes a selected entry from the external DNS server list. Select the entry you want to remove, and then click Remove.

   - **Move Up**   Moves the selected entry up in the priority list. Select the entry you want to change, and then click Move Up.

   - **Move Down**   Moves the selected entry down in the priority list. Select the entry you want to change, and then click Move Down.

7. Click OK three times.

Controlling Authentication for Incoming SMTP Connections

Exchange Server 2003 supports three authentication methods for incoming SMTP connnections:

- **Anonymous authentication**   With anonymous authentication, users can log on with an anonymous or guest account. This allows users to access server resources without being prompted for user name and password information.

- **Basic authentication**   With basic authentication, users are prompted for logon information. When entered, this information is transmitted unencrypted across the network. If you've configured secure communications on the server as described in the section of this chapter entitled "Controlling Secure Communications for Incoming Connections," you can require clients to use SSL. When you use SSL with basic authentication, the logon information is encrypted before transmission.

- **Integrated Windows authentication**   With integrated Windows authentication, Exchange Server uses standard Windows security to validate the user's identity. Instead of prompting for a user name and password, clients relay the logon credentials that users supply when they log on to Windows. These credentials are fully encrypted without the need for SSL, and they include the user name and password needed to log on to the network.

In most cases, only the basic and integrated Windows authentication methods should be enabled for SMTP. With this configuration, the logon process looks like this:

1. Exchange Server attempts to obtain the user's Windows credentials. If the credentials can be validated and the user has the appropriate access permissions, the user is allowed to log on to the virtual server.

2. If validation of the credentials fails or no credentials are available, the server uses basic authentication and tells the client to display a logon prompt. When the logon information is submitted, the server validates the logon. If the credentials can be validated and the user has the appropriate access permissions, the user is allowed to log on to the virtual server.

3. If validation fails or the user doesn't have appropriate access permissions, the user is denied access to the virtual server.

As necessary, you can enable or disable support for these authentication methods by completing the following steps:

1. Start System Manager. If administrative groups are enabled, expand the administrative group in which the server you want to use is located.

2. In the console tree, navigate to the Protocols container. Expand Servers, expand the server you want to work with, and then expand Protocols.

3. In the console tree, expand SMTP. Right-click the virtual server that you want to work with, and then select Properties.

4. On the Access tab, click Authentication. This displays the Authentication dialog box shown in Figure 15-7.

Figure 15-7. *You can use the Authentication dialog box to enable or disable authentication methods to meet the needs of your organization. With basic authentication, it's often helpful to set a default domain as well.*

5. Select or clear the Anonymous Access check box to enable or disable anonymous access. If you enable anonymous access, no user name or password is required to access the SMTP virtual server.

6. Select or clear the Basic Authentication check box to enable or disable this authentication method. If you disable basic authentication, keep in mind that this might prevent some clients from accessing mail remotely. Clients can log on only when you enable an authentication method that they support.

7. A default domain isn't set automatically. If you enable basic authentication, you can choose to set a default domain that should be used when no domain information is supplied during the logon process. Setting the default domain is useful when you want to ensure that clients authenticate properly.

8. Select or clear the Integrated Windows Authentication check box to enable or disable this authentication method.

9. Click OK twice.

Configuring Outbound Security

By default, SMTP virtual servers deliver messages to other servers without authenticating themselves. This mode of authentication is referred to as *anonymous*. You can also configure SMTP virtual servers to use basic or integrated Windows authentication. However, you'll rarely use an authentication method other than anonymous when configuring an SMTP virtual server's outbound security.

In fact, one of the only times you'll use basic or integrated Windows authentication with an SMTP virtual server's outbound security is when the server must deliver all e-mail to a specific server or e-mail address in another domain. That is, the server delivers mail to only one destination and doesn't deliver mail to other destinations. If you need to configure authentication for e-mail delivered to a particular server and also need to deliver mail to other servers, you should configure an Exchange connector to send mail to that specific server and use anonymous authentication for all other mail.

To view or change the outbound security settings for an SMTP virtual server, complete the following steps:

1. Start System Manager. If administrative groups are enabled, expand the administrative group in which the server you want to use is located.

2. In the console tree, navigate to the Protocols container. Expand Servers, expand the server you want to work with, and then expand Protocols.

3. In the console tree, expand SMTP. Right-click the virtual server that you want to work with, and then select Properties.

4. On the Delivery tab, click Outbound Security. To use standard delivery for outgoing messages, click Anonymous Access.

5. To set basic authentication for outgoing messages, click Basic Authentication. Under User Name and Password, type the account name and password that are required to connect to the remote server.

6. To set integrated Windows authentication for outgoing messages, select Integrated Windows Authentication, and then under Account and Password, type the Windows account name and password that are required to connect to the remote server.

7. Click OK twice.

Configuring Outgoing Connections

With SMTP virtual servers you have much more control over outgoing connections than you do over incoming connections. You can limit the number of simultaneous connections and the number of connections per domain. These limits set the maximum number of simultaneous outbound connections. By default, no maximum is set, and this can cause performance problems. To improve performance, you should optimize these values based on the size of your Exchange environment and the characteristics of your server hardware.

You can set a connection time-out that determines when idle connections are disconnected. Normally, outbound connections time out after they've been idle for 10 minutes. Sometimes you'll want to increase the time-out value, primarily when you're experiencing connectivity problems and messages aren't getting delivered.

You can also map outbound SMTP connections to a TCP port other than port 25. If you're connecting through a firewall or proxy, you might want to map outgoing connections to a different port and then let the firewall or proxy deliver the mail over the standard SMTP port (port 25).

You set outgoing connection controls by completing the following steps:

1. Start System Manager. If administrative groups are enabled, expand the administrative group in which the server you want to use is located.

2. In the console tree, navigate to the Protocols container. Expand Servers, expand the server you want to work with, and then expand Protocols.

3. In the console tree, expand SMTP. Right-click the virtual server that you want to work with and select Properties.

4. On the Delivery tab, click Outbound Connections. This displays the Outbound Connections dialog box shown in Figure 15-8.

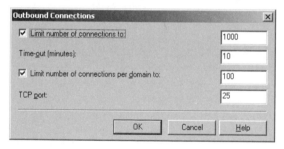

Figure 15-8. *Use the Outbound Connections dialog box to set limits on outbound SMTP traffic. Administrators have much more control over outbound SMTP connections than they do over incoming SMTP connections.*

5. To remove outgoing connection limits, clear Limit Connections To. To set an outgoing connection limit, select the Limit Number Of Connections To check box, and then type the limit value. Valid values are from 1 to 1,999,999,999.

6. The Time-Out field controls the connection time-out. Type the new time-out value in minutes. Valid values are from 30 to 99,999,999. In most cases, you'll want to use a time-out value between 30 and 90 minutes.

7. To set an outgoing connection limit per domain, select the Limit Number Of Connections Per Domain To check box, and then type the limit value. Valid values are from 1 to 1,999,999,999. You can remove the per domain limit by clearing this check box.

8. To map outgoing connections to a different port, in the TCP Port field, type the outbound port that the firewall or proxy expects.

9. Click OK twice.

Managing Messaging Limits for SMTP

You can use messaging limits to control Exchange usage and to improve throughput for message delivery. You can set the maximum allowable message size. Clients who attempt to send a message larger than this size get an NDR that states the message exceeds this limit. The default limit is 4096 KB.

Note You can set message size limits that apply to both incoming and outgoing mail globally on all user mailboxes and individually on specific mailboxes. You set global limits through Message Delivery under Global Settings. You set individual limits in the user's Properties dialog box.

You can set the maximum size of all messages that can be sent in a single connection. You should always set the session limit so that it's several times larger than the message size limit. The default limit is 10240 KB.

You can control the number of messages that can be sent in a single connection. When the number of messages exceeds this value, Exchange Server starts a new connection and transfer continues until all messages are delivered. Optimizing this value for your environment can improve server performance, especially if users typically send large numbers of messages to the same external domains. The default is 20. If you had 50 messages queued for delivery to the same destination server, Exchange Server would open three connections and use these connections to deliver the mail. Because message delivery would take less time, you could considerably enhance Exchange Server's performance.

You can also control the number of recipients for a single message. When the number of recipients exceeds this value, Exchange Server opens a new connection and uses this connection to process the remaining recipients. The default value is 64,000, but a more practical limit is 1000. Using the limit of 1000, a message queued for delivery to 2500 recipients would be sent over three connections. Again, because message delivery would take less time, you could considerably enhance Exchange Server's performance.

You set messaging limits by completing the following steps:

1. Start System Manager. If administrative groups are enabled, expand the administrative group in which the server you want to use is located.

2. In the console tree, navigate to the Protocols container. Expand Servers, expand the server you want to work with, and then expand Protocols.

3. In the console tree, expand SMTP. Right-click the virtual server that you want to work with and select Properties.

4. Click the Messages tab, shown in Figure 15-9.

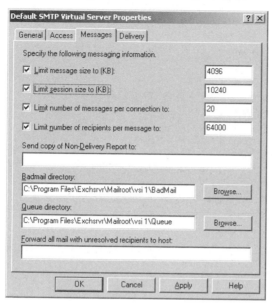

Figure 15-9. *Use the Messages tab to set limits to control Exchange usage and to improve performance.*

5. Use the message size limit settings to strictly control the maximum message size. To disable this limit, clear the Limit Message Size To (KB) check box. Otherwise, select the Limit Message Size To (KB) check box and use the related field to set a message size limit.

 Tip Message size limits apply to messages being sent through SMTP clients. In most environments, you'll find that the default message size limit is too restrictive. You'll usually want to increase this limit to at least 8192 KB.

6. Use session limits to strictly control the maximum size of all messages that can be sent in a single session. To disable this limit, clear the Limit Session Size To (KB) check box. Otherwise, select the Limit Session Size To (KB) check box and use the related field to set a session size limit.

7. Use the messages per connection limit to force Exchange Server to open new connections when multiple messages are queued for delivery to the same destination. To disable this limit, clear the Limit Number Of Messages Per Connection To check box. Otherwise, select the Limit Number Of Messages Per Connection To check box and use the related field to set a limit.

8. Use recipient limits to force Exchange Server to open new connections when messages are addressed to many recipients. To disable this limit, clear the Limit Number Of Recipients Per Message To check box. Otherwise, select the Limit Number Of Recipients Per Message To check box and use the related field to set a limit.

9. Click OK.

Handling Nondelivery, Bad Mail, and Unresolved Recipients

When a message is undeliverable or a fatal error occurs during delivery, Exchange Server generates an NDR and attempts to deliver it to the sender. SMTP virtual server options provide several ways that you can configure how Exchange Server handles nondelivery.

For tracking purposes, you can send a copy of all NDRs to a specific e-mail address such as the organization's postmaster account. The e-mail address specified is also placed in the Reply-To field of the NDR. This allows users to respond to the error message and potentially reach someone who can help resolve the problem.

If an NDR can't be delivered to the sender, a copy of the original message is placed in the "bad" mail directory. Messages placed in this directory can't be delivered or returned. You can use the bad mail directory to track potential abuse of your messaging system. By default, the bad mail directory is located at *root*:\Exchsrvr\Mailroot\Vsi#\BadMail, where *root* is the install drive for Exchange Server and # is the number of the SMTP virtual server, such as C:\Exchsrvr\Mailroot\vsi 1\BadMail. You can change the location of the bad mail directory at any time.

If you have another mail system in your organization that handles the same mail as the SMTP virtual server, you might want to have the SMTP virtual server forward unresolved recipients to this server. In this way, when Exchange Server receives e-mail for a user it can't resolve, it forwards the e-mail to the other mail system, where the recipients can be resolved. For example, if your organization has an Exchange server and a Sendmail server, Exchange Server might receive mail intended for users on the Sendmail server. When Exchange Server can't resolve these users, it forwards the mail to the Sendmail server.

Caution When forwarding is enabled, Exchange Server won't generate NDRs for unresolved mail. Because of this, you should make sure that another mail system is able to send NDRs if necessary. You should also ensure that mail sent to your organization is first delivered to Exchange Server and then forwarded as necessary.

You can configure these nondelivery options by completing the following steps:

1. Start System Manager. If administrative groups are enabled, expand the administrative group in which the server you want to use is located.

2. In the console tree, navigate to the Protocols container. Expand Servers, expand the server you want to work with, and then expand Protocols.

3. In the console tree, expand SMTP. Right-click the virtual server that you want to work with, and select Properties.

4. Click the Messages tab, shown previously in Figure 15-9.

5. In the Send Copy Of Non-Delivery Report To field, type the e-mail address of the organization's postmaster account or other account that should receive a copy of NDRs.

6. In the Badmail Directory field, type the full path to the directory in which you want to store bad mail. If you don't know the full path, click Browse, and then use the Browse For Folder dialog box to find the folder you want to use.

7. If you have another mail system in your organization that handles the same mail as the SMTP virtual server, type the host name in the Forward All Mail With Unresolved Recipients To Host field.

8. Click OK.

Setting and Removing Relay Restrictions

Mail relaying can occur when users outside the organization use your mail system to send messages bound for another organization. However, Exchange Server normally prevents unauthorized users and computers from relaying mail through your organization—and this is the behavior that you'll typically want to use. In this way, only users and computers that are able to authenticate themselves can use your mail system to relay messages.

If necessary, you can grant or deny relaying permissions, overriding the default configuration. To do this, follow these steps:

1. Start System Manager. If administrative groups are enabled, expand the administrative group in which the server you want to use is located.

2. In the console tree, navigate to the Protocols container. Expand Servers, expand the server you want to work with, and then expand Protocols.

3. In the console tree, expand SMTP. Right-click the virtual server that you want to work with, and select Properties.

4. Click the Access tab, and then click Relay. You should now see the Relay Restrictions dialog box, shown in Figure 15-10.

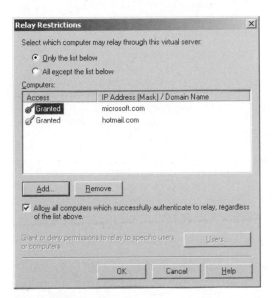

Figure 15-10. *If necessary, you can use the Relay Restrictions dialog box to grant some computers the right to relay mail through your organization.*

5. To grant relay rights to specific computers and deny relay rights to all others, select Only The List Below.

6. To deny relaying for specific computers and grant all others the right to relay, select All Except The List Below.

7. Create the grant or deny list. Click Add, and then in the Computer dialog box, specify Single Computer, Group Of Computers, or Domain.

   • For a single computer, type the IP address for the computer, such as 192.168.5.50.

   • For groups of computers, type the subnet address, such as 192.168.5, and the subnet mask, such as 255.255.0.0.

   • With a domain name, type the FQDN, such as eng.microsoft.com.

Caution When you grant or deny relaying by domain, Exchange Server 2003 must perform a reverse DNS lookup on each connection to determine if the connection comes from the domain. These reverse lookups can severely affect the performance of Exchange Server, and this performance impact increases as the number of concurrent users and connections increases.

8. If you want to remove an entry from the grant or deny list, select the entry in the Computers list, and then click Remove.

9. Click OK.

Managing IMAP4

You use IMAP4 virtual servers to read mail and access public folders on remote servers. Clients can log on to an Exchange server and use IMAP4 to download message headers, and then read messages individually while online.

Most of the tasks you perform with IMAP4 virtual servers were discussed earlier in the section "Mastering Core SMTP, IMAP4, and POP3 Administration." This section examines the few tasks that are unique to IMAP4.

Creating IMAP4 Virtual Servers

When you first install Exchange Server 2003 in an organization and configure it for messaging, a default IMAP4 virtual server is created. The default IMAP4 virtual server allows Internet clients to download message headers and then read messages individually while online. Normally, you won't need to create additional IMAP4 virtual servers, but you can do so if you want to support multiple domains or build fault tolerance into the organization.

You can create additional IMAP4 virtual servers by completing the following steps:

1. If you're installing the virtual server on a new Exchange server, ensure that messaging services have been installed on the server.

2. If you want the IMAP4 virtual server to use a new IP address, you must configure the IP address before installing the IMAP4 virtual server. For details, see "Configuring Static IP Addresses" in Chapter 16 of *Microsoft Windows Server 2003 Administrator's Pocket Consultant*.

3. Start System Manager. If administrative groups are enabled, expand the administrative group in which the server you want to use is located.

4. In the console tree, navigate to the Protocols container. Expand Servers, expand the server you want to work with, and then expand Protocols.

5. In the console tree, right-click IMAP4, point to New, and then select IMAP4 Virtual Server. As shown in Figure 15-11, this starts the New IMAP4 Virtual Server Wizard.

Figure 15-11. *Use the New IMAP4 Virtual Server Wizard to create the additional virtual server.*

6. Type a descriptive name for the virtual server, and then click Next.

7. Use the IP Address drop-down list to select an available IP address. Choose (All Unassigned) to allow IMAP4 to respond on all unassigned IP addresses that are configured on the server. The TCP port is mapped automatically as port 143.

Note The IP address/TCP port combination must be unique on every virtual server. Multiple virtual servers can use the same port as long as the servers are configured to use different IP addresses.

8. Click Finish to create the virtual server. If the default startup setting for the Microsoft Exchange IMAP4 service is set to Automatic, the new IMAP4 virtual server starts automatically as well. If the server doesn't start automatically, you might have selected an IP address/TCP port combination that's already in use.

9. Configure the server using the tasks outlined in this section and the section of this chapter entitled "Mastering Core SMTP, IMAP4, and POP3 Administration."

Controlling Authentication for Incoming IMAP4 Connections

Exchange Server 2003 supports two authentication methods for incoming IMAP4 connections:

- **Basic authentication** With basic authentication, users are prompted for logon information. When it's entered, this information is transmitted unencrypted across the network. If you've configured secure communications on the server as described in the section of this chapter entitled "Controlling Secure Communications for Incoming Connections," you can require clients to use SSL. When you use SSL with basic authentication, the logon information is encrypted before transmission.

- **Simple Authentication and Security Layer** With Simple Authentication and Security Layer (SASL), Exchange Server uses NT LAN Manager (NTLM) and standard Windows security to validate the user's identity. Instead of prompting for a user name and password, clients relay the logon credentials that users supply when they log on to a Windows domain. These credentials are fully encrypted without the need for SSL, and they include the user name and password needed to log on to the network.

Both authentication methods are enabled by default for IMAP4. Because of this, the default logon process looks like this:

1. Exchange Server attempts to obtain the user's Windows credentials using NTLM. If the credentials can be validated and the user has the appropriate access permissions, the user is allowed to log on to the virtual server.

2. If validation of the credentials fails or no credentials are available, the server uses basic authentication and tells the client to display a logon prompt. When the logon information is submitted, the server validates the logon. If the credentials can be validated and the user has the appropriate access permissions, the user is allowed to log on to the virtual server.

3. If validation fails or the user doesn't have appropriate access permissions, the user is denied access to the virtual server.

As necessary, you can enable or disable support for these authentication methods by completing the following steps:

1. Start System Manager. If administrative groups are enabled, expand the administrative group in which the server you want to use is located.

2. In the console tree, navigate to the Protocols container. Expand Servers, expand the server you want to work with, and then expand Protocols.

3. In the console tree, expand IMAP4. Right-click the virtual server that you want to work with, and then select Properties.

4. On the Access tab, click Authentication. This displays the Authentication dialog box shown in Figure 15-12.

5. Select or clear the Basic Authentication check box to enable or disable this authentication method. If you disable basic authentication, keep in mind that this might prevent some clients from accessing mail remotely. Clients can log on only when you enable an authentication method that they support.

6. Select or clear the Simple Authentication And Security Layer check box to enable or disable this authentication method.

7. Click OK twice.

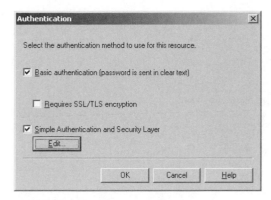

Figure 15-12. *You can use the Authentication dialog box to enable or disable authentication methods to meet the needs of your organization.*

Allowing Public Folder Requests and Fast Message Retrieval

With IMAP4 virtual servers, you can control public folder and message retrieval in two ways. You can do the following:

- Allow clients to download a list of all public folders or just a list of their private folders.

- Specify that Exchange Server should approximate message sizes instead of calculating message sizes exactly during transmission.

Both configuration settings can affect the performance of the virtual server. If your organization uses numerous public folders, you'll usually want to disable automatic downloading of all public folder lists. This allows clients to access their e-mail and private folders more quickly. If the IMAP4 server has a heavy load, you can reduce some of the load and hasten the message retrieval process by allowing the server to approximate message sizes instead of calculating them exactly.

You set these options by completing the following steps:

1. Start System Manager. If administrative groups are enabled, expand the administrative group in which the server you want to use is located.

2. In the console tree, navigate to the Protocols container. Expand Servers, expand the server you want to work with, and then expand Protocols.

3. In the console tree, expand IMAP4. Right-click the virtual server that you want to work with and select Properties. As shown in Figure 15-13, you want to work with options on the General tab.

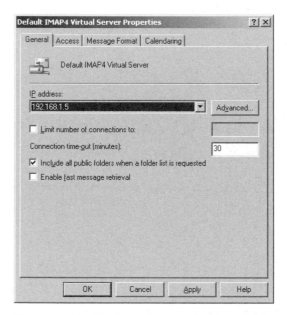

Figure 15-13. *Use the options on the General tab to configure public folder and message retrieval.*

4. To allow clients to download a list of all public folders, select the Include All Public Folders When A Folder List Is Requested check box. Clear this check box to disable automatic downloading of public folder lists.

5. To have Exchange Server 2003 approximate message sizes instead of calculating them exactly, select the Enable Fast Message Retrieval check box. Clear this check box to force Exchange Server to calculate message size exactly.

6. Click OK.

Setting Message Formats

Message format options allow you to set rules that IMAP4 servers use to format messages before clients read them. By default, when Messaging Application Programming Interface (MAPI) clients in the organization send messages, the message body is converted from Exchange Rich Text Format to Multipurpose Internet Mail Extensions (MIME) and message attachments are identified with a MIME content type based on the attachment's file extension. You can change this behavior by applying new rules.

Two key aspects of message formatting are encoding and character set usage. Message encoding rules determine the formatting for elements in the body of a message. Only MIME encoding is available. Character set usage determines which character sets are used for reading and writing messages. If users send messages with text in more than one language, the character set used determines how multilingual text is displayed.

To set message encoding and character set usage for an IMAP4 virtual server, follow these steps:

1. Start System Manager. If administrative groups are enabled, expand the administrative group in which the server you want to use is located.

2. In the console tree, navigate to the Protocols container. Expand Servers, expand the server you want to work with, and then expand Protocols.

3. In the console tree, expand IMAP4. Right-click the virtual server that you want to work with and select Properties.

4. Click the Message Format tab shown in Figure 15-14, then choose one of the following options for MIME encoding:

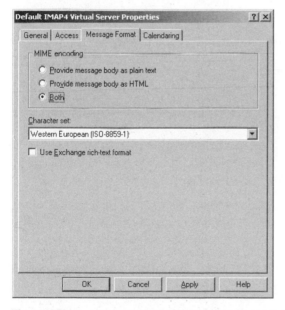

Figure 15-14. *You can use the Message Format tab to set per server defaults for message encoding and character set usage.*

- **Provide Message Body As Plain Text**   Exchange Server converts the message body to text format, and any other elements, such as graphics, are replaced with textual representations.

- **Provide Message Body As HTML**   Exchange Server converts the message body to Hypertext Markup Language (HTML). This allows compliant client applications to display the message body with graphics, hypertext links, and other elements. However, clients that don't support HTML display the actual markup tags mixed in with the text, which can make the message difficult to read.

- **Both** Exchange Server delivers messages with their original formatting, which can be either plaintext or HTML. Use this option to allow the sender to choose the message format.

 Note Exchange Server also supports a third message encoding. This format is called Exchange Rich Text Format and selecting the Use Exchange Rich-Text Format check box enables it. Exchange Rich Text Format is displayed only when clients elect to use this format and you've set the message format as either Provide Message Body As Plain Text or Both.

5. Select the character set to use. The default character set is Western European (ISO-8859-1). All text in the affected messages uses the character set you specify.

6. Click OK to apply the changes.

Managing POP3

You use POP3 virtual servers to read mail on remote servers. Clients can log on to an Exchange server and then use POP3 to download their mail for offline use.

Most of the tasks you perform with POP3 virtual servers were discussed earlier in the section "Mastering Core SMTP, IMAP4, and POP3 Administration." This section examines the few tasks that are unique to POP3.

Creating POP3 Virtual Servers

When you first install Exchange Server 2003 in an organization and configure it for messaging, a default POP3 virtual server is created. The default POP3 virtual server allows Internet clients to download mail for offline use. Normally, you won't need to create additional POP3 virtual servers, but you can do so if you want to support multiple domains or build fault tolerance into the organization.

You can create additional POP3 virtual servers by completing the following steps:

1. If you're installing the virtual server on a new Exchange server, ensure that messaging services have been installed on the server.

2. If you want the POP3 virtual server to use a new IP address, you must configure the IP address before installing the POP3 virtual server. For details, see "Configuring Static IP Addresses" in Chapter 16 of *Microsoft Windows Server 2003 Administrator's Pocket Consultant.*

3. Start System Manager. If administrative groups are enabled, expand the administrative group in which the server you want to use is located.

4. In the console tree, navigate to the Protocols container. Expand Servers, expand the server you want to work with, and then expand Protocols.

5. In the console tree, right-click POP3, point to New, and then select POP3 Virtual Server. As shown in Figure 15-15, this starts the New POP3 Virtual Server Wizard.

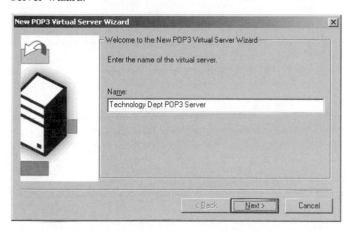

Figure 15-15. *Use the New POP3 Virtual Server Wizard to create the additional virtual server.*

6. Type a descriptive name for the virtual server, and then click Next.

7. Use the IP Address drop-down list to select an available IP address. Choose (All Unassigned) to allow POP3 to respond on all unassigned IP addresses that are configured on the server. The TCP port is assigned automatically as port 110.

Note The IP address/TCP port combination must be unique on every virtual server. Multiple virtual servers can use the same port as long as the servers are configured to use different IP addresses.

8. Click Finish to create the virtual server. If the default startup setting for the Microsoft Exchange POP3 service is set to Automatic, the new POP3 virtual server starts automatically as well. If the server doesn't start automatically, you might have selected an IP address/TCP port combination that's already in use.

9. Configure the server using the tasks outlined in this section and the section of this chapter entitled "Mastering Core SMTP, IMAP4, and POP3 Administration."

Controlling Authentication for Incoming POP3 Connections

Exchange Server 2003 supports two authentication methods for incoming POP3 connections:

- **Basic authentication** With basic authentication, users are prompted for logon information. When entered, this information is transmitted unencrypted across the network. If you've configured secure communications on the server as described in the section of this chapter entitled "Controlling Secure Communications for Incoming Connections," you can require clients to use SSL. When you use SSL with basic authentication, the logon information is encrypted before transmission.

- **Simple Authentication and Security Layer** With SASL, Exchange Server uses NTLM and standard Windows security to validate the user's identity. Instead of prompting for a user name and password, clients relay the logon credentials that users supply when they log on to a Windows domain. These credentials are fully encrypted without the need for SSL, and they include the user name and password needed to log on to the network.

Both authentication methods are enabled by default for POP3. Because of this, the default logon process looks like this:

1. Exchange Server attempts to obtain the user's Windows credentials using NTLM. If the credentials can be validated and the user has the appropriate access permissions, the user is allowed to log on to the virtual server.

2. If validation of the credentials fails or no credentials are available, the server uses basic authentication and tells the client to display a logon prompt. When the logon information is submitted, the server validates the logon. If the credentials can be validated and the user has the appropriate access permissions, the user is allowed to log on to the virtual server.

3. If validation fails or the user doesn't have appropriate access permissions, the user is denied access to the virtual server.

As necessary, you can enable or disable support for these authentication methods by completing the following steps:

1. Start System Manager. If administrative groups are enabled, expand the administrative group in which the server you want to use is located.

2. In the console tree, navigate to the Protocols container. Expand Servers, expand the server you want to work with, and then expand Protocols.

3. In the console tree, expand IMAP4. Right-click the virtual server that you want to work with, and then select Properties.

4. On the Access tab, click Authentication. This displays the Authentication dialog box shown in Figure 15-16.

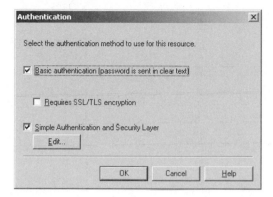

Figure 15-16. *You can use the Authentication dialog box to enable or disable authentication methods to meet the needs of your organization.*

5. Select or clear the Basic Authentication check box to enable or disable this authentication method. If you disable basic authentication, keep in mind that this might prevent some clients from accessing mail remotely. Clients can log on only when you enable an authentication method that they support.

6. Select or clear the Simple Authentication And Security Layer check box to enable or disable this authentication method.

7. Click OK twice.

Setting Message Formats

Message format options allow you to set rules that POP3 servers use to format messages before clients read them. By default, when MAPI clients in the organization send messages, the message body is converted from Exchange Rich Text Format to MIME and message attachments are identified with a MIME content type based on the attachment's file extension. You can change this behavior by applying new rules.

Two key aspects of message formatting are encoding and character set usage. Message encoding rules determine the formatting for elements in the body of a message. With POP3, you can use either MIME or UUEncode. Character set usage determines which character sets are used for reading and writing messages. If users send messages with text in more than one language, the character set used determines how multilingual text is displayed.

To set message encoding and character set usage for a POP3 virtual server, follow these steps:

1. Start System Manager. If administrative groups are enabled, expand the administrative group in which the server you want to use is located.

2. In the console tree, navigate to the Protocols container. Expand Servers, expand the server you want to work with, and then expand Protocols.

3. In the console tree, expand POP3. Right-click the virtual server that you want to work with, and select Properties.

4. Click the Message Format tab, shown in Figure 15-17. Exchange Server can format messages using either UUEncode or MIME. To use UUEncode, select UUEncode, and then, if you wish, select the Use BinHex For Macintosh check box to deliver messages to Macintosh clients using the native binary encoding format. To use MIME, select MIME in the Message Encoding panel, and then choose one of the following options:

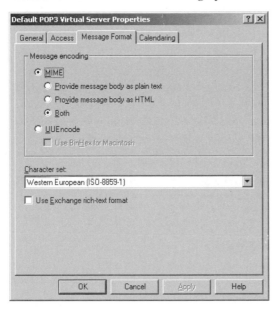

Figure 15-17. *You can use the Message Format tab to set per server defaults for message encoding and character set usage.*

- **Provide Message Body As Plain Text** Exchange Server converts the message body to text format and any other elements, such as graphics, are replaced with textual representations.

- **Provide Message Body As HTML** Exchange Server converts the message body to HTML. This allows compliant client applications to display the message body with graphics, hypertext links, and other elements. However, clients that don't support HTML display the actual markup tags mixed in with the text, which can make the message difficult to read.

- **Both** Exchange Server delivers messages with their original formatting, which can be either plaintext or HTML. Use this option to allow the sender to choose the message format.

Note   Exchange Server also supports a third message encoding. This format is called Exchange Rich Text Format and selecting the Use Exchange Rich-Text Format check box enables it. Exchange Rich Text Format is displayed only when clients elect to use this format and you've set the message format as either Provide Message Body As Plain Text or Both.

5. Select the character set to use. The default character set is Western European (ISO-8859-1). All text in the affected messages uses the character set you specify.

6. Click OK to apply the changes.

Chapter 16

Managing HTTP Virtual Servers for Web and Mobile Access Users

Microsoft Outlook Web Access and Outlook Mobile Access are essential technologies for enabling users to access Microsoft Exchange anywhere at any time. As you know from previous discussions, Outlook Web Access lets users access Exchange over the Internet or over a wireless network using a standard Web browser, and Outlook Mobile Access lets users access Exchange through a wireless carrier using mobile devices, such as smart phones and Pocket PCs. When users access Exchange mail and public folders over the Internet or a wireless network, Hypertext Transfer Protocol (HTTP) virtual servers hosted by Microsoft Exchange Server 2003 are working behind the scenes to grant access and transfer files. As you'll learn in this chapter, managing HTTP virtual servers is a bit different from other tasks you'll perform as an Exchange administrator—and not only because you'll use the Internet Information Services (IIS) Manager snap-in to perform many of the management tasks.

Using Front-End and Back-End Server Configurations for Web and Mobile Access

When you install Exchange Server 2003, Outlook Web Access and Outlook Mobile Access are automatically configured for use. This makes them fairly easy to manage, but there are some essential concepts you need to know to manage these implementations more effectively. This section explains these concepts.

Using Outlook Web Access and Outlook Mobile Access with HTTP Virtual Servers

Outlook Web Access, Outlook Mobile Access, and a default HTTP virtual server are installed automatically when you install Exchange Server 2003. In most cases you only need to open the appropriate ports on your organization's firewall to allow users to access Exchange data. Then you simply tell users the Uniform Resource Locator (URL) path that they need to type in their browser's Address field.

The users can then access Outlook Web Access or Outlook Mobile Access when they're off-site. The URLs for Outlook Web Access and Outlook Mobile Access are different. Typically, the Outlook Web Access URL is *http://yourmicrosoft.com/exchange* and the Outlook Mobile Access URL is *http://yourmicrosoft.com/oma*.

You can configure Outlook Web Access and Outlook Mobile Access for single-server and multiserver environments. In a single-server environment, you use one server for all your messaging needs. Here, the HTTP virtual server used by Outlook Web Access and Outlook Mobile Access is configured directly on the Exchange server and you don't need to change any configuration options.

In a multiserver environment, such as the one shown in Figure 16-1, you have separate servers for different messaging needs. Here, the HTTP virtual server used by Outlook Web Access and Outlook Mobile Access might reside on a different server than the servers used for Simple Mail Transfer Protocol (SMTP), Internet Message Access Protocol 4 (IMAP4), and Post Office Protocol 3 (POP3). To make the best use of Outlook Web Access and Outlook Mobile Access in a multiserver environment, you should designate an Exchange front-end server. The front-end server is the server running the HTTP virtual server and is the one to which users connect when they want to use Outlook Web Access or Outlook Mobile Access.

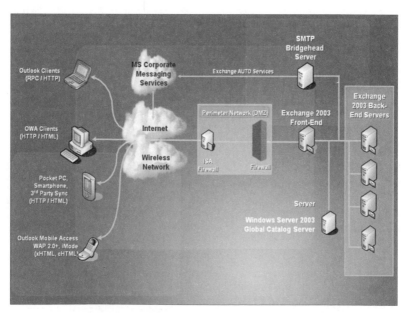

Figure 16-1. *You can configure Outlook Web Access and Outlook Mobile Access in single-server or multiserver environments; these technologies provide access to off-site users over the Internet or wireless connections.*

Configuring Front-End and Back-End Servers for Multiserver Organizations

In multiserver environments, Microsoft recommends that you use a front-end/ back-end deployment scenario for Outlook Mobile Access and Outlook Web Access. In this configuration, front-end servers handle client requests and establish the connections. Once a connection is open, the front-end server uses Lightweight Directory Access Protocol (LDAP) to query Active Directory and determine the back-end server on which the needed mailbox or public folder is located. The front-end server then delivers the request to the appropriate back-end server. When ready, the front-end server passes the back-end server's response to the client.

Additionally, if Secure Sockets Layer (SSL) is used, the front-end server is responsible for encrypting and decrypting message traffic. This means that the front-end server decrypts a client request before delivering it to a back-end server and then encrypts the back-end server's response before sending it to the client.

Tip   Although the focus of this chapter is on HTTP virtual servers, front-end servers can handle SMTP, POP3, and IMAP4 as well. To enable handling of these protocols, all you need to do is to configure clients to use a front-end server rather than the back-end server on which these protocols are configured. The front-end server uses Active Directory to determine where to forward requests.

As you might have already realized, a front-end/back-end deployment strategy has several benefits:

- You can use a front-end server to handle connections and perform directory lookups, which reduces the load on the back-end servers.

- You can use a front-end server to encrypt and decrypt SSL traffic, which again reduces the load on the back-end servers.

- You can use a front-end server to direct requests to multiple back-end servers, which makes it easier to configure clients in large enterprises.

Here's how a typical front-end/back-end deployment works:

1. You install Exchange Server 2003 on the back-end servers and then configure the information stores and virtual servers that are needed by these servers.

2. When you create user mailboxes and public folders, you do so in the information stores on the back-end servers.

3. You install Exchange Server 2003 on the front-end servers. You can place these servers behind the organizational firewall as discussed in the section of this chapter entitled "Using Outlook Web Access and Outlook Mobile Access with Firewalls."

Afterward, you use System Manager to identify the front-end servers. To do that, complete the following steps:

1. Start System Manager. If administrative groups are enabled, expand the administrative group in which the server you want to use is located.

2. Expand Servers. Right-click the server you want to designate as the front-end server, and then select Properties.

3. On the General Tab, select This Is A Front End Server. Click OK.

4. Restart the front-end server. Repeat Steps 1 through 3 for other front-end servers.

5. To complete the deployment, you configure clients to connect to the front-end servers. The front-end servers then act as proxies for the organization.

Using Outlook Web Access and Outlook Mobile Access with Firewalls

You can use Outlook Web Access and Outlook Mobile Access with firewalls. If you configure your network to use a perimeter network with firewalls in front of the designated front-end server, you can use a configuration similar to the one shown previously in Figure 16-1. In this setup, you configure Outlook Web Access and Outlook Mobile Access by completing the following steps:

1. Install the perimeter network and the organizational firewalls. Open ports 80 and 443 to the front-end server's Internet Protocol (IP) address.

2. Install Exchange Server 2003 and then configure the server as a front-end server that will provide Outlook Web Access and Outlook Mobile Access services.

3. The front-end server makes connections to back-end servers and to the organization's global catalog server, which provides information needed for logon and directory searches.

 Note If SSL is enabled, and you want all Web browsers to use SSL exclusively, you don't need to open port 80 on the perimeter network firewall. However, you still need to open port 80 on the organizational firewall.

Your perimeter network could also be configured as shown in Figure 16-2. In this configuration, your front-end server is within the perimeter network and there is a firewall in front of and behind it. In this configuration, you would need to configure Outlook Web Access and Outlook Mobile Access by completing the following steps:

1. Install the perimeter network and the organizational firewalls. On the firewall connected directly to the Internet, open ports 80 and 443 to the front-end server's IP address.

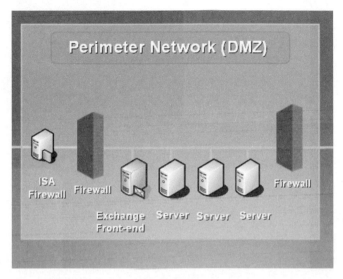

Figure 16-2. *The front-end server can be placed within the perimeter network with a firewall in front of and behind it.*

2. Install Exchange Server 2003 and then configure the server as a front-end server that will provide Outlook Web Access and Outlook Mobile Access services.

3. The front-end server makes connections to back-end servers and to the organization's global catalog server, which provides information needed for logon and directory searches. On the organizational firewall, open port 80 to the IP addresses for the back-end servers. Then open ports 389 and 3268 to the IP address for the global catalog server.

Note As before, if SSL is enabled, and you want all Web browsers to use SSL exclusively, you don't need to open port 80 on the perimeter network firewall. However, you still need to open port 80 on the organizational firewall.

Creating Additional HTTP Virtual Servers

When you install Exchange Server 2003, a default HTTP virtual server is installed and configured for use. The default HTTP virtual server allows authenticated users to access their mailboxes and public folder data. As your organization grows, you might find that you need additional HTTP virtual servers to handle the needs of remote users or that you want to offload HTTP services to separate Exchange servers. You can handle both of these tasks by installing Exchange Server 2003 on new servers and then creating additional HTTP virtual servers as necessary.

You can create additional HTTP virtual servers by completing the following steps:

1. If you're installing the virtual server on a new Exchange server, make sure that messaging services have been installed on the server.

2. If you want the HTTP virtual server to use a new IP address, you must configure the IP address before installing the HTTP virtual server. For details, see "Configuring Static IP Addresses" in Chapter 16 of *Microsoft Windows Server 2003 Administrator's Pocket Consultant* (Microsoft Press, 2003).

3. Start System Manager. If administrative groups are enabled, expand the administrative group in which the server you want to use is located.

4. Navigate to the Protocols container in the console tree. Expand Servers, expand the server you want to work with, and then expand Protocols.

5. Right-click HTTP in the console tree, point to New, and then select HTTP Virtual Server. You should see the Properties dialog box shown in Figure 16-3.

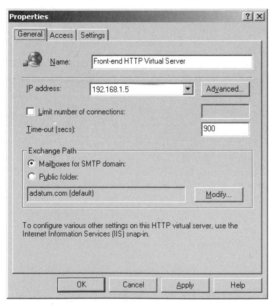

Figure 16-3. *Use the Properties dialog box to configure a new HTTP virtual server.*

6. In the Name field, type a descriptive name for the virtual server.

7. Use the IP Address selection list to select an available IP address. Choose (All Unassigned) to allow HTTP to respond on all unassigned IP addresses that are configured on the server. The Transmission Control Protocol (TCP) port is assigned automatically as port 80 for HTTP and port 443 for SSL.

8. To set additional identities, click Advanced on the General tab. Use the following options in the Advanced dialog box to modify the server's identity:

- **Add**   Adds a new identity. Click Add, select the IP address you want to use, and then type a host name, TCP port, and SSL port. Click OK when you're finished.

- **Modify**   Allows you to modify the currently selected entry in the Identities list box.

- **Remove**   Allows you to remove the currently selected entry from the Identities list box.

Note   The IP address/TCP port combination must be unique on every virtual server. Multiple virtual servers can use the same port, provided that the servers are configured to use different IP addresses.

9. Connection limits control the maximum number of simultaneous connections. To set a connection limit, select the Limit Number Of Connections check box and then type a limit.

10. The Time-Out (Secs) field controls the connection time-out. The default is 900 seconds. As necessary, type a new time-out value.

11. When you create HTTP virtual servers, you have the option of configuring the server for access to the following:

- **Mailboxes for SMTP Domain**   If you want to provide access to mailboxes, select this option. The current domain is configured as the default. To choose a different SMTP domain, click Modify, and then in the Select SMTP Domains dialog box, choose the SMTP domain to use.

- **Public Folders**   If you want to provide access to public folders, select this option. The All Public Folders Tree is configured as the default. To choose a different public folder tree or a specific public folder within a tree, click Modify and then in the Public Folder Selection dialog box choose the public folder to use.

12. Click Finish to create the virtual server.

Managing HTTP Virtual Servers

HTTP virtual servers provide the transport services you need to access public folders and mailboxes from the Web. You can also use HTTP virtual servers to publish documents that can be accessed by off-site users or the general public. If you examine the directory structure for HTTP virtual servers, you'll find several important directories, including:

- **Exadmin**   Exadmin is used for web-based administration of the HTTP virtual server. By default, this directory is configured for integrated authentication only.

- **Exchange** Exchange is the directory to which users connect to access their mailboxes. By default, this directory is configured for both basic and integrated Windows authentication with the default domain set to the pre-Windows 2000 domain name, such as ADATUM.

- **ExchWeb** ExchWeb is used with Outlook Web Access and provides calendaring, address book and other important control functions. By default, this directory is configured for anonymous access but the bin directory which provides the controls is restricted and uses both basic and integrated Windows authentication.

- **OMA** OMA is the directory to which Outlook Mobile Access users connect to access their Exchange data. By default, this directory is configured for basic authentication with the default domain set to \.

- **Public** Public is the directory to which users connect to access the default Public Folders tree. By default, this directory is configured for both basic and integrated Windows authentication with the default domain set to the pre-Windows 2000 domain name, such as ADATUM.

This section examines key tasks that you use to manage HTTP virtual servers and their related directories.

Configuring Ports, IP Addresses, and Host Names Used by HTTP Virtual Servers

Each HTTP virtual server is identified by a unique TCP port, SSL port, IP address, and host name. The default TCP port is 80. The default SSL port is 443. The default IP address setting is to use any available IP address. The default host name is the Exchange server's Domain Name System (DNS) name.

When the server is multihomed or when you use it to provide Outlook Web Access or Outlook Mobile Access services for multiple domains, the default configuration isn't ideal. On a multihomed server, you'll usually want messaging protocols to respond on a specific IP address, and to do this, you need to change the default setting. On a server that provides Outlook Web Access and Outlook Mobile Access services for multiple domains, you'll usually want to specify an additional host name for each domain.

To change the identity of an HTTP virtual server, complete the following steps:

1. If you're configuring a new Exchange server, ensure that messaging services have been installed on the server.

2. If you want the HTTP virtual server to use a new IP address, you must configure the IP address before trying to specify the IP address on the HTTP virtual server. For details, see "Configuring Static IP Addresses" in Chapter 16 of *Microsoft Windows Server 2003 Administrator's Pocket Consultant* (Microsoft Press, 2003).

3. Start IIS Manager. Click Start, point to Programs or All Programs as appropriate, point to Administrative Tools, and select Internet Information Services (IIS) Manager.

Note   By default, IIS Manager connects to the services running on the local computer. If you want to connect to a different server, right-click Internet Information Services in the console tree, and then select Connect. In the Connect To Computer dialog box, type the name of the computer to which you want to connect, and then click OK.

4. In IIS Manager, each HTTP virtual server is represented as a Web site. The Default Web Site represents the default HTTP virtual server. Double-click the entry for the server you want to work with and then double-click Web Sites.

5. Right-click the Web site that you want to manage, and then select Properties.

6. On the Web Site tab, click Advanced. As Figure 16-4 shows, you can now use the Advanced Web Site Identification dialog box to configure multiple identities for the virtual server.

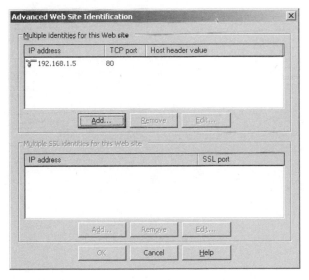

Figure 16-4. *You can use the Advanced Web Site Identification dialog box to configure multiple identities for the virtual server.*

7. Use the Multiple Identities For This Web Site panel to manage TCP port settings:

   • **Add**   Adds a new identity. Click Add, select the IP address you want to use, and then type the TCP port and host name. Click OK when you're finished.

   • **Remove**   Allows you to remove the currently selected entry from the Multiple Identities For This Web Site list.

   • **Edit**   Allows you to edit the currently selected entry in the Multiple Identities For This Web Site list.

8. Use the Multiple SSL Identities For This Web Site panel to manage SSL port settings. Click Add to create new entries. Use Edit or Remove to modify or delete existing entries.

 More Info If the SSL options are unavailable, as shown previously in Figure 16-4, you haven't installed SSL. To enable SSL and the related options, you need to obtain and install an SSL certificate as discussed in the next section of this chapter.

9. Click OK twice.

Enabling SSL on HTTP Virtual Servers

SSL is a protocol for encrypting data that is transferred between a client and a server. Without SSL, servers pass data in cleartext to clients, and this could be a security risk in an enterprise environment. With SSL, servers pass data encoded using 40-bit or 128-bit encryption.

Although HTTP virtual servers are configured to use SSL on port 443 automatically, the server won't use SSL unless you've created and installed an X.509 certificate. You can create and install an X.509 certificate for an HTTP virtual server by completing the following steps:

1. Start IIS Manager. Click Start, point to Programs or All Programs as appropriate, point to Administrative Tools, and then select Internet Information Services (IIS) Manager.

 Note By default, IIS Manager connects to the services running on the local computer. If you want to connect to a different server, right-click Internet Information Services in the console tree, and then select Connect. In the Connect To Computer dialog box, type the name of the computer to which you want to connect, and then click OK.

2. In IIS Manager, each HTTP virtual server is represented by a Web site. The Default Web Site represents the default HTTP virtual server. Double-click the entry for the server you want to work with, and then right-click the Web site that you want to manage, and choose Properties.

3. On the Directory Security tab, click Server Certificate. This starts the Web Server Certificate Wizard. Use the wizard to create a new certificate. For additional virtual servers on the same Exchange server, you'll want to assign an existing certificate.

4. Send the certificate request to your certification authority (CA). When you receive the certificate back from the CA, access the Web Server Certificate Wizard from the virtual server's Properties dialog box again. Now you'll be able to process the pending request and install the certificate.

Restricting Incoming Connections and Setting Time-Out Values

You control incoming connections to an HTTP virtual server in two ways. You can set a limit on the number of simultaneous connections, and you can set a connection time-out value.

Normally, virtual servers accept an unlimited number of connections, and this is an optimal setting in most environments. However, when you're trying to prevent a virtual server from becoming overloaded, you might want to limit the number of simultaneous connections. Once the limit is reached, no other clients are permitted to access the server. The clients must wait until the connection load on the server decreases.

The connection time-out value determines when idle user sessions are disconnected. With the default HTTP virtual server, sessions time out after they've been idle for 900 seconds (15 minutes). Although 15 minutes might seem to be a short time, it's sound security policy to disconnect idle sessions and force users to log back on to the server. If you don't disconnect idle sessions within a reasonable amount of time, unauthorized persons could gain access to your messaging system through a browser window left unattended on a remote terminal.

You can modify connection limits and time-outs by completing the following steps:

1. Start IIS Manager. Click Start, point to Programs or All Programs as appropriate, point to Administrative Tools, and then select Internet Information Services (IIS) Manager.

Note   By default, IIS Manager connects to the services running on the local computer. If you want to connect to a different server, right-click Internet Information Services in the console tree, and then select Connect. In the Connect To Computer dialog box, type the name of the computer to which you want to connect, and then click OK.

2. In IIS Manager, each HTTP virtual server is represented by a Web site. The Default Web Site represents the default HTTP virtual server. Double-click the entry for the server you want to work with.

3. Right-click the Web site that you want to manage, and then select Properties. Click the Performance tab, as shown in Figure 16-5.

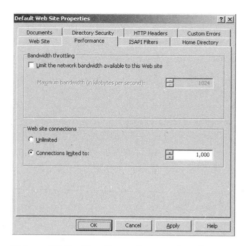

Figure 16-5. *Use the Web Site tab to limit connections and set time-out values for each virtual server.*

4. To remove connection limits, select Unlimited on the Connections panel. To set a connection limit, select Connections Limited To and then type a limit.

5. The Connection Timeout field controls how long idle user sessions remain connected to the server. Type a new value to change the current time-out value.

6. Click OK.

Controlling Access to the HTTP Server

HTTP virtual servers support five authentication methods:

- **Anonymous authentication** With anonymous authentication, IIS automatically logs users on with an anonymous or guest account. This allows users to access resources without being prompted for user name and password information.

- **Basic authentication** With basic authentication, users are prompted for logon information. When entered, this information is transmitted unencrypted (cleartext) across the network. If you've configured secure communications on the server as described in the section of this chapter entitled "Enabling SSL on HTTP Virtual Servers," you can require that clients use SSL. When you use SSL with basic authentication, the logon information is encrypted before transmission.

- **Integrated Windows authentication** With integrated Windows authentication, IIS uses standard Windows security to validate the user's identity. Instead of prompting for a user name and password, clients relay the logon credentials that users supply when they log on to Windows. These credentials are fully encrypted without the need for SSL, and they include the user name and password needed to log on to the network. Only Microsoft Internet Explorer browsers support this feature.

- **Digest authentication**   With digest authentication, user credentials are transmitted securely between clients and servers. Digest authentication is a feature of HTTP 1.1 and uses a technique that can't be easily intercepted and decrypted. This feature is available only when IIS is configured on a server running Microsoft Windows Server 2003 server and is part of a Microsoft Windows 2000 Server or later Active Directory domain. The client is required to use a domain account and the request made by Internet Explorer 5.0 or later.

- **.NET Passport authentication**   With .NET Passport authentication, the user credentials aren't checked directly. Instead, the server checks for a Passport Authentication ticket as one of the cookie files on the user's computer. If the ticket exists and has valid credentials, the server authenticates the client. If the ticket doesn't exist or the credentials aren't valid, the user is redirected to the Passport Logon Service. Once the user logs on to the Passport service, the user is directed back to the original URL.

By default, both basic and integrated Windows authentication are enabled on the Exchange and Public directories used by the HTTP virtual server, and you should rarely change this setting. However, if your organization has special needs, you can change the authentication settings at the virtual directory level. A virtual directory is simply a folder path that is accessible by a URL. For example, you could create a virtual directory called Data that is physically located on C:\CorpData\Data and accessible using the URL *http://myserver.microsoft.com/Data*.

The default public folder tree and any other public folder trees you've created are accessible through basic and integrated Windows authentication. If you want to grant public access to these folder trees or restrict them so that only integrated Windows authentication is allowed, you can do so by editing the individual security settings on the related virtual directory.

Although the mailbox tree is accessible through basic and integrated Windows authentication as well, access to mailboxes is restricted, just as it is from Microsoft Office Outlook 2003. As a result of this security, only William Stanek can access William Stanek's mailbox—unless you've granted special permissions to other users. You should rarely—if ever—change the authentication settings on the Mailbox virtual directory.

The authentication settings on virtual directories are different than authentication settings on the virtual server itself. By default, the virtual server allows anonymous access. This means that anyone can access the server's home page without authenticating himself or herself. If you disable anonymous access at the server level, users need to authenticate themselves twice: once for the server and once for the virtual directory they want to access.

You can change the authentication settings for an entire site or a particular virtual directory by completing the following steps:

1. Start IIS Manager. Click Start, point to Programs or All Programs as appropriate, point to Administrative Tools, and then select Internet Information Services (IIS) Manager.

 Note By default, IIS Manager connects to the services running on the local computer. If you want to connect to a different server, right-click Internet Information Services in the console tree, and then select Connect. In the Connect To Computer dialog box, type the name of the computer to which you want to connect, and then click OK.

2. In IIS Manager each HTTP virtual server is represented by a Web site. The Default Web Site represents the default HTTP virtual server. Double-click the entry for the server you want to work with.

3. Right-click the site or virtual directory that you want to manage, and then select Properties.

4. On the Directory Security tab, click Edit on the Anonymous Access And Authentication Control panel. This displays the Authentication Methods dialog box shown in Figure 16-6.

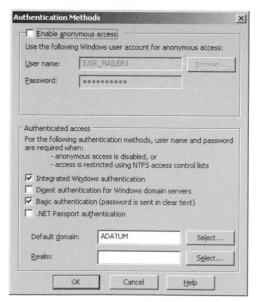

Figure 16-6. *Use the Authentication Methods dialog box to set access control on virtual directories. Virtual directories can have different authentication settings than the virtual server.*

5. To allow anonymous access, select the Enable Anonymous Access check box. To disable anonymous access, clear this check box.

Note In most cases the anonymous user account is named IUSR_ServerName, such as IUSR_Mailer1. If you use this account, you don't need to set a password. Instead, let IIS manage the password. If you want to use a different account, click Browse,s and then use the Select User dialog box to select the anonymous user account.

6. Configure the authentication methods you want to use. Keep the following in mind:

   • Disabling basic authentication might prevent some clients from accessing resources remotely. Clients can log on only when you enable an authentication method that they support.

   • A default domain isn't set automatically. If you enable basic or .NET Passport authentication, you can choose to set a default domain that should be used when no domain information is supplied during the logon process. Setting the default domain is useful when you want to ensure that clients authenticate properly.

   • With basic and digest authentication, you can optionally define the realm or realms that can be accessed. Essentially, a realm is a level within the metabase hierarchy. The default realm name is the computer name, which provides access to all levels within the metabase hierarchy. You could limit this by defining specific realms, such as W3SVC (for the Web Site's root) or W3SVC/1/Root (for the root of the first Web instance).

   • If you enable .NET Passport authentication, all other authentication settings are ignored. As a result, the server only authenticates using this technique for the specified resource.

7. Click OK. Before applying changes, IIS checks the existing authentication methods in use for all Web sites and directories within Web sites. If a site or directory node uses a different value, an Inheritance Overrides dialog box is displayed. Use this dialog box to select the site and directory nodes that should use the new setting, and then click OK.

Configuring Mailbox and Public Folder Access on a Virtual Server

The default HTTP virtual server provides access to mailboxes and public folders in the Exchange server's local domain. You can also configure additional HTTP virtual servers you've created to access mailboxes and public folders in the local domain or other domains.

To provide access to a public folder or public folder tree on a new HTTP virtual server, follow these steps:

1. Start System Manager. If administrative groups are enabled, expand the administrative group in which the server you want to use is located.

 Note You can't configure the default HTTP virtual server (Exchange Virtual Server) using this procedure. Instead, start IIS Manager, right-click the Default Web Site, and then select Properties. You can now configure this site as discussed in Steps 4 through 6.

2. Navigate to the Protocols container in the console tree. Expand Servers, expand the server you want to work with, and then expand Protocols.

3. In the console tree, select HTTP. Right-click the HTTP virtual server that you want to work with and then select Properties.

4. On the General tab, select Public Folder, and then click Modify.

5. As shown in Figure 16-7, choose the public folder or public folder tree that you want to make accessible on the virtual server. If the public folder tree is on a different server than the default, click Change Server. Afterward, select the Exchange Server and the public store containing the public folder tree you want to use and then click OK.

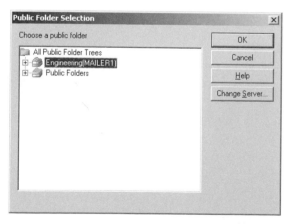

Figure 16-7. *In the Public Folder Selection dialog box, choose the public folder or public folder tree that you want to make accessible on the server.*

6. Click OK. Users can now access the public folder by typing the server or folder URL in their browser's Address field.

Note If the public folder or public folder tree you want to use isn't displayed, click Change Server and then select the public folder store where the element you want is located. Click OK. You can then choose the element in the list.

To provide access to mailboxes in an SMTP domain, follow these steps:

1. Start System Manager. If administrative groups are enabled, expand the administrative group in which the server you want to use is located.

Note You can't configure the default HTTP virtual server (Exchange Virtual Server) using this procedure. Instead, start IIS Manager, right-click the Default Web Site and then select Properties. You can now configure this site as discussed in Steps 4 through 6.

2. Navigate to the Protocols container in the console tree. Expand Servers, expand the server you want to work with, and then expand Protocols.

3. In the console tree, select HTTP. Right-click the HTTP virtual server that you want to work with and then select Properties.

4. On the General tab, select Mailboxes For, and then click Modify.

5. As shown in Figure 16-8, select an SMTP domain, and then click OK.

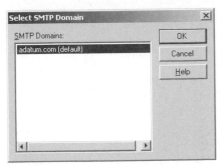

Figure 16-8. *In the Select SMTP Domain dialog box, select the SMTP domain that you want to make accessible on the server.*

6. Click OK again. Users can now access mailboxes for the selected domain.

Creating Virtual Directories for Additional Mailboxes and Public Folders

To provide access to additional SMTP domains or public folder trees, you must create additional virtual directories for the server. These virtual directories serve as the root from which users can access additional resources. For example, you could configure an HTTP virtual server with the fully qualified domain name of mail.microsoft.com to access resources in microsoft.com, boston.microsoft.com, and chicago.microsoft.com. To do this, you would follow these steps:

1. Configure the local SMTP domain (microsoft.com) for access as discussed in the section of this chapter entitled "Configuring Mailbox and Public Folder Access on a Virtual Server." Users can then access mailboxes using the URL *http://mail.microsoft.com/Exchange/alias/*, where *alias* is the user's Exchange alias.

2. Create a new virtual directory on the HTTP virtual server named boston and set the directory to access boston.microsoft.com as the SMTP domain. Users can then access mailboxes using the URL *http://mail.microsoft.com/boston/alias/*, where *alias* is the user's Exchange alias.

3. Create a new virtual directory on the HTTP virtual server named chicago and set the directory to access chicago.microsoft.com as the SMTP domain. Users can then access mailboxes using the URL *http://mail.microsoft.com/chicago/alias/*, where *alias* is the user's Exchange alias.

Procedures for creating virtual directories are examined next.

Creating Virtual Directories for Public Folder Trees

To create a virtual directory for accessing an additional public folder tree, complete the following steps:

1. Start System Manager. If administrative groups are enabled, expand the administrative group in which the server you want to use is located.

2. Navigate to the Protocols container in the console tree. Expand Servers, expand the server you want to work with, and then expand Protocols.

3. In the console tree, select HTTP. Right-click the HTTP virtual server that you want to work with, point to New, and then select Virtual Directory.

4. Type a name for the virtual directory. This name will be used in the folder path of the URL, so be sure to keep it simple.

5. Select Public Folder, and then click Modify.

6. In the Public Folder Selection dialog box, choose the public folder or public folder tree that you want to make accessible on the virtual server.

7. Click OK. Users can now access the public folder by typing the server or folder URL in their browser's Address field.

Creating Virtual Directories for SMTP Domains

To create a virtual directory for accessing an additional SMTP domain, complete the following steps:

1. Start System Manager. If administrative groups are enabled, expand the administrative group in which the server you want to use is located.

2. Navigate to the Protocols container in the console tree. Expand Servers, expand the server you want to work with, and then expand Protocols.

3. In the console tree, select HTTP. Right-click the HTTP virtual server that you want to work with, point to New, and then select Virtual Directory.

4. Type a name for the virtual directory. This name will be used in the folder path of the URL, so be sure to keep it simple.

5. Select Mailboxes For, and then click Modify.

6. Select an SMTP domain, and then click OK.

7. Click OK again. Users can now access mailboxes for the selected domain.

Starting, Stopping, and Pausing HTTP Virtual Servers

HTTP virtual servers run under a server process that you can start, stop, and pause much like other server processes. For example, if you're changing the configuration of a virtual server or performing other maintenance tasks, you might need to stop the virtual server, make the changes, and then restart it. When a virtual server is stopped, it doesn't accept connections from users and can't be used to deliver or retrieve mail.

An alternative to stopping a virtual server is to pause it. Pausing a virtual server prevents new client connections, but it doesn't disconnect current connections. When you pause an HTTP virtual server, active clients can continue to retrieve documents, messages, and public folder data in their Web browser. No new connections are accepted, however.

The master process for all HTTP virtual servers is the World Wide Web Publishing Service. Stopping this service stops all virtual servers using the process and all connections are disconnected immediately. Starting this service restarts all virtual servers that were running when you stopped the World Wide Web Publishing Service.

You can start, stop, or pause an HTTP virtual server by completing the following steps:

1. Start System Manager. If administrative groups are enabled, expand the administrative group in which the server you want to use is located.

2. Navigate to the Protocols container in the console tree. Expand Servers, expand the server you want to work with, and then expand Protocols.

3. In the console tree, expand HTTP and then right-click the virtual server you want to manage. You can now do the following:

- Select Start to start the virtual server.
- Select Stop to stop the virtual server.
- Select Pause to pause the virtual server.

You can start, stop, or pause the World Wide Web Publishing service by completing these steps:

1. Open the Computer Management console.

2. Right-click the Computer Management entry in the console tree and select Connect To Another Computer from the shortcut menu. You can now choose the Exchange server for which you want to manage services.

3. Expand the Services And Applications node by clicking the plus sign (+) next to it, and then choose Services.

4. Right-click World Wide Web Publishing Service, and then select Start, Stop, or Pause as appropriate. You can also choose Restart to have Windows stop and then start the service after a brief pause. Additionally, if you pause a service, you can use the Resume option to resume normal operation.

Chapter 17

Microsoft Exchange Server 2003 Maintenance, Monitoring, and Queuing

With the exception of backup and recovery, no administration tasks are more important than maintenance, monitoring, and queue tracking. You must maintain Microsoft Exchange Server 2003 to ensure proper flow and recoverability of message data. You need to monitor Exchange Server to ensure that services and processes are functioning normally, and you need to track Exchange Server queues to ensure that messages are being processed.

Tracking and Logging Activity in the Organization

This section examines message tracking, protocol logging, and diagnostic logging. You use these features to monitor Exchange Server and to troubleshoot messaging problems.

Using Message Tracking

You use message tracking to monitor the flow of messages into the organization and within it. With message tracking enabled, Exchange Server maintains daily log files with a running history of all messages transferred within the organization. You use the logs to determine the status of a message, such as whether a message has been sent, received, or is waiting in the queue to be delivered. Because Exchange Server handles postings to public folders in much the same way as e-mail messages, you can also use message tracking to monitor public folder usage.

Tip Tracking logs can really save the day when you're trying to troubleshoot delivery and routing problems. The logs are also useful in fending off problem users who blame e-mail for their woes. Users can't claim they didn't receive e-mails if you can find the messages in the logs.

Enabling Messaging Logging

Each Exchange server in your organization can have a different message logging setting. Standard message tracking allows you to search for messages by standard header information (date, time, message ID), as well as by sender and recipient. Extended message tracking allows you to perform searches based on message subject lines, header information, sender, and recipient.

To configure message logging, complete the following steps:

1. Start System Manager. If administrative groups are enabled, expand the administrative group in which the server you want to use is located.

2. Expand Servers, right-click the server you want to work with, and then select Properties. This displays the dialog box shown in Figure 17-1.

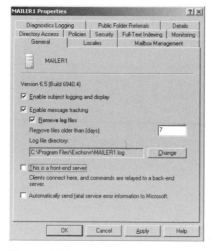

Figure 17-1. *Use the server's Properties dialog box to configure message tracking, but keep in mind that the log files can use a considerable amount of disk space.*

3. To enable standard logging, select the Enable Message Tracking check box.

4. To enable extended logging, select the Enable Subject Logging And Display check box and then select the Enable Message Tracking check box.

5. When prompted, note the path to the network share used for logging, such as \\Mailer1\Mailer1.log, and then click OK. You need to grant read access on this network share to users performing message tracking.

6. If you want Exchange to delete log files periodically, select the Remove Log Files check box and then type the logging interval in the Remove Files Older Than (Days) field. You must enter a value between 1 and 99. In most cases, you'll want to keep log files at least 7 days.

7. Click OK.

Caution   Message log files can use a considerable amount of disk space. In most cases you want Exchange Server to delete log files after a certain period of time. If you don't do this, the log files could use up all the space on the hard disk.

Searching Through the Tracking Logs

You use the Message Tracking Center to search through the message tracking logs. The tracking logs are very useful in troubleshooting problems with routing and delivery. You can search the logs in several ways:

- By message ID
- By sender
- By server that processed the messages
- By recipient
- By date

To begin a search, you must specify one or more of the previously listed identifiers as the search criteria. You must also identify a server in the organization that has processed the message in some way. This server can be the sender's server, the recipient's server, or a server that relayed the message.

To search through the message tracking logs, complete the following steps:

1. Start System Manager and then, in the console tree, double-click Tools and then select Message Tracking Center. You should now see the Message Tracking Center in the details pane as shown in Figure 17-2.

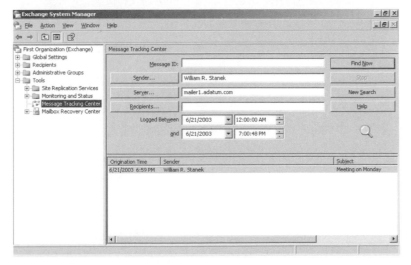

Figure 17-2. *Use the Message Tracking Center to search for user messages, system messages, and postings to public folders.*

Tip If you want to open the Message Tracking Center in a new window, right-click Message Tracking Center and then select New Window From Here.

2. Set the search criteria using the following options:

- **Message ID** Specifies the ID of the message you want to search for
- **Sender** Sets the sender's e-mail address
- **Server** Sets the name of one or more servers that processed the message within the organization
- **Recipients** Sets the e-mail address of one or more recipients
- **Logged Between** Searches for messages from a starting date and time to an ending date and time

 Note To search for messages, you're required to identify only the name of a server that processed the message within the organization and the search interval. All other search parameters are optional. Keep in mind that only messages that match *all* the search criteria you've specified are displayed. If you want to perform a broad search, specify a limited number of parameters. If you want to focus the search precisely, specify multiple parameters.

3. Click Find Now to begin the search. Messages matching the search criteria are displayed. If you need to cancel the search operation, click Stop.

4. Select a message to view its message tracking history, as shown in Figure 17-3.

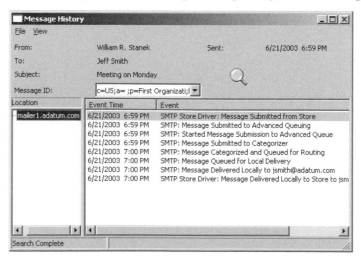

Figure 17-3. *The Message History dialog box tells you how the message was processed.*

Reviewing Message Tracking Logs Manually

Exchange Server creates message tracking logs daily and stores them in the Exchsrvr*ServerName*.log directory, where *ServerName* is the name of the Exchange server. Each log file is named by the date on which it was created, using the format *YYYYMMDD*.log, such as 20030925.log.

The log files are written as tab-delimited text, and they begin with a header that shows the following information:

- A statement that identifies the file as a message tracking log file
- The version of the Exchange System Attendant that created the file
- A tab-delimited list of fields contained in the body of the log file

You can view the log files with any standard text editor, such as Microsoft Notepad. You can also import the log files into a spreadsheet or a database. Follow these steps to import a log file into Microsoft Office Excel 2003:

1. Start Excel 2003. Choose Open from the File menu. Use the Open dialog box to select the log file you want to open. Click Open.

2. The Text Import Wizard starts automatically. The wizard should detect all the appropriate settings, so click Finish immediately.

3. The log file should now be imported. You can view, search, and print the log as you would any other spreadsheet.

Saving or Deleting Message Tracking Logs

By default, Exchange Server saves all tracking log files. If you'd like to delete log files after a specified period of time, you'll need to change the default settings by completing the following steps:

1. Start System Manager. If administrative groups are enabled, expand the administrative group in which the server you want to use is located.

2. Expand Servers, right-click the server you want to work with, and then select Properties.

3. If you'd like to keep all log files, clear Remove Log Files. If you'd like Exchange Server to automatically delete log files at a specified interval, select Remove Log Files, and then type the logging interval in the Remove Files Older Than (Days) field. The logging interval must be a value between 1 and 99.

4. Click OK.

Using Protocol Logging

Protocol logging allows you to track commands that virtual servers receive from clients. You use protocol logging to troubleshoot problems with Hypertext Transfer Protocol (HTTP), Simple Mail Transfer Protocol (SMTP), and Network News Transfer Protocol (NNTP). However, you shouldn't use protocol logging to monitor Exchange activity. This is primarily because protocol logging is process and resource intensive, which means that Exchange server has to perform a lot of work to log activity related to a particular protocol.

Working with Protocol Logging Properties and Fields

When you enable protocol logging, you specify the properties that you want to track. The more properties you track, the more system resources protocol logging requires.

Table 17-1 summarizes key properties that you'll want to track. The first column shows the name of the logging property. The second column shows the name of the field in the protocol log file.

Table 17-1. Key Protocol Logging Properties and Fields

Property Name	Log Field	Description
Date	date	Connection date.
Time	time	Connection time.
Client IP Address	c-ip	IP address of the client making the request.
User Name	cs-username	Account name of an authenticated user.
Service Name	s-sitename	Name of the service processing the command.
Server Name	s-computername	Server on which the log entry was generated.
Server IP Address	s-ip	IP address of the server on which the log entry was generated.
Method	cs-method	Protocol command sent by the client.
Protocol Status	sc-status	Protocol reply code.
Win32 Status	sc-win32-status	Microsoft Windows status or error code. Zero indicates success.
Bytes Sent	sc-bytes	Bytes sent by the server.
Bytes Received	cs-bytes	Bytes received by the server.
Time Taken	time-taken	Length of time the action took in milliseconds.

HTTP, SMTP, and NNTP support a slightly different set of properties. If a protocol doesn't support a property, the related field is recorded with a dash (-) or a zero (0).

Enabling Protocol Logging for HTTP

You enable protocol logging on each virtual server separately. You use HTTP virtual servers to track protocol logging for HTTP, Outlook Web Access, and Outlook Mobile Access.

To enable protocol logging for HTTP, complete the following steps:

1. Start Internet Information Services (IIS) Manager, right-click the Web site you want to work with, and then select Properties. In most cases, the Default Web Site is the one configured as the default HTTP virtual server.

2. On the General tab, select the Enable Logging check box. Use the Active Log Format selection list to choose one of the following log formats:

- **W3C Extended Log File Format**   Writes the log in ASCII text following the World Wide Web Consortium (W3C) extended log file format. Fields are space-delimited, and each entry is written on a new line. This style is the default.

- **Microsoft IIS Log File Format**   Writes the log in ASCII text following the IIS log file format. Fields are tab-delimited, and each entry is written on a new line.

- **NCSA Common Log File Format**   Writes the log in ASCII text following the National Center for Supercomputing Applications (NCSA) Common log file format. Fields are space-delimited and each entry is written on a new line.

- **ODBC Logging**   Writes each entry as a record in the Open Database Connectivity (ODBC)-compliant database you specify.

Tip W3C Extended Log File Format is the preferred logging format. Unless you're certain that another format meets your needs, you should use this format with HTTP, SMTP, and NNTP protocol logging.

3. Click Properties to display a dialog box similar to the one shown in Figure 17-4. You can now set the log time period. In most cases you'll want to create daily or weekly logs, so select either Daily or Weekly.

Figure 17-4. *Use the Logging Properties dialog box to set the log time period, directory, and other properties.*

4. Use the Log File Directory field to set the main folder for log files. By default, log files are written to a subdirectory of %SystemRoot%\System32\LogFiles.

5. Use the Log File Name field to determine the subdirectory and the name format used with the log files. The specific directory used for logging and the log file name depend on the type of virtual server you're configuring and the log time period. For example, if you're configuring the default SMTP virtual server with daily log files, the full path to the log file subdirectory is %SystemRoot%\System32\LogFiles\SmtpSvc1 and the log file is named using the format EXYYMMDD.log, such as EX000925.log.

6. If you selected W3C Extended Log File Format, click the Advanced tab, and then choose the fields that should be recorded in the logs.

7. Click OK twice.

Enabling Protocol Logging for NNTP and SMTP

You enable protocol logging on each virtual server separately. You use SMTP virtual servers to track protocol logging for SMTP mail submission and SMTP mail transport. You use NNTP virtual servers to track protocol logging for NNTP newsgroups.

To enable protocol logging for SMTP or NNTP, complete the following steps:

1. Start System Manager. If administrative groups are enabled, expand the administrative group in which the server you want to use is located.

2. In the console tree, navigate to the Protocols container. Expand Servers, expand the server you want to work with, and then expand Protocols.

3. Expand SMTP or NNTP as appropriate. Right-click the virtual server you want to work with, and then select Properties.

4. On the General tab, select the Enable Logging check box. Use the Active Log Format selection list to choose one of the following log formats:

    - **W3C Extended Log File Format** Writes the log in ASCII text following the W3C extended log file format. Fields are space-delimited, and each entry is written on a new line. This style is the default.

    - **Microsoft IIS Log File Format** Writes the log in ASCII text following the IIS log file format. Fields are tab-delimited, and each entry is written on a new line.

    - **NCSA Common Log File Format** Writes the log in ASCII text following the NCSA Common log file format. Fields are space-delimited and each entry is written on a new line.

    - **ODBC Logging** Writes each entry as a record in the ODBC-compliant database you specify.

 Tip W3C Extended Log File Format is the preferred logging format. Unless you're certain that another format meets your needs, you should use this format with HTTP, SMTP, and NNTP protocol logging.

5. Click Properties to display a dialog box similar to the one shown previously in Figure 17-4. You can now set the log time period. In most cases you'll want to create daily or weekly logs, so select either Daily or Weekly.

6. Use the Log File Directory field to set the main folder for log files. By default, log files are written to a subdirectory of %SystemRoot%\System32\LogFiles.

7. Use the Log File Name field to determine the subdirectory and the name format used with the log files. The specific directory used for logging and the log file name depend on the type of virtual server you're configuring and the log time period. For example, if you're configuring the default SMTP virtual server with daily log files, the full path to the log file subdirectory is %SystemRoot%\System32\LogFiles\SmtpSvc1 and the log file is named using the format EXYYMMDD.log, such as EX000925.log.

8. If you selected W3C Extended Log File Format, click the Extended Properties tab and then choose the fields that should be recorded in the logs.

9. Click OK twice.

Working with Protocol Logs

Protocol log files can help you detect and trace problems with HTTP, SMTP, and NNTP. By default, protocol log files are written to a subdirectory of %SystemRoot%\System32\LogFiles. You can use the logs to determine the following:

- Whether a client was able to connect to a specified virtual server and if not, what problem occurred

- Whether a client was able to send or receive protocol commands and if not, what error occurred

- Whether a client was able to send or receive data

- How long it took to establish a connection

- How long it took to send or receive protocol commands

- How long it took to send or receive data

- Whether server errors are occurring and if so, what types of errors are occurring

- Whether server errors are related to Windows or to the protocol itself

- Whether a user is connecting to the server using the proper logon information

Most protocol log files are written as ASCII text. This means you can view them in Notepad or another text editor. You can import these protocol log files into Excel 2003 in much the same way as you import tracking logs.

Log files, written as space-delimited or tab-delimited text, begin with a header that shows the following information:

- A statement that identifies the protocol or service used to create the file

- The protocol, service, or software version

- A date and time stamp

- A space-delimited or tab-delimited list of fields contained in the body of the log file

If you recorded the log files in an ODBC database, you'll need to perform database queries to search for log entries. Contact your database administrator for assistance.

Using Diagnostic Logging

You use diagnostic logging to detect performance problems related to Exchange services. Unlike other logging methods, diagnostic logs aren't written to separate log files. Instead, log entries are written to the Windows event logs and you use Event Viewer to monitor the related events.

Understanding Diagnostic Logging

All Exchange services record significant events in the Windows event logs. For key services, however, you can configure additional levels of logging and then use the additional information to diagnose performance problems.

Like protocol logging, diagnostic logging can significantly affect the performance of Exchange Server. For this reason, you should enable diagnostic logging only when you're trying to troubleshoot a performance problem. When you do enable it, you should select the level of logging that makes the most sense.

Exchange Server supports four levels of diagnostic logging:

- **None** The default level of diagnostic logging. At this level, Exchange Server records only significant events. These events are written to the application, system, and security event logs along with other information, warnings, and error events generated by Exchange services.

- **Minimum** Writes summary entries in the event logs. At this level, Exchange Server records one entry for each major task it performs. You can use minimum logging to help identify where a problem might be occurring but not to pinpoint the exact problem.

- **Medium** Writes both summary and detailed entries in the event logs. At this level, Exchange Server records entries for each major task performed and for each step required to complete a given task. Use this logging level once you've identified where a problem is occurring and need to get more information to resolve it.

- **Maximum** Provides a complete audit trail of every action that a service performs. At this level, Exchange Server records everything it is doing, and, as a result, server performance is severely affected. You'll need to watch the log files closely when you use this level. If you don't, they might run out of space.

Table 17-2 provides a summary of Exchange services that support diagnostic logging. Entries written to the event logs are recorded according to the event source that generated the event. The event source relates directly to an

Exchange service that you've configured for diagnostic logging. You can use the category of an event to determine what major task is being performed by the event source and thus troubleshoot a related problem.

Table 17-2.   Exchange Services That Support Diagnostic Logging

Service Name	Event Source	Description
-	MSExchangeActiveSyncNotify	Provides Microsoft Active-Sync notification services
Microsoft Exchange Calendar Connector	MSExchangeCalCon	Allows sharing of Lotus Notes and Novell Group-Wise Free/Busy information
-	MSExchangeDSAccess	Allows Exchange to access Active Directory
-	MSExchangeAL	Allows users to address e-mail using address lists
-	MSExchangeMU	Replicates Exchange config-uration information to the IIS metabase
Microsoft Exchange Connector for Novell GroupWise	LME-GWISE	Links Exchange Server and Novell GroupWise
Microsoft Exchange Connector for Lotus Notes	LME-Notes	Links Exchange Server and Lotus Notes
Microsoft Exchange Router for Novell GroupWise	MSExchangeGWRtr	Routes messages between Exchange Server and Novell GroupWise
Microsoft Exchange Directory Synchronization	MSExchangeADDXA	Synchronizes Active Direc-tory with previous versions of Exchange Server
Microsoft Exchange IMAP4	IMAP4Svc	Provides Microsoft Exchange IMAP4 Services
Microsoft Exchange Information Store	MSExchangeIS	Manages Microsoft Exchange Information Store
Microsoft Exchange MTA Stacks	MSExchangeMTA	Provides Microsoft Exchange X.400 Services
Microsoft Exchange POP3	POP3Svc	Provides Microsoft Exchange POP3 Services
Microsoft Exchange Routing Engine	MSExchangeTransport	Processes Microsoft Exchange message routing and link state information for SMTP

(continued)

Table 17-2. Exchange Services That Support Diagnostic Logging   *(continued)*

Service Name	Event Source	Description
Microsoft Exchange Site Replication Service	MSExchangeSRS	Replicates Exchange information within the organization
Microsoft Exchange System Attendant	MSExchangeSA	Provides monitoring, maintenance, and Active Directory lookup services

Enabling and Disabling Diagnostic Logging

You configure diagnostic logging separately for each Exchange server in the organization. Logging begins immediately at the level you specify. The default logging level is None.

To enable diagnostic logging, complete the following steps:

1. Identify the performance problems that users are experiencing and use Table 17-2 to identify services on which you might want to configure diagnostic logging to resolve the performance problems.

2. Start System Manager. If administrative groups are enabled, expand the administrative group in which the server you want to use is located.

3. Expand Servers. Right-click the server you want to work with, and then select Properties.

4. Click the Diagnostics Logging tab shown in Figure 17-5.

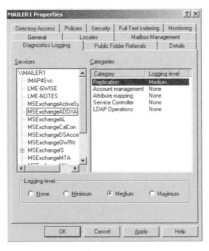

Figure 17-5. *Use the Diagnostics Logging tab to configure diagnostic logging separately for each Exchange server in the organization.*

5. Use the Services list to select a service you want to track. The Categories list should now display a list of major activities that you can track, such as replication, authentication, or connection.

6. In the Categories list, select an activity to track and then choose a logging level—Minimum, Medium, or Maximum. Repeat this step for other activity categories that you want to track.

7. As necessary, repeat Steps 5 and 6 for other services that you want to track.

8. Click OK.

To disable diagnostic logging, complete the following steps:

1. Start System Manager. If administrative groups are enabled, expand the administrative group in which the server you want to use is located.

2. Expand Servers. Right-click the server you want to work with, and then select Properties.

3. Click the Diagnostics Logging tab. Use the Services list to select each service in turn. Watch the Categories list. If any activities are being tracked, select the activity to track and then choose a logging level of None.

4. Click OK.

Viewing Diagnostic Events

Events generated by diagnostic logging are recorded in the Windows event logs. The primary log that you'll want to check is the application log. In this log you'll find the key events recorded by Exchange services. Keep in mind that related events might be recorded in other logs, including the directory service, DNS server, security, and system logs. For example, if the server is having problems with a network card and this card is causing message delivery failure, you'll have to use the system log to pinpoint the problem.

You access the application log by completing the following steps:

1. Start Computer Management. Click Start, point to Programs, point to Administrative Tools, and then select Computer Management.

2. In the console tree, right-click the Computer Management entry and choose Connect To Another Computer from the shortcut menu. You can now choose the server for which you want to manage logs.

3. Expand the System Tools node by clicking the plus sign (+) next to it, and then double-click Event Viewer. You should now see a list of logs as shown in Figure 17-6 on the following page.

4. Select Application.

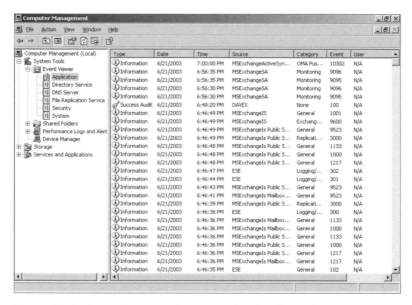

Figure 17-6. *Event Viewer displays events for the selected log.*

Entries in the main panel of Event Viewer provide an overview of when, where, and how an event occurred. To obtain detailed information on an event, double-click its entry. The event type precedes the date and time of the event. Event types include the following:

- **Information**   An informational event, generally related to a successful action.
- **Warning**   Details for warnings are often useful in preventing future system problems.
- **Error**   An error such as the failure of a service to start.

In addition to type, date, and time, the summary and detailed event entries provide the following information:

- **Source**   The application, service, or component that logged the event.
- **Category**   The category of the event, which is sometimes used to further describe the related action.
- **Event**   An identifier for the specific event.
- **User**   The user account that was logged on when the event occurred.
- **Computer**   The name of the computer where the event occurred.
- **Description**   In the detailed entries, this provides a text description of the event.
- **Data**   In the detailed entries, this provides any data or error code output created by the event.

Use the event entries to detect and diagnose Exchange performance problems.

Monitoring Connections, Services, Servers, and Resource Usage

As an Exchange administrator, you should routinely monitor connections, services, servers, and resource usage. These elements are the keys to ensuring that the Exchange organization is running smoothly. Because you can't be onsite 24 hours a day, you can set alerts to notify you when problems occur.

Checking Server and Connector Status

The Tools node in System Manager has a special area that you can use to track the status of Exchange servers and connectors. To access this area, follow these steps:

1. Start System Manager.
2. Expand Tools, and then expand Monitoring And Status.
3. Select Status in the console tree.

Note By default, you are connected to the local Exchange server or the last server you worked with. To connect to a different Exchange server, right-click Status and then select Connect To. Use the Select Exchange Server dialog box to select the server you want to view.

In the right pane, you should now see the status of the current Exchange server and each connector configured for use on this server. The status is listed as either of the following:

- **Available** The server or connector is available for use.
- **Unreachable** The server or connector isn't available and a problem might exist.

In the Name column you might also see icons that give further indication of the status of a given server or connector:

- A red circle with an X indicates that a critical monitor has exceeded its threshold value or the connector or server is unreachable.
- A yellow triangle with an exclamation point (!) indicates that a warning monitor you've set for a server has exceeded its threshold value.

Tip To get the latest status on a server and its connectors, right-click the Status node in the console tree, and then select Refresh. This refreshes the view, ensuring that you have the latest information.

You'll learn more about configuring server monitors in the following section, "Monitoring Server Performance and Services."

Monitoring Server Performance and Services

Exchange monitors provide a fully automated method for monitoring server performance and tracking the status of key services. You can use Exchange monitors to track the following:

- Virtual memory usage
- CPU utilization
- Free disk space
- SMTP and X.400 queues
- Windows service status

Using notifications, you can then provide automatic notification when a server exceeds a threshold value or when a key service stops.

 Note Windows performance monitors are an alternative to Exchange monitors. You use these monitors in the Windows Performance Monitor utility as discussed in Chapter 3 of *Microsoft Windows Server 2003 Administrator's Pocket Consultant* (Microsoft Press, 2003).

Setting Virtual Memory Usage Monitors

Virtual memory is critical to normal system operation. When a server runs low on virtual memory, system performance can suffer and message processing can grind to a halt. To counter this problem, you should set monitors to watch virtual memory usage. You can then increase the amount of virtual memory available on the server or add additional RAM as needed.

You configure a virtual memory monitor by completing the following steps:

1. Start System Manager. If administrative groups are enabled, expand the administrative group in which the server you want to use is located.

2. Expand Servers. Right-click the server you want to work with, and then select Properties.

3. On the Monitoring tab, click Add. In the Add Resource dialog box, select Available Virtual Memory, and then click OK. As shown in Figure 17-7, you'll see the Virtual Memory Thresholds dialog box.

4. In the Duration (Minutes) field, type the number of minutes that the available virtual memory must be below a threshold to change the state. Normally, you'll want to set a value of 5 to 10 minutes.

5. To set a warning state threshold, select the Warning State (Percent) check box, and then select the smallest percentage of virtual memory your server can operate on before issuing a warning state alert. In most cases you'll want to issue warnings when less than 10 percent of virtual memory is available for an extended period of time.

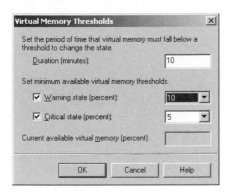

Figure 17-7. *Use the Virtual Memory Thresholds dialog box to set warning thresholds for virtual memory usage.*

6. To set a critical state threshold, select the Critical State (Percent) check box, and then select the smallest percentage of virtual memory your server can operate on before issuing a critical state alert. In most cases you'll want to issue critical alerts when less than 5 percent of virtual memory is available for an extended period of time.

Note If you also set a warning state threshold, this value must be larger.

7. Click OK. For automated notification, you must configure administrator notification.

Setting CPU Utilization Monitors

You can use a CPU utilization monitor to track the usage of a server's CPUs. When CPU utilization is too high, Exchange Server can't effectively process messages or manage other critical functions. As a result, performance can suffer greatly. CPU utilization at 100 percent for an extended period of time can be an indicator of serious problems on a server. Typically, you'll need to reboot a server when the CPU utilization is stuck at maximum utilization (100 percent).

You configure a CPU monitor by completing the following steps:

1. Start System Manager. If administrative groups are enabled, expand the administrative group in which the server you want to use is located.

2. Expand Servers. Right-click the server you want to work with, and then select Properties.

3. On the Monitoring tab, click Add. In the Add Resource dialog box, select CPU Utilization, and then click OK. As shown in Figure 17-8 on the following page, you'll see the CPU Utilization Thresholds dialog box.

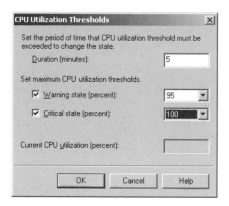

Figure 17-8. *Use the CPU Utilization Thresholds dialog box to set warning thresholds for CPU usage.*

4. In the Duration (Minutes) field, type the number of minutes that the CPU usage must exceed to change the state. Normally, you'll want to set a value of 5 to 10 minutes.

5. To set a warning state threshold, select the Warning State (Percent) check box, and then select the maximum allowable CPU before issuing a warning state alert. In most cases you'll want to issue warnings when CPU usage is 95 percent or greater for an extended period.

6. To set a critical state threshold, select the Critical State (Percent) check box, and then select the maximum allowable CPU before issuing a critical state alert. In most cases you'll want to issue warnings when CPU usage is at 100 percent for an extended period.

 Note If you also set a warning state threshold, this value must be larger.

7. Click OK. For automated notification, you must configure administrator notification.

Setting Free Disk Space Monitors

Exchange Server uses disk space for data storage, logging, tracking, and virtual memory. When hard disks run out of space, the Exchange server malfunctions and data gets lost. To prevent serious problems, you should monitor free disk space closely on all drives used by Exchange Server.

You configure a disk monitor by completing the following steps:

1. Start System Manager. If administrative groups are enabled, expand the administrative group in which the server you want to use is located.

2. Expand Servers. Right-click the server you want to work with, and then select Properties.

3. On the Monitoring tab, click Add. In the Add Resource dialog box, select Free Disk Space, and then click OK. As shown in Figure 17-9, you'll see the Disk Space Thresholds dialog box.

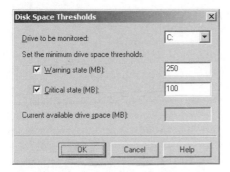

Figure 17-9. *Use the Disk Space Thresholds dialog box to set the thresholds that monitor the available disk space on key drives.*

4. Use the Drive To Be Monitored selection list to choose a drive you want to monitor, such as C:.

5. To set a warning state threshold, select the Warning State (MB) check box, and then select the smallest disk space (in MB) the server can operate on before issuing a warning state alert. Typically, you want Exchange Server to issue a warning when a drive has less than 100 MB of disk space.

6. To set a critical state threshold, select the Critical State (MB) text box, and then select the smallest disk space (in MB) your server can operate on before issuing a critical state alert. Typically, you'll want Exchange Server to issue a critical alert when a drive has less than 25 MB of disk space.

Note If you also set a warning state threshold, this value must be smaller.

7. Click OK. Repeat this procedure for all the drives that Exchange Server uses except M. For automated notification, you must configure administrator notification.

Setting SMTP and X.400 Queue Monitors

If a messaging queue grows continuously, it means that messages aren't leaving the queue and aren't being delivered as fast as new messages arrive. This can be an indicator of network or system problems that might need your attention.

You configure a queue monitor by completing the following steps:

1. Start System Manager. If administrative groups are enabled, expand the administrative group in which the server you want to use is located.

2. Expand Servers. Right-click the server you want to work with, and then select Properties.

3. On the Monitoring tab, click Add. To set an SMTP queue monitor, select SMTP Queue Growth, and then click OK. To set an X.400 queue monitor, select X.400 Queue Growth, and then click OK.

4. To set a warning state threshold, select Warning State, and then type the number of minutes that the queue can grow continuously before issuing a warning state alert. A queue that's growing continuously for more than 10 minutes is usually an indicator of a potential problem.

5. To set a critical state threshold, select Critical State, and then type the number of minutes that the queue can grow continuously before issuing a critical state alert. In most cases a queue that's growing continuously for more than 30 minutes indicates a serious problem with the network or the server.

 Note If you also set a warning state threshold, this value must be longer.

6. Click OK. For automated notification, you must configure administrator notification.

Setting Windows Service Monitors

Exchange monitors can track the status of Windows services as well. If a service you've configured for monitoring is stopped, Exchange Server generates a warning or critical alert.

When you install an Exchange server, certain critical services are automatically configured for monitoring. These services are displayed on the Monitoring tab under the heading Default Microsoft Exchange Services, and they're generally the following services:

- Microsoft Exchange Information Store
- Microsoft Exchange Message Transfer Agent (MTA) Stacks
- Microsoft Exchange Routing Engine
- Microsoft Exchange System Attendant
- Simple Mail Transport Protocol (SMTP)
- World Wide Web Publishing Service

When you configure service monitors, you can add them to the Default Microsoft Exchange Services heading or you can create your own heading for additional services. The key reason for grouping services under a common heading is to ease the administrative burden. Instead of having to configure separate entries for each service, you create a single entry, add services to it, and then set the alert type for all the services in the group.

You configure service monitors by completing the following steps:

1. Start System Manager. If administrative groups are enabled, expand the administrative group in which the server you want to use is located.

2. Expand Servers. Right-click the server you want to work with, and then select Properties.

3. On the Monitoring tab, click Add. In the Add Resource dialog box, select Windows 2000 Service, and then click OK. As shown in Figure 17-10, you'll see the Services dialog box.

Figure 17-10. *In the Services dialog box, type a name for the group of services you want to monitor. After adding the services, set the type of alert as either warning or critical.*

4. Type a name for the group of services for which you're configuring the monitor.

5. Click Add. Select a service to add to the monitor, and then click OK. Repeat as necessary.

6. When any of the selected services stops running, an alert is issued. This can be either a warning alert or a critical alert, depending on the value you select in the When Service Is Not Running Change State To field.

7. Click OK. For automated notification, you must configure administrator notification as described in the section of this chapter entitled "Configuring Notifications."

Removing Monitors

If you don't want to use a particular monitor anymore, you can remove it by completing the following steps:

1. Start System Manager. If administrative groups are enabled, expand the administrative group in which the server you want to use is located.

2. Expand Servers. Right-click the server you want to work with, and then select Properties.

3. Click the Monitoring tab. You should now see a list of all monitors configured on the server.

4. Select the monitor you want to delete, and then click Remove.

5. Click OK.

Disabling Monitoring

When you're troubleshooting Exchange problems or performing maintenance, you might want to temporarily disable monitoring and in this way stop Exchange Server from generating alerts. To disable monitoring, complete the following steps:

1. Start System Manager. If administrative groups are enabled, expand the administrative group in which the server you want to use is located.

2. Expand Servers. Right-click the server you want to work with, and then select Properties.

3. Click the Monitoring tab. You should now see a list of all monitors configured on the server.

4. Select the Disable All Monitoring Of This Server check box, and then click OK.

 Caution When you're finished testing or troubleshooting, you should repeat this procedure and clear the Disable All Monitoring Of This Server check box. If you forget to do this, administrators won't be notified when problems occur.

Configuring Notifications

One of the key reasons to configure monitoring is to notify administrators when problems occur. You can configure two types of notification:

- **E-Mail**   Used to send e-mail to administrators when a server or connector enters a warning or critical state

- **Script**   Used to have Exchange Server execute a script when a server or connector enters a warning or critical state

The sections that follow explain how you can create and manage notifications.

Notifying by E-mail

You use e-mail notification to send e-mail to administrators when a server or connector enters a warning or critical state. You can select multiple recipients to be notified and you can select a specific server to use in generating the e-mail.

To configure e-mail notification, follow these steps:

1. Start System Manager.

2. Expand Tools, and then expand Monitoring And Status.

3. Right-click the Notification folder, point to New, and then click E-mail Notification. This displays the Properties dialog box shown in Figure 17-11.

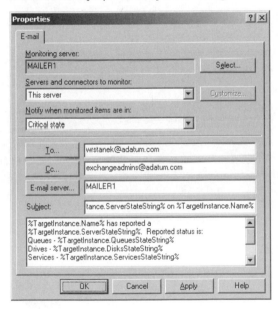

Figure 17-11. *Use the Properties dialog box to configure e-mail notification.*

4. To specify the server that will monitor and notify users by e-mail, click Select, and then choose a server.

5. Use the Servers And Connectors To Monitor list box to choose the servers or connectors you want administrators to be notified about. The available options are as follows:

   - This Server
   - All Servers
   - Any Server In The Routing Group
   - All Connectors
   - Any Connector In The Routing Group

- Custom List Of Servers
- Custom List Of Connectors

 Note To create a custom list of servers or connectors, select Custom List Of Servers or Custom List Of Connectors, and then click Customize. Afterward, in the Custom List windows, click Add, and then choose a server or connector to add to the custom list.

6. You can configure notification for either warning alerts or critical state alerts. Use Notify When Monitored Items Are In to choose the state that triggers notification.

7. Click To, and then select a recipient to notify. You can notify multiple users by selecting an appropriate mail-enabled group.

8. Click Cc, and then select additional recipients to notify. Again, you can notify multiple users by selecting an appropriate mail-enabled group.

9. Click E-mail Server, and then choose the e-mail server that should generate the e-mail message.

10. Use the Subject field to set a subject for the notification message. The default subject line specifies the type of alert that occurred and the item on which the alert occurred. These values are represented by the subject line %TargetInstance.ServerStateString% on %TargetInstance.Name%.

11. The message box at the bottom of the window sets the body of the message. In most cases you'll want to edit the default message body. The default text tells administrators the following information:

   - %TargetInstance.Name% is the name of the server or connector that triggered the notification.
   - %TargetInstance.ServerStateString% is the type of alert.
   - %TargetInstance.QueuesStateString% is the reported status of queues.
   - %TargetInstance.DisksStateString% is the reported status of drives.
   - %TargetInstance.ServicesStateString% is the reported status of services.
   - %TargetInstance.MemoryStateString% is the reported status of virtual memory.
   - %TargetInstance.CPUStateString% is the reported status of CPUs.

12. Click OK. Repeat this procedure to configure notification for other servers and connectors.

Using Script Notification

You use script notification to have Exchange Server execute a script when a server or connector enters a warning or critical state. The script can execute commands that restart processes, clear up disk space, or perform other actions needed to resolve a problem on the Exchange server. The script could also generate an e-mail through an alternate gateway, which is useful if the Exchange server is unable to deliver e-mail.

To configure script notification, follow these steps:

1. Start System Manager.

2. Expand Tools, and then expand Monitoring And Status.

3. Right-click the Notification folder, point to New, and then click Script Notification. This displays the Properties dialog box shown in Figure 17-12.

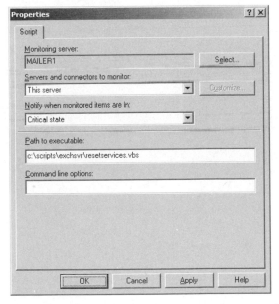

Figure 17-12. *Use the Properties dialog box to configure script notification.*

4. To specify the server that will monitor and notify users by e-mail, click Select, and then choose a server.

5. Use the Servers And Connectors To Monitor list box to choose the servers or connectors you want administrators to be notified about. The available options are as follows:

   • This Server

   • All Servers

- Any Server In The Routing Group
- All Connectors
- Any Connector In The Routing Group
- Custom List Of Servers
- Custom List Of Connectors

 Note To create a custom list of servers or connectors, select Custom List Of Servers or Custom List Of Connectors, and then click Customize. Afterward, in the Custom List windows, click Add, and then choose a server or connector to add to the custom list.

6. You can configure notification for either warning alerts or critical state alerts. Use the Notify When Monitored Items Are In selection list to choose the state that triggers notification.

7. In the Path To Executable field, type the complete file path to the script you want to execute, such as C:\Scripts\Mynotificationscript.vbs. You can run any type of executable file, including batch scripts with the .bat or .cmd extension and Windows scripts with the .vb, .js, .pl, or .wsc extensions.

 Note The Exchange System Attendant must have permission to execute this script, so be sure to grant access to the local system account or any other account that you've configured to run this service.

8. To pass arguments to a script or application, type the options in the Command Line Options field.

9. Click OK.

Viewing and Editing Current Notifications

You can view all notifications configured in the organization with the Notification entry in System Manager. Start System Manager, expand Tools, expand Monitoring And Status, and then select Notifications.

Each notification is displayed with summary information depicting the following:

- Name of the monitoring server
- Items monitored
- Action performed
- State that triggers notification

To edit a notification, double-click it, and then modify the settings as necessary. When you're finished, click OK.

To delete a notification, right-click it, and then select Delete. When prompted to confirm the action, click Yes.

Working with Queues

As an Exchange administrator, it's your responsibility to monitor Exchange queues regularly. Exchange Server uses queues to hold messages while they're being processed for routing and delivery. If messages remain in a queue for an extended period, there could be a problem. For example, if an Exchange server is unable to connect to the network, you'll find that messages aren't being cleared out of queues.

Understanding System and Link Queues

Exchange Server supports two types of queues:

- **System queues**   The default queues in the organization. There are three providers for system queues: SMTP, Microsoft MTA (X.400), and Messaging Application Programming Interface (MAPI).

- **Link queues**   Created by Exchange Server when there are multiple messages bound for the same destination. These queues are accessible only when they have messages waiting to be routed.

You have direct access to MAPI, SMTP, and X.400 queues through the queue viewer. MAPI queues are used with connectors, such as Connector for Novell GroupWise or Connector for Lotus Notes. X.400 queues are used with the Microsoft MTA, which provides addressing and routing information for sending messages from one server to another. The MTA relies on X.400 transfer stacks to provide additional details for message transfer, and these stacks are similar in purpose to the Exchange virtual servers used with SMTP.

The key queues used with the Microsoft MTA are the following:

- **SMTP Mailbox Store**   Contains SMTP messages in the mailbox store for MTA

- **Messages Waiting To Be Routed**   Contains messages that are waiting to be routed

Each SMTP virtual server has several system queues associated with it. SMTP queues are used to hold messages in various stages of routing. The SMTP queues are as follows:

- **DSN Messages Pending Submission**   Contains data source name (DSN) messages that have been acknowledged and accepted by the SMTP service but haven't been processed yet.

- **Failed Message Retry Queue**   Contains messages that can't be routed because the destination server is unreachable.

- **Local Delivery**   Contains messages that are queued for local delivery—that is, messages that the Exchange server is waiting to deliver to a local Exchange mailbox.

- **Messages Awaiting Directory Lookup**   Contains messages to recipients who have not yet been resolved in Active Directory.

- **Messages Pending Submission** Contains messages that have been acknowledged and accepted by the SMTP service but haven't been processed yet.

- **Messages Queued for Deferred Delivery** Contains messages that are queued for deferred delivery.

- **Messages Waiting To Be Routed** Contains messages waiting to be routed to a destination server. Messages move from here to a link queue.

Accessing the Queue Viewer

You access system and link queues by completing the following steps:

1. Start System Manager. If administrative groups are enabled, expand the administrative group in which the server you want to use is located.

2. Expand Servers, expand the server you want to work with, and then select Queues.

3. As shown in Figure 17-13, the Queue Viewer provides an overview of the status of each queue:

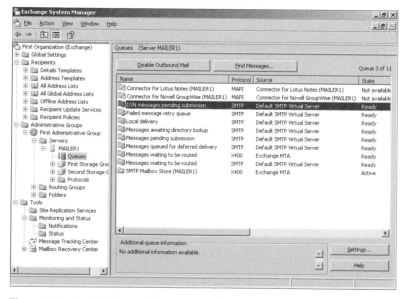

Figure 17-13. *The Queue Viewer provides an overview of the status of each queue.*

- A folder icon indicates an active state.

- A folder icon with a green check mark indicates the queue has a reader status.

- A folder icon with a red exclamation point indicates a warning state such as Not Available or Error.

Changing the SMTP Queue Directory

On a busy server, messages are written to and read from the SMTP queue directory in rapid succession. Because of this, the disk drive used with the SMTP queue directory should be optimized for read/write performance. If it isn't, Exchange might not be able to process messages fast enough, which could result in message processing delays of a few seconds, a few minutes, or even a few hours.

By default, the SMTP queue directory is placed on the same drive as the Exchange server installation: *root*\Exchsrvr\Mailroot\vsi#\Queue, where *root* is the install drive for Exchange Server and # is the number of the SMTP virtual server, such as C:\Exchsrvr\Mailroot\vsi1\Queue. You can change the location of the queue directory at any time. However, before you do this, you must stop the associated SMTP virtual server, which temporarily stops message processing. Because of this, you probably should make this change during nonbusiness or nonpeak usage hours.

To change the SMTP queue directory, complete the following steps:

1. Start System Manager. If administrative groups are enabled, expand the administrative group in which the server you want to use is located.

2. In the console tree, navigate to the Protocols container. Expand Servers, expand the server you want to work with, and then expand Protocols.

3. In the console tree, expand SMTP. Right-click the virtual server that you want to work with, and then select Stop to halt message processing.

4. Right-click the virtual server entry again and then select Properties.

5. On the Messages tab, the Queue Directory field shows the current location of the SMTP queue. To change the queue directory location, click Browse and then use the Browse For Folder dialog box to choose a new queue directory.

6. Click OK to close the Properties dialog box. Next, right-click the virtual server entry in System Manager, and then select Start to resume message processing.

7. Select the Queues node and then click Refresh. The SMTP queues should be in the Ready state. Watch the queues to ensure messages are processing. If messages aren't being processed, you might need to double-check the directory settings, the permissions, and the availability of drive space on the related hard drive.

Managing Queues

You usually won't see messages in queues because they're processed and routed quickly. Messages come into a queue, Exchange Server performs a lookup or establishes a connection, and then Exchange Server either moves the message to a new queue or delivers it to its destination.

Understanding Queue Summaries and Queue States

Messages remain in a queue when there's a problem. To check for problem messages, use the Queue Viewer to examine the number of messages in the queues. If you see a queue with a consistent or growing number of messages, there might be a problem. Again, normally messages should come into a queue and then be processed fairly quickly. Because of this, the number of messages in a queue should gradually decrease over time as the messages are processed, providing no new messages come into the queue.

Whenever you click a Queues node in System Manager, you get a summary of the currently available queues for the selected node. These queues can include both system and link queues, depending on the state of the Exchange server.

Although queue summaries provide important details for troubleshooting message flow problems, you do have to know what to look for. The connection state is the key information to look at first. This value tells you the state of the queue. States you'll see include these:

- **Active** An active queue is needed to allow messages to be transported out of a link queue.

- **Ready** A ready queue is needed to allow messages to be transported out of a system queue. When link queues are ready, they can have a connection allocated to them.

- **Retry** A connection attempt has failed and the server is waiting to retry.

- **Scheduled** The server is waiting for a scheduled connection time.

- **Remote** The server is waiting for a remote dequeue command (TURN/ ETRN).

- **Frozen** The queue is frozen, and none of its messages can be processed for routing. Messages can enter the queue, however, as long as the Exchange routing categorizer is running. You must unfreeze the queue to resume normal queue operations.

Administrators can choose to enable or disable connections to queues. If connections are disabled, the queue is unable to route and deliver messages.

You can change the queue state to Active by using the FORCE CONNECTION command. When you do this, Exchange Server should immediately enable a connection for the queue, which allows messages to be routed and delivered from it. You can force a connection to change the Retry or Scheduled state as well.

Here is some other summary information that you might find useful in trouble-shooting:

- **Time Oldest Message Submitted** Tells you when the oldest message was sent by a client. Any time the oldest message has been in the queue for several days, you have a problem with message delivery. Either Exchange Server is having a problem routing that specific message, or a deeper routing problem could be affecting the organization.

- **Number Of Messages** Tells you the total number of messages waiting in the queue. If you see a large number of messages waiting in the queue, you could have a connectivity or routing problem.

- **Total Messages Size (KB)** Tells you the total size of all messages in the queue. Large messages can take a long time to deliver, and, as a result, they might slow down message delivery.

- **Time Next Connection Retry** When the connection state is Retry, this column tells you when another connection attempt will be made. You can use FORCE CONNECTION to attempt a connection immediately.

Refreshing the Queue View

Use the queue summaries and queue state information to help you find queuing problems, as discussed in the earlier section of this chapter entitled, "Understanding Queue Summaries and Queue States." By default, the queues view is refreshed every 2 minutes. To change the refresh rate, click Settings in the Queue Viewer and then set a specific refresh rate of 1, 2, 5, or 10 minutes. To refresh the queue immediately, click Refresh on the toolbar or select Action, Refresh.

Finding Messages in Queues

To manage queues, you must enumerate messages. This process allows you to examine queue contents and perform management tasks on messages within a particular queue.

The easiest way to enumerate messages is to do so in sets of 100. To display the first 100 messages in a queue, follow these steps:

1. Start System Manager, and then navigate to the Queues node on the server you want to work with.

2. If you select the Queues node, you should see a list of available queues in the details pane. Double-click the queue to display the Find Message dialog box.

3. Click Find Now. The search results are displayed in the lower portion of the Find Messages dialog box.

4. When a message is displayed in the Find Messages dialog box, you can double-click it to view message details, as shown in Figure 17-14. The details provide additional information that identifies the message, including a message ID that you can use with message tracking.

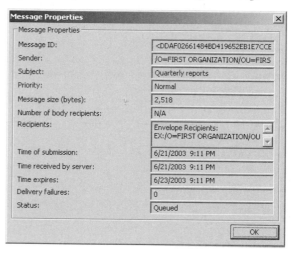

Figure 17-14. *After you enumerate messages in a queue, you can examine message details by double-clicking the entries for individual messages.*

You can also specify message restrictions, including the specific number of messages to enumerate and the message state you want to search for, such as Retry. To do this, follow these steps:

1. Double-click the queue you want to work with. This displays the Find Messages dialog box.

2. Use the Number Of Messages To Be Listed selection list to choose the number of messages to enumerate. The available values are 100, 500, 1000, and 10,000.

3. Use Show Messages Whose State Is to restrict the enumeration by message state. For example, to find messages that are in the Retry state, select Retry, or to find messages that are Frozen, select Frozen.

4. Click Find Now.

Enabling and Disabling Outbound Mail from Queues

Enabling outbound mail from queues makes them available for routing and delivery. Disabling outbound mail from queues makes them unavailable for routing and delivery.

To enable or disable outbound mail from queues, follow these steps:

1. Start System Manager, and then navigate to the Queues node on the server you want to work with.

2. To disable outbound mail from queues, click Disable Outbound Mail. Confirm the action when prompted by clicking Yes.

3. To enable outbound mail from queues, click Enable Outbound Mail. Confirm the action when prompted by clicking Yes.

Forcing Connections to Queues

In most cases you can change the queue state to Active by forcing a connection. Simply right-click the queue and then select Force Connection. When you do this, Exchange Server should immediately enable connections to the queue, and this should allow messages to be routed and delivered from it.

Freezing and Unfreezing Queues

When you freeze a queue, all message transfer out of that queue stops. This means that messages can continue to enter the queue but no messages will leave it. To restore normal operations, you must unfreeze the queue.

You freeze and then unfreeze a queue by completing the following steps:

1. Start System Manager, and then navigate to the Queues node on the server you want to work with.

2. Right-click a queue, and then select Freeze.

3. When you're done troubleshooting, right-click the queue, and then select Unfreeze.

Another way to freeze messages in a queue is to do so selectively. In this way, you can control the transport of a single message or several messages that might be causing problems on the server. For example, if a large message is delaying the delivery of other messages, you can freeze that message until other messages have left the queue. Afterward, you can unfreeze the message to resume normal delivery.

To freeze and then unfreeze individual messages, complete the following steps:

1. Start System Manager, and then navigate to the Queues node on the server you want to work with.

2. Right-click the queue and then select Find Messages. In the Find Messages dialog box, click Find Now.

3. Right-click the problem message, and then select Freeze. You can select multiple messages using Shift and Ctrl.

4. When you're ready to resume delivery of the message, right-click the problem message, and then select Unfreeze.

Deleting Messages from Queues

You can remove messages from queues if necessary. To do this, follow these steps:

1. Start System Manager, and then navigate to the Queues node on the server you want to work with.

2. Right-click the queue and then select Find Messages. In the Find Messages dialog box, click Find Now.

3. Right-click the problem message. You can select multiple messages using Shift and Ctrl and then right-click as well. Select one of the following options from the shortcut menu:

   - **Delete (With NDR)**   Deletes the selected messages from the queue and notifies the sender with a nondelivery report (NDR)

   - **Delete (No NDR)**   Deletes the message(s) from the queue without sending an NDR to the sender

4. When prompted, click Yes to confirm the deletion.

Deleting messages from a queue removes them from the messaging system permanently. You can't recover the deleted messages.

Index

E

About the Author

William R. Stanek has 20 years of hands-on experience with advanced programming and development. He is a leading technology expert and an award-winning author. Over the years, his practical advice has helped millions of programmers, developers, and network engineers all over the world. He has written more than two dozen computer books. Current or forthcoming books include *Microsoft Windows XP Professional Administrator's Pocket Consultant, Microsoft Windows 2000 Administrator's Pocket Consultant 2nd Edition,* and *Microsoft Windows Server 2003 Administrator's Pocket Consultant* and *IIS 6.0 Administrator's Pocket Consultant.*

Mr. Stanek has been involved in the commercial Internet community since 1991. His core business and technology experience comes from more than 11 years of military service. He has substantial experience in developing server technology, encryption, and Internet solutions. He has written many technical white papers and training courses on a wide variety of topics. He is widely sought after as a subject-matter expert.

Mr. Stanek has an MS degree in Information Systems with distinction and a BS degree in Computer Science magna cum laude. He is proud to have served in the Persian Gulf War as a combat crew member on an electronic warfare aircraft. He flew on numerous combat missions into Iraq and was awarded nine medals for his wartime service, including one of the United States of America's highest flying honors, the Air Force Distinguished Flying Cross. Currently, he resides in the Pacific Northwest with his wife and children.